THE
MORMON
PEOPLE

THE
MORMON
PEOPLE

The Making of an American Faith

MATTHEW BOWMAN

RANDOM HOUSE

NEW YORK

Published in the United States by Random House, an imprint of The Random House Publishing Group, a division of Random House, Inc., New York.

RANDOM HOUSE and colophon are registered trademarks of Random House, Inc.

Grateful acknowledgment is made to the following for permission to reprint previously published material:

The Church of Jesus Christ of Latter-day Saints: "The Family: A Proclamation to the World," © by Intellectual Reserve, Inc. Reprinted by permission of The Church of Jesus Christ of Latter-day Saints.

CW McMaster Family Group: Excerpt from "Reverently, Quietly" by Clara McMaster. Reprinted by permission of CW McMaster Family Group, Salt Lake City, Utah.

Phyllis R. Oakes: Excerpt from "I Am a Child of God" by Naomi W. Randall, © by Intellectual Reserve, Inc. Reprinted by permission of Phyllis R. Oakes.

Library of Congress Cataloging-in-Publication Data
Bowman, Matthew Burton.
The Mormon people : the making of an American faith / by Matthew Bowman.
p. cm.
Includes bibliographical references and index.
ISBN 978-0-679-64490-3
eBook ISBN 978-0-679-64491-0
1. Church of Jesus Christ of Latter-day Saints—History. I. Title.
BX8611.B695 2012
289.309—dc23   2011040659

Printed in the United States of America on acid-free paper

www.atrandom.com

246897531

First Edition

Book design by Caroline Cunningham

For Richard Bushman

CONTENTS

———————

PREFACE

From 1820 to 1830, Joseph Smith, Jr., the young son of a farmer living in Manchester Township in rural upstate New York, experienced a series of remarkable visionary experiences. In April of the latter year, at age twenty-five, he organized a new religion. This frontier faith has come to be formally known as the Church of Jesus Christ of Latter-day Saints and is colloquially called Mormonism, named for the Book of Mormon, a new work of scripture Joseph Smith claimed to have translated by the gift and power of God from golden plates an angel gave him. Driven at sword's point from Kirtland, Ohio, in 1838, from Far West, Missouri, in 1839, and from Nauvoo, Illinois, in 1846, the Mormons fled angry dissenters, hostile mobs, and the stern power of state and federal governments to the Great Basin, where in 1847 they began to build their own society and hoped to practice their faith in peace. Forty years later, determined to stamp out the Mormons' de facto theocracy, their economic communalism, and their practice of polygamy, Congress sent federal marshals to Salt Lake City. After half a decade of struggle, the Mormons capitulated and Utah became a state.

Something curious happened over the next century. The Mormons, once radical utopians, social revolutionaries, and, in the eyes of many Protestant Americans, determined heretics, found a way to become fully American as well. In the twentieth century the Mormons embraced patriotism, the Protestant work ethic, and the mores and re-spectability of the American middle class. By the 1960s and 1970s, the Mormon Tabernacle Choir routinely sang at presidential inaugurations and Mormons were rising in the ranks of American business, government, and arts. To them, this was no compromise; rather, they had found a way to integrate their theology with their nation.

But to many other Americans, Mormonism remains a faith on the fringe. The cheerful and successful Mormons in the American public eye still believe, after all, that Joseph Smith conversed with God and received revelation from the hands of angels. Today, at the beginning of the second decade of the twenty-first century, Mormonism looms large in presidential politics and pop culture, and seems poised to undergo the most intense examination it has faced in a century or more. This book is intended as an introduction to the faith of presidential contender Mitt Romney and bestselling author Stephenie Meyer, the faith of basketball star Jimmer Fredette and businessman Stephen Covey. The story of Mormonism is not merely the story of these believers and their ancestors, but the story of America itself. Mormonism has been called the most American of all religions, and this is true in a deeply paradoxical way. While Mormonism's struggles with the nation throw into sharp relief what Americans believe about themselves, its aspirations and ideals no less reflect the dreams of the republic itself.

ACKNOWLEDGMENTS

As all authors know, though we are the ones who sit behind the keyboard the work is not ours alone. I have received advice and help from more people than I can name here. First thanks go to my editors, Ben Steinberg and Jon Meacham, and my production editor, Evan Camfield, whose diligence made this a far better book. My family, Maurice and Rosanne Bowman, John and Amy Pilkington, and Kent and Winnie Burton, who often hosted me as I wrote, are models of the best Mormonism has to offer. Christopher Jones, Max Mueller, and John Turner, rising young students of Mormonism, read the entire manuscript and offered detailed and extraordinarily valuable criticism, as did Steve Tayson, who reviewed the book for Random House; the future of Mormon scholarship could be in no better hands. Katie Blakesley, Spencer Fluhman, Lisa Fraser, Kim Gardner, Steve Gooch, Emily Jones, Rachel Kearl, Liz and Dan Kirk, Cristy Meiners, Ben Park, Jenny Reeder, Ollie Russell, Kathy Wallace, and Richie Wilcox all read portions of the manuscript, caught embarrassments, and offered criticism, insights, reaction, encouragement, and occasionally black bean burgers, trips to the beach, and dutiful willingness to listen to me think out loud about Heber J. Grant. Brittany Chapman at the Church History Library in Salt Lake City accommodated my sometimes ridiculously urgent requests for aid with characteristic cheer. Kristine Haglund possesses, in addition to perfect prose pitch and a deep understanding of what makes Mormons tick, the remarkable and wonderful ability to avoid recoiling when I lob wildly sweeping claims about Mormonism at her. Xarissa Holdaway held her own in a few conversations about how writing works. Nathan Nielson provided great insight into the paradoxes of modern Mormonism. Allison Pond's abounding grace, sympathy, keen editorial eye, and unflinching friendship saw me through a dozen late nights when the project seemed too rushed and demanding to possibly accomplish. Rebecca Rygg's extraordinary dedication, patience, and meticulousness improved my prose and my arguments immeasurably; if semicolons remain herein, they do so despite her strenuous objections.

Lastly, this book is dedicated to Richard Bushman, a mentor and friend, to whom I owe a great deal. The arguments and assertions therein, of course, are mine.

INTRODUCTION

In the late summer of 1830, a twenty-three-year-old farmer left his home in northern Ohio bound for upstate New York, where he had been born. He had sold his farm and was determined to make a new living as an evangelical preacher. His name was Parley Pratt, and he had always been interested in religion. One August night he slept at the home of an old Baptist who gave him a copy of the Book of Mormon, a puzzling new scripture that had been published earlier that very year in the nearby village of Palmyra. Pratt devoured the six hundred pages of the book in two days, finding in it, as he said later, the "fulness of the gospel of a crucified and risen Redeemer."[1]

The next day he walked ten miles to Palmyra in search of the man who had produced the book, a farmer's son named Joseph Smith only two years older than Parley himself. He did not find Joseph, who was in Pennsylvania with his wife's family. Instead, he found a new church of a few dozen members called the Church of Christ flourishing under the guidance of Joseph's brother Hyrum and his friend Oliver Cowdery, a schoolteacher who had served as scribe during the translation of the Book of Mormon. They told Pratt that their faith was based on far more than the book alone. God had chosen this time and this place, upstate New York in the wake of the American Revolution, to restore to earth the true church of Jesus Christ, whose priestly authority had been lost to humanity for more than a millennium. Parley Pratt believed every word, and Cowdery baptized him and ordained him an elder.

Only a few days after Pratt himself read the Book of Mormon—and without meeting Joseph Smith—Pratt left Palmyra as a missionary for the new religion with a bag full of copies of the new work of scripture. Before his death in May 1857, Parley Pratt would travel to Canada, England, the Pacific Islands, and Chile, convert thousands, write books, tracts, and hymns in celebration of the new faith, claim by ordination the mantle of an apostle of Jesus Christ, suffer arrest and escape from prison in Missouri, abandon the United States to join the Mormon Zion in the Salt Lake Valley, and marry eleven more wives— the last of whom had an angry ex-husband who stabbed Pratt to death on a farm in Arkansas. Despite his dreams of the pulpit, this was hardly the life that Pratt had imagined for himself when he sold his farm in Ohio.

Eight years after Pratt's conversion, Joseph Smith changed the name of his church to the Church of Jesus Christ of Latter-day Saints. Only months after its organization, journalists, bemused Protestant ministers, and other curious or hostile people labeled the new church "Mormonites." As one minister wrote, the term applied to those "affected with the Mormon delusion."[2] Soon the epithet shortened to "Mormon," and the Saints themselves adopted it, gladly embracing the nation's scorn. For many years, at least until the 1890s, when they abandoned the practice of plural marriage and embraced statehood for Utah, to which they had fled after Joseph Smith was killed in 1844, their acceptance of the name "Mormon" signified their proud separatism, their confidence that their society would ultimately surpass what the United States might have to offer.

There are a number of different churches derived from Joseph Smith's religious experiments. Most claim the title "Mormon," signifying their inheritance from Joseph Smith, the religious practices he developed, the doctrine he taught, and, more generally, the deep cultural and religious impulses he felt: a profound optimism about human potential, an urge to close the gap between the human and the divine, a preoccupation with familial relationships. The Church of Jesus Christ of Latter-day Saints, headquartered in Salt Lake City, Utah, is by far the largest of these churches, and it is the one I mean in this book when I use the terms "Mormon" or "the church." Recently, in an effort to bolster its Christian credentials, the leadership of the church has urged the media to use its full name on first reference and to refer to its members as "Saints" or "Latter-day Saints"—a sign either of the church's desire for greater inclusion in mainstream culture or of its reach for identification beyond its American nickname and origins to the sacred history of Christianity more generally. By the time of Joseph Smith's death in 1844, he had about fifteen thousand followers; today there are some fourteen million Mormons on the globe. Roughly six million of those are in the United States—many in Utah, but more outside the state than in it.

If God indeed selected frontier America in the early nineteenth century for the restoration of his church, he could hardly have chosen better. Many scholars have called Mormonism the quintessential American faith. For many Americans of Pratt's generation, faith in God and confidence in American democracy went hand in hand. Protestant evangelicals, who insisted that no soul needed a priest to guide it to heaven or to interpret the Bible, found the culture of American individualism particularly congenial. And, for a time, so did the Mormons. The audacity of Joseph Smith's new scripture, dialogues with God, and claim to Christ's ancient priesthood authority had a particularly American flavor—a confident amateurism, an affinity for re-creation, renewal, and resurrection, excitement at the possibilities that religious liberty, nearly unlimited land, and economic prosperity might bring. The Mormons knew it. They often spoke reverently about the Constitution, praising in particular its defense of religious freedom and the principles of liberty it espoused. In December 1833, when Mormons in Missouri were facing great hostility from their neighbors, Joseph Smith dictated a revelation from God declaring that the Mormons should seek government protection. "According to the laws and constitution of the people, which I have suffered to be established," ran the revelation, "every man may act in doctrine and principle pertaining to futurity, according to the moral agency which I have given unto him. For this purpose have I established the Constitution of this land, by the hands of wise men whom I raised up."[3] As they would do in so many different areas, the Mormons here formalized and sacralized what many other believers did merely by implication. Evangelicals might believe that the Constitution was godly, but the Mormons heard a divine voice formally claiming parentage of their nation.

The same totalizing vision that allowed the Mormons to sacralize the Constitution also drove them away from the main currents of American culture, for they sought not merely to create a new faith but to build a new society. Although the Mormons valued many elements of American political culture, they were committed to other visions as well. The struggle in Missouri was not a conventional conflict over property rights, because Joseph Smith had named Jackson County, Missouri, the literal location of the millennial Zion, the New Jerusalem, seat of the coming Kingdom of God on earth. In the early 1830s, hundreds of Mormons flocked there, advocating prophecy, millennialism, spiritual gifts, and the transformation of the frontier into a utopian society. Joseph Smith introduced to his people the United Order, a form of utopian socialism that required all Saints to turn over ownership of their property to an increasingly elaborate priesthood hierarchy.

Mormon religious life was based on the construction of and participation in communities that often drew them away from the mores and values of American democratic culture. It is little wonder that their neighbors grew uneasy. For those Americans who feared the Mormons, they were, as the Presbyterian minister Jonathan Turner claimed a few years after the Missouri conflict, "in truth, the most dangerous and virulent enemies to our political and religious purity, and our social and civil peace, that now exist in the Union."[4] The litany of protests grew from there: the Mormons were fanatics; they were authoritarian; they were heretics. And when they moved to Utah and their polygamy became widely known, the accusations grew harsher. Dime novels like Arthur Conan Doyle's *A Study in Scarlet* and Zane Grey's *The Riders of the Purple Sage* presented a Mormon kingdom in Utah built on assassination, the enslavement of polygamous wives, and cultish worship of Brigham Young. And just like that, the Mormons reached the limits of what American culture would tolerate.

Mormons consider themselves Christian, but they have consistently encountered the same ambivalent struggle with others who claim that term as they have with other Americans. They believe in a creator God, a supreme deity, God the Father, whom they often call Heavenly Father. They believe that his son, Jesus Christ, was born to a virgin on the earth and was crucified and resurrected to redeem the world from sin. They also believe in the Holy Spirit. But they reject the orthodox theology of the Trinity to which virtually all other Christians subscribe; Mormons teach that God the Father and Jesus Christ both possess bodies of flesh and bone and thus are separate beings bound into the Trinity by mind, will, and purpose rather than being, as the Nicene Creed puts it, of one substance. Mormons believe in the Bible, though Joseph Smith taught that errors and mistranslations might sometimes compromise its text. They also use three other works of scripture: the Book of Mormon, the record of an ancient American civilization the resurrected Christ visited; the Doctrine and Covenants, a collection of revelations given to Joseph Smith; and the Pearl of Great Price, a collection of inspired texts mostly produced by Joseph Smith.

Mormons believe that Christ established a church before his crucifixion, placed Peter at its head, and gave that church priesthood authority to perform the sacraments of salvation: baptism, confirmation, the Lord's Supper, and other ordinances. But this authority and this church were lost in the intervening centuries, and Mormons believe that God chose Joseph Smith to restore them and, providentially, the United States of America as the place where they could be restored. They combine a sacramentalism and priesthood reminiscent of Catholicism with a decidedly Protestant devotion to scripture and suspicion of trained clergy.

In the strictest sense, Mormons do not believe that Joseph Smith established a "new" church at all. For Mormons, the history of humanity is much like the history of the Israelites in the Bible writ large: a cycle in which God blesses his people with prosperity, followed by a period of corruption, wickedness, and collapse, after which God reaches out to offer a second chance, a redemption, a restoration. This is the form of history the civilizations in the Book of Mormon experience. It is also the history of God's true church, which Mormons believe was given first to Adam, whom angels baptized and taught of Jesus Christ, before his descendants collapsed into the wickedness from which Noah was sent to save them. As was Abraham, as was Moses, as was, eventually, Joseph Smith himself. Each time humanity fell, God sent a priestly prophet to reorganize true worship and teach true doctrine.

Mormons share with Protestants the belief that the centuries after Christ's death saw this sort of corruption; the Mormons call this period "the Great Apostasy." Unlike those Protestants, Mormons believe that purity was not regained until Joseph Smith appeared on the American frontier. The name of the church, then—the Church of Jesus Christ of Latter-day Saints—possesses the modifier "Latter-day" to distinguish it from its other manifestations in history as well as from the churches of the present day. Joseph Smith's church is the last incarnation—or, to use Mormon parlance, the last dispensation—before Christ's Second Coming. Mormons believe that this time God has established his kingdom so firmly, and in such fertile ground, that it will not fall again.

Mormons believe that their church has been given not only the gift of the restored gospel, but also the mandate to prepare the earth for the Second Coming of Jesus Christ, and this means that they still, to a considerable extent, perceive a strong sense of difference from the world around them. They have always insisted on defining their own community on their own terms, whether that be the theocratic kingdom Brigham Young built in the West or the Mormons in contemporary America who avoid cocktails at company parties. Years after violence broke out in Missouri and the Mormons were driven from the state, eventually fleeing to the Utah Territory, Parley Pratt would write with bitterness, "The struggle was now over, our liberties were gone, our homes to be deserted and possessed by a lawless banditti; and all this in the United States of America."[5] For many Mormons in the nineteenth century, the true hope for those virtues they valued in the Constitution lay not in the United States but among the Mormons themselves.

Pratt illustrated that conviction when he imagined a future in which the United States had collapsed and only the Mormons, "the remnant who fled into the wilderness and rallied to the standard of liberty," survived to erect "the foundation of the perfect form of government."[6] As Brigham Young declared, "The exodus of the nation of the only true Israel from these United States to a far distant region of the West, where bigotry, intolerance and insatiable oppression lose their power over them—forms a new epoch."[7] In Brigham Young's language, the making of the Mormon people found expression: they were no longer merely another denomination, a Christian sect, but a nation, a new Israel, a people bound as much by heritage and identity as belief. As the scholar Jan Shipps has suggested, the Mormons' abandonment of the United States and trek to the Salt Lake Valley made them more than a denomination; it made them a "faith tradition," rooted in common faith but encompassing as well a shared language, history, culture, and folkways. In response to the persecution they faced in the United States, the Mormons made of themselves a people.

One hundred and fifty years after the death of his ancestor, Parley Pratt's great-great-grandson Mitt Romney announced his bid for the Republican Party's nomination for the presidency of the United States. While Parley Pratt struggled to reconcile his loyalty to his nation with his religious beliefs, Mitt Romney, a fourth-generation Mormon, seemed to see no struggle at all. He had served as governor of Massachusetts, and his father, George, as governor of Michigan. Both Romneys had remarkable success as businessmen in archetypically American industries: the elder Romney in automobiles in the 1940s and 1950s, the younger in the financial and capital markets in the 1980s and 1990s. And both were lifelong practicing Latter-day Saints. Like their ancestor, both served missions: George to the British Isles, Mitt to France. Both served in high offices in the church: as bishops (leaders of a single congregation called a ward and thus comparable to a pastor or Catholic priest) and stake presidents (presiding over a stake, a collection of several wards, comparable to a Catholic diocese).

Neither George nor his son Mitt seemed troubled by the fierce, combative tension between their faith and American culture that had so plagued their ancestor. By their time, Mormonism had self-consciously surrendered its attempt to build an independent kingdom of God in the West and had instead found ways to articulate its values in the language of American virtue. Indeed, to the younger Romney, his religion enriched his decision to seek the presidency. Invoking traditional Mormon praise for the Constitution's defense of religious freedom, which he called "fundamental to America's greatness," Romney argued that "freedom requires religion, just as religion requires freedom."[8] Placing his own faith alongside Catholicism, Protestantism, and Judaism, Romney argued that Mormonism could buttress the American civic religion as well as any other faith, that it upheld the values of individual responsibility, character, and democracy that Americans judged essential in any aspirant to the presidency.

He dismissed those who voiced suspicion of his faith as pedants quibbling over theology, matters he believed should not influence a voter's choice. So it was perhaps a surprise to Romney when he became the target of salvos that had been lobbed at the Mormons since Pratt's time. In *The New Republic* Damon Linker warned that the Mormons were subject to the potentially arbitrary command of a prophetic leader. *Slate*'s Jacob Weisberg argued that Mormons were credulous dupes obeying con men.[9] The Florida evangelist Bill Keller labeled the Mormons clannish, secretive, and heretical, cardinal sins in the rambunctious public square of American culture and politics. Mitt Romney, whose family for two generations had been archetypical American success stories, whose happy marriage and large family seemed almost too perfectly American, found himself in the role of defender for a faith that, it turned out, many Americans still found rather odd.

The extent to which Romney's Mormonism cost him the Republican nomination in 2008 is hard to judge. But his experience, particularly when seen in the light of the Mormon past, illuminates the tumultuous relationship between the Mormon faith and the nation with which it is so often identified. Over the course of its (by now) nearly two centuries of history, Americans have admired Mormons for their diligence, their rectitude, their faith, and their honesty; they have feared them for their zealotry, their polygamy, and their heresy. Mormons have been the model minority and a dangerous cancer on the republic—and sometimes both at the same time. From prophecy to polygamy to debates over gay marriage, Mormonism has frequently—

incongruously—lain at the center of America's debate over what sort of nation it wishes to be.

Similarly, Mormons have found in the United States inspiration and repression, each in a multitude of forms. Mormons have made American culture a mirror for their own aspirations, embracing its democratic culture and bootstrap ideology as expressions of their own profoundly optimistic theology. But Mormonism also began as a radical movement with a profoundly transformative vision of what American society might become. And despite its transformation into the all-American religion of the Romneys, that is still what it is; it presses at the boundaries of American life in a number of ways, challenging its norms as any prophetic religion must. From a faith with such a powerful sense of identity, such a vivid and compelling story of origin, such a profound hold on the spiritual life of its followers, anything less would be disappointing.

This book is a work of synthesis. Over the past forty years Mormon history has enjoyed a renaissance of sorts. In the 1970s and 1980s Mormons themselves began seeking graduate training in history, sociology, religious studies, and other disciplines, and these academics, together with an enthusiastic and remarkably diligent cadre of amateur Mormon scholars, turned the tools of their training on their own past. More recently, in the 1990s and 2000s, non-Mormon academics have taken an interest in what the Mormon experience might say about American life in general. These three groups have produced a remarkable amount of scholarship, and it is my aim to weave it into a coherent narrative, finding in this astonishing amount of timber something like the unity of a forest. Though I cite only primary quotations in the text, the bibliographic essay at the end of the book discusses the scholarship on which I relied in further detail.

MATTHEW BOWMAN
HAMPDEN-SYDNEY COLLEGE
JUNE 24, 2011–SEPTEMBER 14, 2011

THE
MORMON
PEOPLE

ONE

JOSEPH SMITH AND THE FIRST MORMONS

To 1831

O n a Monday morning in November 1835 a slender man in his middle forties, curiously dressed in a sea-green coat and pants and sporting a curling grey beard, picked his way into the muddy frontier town of Kirtland, Ohio, twenty miles northeast of Cleveland along the Chagrin River. He had come from New York City to visit Joseph Smith, Jr.: a national curiosity, twenty-nine years old, a self-declared prophet of God and leader of a people most often called the Mormons. Shortly after ten in the morning, Joseph's visitor found the prophet in his home in a row of cabins that lined a dirt road for perhaps a mile as it wound up a hillside from the river and toward an impressively large, if still incomplete, sandstone and lumber hall. The Mormons were building a temple, and the man, who rather evasively identified himself only as "Joshua the Jewish minister," must have gazed on it with awe and perhaps a little bit of envy. Joseph Smith, rarely humble, could not resist his visitor's apparent desire to discuss religion. The two spent the afternoon and evening together. Joseph told his visitor of his own visions of God, of the angel Moroni that had given him charge of golden plates that bore an ancient Christian scripture, and of his divine mandate to restore the Biblical church of Christ to the earth.

Joseph's scribe reported that the visitor seemed "highly entertained" at these stories, and well might he have been. After preaching to the prophet and some other Mormons on the impending degradation and collapse of American society, which he likened to the satanic Babylon of scripture, the man confirmed that he was in fact Robert Matthews, infamous in the press as "the Prophet Matthias." He claimed to be a true Israelite, the New Testament apostle Matthias reborn, divinely ordained to the "priestly" office that the Biblical name Joshua, with its echo of Mount Sinai and the Exodus, implied, and the embodied "spirit of truth."[1] Three years earlier, Matthews had converted a handful of well-off New Yorkers, rearranged their marriages, squandered their money, introduced a version of Jewish dietary codes, and prophesied that his child would be the Messiah. His small urban kingdom had crashed to the ground when he was indicted for the murder of one of his followers. Though not convicted of that crime, Matthews served several months for beating his daughter and for contempt of court, as he routinely shouted and preached during his trial. When he surveyed the town of Kirtland several months after his release, friendless and destitute, Matthews no doubt envied the younger prophet. Joseph Smith had produced scripture and attracted hundreds of followers, and his temple was rising yards from his front door. The town of Kirtland had itself become a projection of his vision and his will. Matthews came as a supplicant.

Despite their differences, the two prophets sprang from similar cultures and impulses. The young American nation fostered prophets. Life in the early republic was quite different from that of the small kingdoms of the British emigrants who had settled the land a century and a half before. The Puritans had dreamed of spiritually united communities in which both church and state served the righteous desires of God's elect, a society orderly, regular, and clear-eyed in its devotions. But two centuries after the first Puritans had waded to the shores of Massachusetts, the vision had come unraveled. The surge of individualism that followed the American Revolution and the Constitution's disestablishment of religion upset the old structures of authority. Such excitement for the experiment in self-government joined with a booming market economy growing through the eighteen century to produce a peculiar democratic tide that washed over the culture, society, and industry of early-nineteenth-century America. It offered Americans the opportunity to master their own lives rather than subordinate themselves to the collective. It trained them in individualism, in self-reliance, in risk-taking, and in the pursuit of opportunity. It fostered respect for refinement, for culture, for economic success. It taught that these qualities would come through rectitude, discipline, and hard work, and its way of life spread across the nation.

The prophets were children of this age. Their grand religious experiments were possible only in the chaotic freedom of the time. But each man in Kirtland that November morning longed for a cosmos ordered in ways far more permanent than the ceaseless whirl of democracy and trade seemed capable of offering, and each seemed to find such rest in marriage, family, and community. They preached salvation, the coming millennium, the great judgment of Christ on the chaos of their time, and they warned that only in their own ranks could salvation be found.

When Matthews claimed to be the product of reincarnation, Joseph Smith decided he had heard enough; he accused the older man of being possessed of a devil and cast him from Kirtland. Today, nearly two hundred years after their meeting, Robert Matthews lies buried and forgotten; even the date of his death remains uncertain.

Joseph Smith's grave, however, has become a pilgrimage site, his name recited and blessed in sermon and testimony by millions, the scripture he spoke and the rituals he taught cherished across the globe as the true and ordained way to God. His triumph sprang in part from the force and creativity of his religious imagination, his unswerving faith in his own capacities as a conduit for divine revelation, and his will to see his dreams made reality. But it grew also from the vision and dedication of those who chose to follow him: those who accepted and interpreted his ideas, who built in wood and stone the cities he saw in vision, and who, most of all, embodied in a holy community the divine experiences he craved. Men such as Joseph and the prophet Matthias were often assailed for theocracy, for rejecting democracy and establishing religious tyranny. But Mormonism was as much the construction of Joseph Smith's followers as of Smith himself. It was a sacramental community bound together through ritual, priesthood, and ordinance, and his people became the society of which Joseph had dreamed: a firm rock in an unreliable world, a faithful community that itself became, in a way, the salvation its followers sought.

In 1816 Joseph Smith, Sr., and his wife, Lucy Mack Smith, gathered their children, including ten-year-old Joseph Jr., and left their home in Vermont to chase opportunity west. They were part of a New England exodus across the Great Lakes region in the eighteenth and early nineteenth centuries, children of the decaying utopia of Puritan New England following paths since wrenched askew from those of their ancestors. There had been Smiths in Massachusetts and Macks in Connecticut since the seventeenth century, farmers and small merchants, though by the generation of Joseph and Lucy both families seemed interested in trying something new. Joseph Sr.'s father, Asael, took his family from urban Massachusetts to eighty-three acres of raw land in Tunbridge, Vermont, in 1791, while Lucy's father, Solomon Mack, and brother Stephen found prosperity as merchants in the burgeoning towns of Vermont. When Lucy and Joseph were wed, they received its fruits: part ownership of the farm from Asael and a thousand dollars for Lucy from Stephen.

Though Vermont might once have been isolated, in the first years of the nineteenth century the arteries of trade had reached its mountains: a weekly stage line to Boston in 1801, a canal reaching Connecticut a year later. The pulse of commerce began to move back and forth, and Joseph Smith, Sr., sought to ride it. He bought a host of goods on credit from Boston and opened a small general store in Tunbridge. For a time he was successful, enough so that in 1803 he banked his career on ginseng, an herb whose popularity in China was making American merchants rich. But when the ship that carried Joseph Sr.'s investment in the East returned, word that his shipment had earned only the price of a case of tea came with it. Outraged, Stephen Mack hunted down a merchant who admitted that he had stolen Joseph's due before fleeing to Canada. Joseph Sr. was left with nothing but debt to his Boston creditors, and he and Lucy sacrificed their wedding gifts to pay it: Joseph sold his share of the farm, and Lucy surrendered the thousand dollars of her dowry.

Joseph Smith, Sr., had glimpsed the fantastic possibilities this new society offered—he, the son of a farmer, trading with such an exotic locale as China, growing wealthy because of his acumen and confidence. But through no fault of his own, save perhaps desire and ambition, he instead fell through its cracks. The Smiths sank from the respectable upwardly mobile middle class into which Joseph and Lucy were born to the desperate lives of tenant farmers. Economic insecurity and social anxiety would plague them and their children for the rest of their lives. As Lucy stiffly described the choice to pay off her husband's debt, "This was considerable of a trial to us for it deprived us at once not only of the comforts and conveiniences of life but also of a home of any discription."[2] It was a bitter lesson that Joseph's children would have to learn vicariously, for the oldest living, Alvin, was barely five, with a younger brother, Hyrum, and an infant sister, Sophronia. The Smith child who worked hardest to overturn the systems of the world his parents struggled with, Joseph Jr., would not be born for another two years.

For a dozen years following the disaster, the Smith family drifted from farm to farm, from state to state. They lived in New Hampshire, Vermont, and Connecticut. Joseph Sr. worked variously as a schoolteacher, a day laborer, and a tenant farmer, cultivating land rented from other men. And they had more children: four sons, and another daughter. The oldest of these, born on December 23, 1805, was named Joseph Jr. He entered the world in a small cabin on a cold, windswept hill in Sharon, Vermont, on land rented from Lucy's father. A hundred years later, a group of well-dressed Mormons would travel there by train to erect a granite monument to the boy's life, but before he was two years old his ragged family left Sharon carrying their possessions on their backs, doggedly pursuing a stability that would never come.

Later, in her memoirs, Lucy devoted an entire chapter to her son Joseph Jr.'s bout with typhoid in 1813. The Smiths were then in New Hampshire, and the disease had killed thousands all across New England that year. Young Hyrum brought it home from his school, and the Smith parents prayed hand in hand through the night at the bedsides of their children who fell ill and recovered in turn. Just as the exhaustion and fear had passed, seven-year-old Joseph, seemingly recovered, complained of pain in his armpit and leg. Infection had set in. He was bled and lanced, but the disease had crept into his bone. Lucy recalled Hyrum sitting for hours with his brother's leg in his hands, applying pressure that allowed Joseph to sleep, and when doctors recommended that Joseph's leg be amputated, she refused to allow them into the boy's room. They instead agreed to peel back the flesh and chip away the diseased bone, which came off in three large chunks. As Lucy told the story, her seven-year-old son exhibited preternatural poise and compassion, ordering his mother to leave the room rather than to see her child in such pain and declaring that he would take no alcohol to numb his senses but instead should be held in the steady embrace of his father, who, he insisted, could "stand it" when his son screamed in his arms. And Joseph Sr., white-faced, did just that, while his wife agonized on the stoop, clinging to her son's declaration that "the Lord will help me, and I shall get through with it."[3]

Lucy's memories taught her readers of the Smith family religion. Neither she nor her husband was a member of any church, but this was not due to lack of faith or longing. The Smiths had a strong sense of the power of God's providence in their lives, and they measured it by the strong bonds that held the family together. Her son's prodigious spiritual insights and firm confidence in God's will was to Lucy an example to them all. She explained that during Joseph's recovery "we felt to acknowledge the hand of God, more in preserving our lives through such a tremendous scene of affliction, than if we had, during this time, seen nothing but health and prosperity." Lucy's mother, Lydia, a dutiful Congregationalist, had imparted to her daughter her stern piety: Lucy passionately prayed and studied scripture throughout her life and taught her children to do so as well. She was firmly convinced that direct appeals to God had saved various family members from a plague of consumption in her youth. While herself deathly ill several years into her marriage she pled that God would "let me live, if I am faithful to the promise which I made to him, to be a comfort to my mother, my husband, and my children."[4] Upon recovery she sought and found a minister who would baptize her without a subsequent obligation to join any congregation: though she longed for guidance and instruction, her church was her family.

She found her husband to be like her a seeker, but somewhat less orthodox. Joseph Sr.'s father, Asael, had abandoned Congregationalism for Universalism, the doctrine that Christ's crucifixion saved all humanity, without exception. To Calvinists this was heresy. But by 1797, the Tunbridge Universalist Society recorded among its members Asael, his brother Jesse—and Asael's son Joseph. As Asael insisted to his children late in his life, Christ "can as well Save all, as aney."[5] In Tunbridge, Lucy prevailed upon her husband to attend a Methodist service, which proved to be not to his tastes and led to scorn from his father. But he regularly had dreams—dreams like those of Joseph of Egypt, like those of Daniel, like those of Ezekiel. In them he wandered across barren and broken landscapes, guided toward some elusive salvation by ministering spirits but constantly threatened by shadowy forces and terrible beasts. Lucy said that one dream featured "horned cattle, and roaring animals . . . tearing the earth, tossing their horns, and bellowing most terrifically" that reared up against him when he happened upon salvation. In multiple dreams, he was brought to a door or a gateway, to a garden or a great building where he "prayed earnestly for admittance"—but when the door cracked he always awoke, dissatisfied, before he could enter.[6] Joseph Sr. wanted more than anything to walk into that church, but he found no faith in America that satisfied him.

A wistful seeker's faith followed the Smith family over the next ten years, even as they struggled toward some measure of economic stability. In 1816, the infamous year without a summer (also called "Eighteen Hundred and Froze to Death"), frost persisted into June and July and rivers remained icy all summer as far south as Pennsylvania. Like thousands of others, the Smith family lost their crops. By the end of that year they had followed Joseph Sr.'s brother Jesse to western New York. They settled just east of Rochester in a bustling village called

Palmyra, a series of farms scattered around a small crossroads, where sat a Presbyterian church, a printing shop, and a handful of other commercial businesses. There, they once again began to plant roots: Joseph Sr. and his older sons hired out as laborers, and they gradually earned enough to purchase a farm a mile or two from town in 1819. They routinely struggled to meet their mortgage payments, but Lucy spoke with relief of their "snug comfortable though humble habitation built and neatly furnished by our own industry."[7]

The Smiths had unwittingly moved into an ideal location for a family with unresolved spiritual yearnings, the center of what one historian has called "the antebellum spiritual hothouse" and another "the burned-over district." Work began on the Erie Canal, which passed through Palmyra, in 1817 and concluded in 1825, but even before it was completed the canal made upstate New York the bustling highway of American commerce: farmers shipped their grain down the canal east; merchants sent the luxuries of Boston and New York back. Through its connection to the Great Lakes, the canal became a major thoroughfare to the western settlements in Illinois and Indiana, and along its banks boomtowns such as Palmyra thrived. Canal workers, settlers, and farmers traveled back and forth, beginning a great age of American migration, and so did the prophets.

The optimism, instability, and freedom of the New York frontier were life's blood to the eclecticism and experimentation always to be found at the margins of mainstream Christianity. The Shakers, for instance, so named for their physical worship services, had fled to America from a disapproving Britain under the leadership of Ann Lee, whom they believed to be Christ reincarnated. In the United States they found fertile ground for both converts and settlement, and in 1826 they established a colony less than thirty miles from Palmyra. Another reincarnated Jesus, the ex-Quaker Jemima Wilkinson, founded her own community in Jerusalem, New York. Farther east along the canal lay Oneida, where John Humphrey Noyes taught that as the Second Coming had already occurred, it now fell to the elect to build sanctuaries of "Bible communism," where the conventions of marriage and commercial capitalism that ruled the rest of the country would be set aside. North of Albany, the farmer William Miller sat by the fire in his home in Low Hampton, New York, feverishly working out the precise date of the Second Coming from the book of Daniel for his thousands of followers, who were convinced that they needed no trained pastors to interpret scripture for them.

But the Smiths had always been drawn—particularly Lucy—not to such visionaries but to the more mainstream ecstasies of evangelical revivalism. The force behind revivalism was the Methodists, who rejected the Calvinist teaching that God had already selected those who would be saved and instead urged potential converts to embrace Christ in a personal divine encounter. At Methodist camp meetings, itinerant preachers, though frequently uneducated and even unlettered, learned how to rouse the Holy Spirit among their listeners. Between rousing and sometimes raucous gospel hymns, they offered not prepared sermons on doctrinal topics but emotional appeals, promising forgiveness, warning of hell, reaching their hands to the heavens, and pleading with the crowd to leave sin behind and walk forward to be saved in the arms of Christ. Speakers, some lay, some ordained, would rotate on the platform for days at a time, and masses of unchurched farmers, laborers, and the poor would gather to learn of their eternal fate. "Men are so spiritually sluggish," declared Charles Grandison Finney, the great revivalist of the age, "that they must be so excited that they will break over their countervailing influences before they will obey God."[8] Finney's talents shone in a months-long revival in 1830–31 in Rochester, a few miles from Palmyra, in which he converted hundreds. When Finney learned after years of successful revivalism throughout New York and New England that his denomination officially embraced Calvinist predestination theologies, he abandoned Presbyterianism in horror.

The sort of spiritual manifestations the Smith family had already experienced were not new to most revivalists. Portentous dreams were common particularly among itinerant Methodist preachers, as were the type of healings and providential manifestations Lucy had experienced. At some Methodist camp meetings many spoke in tongues, had visions of Christ, and experienced bodily convulsions, dreams, and trances. When the Smiths arrived in Palmyra in the midst of a revival that stretched from 1816 to 1817, they were naturally interested. The number of Presbyterians in the town doubled over those years, and Lucy herself joined the church, frequently taking her sons Hyrum and Samuel and daughter Sophronia with her.

It was in this atmosphere that Joseph Jr., then a young teenager, began thinking about religion. Lucy was curious about her third son. She recalled him "much less inclined to the perusal of books than any of the rest of our children, but far more given to meditation and deep study," though from his later writings it seems clear that his mind and language were drenched in the rhythms, phrases, and ideas of the Bible.[9] The young man seemed fascinated with the revival. As he said later, he was "somewhat partial to the Methodist sect." But even though he wanted "to get Religion too wanted to feel & shout like the Rest," he could "feel nothing."[10] Though the revivalists promised a personal encounter with Christ, to Joseph the spiritual "feelings" that he craved "were entirely lost in a strife of words and a contest about opinions."[11] The boy who had learned from his dreaming father and faithful mother to value spiritual community above all saw it dissolved in the tumult of the revival, where individual experience trumped all. Mormons today, confident in the importance of membership in their church, interpret Joseph's confusion as distress over which denomination he should join. Joseph does mention this, but it seems clear that his spiritual anxiety went deeper: like his parents, he was disturbed by the chaos and uncertainty in the world around him. From God he wanted security, not dramatics. And so, after encountering the verses in the First Epistle of James which direct the faithful that "If any of you lack wisdom, let him ask of God," Joseph decided to ask. Like Thoreau or Muhammad or Moses, Joseph Smith sought God in the wilderness. Probably at age fourteen, in the spring of 1820, he went to the woods behind his father's farm to pray.

He recorded the experiences that happened next in at least three later manuscripts, one in 1832, one in 1835 (in his scribe's record of the story told to Matthias), and one in 1838. Each describes slightly different details. Today Mormons call the event "the First Vision," seeing in it the inauguration of the restoration of truth, the beginning of the last dispensation of Christ's church. But for the young Joseph, the event was more likely not so different from the prophetic dreams his father had had or the revelations other revivalists reported. It was a personal vision in a visionary age, the experience that confirmed to him that God was offering him salvation. This is how Joseph recorded the experience in 1832, saying that "a pillar of light above the brightness of the sun at noon day come down from above and rested upon me and I was filled with the spirit of god and the Lord opened the heavens . . . and he spake to me saying Joseph my Son thy sins are forgiven thee, go thy way walk in my statutes and keep my commandments."[12] Later, he expanded his account. The 1838 version introduces the presence of Christ as well, describing in "a pillar of light . . . two Personages, whose brightness and glory defy all description," and follows Joseph's forgiveness of sins with direction to join no church, "for they were all wrong." Joseph testified, "The Personage who addressed me said that all their creeds were an abomination in his sight."[13]

When the spectacular shaft of light receded, Joseph remembered lying dazed on his back in the quiet grove, no doubt baffled and overwhelmed. He returned to his house and said very little about his experience. He later said that all he told his mother was that he had learned for himself that Presbyterianism was not true. Lucy would later conflate his teenage reluctance to join a church with his later experiences with angels, not with any vision of God the boy might have had. Indeed, to his parents, little seemed changed about their son for several years. As usual, there was work to do, for the Smiths were constantly struggling to afford their mortgage, and, as he frequently did, Joseph Sr. had made an unwise financial choice: to build a relatively extravagant frame house to replace the family cabin. Other than this, the next several years were quiet.

And then, late in the night of September 21, 1823, an angel appeared by Joseph's bedside while he prayed. "His whole person was glorious beyond description," Joseph wrote, "and his countenance truly like lightening." Finally, for the first time, Joseph was told that "God had a work for me to do." The angel identified himself as "Moroni" and told Joseph that in a hill nearby was "a book deposited, written upon gold plates, giving an account of the former inhabitants of this continent . . . he also said that the fullness of the everlasting Gospel was contained in it, as delivered by the savior to the ancient inhabitants."[14] Moroni then recited several passages from the Bible—from Malachi, Acts, Joel, and Isaiah—verses familiar to Joseph, who understood their millenarian import: Moroni was advising him that the last days were at hand, that the time had come to repent and prepare for the Second Coming of Christ. Then he vanished, only to reappear shortly thereafter. Moroni appeared to Joseph three times that night, each time repeating all he had said, and again the next day, as the exhausted boy was leaving the fields upon finding himself too weary to work. To his last visit, Moroni appended a command that Joseph should tell his father everything. Joseph Sr., a man comfortable with visions, advised his son to obey.

Mormons today call the hill "Cumorah," the name of such a site in the Book of Mormon. It sits some three miles south of the Smith homestead, and Joseph probably walked there later that September afternoon. He found the stone Moroni described on the western side and used a log to pry it up, revealing a crude stone box containing both the plates and two stones set in a silver bow attached to a breastplate. Moroni had identified these as a "Urim and Thummim," a device for translation described in the Bible. Joseph reached for them and was hurled backward. Moroni appeared and informed the boy that he was tempted by the gold of the plates rather than the divine message they contained. He would have to wait four years and prove himself by returning to the hill faithfully each September 22 before he would be allowed to recover them.

That night, Joseph told his family everything, and they believed every word. Lucy recalled the occasion with joy, noting that Joseph's mission "caused us greatly to rejoice, the sweetest union and happiness pervaded our house, and tranquility reigned in our midst."[15] Lucy remembered that many nights afterward he would gather them together and distract them from their troubles by telling stories of Moroni.

But as so frequently seemed to happen to the Smiths, their short happiness was shattered. Early the next year Alvin, the eldest Smith son, died, either of appendicitis or of accidental calomel poisoning. His last words urged his brother Joseph to recover the lost plates. According to Joseph's younger brother William, at Alvin's funeral a minister warned that the dead man, who had never joined a church, might well be suffering in hell, a proposition to which the Smiths reacted violently. But mostly they mourned, Joseph, who had idolized his brother, particularly so. They also faced a hard reality. Alvin had in his early twenties become the family's financial engine; he had cosigned for the farm with his father and was building his parents' frame house. By 1825, the family fell behind on their mortgage again, and Joseph Sr., who seemed to have little energy left, managed to save the land only by persuading a friend to purchase it and rent it out to the hapless family.

Perhaps the Smiths found Joseph's tale easy to believe because Moroni's behavior would not have seemed so incongruous to Americans accustomed to dramatic religious experience, objects of mysterious power, or even buried treasure. Since the time of the Puritans, who regularly divined omens from the weather, used herbs to heal, and sought protection from rituals and wards, folk practices that ministers angrily labeled "magic" or "superstition" had thrived in America. But despite the clergy's complaints, many of their flock saw little difference between angels or the miracles of the New Testament and the possibility that dowsers could locate water with a birch rod, as Joseph Sr. sometimes did, or that gazing into a particular stone might show one with the gift visions of lost and hidden objects. The year before his encounter with Moroni, Joseph had found such a stone while digging a well, and he later acquired another. His mother said that with these seerstones he could scry, or see things invisible to the natural eye.

Joseph was not alone; a neighbor named Sally Chase, a member of a respectable Methodist family, could find money and other lost objects with a stone of her own. Her brother Willard was there when Joseph found his stone, and the two seers developed something of a rivalry. Other neighbors consulted various means of fortune-telling, drew magical symbols on parchment to guard their sleep, and sought charms to ward off disease.

Particularly appealing to these magicians was the quest for buried treasure. Stories of lost riches in the hills of New York, left by pirates or Spanish conquistadores or lost native civilizations and guarded by the spirits of the dead, were popular in Palmyra. The spirits were said to have demands for any who sought it, and scryers and magicians hoped they possessed the talents to meet these challenges. Surrounding Palmyra were the burial sites of a number of Native American tribes, and it was quite common for children to come home with beads, carvings, and other artwork. It is hard not to see Moroni fitting into young Joseph's world, hard not to imagine Joseph pointing to the tumuli standing silently out in the night as he told his gathered family stories of Moroni and his ancient civilization.

In 1825 a man named Josiah Stowall, a middle-aged Presbyterian businessman and farmer, heard of Joseph Smith, Jr.'s talents and hired the young man and his father to come to Harmony, Pennsylvania, some 150 miles south of Palmyra. Stowall was convinced that an ancient Spanish silver mine lay near his land there, and he wanted Joseph to find it. To Stowall, an American in a world where business and magic existed side by side, this was an investment as sure as his farm. Quite aware of what Stowall's money—and perhaps Spanish silver— would mean to his parents, Joseph Smith spent most of 1825 and 1826 in Pennsylvania, digging and scrying. He found no silver. In 1826 Stowall's nephew, believing Joseph to be a swindler, brought a complaint against the Smiths in court. Stowall himself testified to his confidence in the young man's gifts. Joseph had, it seemed, proved able to find lost objects and help neighbors locate cattle; the old farmer seemed sure that it would only be a matter of time before the silver came to light. Joseph appears to have been released with virtually no sentence.

He did seem increasingly embarrassed by his association with the treasure diggers. While in Harmony he met and courted Emma Hale, the twenty-two-year-old daughter of a local farmer named Isaac Hale, whose solid prosperity as much as his strict Methodism led him to doubt the young seer's petitions for his daughter. Hale was a man of the marketplace, and he immediately recognized that Joseph Smith, Jr., was not of his persuasion. He seemed largely uninterested in the young man's heresies. Rather, Isaac's concerns about Joseph were roused when he considered his would-be son-in-law's capacity for supporting Emma. He complained that though the Smiths boarded at his home, they never paid their rent and later said that he rejected Joseph's request for Emma's hand because the young man "followed a business I could not approve."[16] A few years later, after Joseph had recovered the golden plates, Isaac wanted to heft the chest that held them, but he quickly lost interest when told he was not allowed to look inside, counseling Joseph to remove it from the house so that curious neighbors would not come looking for a glimpse.

Emma, tall, with a serious face and dark hair, had a firmness in her. In January 1827, she visited Joseph at the Stowall home, and he pled with her to elope with him. Exhibiting the steady tenacity that later trials would require of her, she concluded that though "my folks were bitterly opposed to him . . . preferring to marry him to any other man I knew, I consented."[17] The two were married in the living room of one of Stowall's friends and immediately traveled to Palmyra. It was just after Joseph's twenty-first birthday, but the young man was already tall and barrel-chested, with a prominent nose and light brown hair and an intensity in his gaze that captivated many he encountered.

In the summer of 1827 the couple returned to Harmony to claim some of Emma's possessions. During this visit they had a tense encounter with Isaac Hale. Joseph assured his father-in-law that "he expected to work hard for a living and was willing to do so," promising that his days as a treasure seeker were over.[18] This was precisely the thing to say. Isaac proved to possess a capacity for tolerance, and offered his new son-in-law work and the couple a place to stay on the Hale family property. But soon—and likely to Isaac's chagrin—Joseph and Emma left for Palmyra again. September 22, 1827, the fourth anniversary of Joseph's visit to the hill, was approaching.

The events from the fall of 1827 through early 1829 appear in retrospect archetypal. These first patterns of behavior, reaction, and preoccupation left their imprint on the burgeoning Mormon movement, and it would bear their mark for decades thereafter. That September, Joseph retrieved the plates and seemed dismayed that he was met not with praise and awe but skepticism and hostility. That reception forced him to desperation and flight, to reliance on his own people. If there is a point at which the Mormon sense of otherness, its conviction that its own identity was formed in the fires of persecution, was born, this may be it. Joseph found that the message, which seemed to him so glorious and essential, was met with doubt and scorn. Late on September 21, 1827, most of the Smith household seemed to be awake and tense with anticipation. Joseph found his mother and asked if she had a chest with a sturdy lock. She did not. Joseph instead located Emma, and the two left for the hill shortly after midnight in a borrowed wagon. They did not return till late the next morning—and they did not have the plates.

Joseph had not been shy about sharing the story of Moroni. Josiah Stowall and Joseph Knight, another friend of Joseph's from his time in Harmony, had come to Palmyra to witness whatever might occur that night. Moreover, Joseph's fellow treasure seekers seemed to believe they had finally struck gold. Upon returning to Palmyra Joseph found Willard Chase and others eager to claim a share of whatever their former compatriot may have found, and he warned his parents to avoid certain neighbors. When he returned home, Joseph reported that he had concealed the plates in a hollow log to hide them from the treasure diggers and that he was to show them to no one. He instead showed his mother the breastplate and handed her what felt rather like "old fashioned spectacles" wrapped in a handkerchief, but with a longer bow and strangely thick and round lenses: the Urim and Thummim.[19] Joseph moved the plates several times over the next few days, but Willard Chase and the other money diggers were persistent, even violent. One night Joseph arrived home with a dislocated finger, bruised and battered, reporting that he had been attacked while lugging the plates—which weighed some fifty pounds, according to others who hefted them—home from the log. Chase hired a conjurer to find the plates and enlisted his sister, whose own seerstone led a mob to the Smiths' barn. One night it was ransacked, but the plates were not there.

So, for the first time in Mormon history, but hardly the last, the believers fled, finding the mission Joseph believed to be divinely inspired forced into compromise with the rough-and-tumble world of the American frontier. As the Smiths had so often done, and as Mormons would do again and again, they retreated to their own people. After the barn was raided Joseph threw himself on the mercy of family; soon Emma's brother arrived in Palmyra to cart the couple and the plates back to Harmony.

Over the next months of his life, Joseph Smith found himself dependent upon the generosity of two older men, whose divergent responses to the boy reflected not only their own preoccupations but American culture in the early republic. The first was Isaac Hale. Rather exasperated at Joseph and his golden plates, he nonetheless took the couple in, gave Joseph work, and eventually sold him a house on his property. The young man proved himself to his father-in-law by paying off the house in 1830.

The second was Martin Harris, an affluent farmer who lived on the north side of Palmyra and had occasionally hired the Smith boys to work on his farm. Harris's fascination with the mystical was as typical of the age as Isaac's pious capitalism was. Like the Smiths, he doubted traditional orthodoxies; claiming that personal inspiration from God had led him to join no church, he scoffed at doctrines that made no sense to him, such as the Trinity: "I cannot find it in any Bible," he would say later.[20] Martin Harris possessed an Enlightenment skepticism and a readiness to accept the supernatural, a combination that might seem curious to modern Americans, but it marked him as very much a man of his time. Antebellum America was full of Harrises—women and men who instinctively doubted the authority of a minister but who heard the voices of angels outside their windows late at night.

When he first heard of the "golden Bible," Harris wondered if the money diggers had found a kettle, but his curiosity led him to the Smith home. He interviewed each Smith individually before approaching Joseph, who astonished the man with an announcement that God had work for Harris to do. Denied a viewing of the plates, Harris went home and stewed, but in early 1828 he appeared in Harmony, convinced by prayer that God wished him to stand at Joseph's side. Like Hale, he was given the plates in a chest to heft, but while the other man's gruff practicality left him little interested, Harris was intrigued; he wanted further evidence. Joseph gave him a scrap of paper covered in strange symbols: this was, he said, "reformed Egyptian," the form of writing on the plates.[21] He sent Harris, paper in hand, to consult with scholars.

Harris went to Charles Anthon, an expert in Semitic languages at Columbia College, but the events of their meeting are under dispute.

According to Harris, Anthon identified the symbols as genuinely ancient and signed a document to that effect. The professor then inquired
about the source of the transcript, and when Harris told him about
Joseph, Moroni, and the plates, Anthon politely asked for his affidavit
back and tore it up. He asked to see the plates himself, and when Harris said they were sealed away, Anthon declared, "I cannot read a sealed
book."[22] Later Anthon would write two letters, in 1834 and 1841,
denying Harris's claims and warning that the farmer was being
scammed. Oddly, he described the scrap as bearing zodiacal signs
mixed with Greek and Hebrew letters, which does not resemble the
transcript later published. No Anthon certification exists; all that stands
is his denial. When Harris returned, Joseph was thrilled, both with
Harris's report and with Anthon's parting words. He turned his King
James Bible to Isaiah 29:11, which described "a book that is sealed,
which men deliver to one that is learned, saying, Read this, I pray thee;
and he saith, I cannot; for it is sealed."

Several years later Joseph would write the story in his own hand,
constructing the dialogue between Harris and Anthon as a close paraphrase of Isaiah. For Joseph, Anthon's rejection of Harris was more
important than the confirmation Harris reported, for two reasons.
First, it broke open a gap between his prophetic authority and that of
experts, the trained men of the world. In Anthon Joseph saw his rejection at the hands of the establishment, the elite, the learned, and he
welcomed it. He would build something better. But Anthon's enact-
ment of Isaiah's prophecy also reawoke in Joseph the sense that he had
possessed since he had heard Moroni quote to him the apocalyptic
verses from Malachi and the rest: the history in which Joseph was living
had ruptured from mundane time. Rather, he was living in the latter
days, the age of prophecy. The separation from the Palmyra money
diggers, the flight to Harmony, Anthon's dismissal—all of these only
whetted the young man's appetite to make for himself a different
world. It would begin with translation.

Harris was completely convinced. He spoke of paying for the publication of the translation and sponsoring Joseph, who decided Harris
would be his scribe. On the upper floor of Joseph's small house in
Harmony, Emma may have hung a blanket to divide the room in two.

Joseph sat on one side, with the Urim and Thummim, Lucy's "spectacles," over his eyes and the plates before him. Harris sat on the other side of the blanket, pen ready as Joseph read aloud. Emma spoke later of touching the plates as they lay on the table under their cloth, after Joseph and Martin had finished for the day, as she said, gingerly "tracing their outline and shape. They seemed to be pliable like thick paper, and would rustle with a metallic sound when the edges were traced by the thumb."[23] From the middle of April to the middle of June 1828, the two men worked slowly, producing 116 pages. And then disaster struck.

By early June, Harris was worried about his wife, like Joseph's mother also named Lucy. She was back in Palmyra, distressed with her husband's apparent determination to throw the family fortune after a country prophet. Harris pled with Joseph to allow him to take the pages home to prove to his wife the worth of his work. His timing was poor, for Emma was just coming to the end of an exhausting and dangerous pregnancy, and Joseph said no. Harris asked again. Joseph again refused, saying that God would not allow it. Harris asked again. Finally, Joseph relented. He instructed Harris that only immediate family members were allowed to see the pages and sent the older man on his way. Only days later, on June 15, Emma nearly died giving birth to a boy: Alvin, who lived for only a few hours. Joseph tended to his wife and grieved. By the end of the month he realized that Harris had not yet returned. Emma, who had marveled at her husband's dictation, urged Joseph to go after him. In Palmyra he gave his parents the sorry news. They invited Harris to breakfast, but for several hours he failed to appear. A little after noon, Lucy looked out the window to see Harris "walking with a slow and measured tread towards the house. . . . On coming to the gate, he stopped instead of passing through and got upon the fence, and sat there some time."[24] Martin Harris had lost the pages, and Joseph despaired.

Joseph had been a visionary and a translator, a man who saw angels and produced scripture, but this new crisis pushed him into prophecy, the proclamation of the Word of God. He stayed in Palmyra for several days, afraid to return and break the news to Emma. But when he returned in July, for the first time Joseph received what he and his followers would later call a "commandment" or a "revelation." As his associates would later describe it, in a voice steady, strong, and slow, the blood drained from his face, he dictated to a scribe what seemed to be the word of God himself—sonorous, formal, distant, and judgmental even upon Joseph himself. As the revelation ran:

> For God doth not walk in crooked paths, neither doth he turn to the right hand nor to the left, neither doth he vary from that which he hath said . . . it is not the work of God that is frustrated, but the work of men. . . . Behold thou art Joseph, and thou wast chosen to do the work of the Lord, but because of transgression if thou art not aware thou wilt fall.[25]

Line after line poured forth, declaring that "my work shall go forth," and "even so, shall the knowledge of a Savior come to my people." As the year progressed, the revelations continued to come, one directed to Joseph's father, declaring in a phrase famous among Mormons today that "a marvelous work is about to come forth among the children of men."[26] As would so often be the case, Joseph Smith returned from failure with an expanded vision: more than merely a book, he now spoke of a "work," some grander effort of which translation would be only a beginning.

By late 1828 Emma had replaced the still-believing but now unreliable Harris as scribe, and Joseph made some efforts at translation. He wrote off the work done with Harris and began fresh, with a different portion of the plates. Progress was halting and slow until April 1829, when Joseph's brother Samuel arrived in Harmony with a lanky young man with sharp features and dark hair. This was Oliver Cowdery, a schoolteacher who had boarded with the Smiths in Palmyra and had heard with fascination the stories of Lucy's remarkable son. The two young men immediately sensed an affinity, and two days after his arrival Cowdery took up the pen to serve as scribe. The second effort at translation moved much more quickly than the first. Joseph had dispensed with the Urim and Thummim and instead sat at the table with his scribe, the plates wrapped in a cloth before him, and stared into his seerstone as the words flowed from his lips. He sometimes placed the stone in the bottom of a hat and pressed it to his face to block out the light.

Mormons today describe Joseph as the "translator" of the Book of Mormon, because that is the word he and his associates used, but it is not, according to common modern definitions of the word, a strictly accurate description. He made no effort to puzzle out the letters on the plates—indeed, while working with Cowdery he did not look at the plates at all. Rather, much as with the revelations, he spoke a sentence or two, paused for Cowdery to write it, and then spoke another. Though Joseph himself never commented on the process of translation, many of his associates—Cowdery, Emma, Harris, Joseph Knight, and others—seemed to believe that words appeared on the stone as Joseph stared. As one witness, David Whitmer, put it, "One character at a time would appear, and under it was the interpretation in English. Brother Joseph would read off the English to Oliver Cowdery."[27] A portion of the manuscript Cowdery transcribed still exists, and the corrections on it indicate that Joseph spelled out proper nouns, and Emma once commented that each morning Joseph "would at once begin where he had left off, without either seeing the manuscript or having any portion of it read to him."[28]

Cowdery arrived in Harmony on April 5, 1829. In the middle of May he and Joseph, again fleeing curious neighbors, moved their work to Fayette, New York, some thirty miles from Palmyra. There they stayed with the family of Peter and Mary Whitmer, friends of Oliver's who quickly became convinced of the importance of Joseph's task. On June 11, Joseph Smith took the title page to a local courthouse and applied for a copyright. This means that Joseph had dictated to Cowdery the bulk of what would become some six hundred pages of closely printed prose in roughly two months, about the same amount of time in which Martin Harris had taken down 116 pages. In October, thanks in part to three thousand dollars from the faithful Harris, a Palmyra printing shop began typesetting the Book of Mormon. It went on sale the following March.

The story to this point seems incredible to many modern Americans, who instinctively dismiss that which seems irrational or unprovable, and that it should. It belongs to a different time, an age when the intellectual revolutions of the Enlightenment still stood locked in uneasy embrace with the intuitive and mystical world of the premodern age. Whether angels, the voice of God, and ancient holy plates appeared in the life of Joseph Smith or not, he and those around him firmly believed that such events were possible, and his followers believed they were very real indeed. For his friends and contemporaries who watched the events of the late 1820s unfold, these events happened as Joseph Smith reported them, and the same is true for modern Mormons. The sharp presence of the supernatural reaches from the early-nineteenth-century frontier into twenty-first-century meetinghouses, where young children are taught of Moroni and golden plates. Just as the miracles performed by Catholic saints or the ecstasies of Pentecostalism bind other believers to the world of the New Testament apostles, these stories bind Mormons today to the world Joseph Smith experienced. For those faithful believers, the New Testament has not yet dissolved into myth; for Mormons, Joseph Smith has yet to either.

But many others, both those contemporary to Joseph Smith and today, find the stories of Moroni and the plates too fantastical to be believed. Though many critics—such as Mark Twain, who famously labeled the book "chloroform in print"—dismissed the Book of Mormon as a slag of dull prose, they still struggle to explain how an unschooled twenty-three-year-old like Joseph Smith could have produced the alien voices and complex narrative within it. Some have suggested that some educated man, most often Joseph's later associate Sidney Rigdon, produced the Book of Mormon, perhaps working from a novel, though efforts to make such theories fit the evidence of what went on in Palmyra and Harmony quickly lurch into the conspiratorial.

More recently, scholars have begun speaking of Joseph Smith as a "religious genius," capable of producing such a text from his own fiery imagination. He was hardly alone among the prophets of the age, many of whom produced revelatory texts: in England, a woman named Joanna Southcott had, a generation earlier, published a voluminous set of revelations that wove dialogues she had had with God into a narrative of her life and visions. In the United States Jemima Wilkinson also received revelations, describing elaborate visions that echoed those of Revelation, as well as Ezekiel and other Biblical prophets. Later in the nineteenth century Ellen G. White, the prophetess of the Seventh-day Adventists, had similar experiences and produced similar texts. Joseph Smith lived in a visionary age, and by any measure he had success because people were open to such possibilities. But even by the measure of such contemporaries, Joseph Smith's revelatory corpus is distinctive precisely for the absence of his own voice. While in their writings Southcott chats with God and Wilkinson sees visions like Paul or the Hebrew prophets, Joseph's voice is nowhere to be heard in the Book of Mormon, and the few times he does appear in the other revelations, he is almost always addressed as a hearer rather than functioning as a participant.

The Book of Mormon is divided into fifteen books, all titled in Biblical style: "The First Book of Nephi," "The Book of Jacob," "The Book of Alma," and so forth; there are some 350 named people and places, from Amalakiah and Abish to Zeniff and Zoram. It presents itself as the work of three main ancient authors who lived in a time spanning the years from just before the fall of Jerusalem to the Babylonians in 587 B.C.E. to sometime just after 400 C.E. Their voices are distinct, their preoccupations, moods, even vocabulary distinguishable. Each of these authors produces his own prose but also works from other sources that he quotes, redacts, or paraphrases on occasion, from the Hebrew Bible (closely, but not precisely, following the King James Version) to records left by other characters within the text. We are given a monetary system, a scale of weights and measures, and a mathematical system that appears to be base 8 rather than base 10. It is an enormously complicated work, written in archaic English vaguely reminiscent of the King James Bible, dense and often repetitive to a degree that often turns off merely curious readers. But the book is self-consciously written to be read. As the last verses, in the voice of Moroni, run:

> And again, if ye by the grace of God are perfect in Christ, and deny not his power, then are ye sanctified in Christ by the grace of God, through the shedding of the blood of Christ, which is in the covenant of the Father unto the remission of your sins, that ye become

holy, without spot. And now I bid unto all, farewell. I soon go to rest in the paradise of God, until my spirit and body shall again reunite, and I am brought forth triumphant through the air, to meet you before the pleasing bar of the great Jehovah, the Eternal Judge of both quick and dead. Amen.[29]

The narrative follows a group of Israelites guided by God out of Jerusalem as the Babylonian armies approach, around 600 B.C.E. They flee to the sea, where they build a ship and sail to a "promised land," which appears to be, though is never identified as, the American continent. Once there, the founding family—a prophet named Lehi, his wife, Sariah, and his several children, most prominently two sons named Nephi and Laman—collapse into infighting, eventually dividing into rival factions that became competing civilizations, the righteous Nephites and the wicked Lamanites. Nephi is the first narrator, and he comes across as a well-intentioned but frustrating young man of great faith and distinct lack of empathy for those like Laman who lack the trust in God and consequent divine experiences Nephi is blessed with. After his death and a few brief interpolations by some of his descendants, the book leaps forward hundreds of years and into the voice of Mormon, a Nephite soldier living in the 300s C.E. He is the primary narrator of the book that bears his name, and he announces his task to be the abridgment of his people's history. Over the next several hundred pages, Mormon narrates the story of kings and wars, missionaries and prophets, inserting occasional letters and sermons, describing the Nephites' struggle to alternately convert and defend themselves against the Lamanites. But the focus of the book is the Nephites' struggle to maintain their humility despite their prosperity. By Mormon's time, the Nephite civilization has succumbed to pride and wickedness, become arrogant and unbending despite the looming inevitability of Lamanite victory. In despair, near the end of the book the old prophet turns the record over to his son, Moroni, who adds a brief history of another civilization, some letters from his father, and his own final thoughts before burying the plates in Cumorah, where they would wait for some fourteen hundred years until Moroni himself, as a resurrected angel, would lead Joseph Smith to unearth them anew.

Despite its politics and wars, the Book of Mormon is ultimately a religious history—a history of the religious affairs of the people it describes, but more important, a history written from a religious perspective. The ultimate cause of all historical events in the Book of Mormon is the nature of a people's relationship with God. The rise and fall of Nephite civilization mirrors the cycle of prosperity and corruption the Israelite civilization of the Hebrew Bible endures; righteousness gains a people wealth, success in war, and happiness, which leads inevitably to arrogance and pride. Consequently they lose their faith and are again brought low. The narrators understand their purpose to be to convince their readers that this is indeed how history works. Mormon frequently ends his stories with a flourish, "And thus we see," followed by an exhortation to trust God and obey his commandments. Compared to the Jews they leave behind, the Nephites are remarkably Christian; beginning with Nephi himself, their prophets possess detailed knowledge about the mission of Jesus, and the text is full of sermons about faith, atonement, and repentance. The centerpiece of the text is the appearance of a resurrected Jesus Christ to the Nephites soon after his ascension in Israel: he blesses their children, heals their sick, teaches them, and ordains twelve Nephite men to serve as apostles, baptizing and blessing and leading a church upon his departure. The existence of the book itself offers a new iteration of scripture, shattering the Bible's primacy as the word of God and conventional Protestant claims to authority and opening the gates for a flood of new scripture. It offers a distinctly American Christianity with a history centuries old.

The Book of Mormon has attracted criticism both for its prose and for its content. Twain and others, even such contemporary critics as Harold Bloom, have dismissed its prose as tendentious and impenetrable. Others have mounted more substantive criticism of its contents, usually finding it suspiciously well-tailored to the concerns of Jacksonian America for a work written by ancient Jews. Alexander Campbell, one of the founders of the Disciples of Christ, read it carefully and declared, "This prophet Smith, through his stone spectacles, wrote on the plates of Nephi, in his book of Mormon, every error and almost every truth discussed in N. York for the last ten years." Campbell found debates over infant baptism, church government, ordination and authority, and a dozen other issues that had raged in revivalist America all conveniently resolved in the "ancient" book.[30] Similarly, many modern readers have found in its pages events similar to evangelical revivals, defenses of civil liberties and egalitarianism, and, in the subversive and conniving "secret combinations" that bring down Nephite governments, a profound antebellum fear of secret societies, particularly Freemasonry.

The process of producing the book broadened Joseph Smith's religious imagination, particularly his understanding of his own role and mission. His partnership with Cowdery was particularly productive; their similarities went beyond their closeness in age and Vermont roots to a visionary bent and an interest in religion. Cowdery had a reputation as a dowser, like Joseph Sr. capable of finding objects under the earth with a rod, and he immediately took to the translation process, even attempting unsuccessfully to produce a few sentences on his own at one point. Later, he would produce a revelation of his own, addressed to "Oliver" in the same stentorian tones as Joseph's. He did these things under Joseph's guidance. The young prophet, product of the tightly knit faith of his family, anxious to create harmony and stability, interested more than anything in companionship and community, sought collaborators. He had a growing vision of not merely a book and a vision, but of a new church. Inheritor of Enlightenment values and a Jacksonian suspicion of authority, he knew that others would only accept his experiences and his authority on the basis of evidence and their own experiences.

To that end, soon after the translation process was complete, when the Harrises and the Smiths had come to the Whitmer farm in Fayette to celebrate, Joseph invited eleven friends and relatives into the woods behind the farm to see the plates. First in early July, he and Oliver recruited Martin Harris and David Whitmer, Oliver's closest friend among the Whitmers and only a few months older than Joseph himself. The four went into the woods to pray, and later that day the three men signed a statement declaring, "We, through the grace of God the Father, and our Lord Jesus Christ, have seen the plates which contain this record . . . we declare with words of soberness, that an angel of God came down from heaven, and he brought and laid before our eyes, that we beheld and saw the plates."[31] Several days later, Joseph invited eight more—including his father, two of his brothers, and several Whitmers—to the same spot, where he passed the plates around, inviting his friends to handle and examine them. All eight signed a similar statement. Both statements were published in the opening leaves of the Book of Mormon.

Joseph had plans for these farmers and teachers. Early the next year he rode from Harmony to Palmyra with his friend Joseph Knight and told him that he intended to organize a church. While translating in Harmony, he and Cowdery had encountered a passage in which Christ gave his Nephite apostles the authority to baptize. Wondering what became of this authority, the two went to the banks of the Susquehanna River and prayed about the question. According to Cowdery, "the vail was parted, and the angel of God came down in glory and delivered the anxiously looked for message, and the keys of the gospel of repentance!"[32] Later, in his 1838 history, Joseph Smith identified this angel as John the Baptist, who gave to the two men what Joseph called "the priesthood of Aaron," which included the authority to baptize and administer certain other sacraments. After commanding the two men to baptize each other, the angel also promised to them a higher priesthood, which Joseph eventually claimed came through the hands of the resurrected New Testament apostles Peter, James, and John.

With this authority Joseph Smith, at age twenty-four, founded a church. On April 6, 1830, he drew together the Whitmers and Harrises, the Joseph Knights and Oliver Cowderys, and Emma and Lucy and Hyrum and Sophronia, probably at the Smith home just north of Palmyra. According to David Whitmer there were some forty or fifty in attendance. There Joseph and Cowdery ordained each other the first and second elders of the Church of Christ. A revelation received that day named Joseph the leader of this new community, calling him "a seer, a translator, a prophet, an apostle of Jesus Christ, an Elder of the church through the will of God the Father and the grace of Jesus Christ." The church was commanded to "give heed unto all his words, and commandments which he shall give unto you, as he receiveth them."[33] Joseph and Cowdery administered the Lord's Supper and then began to baptize and confirm. There were no sermons. From the beginning Joseph Smith's church began to leave the raucous world of evangelical revivalism behind. Instead, the community of the elect would be built not on conversion but on confirmation and ordination, on the bonds the priesthood could create. Joseph transformed farmers into priests, elders, and teachers; he sent them out, still wet from baptism, bearing Books of Mormon to bring others into the fold.

Befitting a church founded by a Smith, the Church of Christ (renamed the Church of Jesus Christ of Latter-day Saints eight years later) initially expanded along family lines, as many young religious movements do. But there was something deeply significant about this fact to Joseph Smith. He baptized his father and collapsed into the man's arms "with greaf and joy," as Joseph Knight recalled, fleeing the crowd to hide his tears, looking like "he wanted to git out of site of every Body, and would sob and crie."[34] Joseph's church was in many ways a formalization and extension of the family bonds that his mother had invested with such spiritual significance. Samuel Smith brought the book to his cousins, the children of Jesse Smith, while in southern New York some two dozen Knights walked into the waters of baptism. In Fayette the Whitmer clan joined en masse. Other families—the Kimballs, the Pratts, the Snows—would also join over the next few years, conversions following bloodlines. A Methodist minister's wife named Rhoda Greene and her brother Phineas Young, for instance, received Books of Mormon from Samuel Smith in June 1830 and within two years they, their families, and their three brothers Joseph, Lorenzo, and Brigham were baptized. By the middle of 1830 the Church of Christ in New York was growing rapidly, centered around these clans, and Joseph and Emma had moved to Fayette with the Whitmers. Emma would never see her parents again, and the possibility seemed to weigh upon her; in mid-July Joseph gave her a revelation mixing rebuke and praise in which God named her "elect lady" but also warned that she should "murmur not."[35] That same month she consented to join her husband's church.

Joseph Smith was always restless, and even after organizing a church he would cast his eyes and thoughts elsewhere. In September 1830 he sent Oliver Cowdery and three other missionaries (including a new convert named Parley Pratt) west, where they were to preach to the Native Americans. These people, Joseph believed, were the last descendants of the Nephites and Lamanites, the scattered house of Israel to be brought back into the fold. With their help, Joseph promised that the New Jerusalem itself, the city of Zion that would herald Christ's Second Coming, could be built on the western American frontier. The mission wove together many of the threads that animated early Mormonism: Joseph Smith's impulse toward reconciliation among divided people, the religious nationalism of the Book of Mormon, the impulse to evangelize, all come together in the dream of a holy city, a new civilization whose honor for God would make it a place of peace and reunion. Even in the tumult of reinvention that Jacksonian America offered its citizens, this was a bold dream.

But word came back earlier than expected: in Ohio, the missionaries had encountered a friend of Parley Pratt's, a minister named Sidney Rigdon. Rigdon was then thirty-seven, older by a decade than most of the Mormon leaders, an imposing orator and educated theologian. Even so he found the Book of Mormon impressive, and Pratt baptized him and several others in November 1830, forming the nucleus of a small Mormon community in Ohio. By that winter, Joseph had decided that the church itself would begin the first leg of its journey west toward Zion. As his parents had fifteen years before, he went west, leaving New York in January 1831, and his church followed. Emma, Martin Harris, the Whitmers, Joseph Knight, Rhoda Greene, and Lucy and Joseph Sr. all abandoned their homes, abandoned the lives of farmers, merchants, and teachers in pursuit of a different world. They were going to Kirtland, Ohio, but the city they saw before them was the New Jerusalem.

TWO

LITTLE ZIONS

1831–1839

The vision of the New Jerusalem grew more than anything else from Joseph Smith's new scripture, which he never stopped producing. His most famous and most influential project, the Book of Mormon itself, was also his first, but in 1831 and 1835 and 1844, various editions of his revelations, faithfully recorded by his eager scribes, also went into print under the title "Doctrine and Covenants." He spent years producing what he called a new translation of the Bible, a set of clarifications, rewordings, and substitutions of the text of the King James Version, and he periodically issued more scripture in the voices of ancient prophets. The great theme emerging from all of these documents, or at least the theme Joseph himself emphasized most passionately, was Zion, the righteous society of believers whose loyalty to God and to one another meant they would live together in bliss and harmony. But though they all promise the possibility of its creation, Joseph Smith's scriptures also detail its fragility: its triumphs are always matched by the possibility of its collapse. This pattern is in large measure the story of the Book of Mormon itself. The Nephite struggle for righteousness brings unity and an end to poverty and separation; their pride and lust for power and wealth lead to their collapse.

This primal cycle, this yearning for Zion, echoes through all the scripture that flowed from Joseph Smith's lips.

Joseph's new scripture appeared in two genres: the form he called "revelations" or "commandments" and the form he called "translations." The commandments and revelations were visions dealt from heaven, often in the voice of God. They generally confronted immediate circumstances, addressing Joseph or his followers by name and offering particular advice or instruction. A few were longer and more elaborate, spinning out extended discussion of theological issues such as the nature of truth, the authority of the priesthood, the last days, or the afterlife. The most dramatic of the revelations came on February 16, 1832, in response to John 5:29: "And shall come forth; they that have done good, unto the resurrection of life; and they that have done evil, unto the resurrection of damnation." While Joseph and Sidney Rigdon pondered the verse, they experienced what Mormon publications later called "the Vision." The two men stared into heaven and for an hour alternately described what they saw: the throne of God, the multitude of the faithful, the fall of Satan. Most importantly, the Vision drew on Saint Paul's description of the varying glories of resurrected bodies, such as the sun, moon, and stars, to describe three levels of heaven: the celestial, terrestrial, and telestial, reserved respectively for those who fully received the ordinances of the gospel, those "honorable men of the earth" who were not valiant Christians, and, at the bottom, the wicked, "the liars and sorcerers and adulterers." All these levels "surpass all understanding in glory." Only a scant handful of humanity, the "sons of perdition" who denied Christ to his face, would receive nothing at all.[1] All others would be granted that glory they were capable of receiving. The Vision fulfilled the wildest dreams of old Asael Smith the Universalist. Its vision of heaven as a community of the like-minded reveals two characteristic features of Mormonism: its understanding of salvation in terms of community and its optimism about humanity's potential to gain it.

The translations, on the other hand, spoke in the voice of ancient authors: Mormon and the other Book of Mormon scribes, eventually Moses and Abraham. They reached into the deep past, offering not strictly doctrinal instruction but narratives of ancient Christian civilizations. These gave the Mormons models for their own form of Christianity, primordial visions of the Zion Joseph Smith sought to build. Some derived from a particularly ambitious project: soon after the printer peeled the Book of Mormon's pages from his press in June 1830, Joseph Smith, seated across the Whitmers' table from Oliver Cowdery, opened a copy of the King James Version of the Bible. They began with Genesis. The Book of Mormon's systematic unfolding of such doctrines as atonement or incarnation that had to be wrested from the terse narratives of the Gospels or the winding letters of Paul convinced Joseph that "many important points touching the salvation of man, had been taken from the Bible, or lost before it was compiled."[2] A revelation commanded Smith and Cowdery to "study it out in your mind" when seeking inspiration, and Joseph did just that: debating the text with his companion, exploring nuances and ambiguities, and eventually adding, with rather breathtaking hubris, emendations, corrections, and clarifications as notes to the text of the King James Version.[3] He would work sporadically on the translation of the Bible over the next seven years with a number of partners, the most productive of whom was Sidney Rigdon, whose education in theology well equipped him as a sparring partner for the enthusiastic but uneducated young prophet.

From the project grew a number of Joseph Smith's translations, which often seem like extended revisions of Biblical stories. The translations beyond the Book of Mormon are called the Book of Moses, which includes the Vision of Enoch and the Book of Abraham. Like the brief emendations of the Bible translations, they are best understood as expansions or elaborations of scriptural narrative rather than a rendering of any original language into English. The Book of Moses draws on the opening chapters of Genesis, particularly the elliptical handful of verses covering the city of Enoch, taken to heaven for its righteousness. The Book of Abraham derives from a collection of Egyptian manuscripts that Joseph purchased in 1835 from a man named Michael Chandler, who made an improbable living showing a handful of mummies and the accompanying papyri in his possession across the country. For several months Joseph worked through the ancient scrolls and produced an account written in the first-person voice of Abraham describing his early life and visions. As with the Book of Mormon and the Book of Moses, he called it a "translation," though later scholars found it had little to do with the text on the fragments of papyrus that survived into the twentieth century.

In all the translations Zion leaps vividly to life. Enoch, a great prophet, gathers together a group of the faithful, of whom it is said, "And the Lord called his people Zion, because they were of one heart and one mind, and dwelt in righteousness; and there was no poor among them." And they build a city. God declares to Enoch that in the last days, the elect will be "looking forth for the time of my coming; for there shall be my tabernacle, and it shall be called Zion, a New Jerusalem." To Joseph Smith, this would have sounded like members of the Nephite society after Jesus Christ's visit in the Book of Mormon, who "had all things common among them; therefore there were not rich and poor, bond and free, but they were all made free, and partakers of the heavenly gift."[4] And, of course, it would have sounded to him like his own dreams.

The history Joseph Smith learned from these stories linked the success of civilizations to their righteousness. In them, God grants Abraham and Moses and Adam knowledge of Jesus Christ, as he did to the Book of Mormon prophets, and all are instructed to govern themselves according to his teachings. Success comes not through the leverage of capital, the amassing of property, or skill at arms but through commitment to God and humility before the commandments of Jesus. Such commitment necessarily fostered the sort of unity Joseph craved. The translations are full of withering denunciations of social divisions born of rank or wealth and, like the Old Testament, diagnose these failures as collective sin. But they are also full of promises of joy for the faithful. They were not like the America Joseph Smith lived in, but they were models for the nation he hoped to build.

Neither the Book of Mormon nor the early revelations offered much that Protestants would have found theologically objectionable (that would come later, in the Book of Abraham's vision of premortal life and in the Vision itself and other revelations), but the very existence of Joseph Smith's new scripture called into question the absolute authority Protestants were accustomed to granting the Bible over matters of faith and practice. Joseph Smith constantly revisited his own productions, revising, clarifying, editing for style and grammar and, less frequently, content, and his restlessness with his own texts is a mirror of his constant social experiments. Like the scripture of other marginal religious movements in America, Joseph Smith's revelations and translations were a form of social criticism, calling for a profound reimagining of American society. He needed his revelations and translations to provide models, directions, and inspiration as he pushed forward the transformation of his people into the Mormon Zion he dreamed of.

Within Joseph Smith burned a powerful conviction that the wrongs of the world could be set right. Unlike many other prophets, he was not simply a doomsayer but a builder. Like them, he saw the millennium approaching. Prophets such as the revolutionary slave Nat Turner, or William Miller, who urged his followers to sell all they owned and await the return of Christ on hilltops, saw society crumbling irretrievably. Joseph Smith sounded similar alarms; as one revelation proclaimed to several followers, "Ye are called to bring to pass the gathering of mine elect . . . to prepare their hearts and be prepared in all things against the day when tribulation and desolation are sent forth upon the wicked."[5] And yet, the bleak urgency of such revelations was tinged with hope. Joseph Smith called for neither revolution nor quietism. The great promise of the last days was neither the destruction of the wicked nor passive redemption at the hands of Christ but the possibility of building Zion. There, poverty would be relieved, anxiety stilled, ruptured families healed. That Christ was coming soon meant only that the work was all the more urgent, for the city must stand to welcome him on his return.

Joseph quickly found the place for Zion. Kirtland proved reasonably hospitable. There were dozens of converts waiting for him when he arrived in February 1831, and more trickled in every week, farmers, shopkeepers, schoolteachers sent back to Kirtland from Illinois or Pennsylvania or even Canada by eager missionaries. The town, a hub of the pulsing and muddy frontier economy, was not so different from Palmyra. Kirtland sat near the ports of Lake Erie, close to busy trading posts, and attracted men like Newel Whitney, an ex-soldier and former Indian trader who opened his store at a busy crossroads in Kirtland, and Isaac Morley, a soldier who had abandoned his family's fading fortunes in Massachusetts and became a wealthy farmer and landowner in Ohio. Both were followers of Sidney Rigdon and became followers of Joseph Smith. Throughout his years in Ohio, Joseph and Emma subsisted on the generosity of the Whitneys, the Morleys, and other families, who took the young couple into their homes and tended Emma when twins born in early 1831 both died. Joseph and Emma found the families generous and hospitable. He marveled at the small economic cooperative they built. With characteristic exuberance he saw in these small things the potential for eternity: the seeds of Zion itself.

In late June 1831, only months after he arrived in Kirtland and found there the people of Zion, Joseph and several companions followed the missionaries he had sent to Missouri west and found the city's location. Oliver Cowdery and several others were already in Jackson County, near a town called Independence, preaching to Native Americans and to the settlers, but the harvest was meager; the Indians showed little interest, and there were no more than a few hundred Americans living in Independence. Joseph was disappointed, but he nonetheless looked out over the Independence fields and declared by revelation that "this is the land of promise, and the place for the city of Zion." Later, he looked over a blossoming prairie on a bluff north of Independence, designating it the Garden of Eden and the valley to which Adam fled after his exile. Calling the valley "Adam-ondi-Ahman," he prophesied that there, in the last days, Adam would come to "visit his people," as described in the Book of Daniel's account of the coming of a personage known as the Ancient of Days in the End Times. There the human family reconstituted from the Fall through the power of the priesthood would gather to honor their ancient father, who would present them to Jesus Christ.[6] In a stroke Joseph sacralized the American continent, finding in its vistas not only the Christianized past of the Garden and the Book of Mormon but also the apocalyptic future of the End Times. To many Americans, the Mormons among them, America offered the promise of new birth and a glorious inheritance. To Joseph Smith, it was the land of Christianity's past and future. He resolved that the Mormons would purchase acres of land around Independence, dedicated it as a divine inheritance, and laid a stone on a lot near the courthouse. There would sit a temple built to God when Zion's people came to settle.

Joseph Smith's ability to transform the mundane into the sacred, to find in a small group of farm families the seedbed of God's kingdom or to see in a Missouri valley the Garden of Eden and the triumphant regathering of the family of God, can seem simultaneously absurd and breathtaking. It is easy to understand this young church as a shadow Joseph Smith, Jr., cast. Setting questions of prophecy aside, he remains a terrifically romantic figure, a seducer of biographers, a man of colossal imagination, will, and vision. His visionary creativity was immense but rarely disciplined. Ideas spun from him like a Catherine wheel; whatever earned his attention would be lit with the fires of heaven, but it required systematization and implementation. From the time he had sought a scribe to take the dictation of the Book of Mormon, he had not wanted to work on his own; that was not his temperament. So he gathered friends around him, leaned on those who were awed by the power of the revelations, but not so awed that they did not have their own visions of the divine. Some of his prophetic utterances they would reject, but more often they would gratefully seize them and seek to shape them into their own worlds. The years in Ohio and Missouri saw the halting construction of Zion, the struggle to bridge the gap between vision and creation, between Joseph Smith's desire to foster a people who had a collective vision of God and his conviction that he had been particularly chosen to guide them to it. Together, they built the religion called Mormonism.

Joseph Smith's religion grew with tremendous rapidity. Only three years after his visit to Missouri, there were some twelve hundred Mormons settled in Independence and two thousand more in Kirtland. Joseph's followers would call this the Gathering. Unlike the Baptists or the Presbyterians or the Methodists, who planted churches in the towns of America as they moved across the continent, pinning their faith to the expansion of the young country itself, Joseph brought his followers to him to build the kingdom of God.

The Mormon missionaries preached the millennium. Theirs was a Zionist faith calling for a reconstructed society free of the churning pressures of frontier America in favor of the utopian Zion Christ had promised. They offered up Joseph Smith's prophetic calling and the Book of Mormon as evidence of the inauguration of the last dispensation of history and the coming advent of Jesus Christ. But they also appealed to Americans' rough-hewn conviction that each of them was individually equipped to judge the truth of any religion and needed no authority to find God. When the schoolteacher William McLellin closed his Paris, Tennessee, schoolhouse early to hear two Mormon missionaries preach in July 1831, these were the things that captured his attention. Harvey Whitlock, he remembered, spoke "some of the Signs of the times" and "expounded the Gospel the plainest I thot I ever heard in my life." Then David Whitmer stood and "bore testimony to having seen a Holy Angel," telling the congregation of the miracles surrounding the appearance of the Book of Mormon.[7]

McLellin sat up late with the missionaries that night, pleading with them to stay longer. They replied that they would not wait but that he was welcome to come with them if he wanted to hear more. McLellin pondered this for the rest of the day and then asked for a week to wrap up his business in Paris. On July 30, he closed his school and left town; on August 21 he was in Missouri, where Hyrum Smith baptized and ordained him an elder. The next day, Hyrum sent him across Illinois to spread the new gospel himself on his way to Ohio. In mid-September, eight weeks after he left class early to hear the Mormons preach, McLellin unlocked the schoolhouse again, carrying copies of Joseph Smith's scripture, and used the space to preach. By October, he had settled in Kirtland.

The Mormons offered much the same thing other movements did. Jemima Wilkinson and William Miller promised prophecy and millennium, John Humphrey Noyes and the Shakers a utopian community. Though many Mormon converts—like McLellin himself, who spent hours in the Missouri woods one Saturday morning in August in "earnest prayr to God to direct me into truth"—reported receiving divine direction, the revivalists also promised spiritual ecstasies and emotional encounters with God. The Mormons sought the resumption of the

New Testament church, but the Restorationist movement did as well. After his sojourn in the woods McLellin sought out Hyrum Smith and told him "I wanted him to baptize me because I wanted to live among a people who were based upon pure principles and actuated by the Spirit of the Living God." In those words were packed a whole host of hungers, the distilled welter of other religious movements into one: for uncorrupted religion, for direct contact with God, for a stable community of people who shared the same desires and values, and all of it reasonable, convincing both to the heart and to the head.

And perhaps most of all, the Mormons had their new scripture. In this America, supernaturalism and skepticism overlapped. It was an age of Enlightenment confidence, and Americans trusted their own spiritual and mental capacities. This did not mean they had left behind folk magic or belief in divine intervention or confidence in the supernatural truths of the Bible, but it did mean that they expected to be able to evaluate such things, rather than accept them on the authority of another. And the Mormons would gladly hand any curious onlooker a copy of Joseph Smith's book and ordain any man to office. As early as June 1830, this had earned them the sobriquet "Mormonite," soon narrowed to "Mormon," a title the church eventually claimed proudly, making of the epithet a symbol of their conviction. McLellin came to the conclusion that "from all the light I could gain by examinations searches and researches I was bound as an honest man to acknowledge the truth and validity of the book of Mormon."[8] Indeed, rarely did missionaries draw on the verses and stories of the Book of Mormon in sermons: it was not to them a source of doctrine. Rather, they brandished the book as tangible proof of Joseph Smith's divine calling, the reopening of the heavens, and the inauguration of the dispensation in the fullness of time.

Many of the New York converts had watched Joseph Smith blossom into prophethood. They were related to or were friends of the witnesses to the plates; they believed in the miracles that surrounded the Book of Mormon. But the Kirtland converts whom they met in Ohio had never seen Joseph Smith. Though Sidney Rigdon and his flock had examined the Book of Mormon, they brought to the faith desires

and presuppositions somewhat different from those of the New Yorkers, things that sometimes hampered and sometimes inspired Joseph
Smith. The converts of the upper Ohio region were in large measure
Restorationists, longing for the recovery of the New Testament church.
The proclamation of a new dispensation of the gospel, a restoration,
was precisely what these people had been waiting for. For them the
dream of Zion was the dream of primitive Christianity.

Many were also charismatics, believers in gifts of the spirit, such as
speaking in tongues and prophecy. Some Restorationists traced their
religious heritage to the massive Cane Ridge revival of 1801, where
prodigious manifestations—tongues, prophecy, trances, bodily contor-
tions, healings—had occurred, and the Methodist revivalists continued
to ride through the land promising the same. Rigdon himself was a
seer who prayed late into the night. He was moody, melancholic, a
visionary. The convert Philo Dibble said, "If angels had administered
to the children of men again, I was glad of it."[9] Elizabeth Ann Whitney, one of Rigdon's followers, observed placidly later of Joseph
Smith's arrival at their home that "I remarked to my husband that it
was the fulfillment of the vision we had seen of a cloud as of glory rest-
ing upon our house."[10] The Mormon missionaries found a flood of
converts confessing dreams and visions that prepared them for the
prophet from Palmyra.

Joseph Smith found the first of these beliefs inspiring and the second
troubling. The idea of restoration spoke to his own visionary experiences, and he was eagerly interested in the ways the Ohio Restorationists dealt with the concept. Sidney Rigdon had spent much of the 1820s
in discussions with a group of ministers, including Alexander Campbell,
wondering how best to chip away the barnacles that had accrued on the
hull of Christianity since the apostolic age. They called themselves simply Christians, or Disciples of Christ, as often as they did Restorationists. Campbell was a rationalist, a researcher, and his great project was
the recovery of the New Testament's form of organization. Like Baptists, he insisted on baptism by immersion because he found it in the
New Testament; unlike Baptists and other low-church Protestants, he
sought to reclaim Biblical offices like "bishop," rejecting titles like
"Reverend" or "Minister," and to worship in the way the New Testa-

ment churches seemed to: with no music, with a rejection of formal confessions of faith, and directed by lay members of the congregation.

Sidney Rigdon was much more a visionary and a millennialist than the methodical Campbell; he sought not merely the primitive church but the community of the Acts of the Apostles with a fervor that sometimes embarrassed his friend. Rigdon was haunted by Acts 4:32: "And the multitude of them that believed were of one heart and of one soul: neither said any of them that ought of the things which he possessed was his own; but they had all things common." In May 1829, a young man named Lyman Wight heard Rigdon preach near Kirtland on "the doctrine of the apostles," which led Wight to consider the church of "the Acts of the Apostles, where they had all things in common."[11] Rigdon directed the young man to Isaac Morley, a parishioner and wealthy farmer. By the winter of 1829, Morley, Wight, a local storekeeper named Newel Whitney, Campbell's in-laws Julia and John Murdock, and a half dozen other families organized what was then called a "communistic society." They called it the Morley Family, because on his farm they worked the land together, surrendered private property, lived in log cabins lined row by row, and prayed together nightly. This was too much for Campbell, for whom such experiments smacked of the theories of Robert Owen, an avowedly secular reformer who had founded a similar society a few hundred miles away in New Harmony, Indiana. But Rigdon's flock pressed on.

Rigdon and Morley, Wight and John Murdock all easily caught Joseph Smith's vision of the New Jerusalem. The Mormon missionaries ordained them all elders and gave them a flock of nearly a hundred converts to tend until the New York Mormons arrived. The discovery of the Morley Family was inspiring to Joseph Smith; almost immediately upon his arrival in Kirtland he pronounced the "law of the church" in a revelation that commanded missionary work, declared that "repentance" and "baptism by water" lay at the heart of the gospel—and then seamlessly began to direct the church toward a radically transformed economic order. Dubbing the practice "consecration," the revelation instructed the faithful to turn over their property to a bishop of the church, who would then return to them enough to meet the needs of their families. The rest would be distributed to the poor, and what remained would be used for "building houses of worship." The revelation declared that this would make every Mormon "accountable to me [God], a steward over his own property," bound to God and the body of believers rather than independent.[12]

Ultimately, the revelation taught that consecration would not merely serve the poor but also change the hearts and souls of those who accepted stewardship. It was, after all, a commandment given that "my covenant people may be gathered in one in that day when I shall come to my temple. And this I do for the salvation of my people." In March 1831 a revelation declared, "But it is not given that one man should possess that which is above another: wherefore the world lieth in sin."[13] A Zion society required a Zion people, and consecration seemed a way to infuse those values into American capitalists. Joseph appointed Newel Whitney and another merchant, a haberdasher and former Campbellite named Edward Partridge, the first bishops of his church in Kirtland and Missouri, and organized a committee called the United Firm to see to the collection and dispersal of property. Converts volunteered to deed their land, and the bishops worked diligently to ensure that none went hungry among the Latter-day Saints. Joseph Smith, who himself often lived on the charity of his followers, prayed that they might mature into a society with no poor among them.

While the idea of restoration inspired Joseph Smith, the Kirtland charismatics troubled him more, forcing him to define the lines of authority in his nascent church. Mormon worshippers gathered in ad hoc groups of believers loosely bound together through friendship or family ties. They had no preachers but would testify to one another, and men ordained to priesthood office would administer the Lord's Supper. In August 1830 a revelation proclaimed that the Mormons should use water for the service if the only wine available was for "purchase" from non-Mormons, saying, "You shall partake of none [wine] except it is made new among you; yea, in this my Father's kingdom which shall be built up on the earth . . . the hour cometh that I will drink the fruit of the vine with you on earth."[14] Every meeting of the Mormons reinforced their apocalyptic difference.

But in Ohio things went far beyond this. Consumed with the Holy

Spirit, converts would fall into fits and trances, rush to and fro about the room, dance in ecstasy, and pronounce visions. The convert Levi Hancock had dreams of Jesus while a youth and actual visions of him while an adult, which he later interpreted as spurs toward baptism at the hands of Parley Pratt. But nonetheless he still complained of worshippers "falling down frothing at the mouth" and of a man named Burr Riggs who would swing from the rafters, "fall like he was dead," then revive and recite the visions he had seen. "Edson Fuller would fall and turn black in the face," Hancock said, rather primly. "Heman Bassett would behave like a baboon."[15]

The evolution of Mormonism is in many ways the struggle in Levi Hancock's mind writ large. On the one hand, the faith rested upon the premise that the heavens stood reopened and its gifts stood newly available. Tongues were not necessarily foreign to the Mormons. Brigham Young, a convert from Methodism who arrived in Kirtland in 1832, had on occasion spoken in tongues in his small Mormon gathering in New York. The difference between Levi Hancock's dreams and Joseph Smith's visions was not so great. And the young prophet seemed to relish his charisma. Several months after his arrival in Kirtland, for instance, Joseph sat quietly in a discussion about the primitive church with the family of Luke Johnson and their minister, a Methodist named Ezra Booth. When someone pointed out that Elsa Johnson sat in the room with an arm paralyzed by arthritis and no New Testament apostles to heal her, Joseph stood, strode forward, seized her arm, and pronounced it whole in the name of Jesus Christ. Then, without another word, he turned and stalked from the room. A moment later, Elsa lifted the arm with ease. The miracle shocked the Johnson family and their minister into conversion.[16]

But repeatedly in the months following the organization of his church, Joseph Smith struck down challenges from rival prophets who claimed to commune with God in the same way as he had. There was Hiram Page, one of the Eight Witnesses to the plates, who received revelations from a small black seerstone; Laura Hubbell, who wandered the streets of Kirtland claiming to be a prophetess; an ex-slave known in the sources as Black Pete, heir to a charismatic form of African American Methodism and revered in Kirtland as "a revelator" who conversed with angels. All of these people accepted the Book of Mormon and hailed the prophetic mission of Joseph Smith. Black Pete and Page were both given priesthood office. Indeed, all seem to have expected, with some justification, that they had found a home for their own gifts. Just as Joseph Smith, heir to a poor farm family, found in his faith empowerment and stability and knowledge that seemed otherwise beyond his reach, so too, it seems, did Laura Hubbell and the ex-slave Black Pete.

But Joseph did not see them as fellows. He was sensitive about challenges to his power, and he and other New York leaders were shaken by the strangeness they found in Kirtland. Parley Pratt complained that "strange spiritual operations were manifested that were disgusting rather than edifying." Joseph Smith's egalitarian instincts and visionary streak coexisted with a profound longing for order and a stubborn insistence on his own authority. Page and Hubbell found themselves rebuked by revelations declaring "Verily, verily, I say unto you, that ye have received a commandment for a law unto my church, through him whom I have appointed unto you to receive commandments and revelations from my hand." Some of those prophets, including perhaps Black Pete, were cut off from the church. In Joseph's church, the strange spirituality of the revelations had to coexist alongside the rationality and stability that so appealed to William McLellin. The burgeoning Mormon vision of salvation was premised on the channeling of ecstatic experience along particular and defined lines of order and community; as the revelation promised, "Ye are to be taught from on high. Sanctify yourselves and ye shall be endowed with power."[17] Glory came through education and the establishment of order.

Midway through a church conference in June 1831, charismatic experience erupted: Lyman Wight leapt onto his bench and began describing a vision of God. Others began rambling in strange tongues. Joseph Smith cast out a devil and then, perhaps as he had planned all along, imposed order. For the first time he described the difference between the lower priesthood, later called "Aaronic," and the higher priesthood, the "Melchizedek." The various Biblical offices such as "deacon," "elder," "Seventy," and so forth that Mormon men had already been given were gradually grouped under one of these priesthoods. The men were divided, ordained, and organized into "quorums" by office, and each quorum was given a president.

Priesthood did three things. First, it made Mormonism a sacramental religion, one in which salvation was gained through rites such as baptism and the Lord's Supper that priesthood was required to administer. Second, Mormons believed the priesthood equipped one to access the power of God: to heal, cast out demons, bless, and dedicate. It made farmers into the emissaries of God—apostles, just like Peter or Paul. And finally, it gave those Mormons who held it a sacred genealogy of their own. In September 1832 a revelation declared that the priesthood was not merely an administrative structure; rather, the priesthood bound together the human family in a way that was critical to its salvation. The revelation opened with a long genealogy of ordinations that reached into the Bible, making Joseph and his fellows "the sons of Moses and of Aaron and the seed of Abraham."[18] While Aaron, brother of Moses and the Bible's first priest, was a familiar figure to these former Methodists or Baptists, Melchizedek was more elusive. Mentioned only in passing in Genesis, he is referred to again in the Epistle to the Hebrews, which calls Jesus a priest of the order of Melchizedek. The deep Old Testament flavor of these ideas took the young religion far from American Protestantism, a faith suspicious of authority and organization. But it allowed the Mormons to imagine themselves not as simply Americans or Christians but as the new Israel, the community of God, joined to the family of Adam, Moses, and Abraham.

The notion of priesthood as adoption, welding the Mormons to the family of the patriarchs, meant that Mormonism surpassed all other social allegiances or divisions. Joseph made his father a "patriarch," charging him to administer special blessings to all the members of the church, as Isaac and Jacob had to their sons, and finally granting to that old man the dignity he had long since lost in American society. Additionally, in 1836, Joseph Smith ordained Elijah Abel, an African American who had escaped slavery, an elder, giving him the Melchizedek priesthood and sending him on missions to Ohio, New York, and Canada. Several years later, in Massachusetts, a free black man and abolitionist named Walker Lewis met Parley Pratt, accepted the Mormon's message, and was baptized and ordained an elder. A barber and Freemason, Lewis was a respected community leader. That he and Abel found a home in this new religious community in the racially charged atmosphere of antebellum America indicates how serious Joseph Smith was about replacing secular community with the divine lineage of the priesthood.

The priesthood was the skeleton of the kingdom of Zion, the community of God. From the early months of the organization of the church, Joseph Smith would routinely convene ad hoc councils of men to consider issues facing the church and to render decisions. In late 1831 Joseph received a revelation designating him as the "president of the high priesthood"; in effect, the president of the church as a whole. Following the conciliar model, he took two counselors to form the "First Presidency" of the church: Rigdon and a schoolteacher named Jesse Gause. Under the First Presidency, the various quorums of elders and priests and deacons convened. In 1834 Joseph announced the formation of the "stakes of Zion," a name drawn from Isaiah. The stakes were the communities preparing Zion, the gathering places from which the tent of Zion would rise. A stake president was called in Kirtland and another in Missouri, each with counselors and a "high council" of high priests to advise him.[19]

A loose collection of elders and deacons and teachers with responsibilities to administer the Lord's Supper or collect offerings would have been familiar to a Methodist or Presbyterian. The word *priesthood* and the growing councils were not; they would have smacked of the tyranny Protestants so feared in Catholicism and the pope's perceived desire to rule politically as well as spiritually. But this was precisely what Joseph Smith imagined. He sent David Whitmer, the president of the Missouri stake, a map called "the plat of Zion," a layout for the entire dreamed city, divided into ten-acre blocks with a complex of temples sitting in the center, the focal point for a millennial kingdom connected through them to God. Thus did the Mormons divide the world between the sacred and the profane and create a geographical vision of salvation; Zion was given a place, an organization, a geography, and boundaries, all brought into being through map and government.

Logically, therefore, the land outside Zion required governance, and it was put in the hands of the Quorum of the Twelve Apostles, which Joseph Smith organized in early 1835. The twelve men selected included William McLellin; Lyman Wight; Parley Pratt and his brother Orson, an amateur philosopher; Joseph's brothers William and Samuel; Luke and Lyman Johnson, the sons of Elsa, whose arm Joseph had healed; and Brigham Young, a Vermont carpenter who had received and read the Book of Mormon from his sister, Rhoda Greene. These men were designated "traveling councilors," with conciliar jurisdiction over the presumably temporary clumps of Mormon believers outside the reach of Zion. Moreover, they were designated the missionaries of the church, regularly dispatched to preach. These men were Joseph's favorites, his friends, closer to him in age and background than the Rigdons or the Gauses.

The councils proved adept at managing the practical as well as the sacred. Even Joseph Smith himself was subject to their jurisdiction. Once when he lost his temper—a fault typical of Joseph, who was mercurial, quick to raise his voice or lash out with words, but also quick to weep and forgive—he ended up before a church council charged with aggressive conduct toward a Seventy. He willingly submitted to the authority of the council and agreed to abide by its judgments. Though a March 1835 revelation declared that all of these councils—the high councils, the Quorum of the Twelve, the First Presidency, and the lower quorums of elders and Seventies when they met in total—were equal in authority, in practice Joseph would lean on the Quorum more than the others, and drew them close to him.

The councils' flexibility, stability, and authority were the critical reason Mormonism would survive Joseph Smith's death. Unlike many other nineteenth-century visionaries and charismatic leaders, Joseph ensured that his church would not depend upon his own presence. The priesthood was egalitarian—every Mormon man held some office, and every Mormon was equally subject to conciliar discipline. Twice a year these leaders were presented to the body of the church in council for common consent, which was nearly always granted. But despite the formality, this was not democracy. They did not value equality, universal participation, or the will of the majority for its own sake.

Women, for instance, were entirely excluded from priesthood leadership; Emma Smith had received a revelatory assignment to compile a hymnbook, coupled with a charge to teach the scriptures and preach, but that was as close as any woman came to receiving office through the revelations. Though women would often speak in the small impromptu testimony meetings that constituted Mormon worship, they were not granted the priesthood. Priesthood government valued liberty and equality less than it did righteousness; its ultimate power rested in the God revealed in scripture and Joseph Smith's revelations, not in the consent of the members. The concerns for civil liberties and property rights that animated American democracy had little weight in the kingdom of God.

By the mid-1830s, Joseph Smith believed that he had laid the foundations for Zion to rise. He soon began to think about building a temple, a focal point for all these changes, a place where the Mormons might seek the power of God in full. In the spring of 1833 revelations began to command the Mormons to build a temple in Kirtland and to promise that "my glory shall be there, and my presence shall be there." As with the temple of Solomon in the books of Samuel and Kings, detailed directions were given through revelation; it was to be "fifty-five by sixty-five feet in the width thereof and the length thereof, in the inner court; and there shall be a lower and a higher court."[20] The temple was to contain on the upper floor offices, on the lower two levels meeting halls, ringed with what the revelations called "altars" but were actually pulpits of seats for the presidents of the various priesthood quorums. Joseph's dedication prayer assigned the temple a wide range of functions: "a house of prayer, a house of fasting, a house of faith, a house of learning, a house of glory, a house of order, a house of God."[21] It was to become the focal point of the Mormons' lives. It hosted social gatherings, council meetings, and an amateur choir and housed rooms for "the school of the prophets," the name, drawn from the Old Testament, given to the regular meetings Joseph convened to study Hebrew, the Bible, and Joseph's revelations.

A church committee bought land for the temple at the top of the hill that rose above Kirtland, and in June 1833 the Mormons began quarrying, digging, making bricks. Most settlements lay along the

Chagrin River, which wound past the hill from Lake Erie. The Whitney store sat at a crossroads next to the river, and Mormon homes began to appear along Chillicothe Road, which climbed the hill toward the temple site: Joseph Smith's small farm, to which he moved in 1834, Sidney Rigdon's and Hyrum Smith's houses, and a series of small cabins hastily built to house other workers. Joseph spent much of his time translating or meeting with councils rather than working; like the followers living around him he was chronically broke and frequently lived on donations from his friends—a hog here, a steak there. Joseph was never careful with money and often seemed content to sign for loan after loan with no concern about debt, the beauty of Zion overwhelming such practical considerations.

Joseph did not care that the temple project was far beyond—horrendously beyond—the resources of his meager community. And neither did many of the others. As a convert named Eliza R. Snow said, "While the brethren labored in their departments, the sisters were actively engaged in boarding and clothing workmen not otherwise provided for—all living as abstemiously as possible so that every cent might be appropriated to the grand object."[22] The temple workers were paid when money—usually in the form of loans and contributions—became available, which was sporadically. Most were volunteers. Jonathan Crosby reported that Brigham Young, then working on the temple windows, came to his home to borrow money: "Brother Young said he had nothing in his house to eat, and he knew not how to get anything."[23] In January 1835, John Tanner, a convert from New York, arrived in Kirtland and brought relief: having recently liquidated his several farms and hotel, he immediately loaned Joseph Smith two thousand dollars and the temple committee thirteen thousand. Though his cash made the construction possible, he was likely never repaid.

But when the temple neared completion, it all seemed worth it. In January 1836, with the building nearing completion and tools still propped in the corners, Joseph Smith began to introduce his ordinances. Joseph struggled to reenact the Bible, to mingle the Old Testament notions of priesthood and temple with the New Testament message of Christ. Throughout that month he invited the Quorum, the high councils, and the presidencies to the temple, where they confessed their faults to one another and washed and anointed one anothers' bodies, melding Old Testament priestly practice with the New Testament rite of foot-washing. These rituals were uncommon in American Protestantism; though some Baptists practiced foot-washing, the full washing and anointing done in the Kirtland temple was a new thing on the American frontier, reflecting Joseph's Old Testament conviction that the salvation of the individual must come through connection to community. And he saw visions that confirmed it; the throne of God, surrounded by Adam, Jesus, and his older brother Alvin. Others saw heaven as well; W. W. Phelps, a journalist and gifted writer, wrote to his wife that "the Spirit of the Lord came upon me so that I could not speak, and I cried as little children cry."[24] Zebedee Coltrin declared that he saw "the Savior extended before him, as upon the cross, and a little after, crowned with glory upon his head above the brightness of the sun"; Roger Orton saw "a mighty angel riding upon a horse of fire with a flaming sword in his hand, followed by five others, encircle the house and protect the saints."[25]

On March 27, they dedicated the temple. To Joseph Smith, the dedication was a rite of organization; he strictly seated his priesthood leaders in particular pulpits reserved to them on either side of the sanctuary. Though Sidney Rigdon preached for nearly three hours, the most significant event was the sustaining. One by one, each quorum was asked to stand and sustain every other quorum, rising to support Joseph and his counselors, rising to support the new Quorum of the Twelve Apostles, and so on down to the presidency of the Seventy and the deacons, confirming to Joseph in solemn ceremony the strength of the church he had built. Joseph then offered a prayer asking God to accept the temple, to grant the missionaries success, to hasten Zion. And then the meeting closed with a Methodist tradition: the congregation shouted "Hosanna!" three times. Joseph was exultant; this was the world he wanted.

On Sunday, April 3, a thousand Mormons gathered to receive the Lord's Supper. After blessing and distributing the bread and wine, Joseph and Oliver Cowdery retreated to a pulpit and drew the curtains around themselves, and a series of spectacular visions commenced. Joseph's journal, kept by Oliver's brother Warren, declared that "they saw the Lord standing upon the breast work of the pulpit before them . . . his eyes were as a flame of fire, the hair of his head was like the pure snow, his countenance shone above the brightness of the sun, and his voice was as the sound of the rushing of great waters, even the Voice of Jehovah." Jesus announced, "I have accepted this house and my name shall be here." After Jesus vanished and Joseph and Oliver sat trembling, "another great and glorious vision burst upon them." Elijah, the great Old Testament prophet, appeared and announced that "the keys of this dispensation are committed into your hands." Quoting Malachi, Elijah announced that "he should be sent before the great and dreadful day of the Lord come, to turn the hearts of the Fathers to the children, and the children to the fathers."[26] The "keys" of which Elijah spoke eventually became central to the Mormon understanding of what their priesthood was: keys were the authority to bind and loose the power Jesus promised to Peter in the New Testament, in order to enact ordinances to seal people to salvation. These were visions that lasted. They confirmed the power of the temple and its rituals and pointed the way to salvation, which would come through the priesthood of Zion that Joseph struggled so ceaselessly to build.

The early years in Ohio were extraordinarily productive: more revelations poured from Joseph Smith's mouth in the early 1830s than at any other point in his life, and his community grew by leaps and bounds as the converts streamed in. By 1835 some two thousand Mormons lived in and around Kirtland. The three years that followed the dedication of the temple in March 1836 were perhaps the most difficult of Joseph Smith's life. As the Mormon community grew, its visions and ambitions expanded. And its ever-growing radicalism not only frightened its neighbors but also turned the community against itself. Its transformation from a religious movement into a community attracted and repelled both its own followers and its neighbors, and the conflicts that ended the Mormon settlements in Ohio and Missouri illustrated both capacities.

Early challenges provided warnings. The former Methodist minister Ezra Booth became the most prominent early Mormon apostate because he came to bridle at the pedantic detail of the revelations. Booth was annoyed when commanded to walk to Jackson County, Missouri, and back, preaching all the way; he found a revelation prescribing a house be built for Joseph Smith suspicious; and most of all he believed the authority the revelations bestowed upon Joseph garish, bordering on blasphemy. The "name of the Lord is substituted for that of Smith," he complained. "When they and the Scriptures are at variance, the Scriptures are wrongly translated." Booth's complaints reflected many Americans' discomfort with Mormonism's authoritarian impulses and presumption to replace the Bible. "When he says he knows a thing to be so," Booth said of Joseph Smith, "thus it must stand without controversy."[27] At a conference in September 1831 Booth, having voiced complaints, was told he must no longer preach, and soon after he abandoned the faith. He was not the only one; some two dozen of those who attended the June conference and received priesthood office abandoned Mormonism. Many, like Booth, later wrote with a slight sense of befuddlement that they had once believed that Joseph Smith had spoken the words of God.

Other critics quickly picked up on Booth's complaints. In 1833 Joseph Smith dictated a revelation famously known as the Word of Wisdom, a commandment on dietary practices. "Inasmuch as any man drinketh wine or strong drink among you behold it is not good," ran the revelation. It warned the Mormons away from tobacco and red meat, instead recommending fruits and grain.[28] The early 1830s was the great blossoming of the American temperance movement; under pressure from the hundreds of thousands of members of the American Temperance Society, many churches implored members to voluntarily give up drink, and beginning in 1835 the Whig Party added anti-alcohol legislation to its platform. Even Eber Howe, editor of the *Painesville Telegraph,* who viewed Mormonism as something of a collective insanity, conceded that "we are inclined measurably to agree with the mandate." But Howe scoffed that, "like all other modern Mormon inspirations, a little improvement is made to God's former will" as recorded in the Bible.[29] Though temperance might be a fine idea, it seemed bizarre to him that God would comment on tobacco and vegetables, and like Booth he was offended that Joseph Smith presumed to command in such detail. The Mormons were developing a reputation for clannishness and authoritarianism.

These suspicions would soon erupt, devastating the Zion that Joseph had seen in the translations and sought to build with consecration and priesthood. In August 1833 Oliver Cowdery arrived at Kirtland with distressing news. Jackson County, Missouri, had always been lightly settled, and by the summer of 1833 the Mormons there numbered nearly a thousand, a third of the population. They had become, inadvertently, a powerful political force. The Mormons bought land; they purchased supplies from merchants of their own faith; they were, almost all of them, northern migrants to a southern state in an age when such regional distinctions mattered a great deal. And they believed that Jackson County was the holy ground of their faith. The native Missourians had no doubt that the Mormons intended to use their strength; as one merchant, Josiah Gregg, remembered, they would "boast of their determination to be the sole proprietors of the Land of Zion."[30] The Mormons' visionary separatism grated on their neighbors, who feared they were not simply a harmless religious minority but a well-organized social force.

On July 20, 1833, anticipating future elections, several hundred citizens of Jackson County gathered to consider the problem. They understood themselves to be protecting democracy from Mormon priesthood and preserving the frontier capitalism that Joseph Smith disliked—defending, in short, the American life that Mormonism seemed to threaten. They accused the Mormons of agitating against slavery, for W. W. Phelps had published an article in the Mormon newspaper describing the law governing free blacks in the state as an aid to the few black converts the Mormons had gathered. Consciously echoing the Declaration of Independence, they signed a manifesto above a pledge of "our lives, fortunes, and sacred honors."[31] They understood themselves to be no mob, but rather a group engaging in a type of civil action common in the early nineteenth century: the town meeting. In many frontier cities, such ad hoc public gatherings debated matters of civic import, settled disputes, and, occasionally, lashed out with all legality against threatening minorities.

After deliberating, they went to the Mormon leaders Phelps and

Edward Partridge, the bishop of Jackson County, and demanded that the Mormons leave the county. When Phelps and Partridge asked for time, the meeting deliberated among itself and decided—again, "with the utmost order"—to raze Phelps's home and printing office.[32] There they destroyed the vast majority of the first printing of the *Book of Commandments,* a collection of Joseph Smith's revelations. They then covered Partridge with warm tar and doused him with feathers from a cut-open pillow, a frontier punishment designed to humiliate as well as to injure. The meeting then dispersed in orderly fashion and left the Mormons time to consider. Against such pressure, Phelps and Partridge on July 23 agreed that the Mormons would begin to leave Jackson County by the end of the year.

The Mormons of Kirtland were stricken by the news but could not have been all that surprised. Only a year before, late on the cold night of March 24, 1832, Joseph Smith awoke to a light tap on the window near the cot where he slept next to Joseph Murdock, one of the twins he and Emma had recently adopted. A moment later the door burst open, and a crowd of men dragged him from his bed and into the street, where his clothes were ripped off and tar was poured over his body. Somebody broke a vial of poison on his teeth. He saw Sidney Rigdon lying nearby, unconscious from a blow to the head. The child died of exposure. Symonds Ryder, a friend of Ezra Booth's and a Campbellite minister, later confessed straightforwardly to participation in the raid "to get rid of them." Ryder, like Booth, had briefly been a Mormon himself. Mormons often credit his apostasy to the seemingly niggling fact that his name was spelled incorrectly in a revelation, but Ryder himself wrote that he blanched at the doctrine of consecration, which he called a "plot" to "take their property from them and place it under the disposal of Joseph Smith."[33] There were similar fears in Missouri.

Upon hearing Cowdery's report, Joseph Smith was characteristically emotional but uncharacteristically indecisive. He considered armed retaliation; he pled with God to defend the Mormons; he could not understand why the cause of Zion had been dealt such a blow and worried that the heavens seemed uncharacteristically silent. Meanwhile, the Missouri Mormons consulted with the governor, who advised them to use the courts. Accordingly, they hired several attorneys, but this only proved to the residents of Jackson County that the Mormons could not be trusted. In late October raiders began assaulting the Mormon settlements again. This time the Mormons resisted, but when shots were exchanged, public opinion recoiled. The Mormons laid down their arms, and a band of Missouri vigilantes began in November to drive them north to the Missouri River and across to Clay County.

In December 1833, after months of agonizing, Joseph announced with relief that a revelation had come. Like the Nephites or the children of Israel, the Mormons were told that for their "transgressions . . . they must needs be chastened and tried" to eliminate the "contentions, and envying, and strifes, and lustful and contentious desires" that ran among them. But nonetheless, God declared, "My bowels are filled with compassion toward them. I will not utterly cast them off." For the first time, the Mormons began to think seriously about their place in American politics. Sensitive to accusations that they had planned to subvert American elections, they protested in July and August that the cause at stake in Missouri was religious freedom, protected by the First Amendment. The revelation counseled the Mormons to refuse to sell their property in Jackson County and to seek aid "according to the laws and constitution of the people"; indeed, startlingly, it claimed that "for this purpose have I established the Constitution of this land, by the hands of wise men whom I raised up unto this very purpose."[34]

Joseph's followers were not so confident. In February 1834 a Missouri court hearing to determine the fate of the Mormon property was indefinitely postponed, and two Mormon leaders, Lyman Wight and Parley Pratt, arrived in Kirtland from Zion, spoiling for an aggressive defense of Jackson County. Soon after their arrival, a revelation announced that "the redemption of Zion must needs come by power" and designated Pratt and Wight to raise five hundred volunteers.[35] That spring the two desperately recruited while Joseph raised money to fund a Mormon company, the equivalent of those that had exiled the Missouri Mormons, to regain for them their land. Neither effort was terribly successful; the temple drained funds and bodies, and when the company Joseph named Zion's Camp set out in May 1834 to march the eight hundred miles to Missouri, barely two hundred men composed its ranks.

Zion's Camp was a disaster. Though under consecration the men were bound to share their food as stores ran low, they squabbled over rations. Joseph Smith and a Seventy named Sylvester Smith fought over a campsite and Joseph's aggressive dog; Joseph, in a pique, prophesied that the man would be set upon by beasts, and Sylvester Smith flung his prophecies back in his face as lies. Though Joseph and his closest associates saw signs of providence in the health of the horses and the availability of animals for game, the camp was plagued with storms, flooding rivers, and, upon reaching Missouri, a cholera outbreak that struck a third of Zion's Camp and killed fourteen. Joseph laid hands upon the sick to no avail; he believed that God was expressing displeasure with the camp's complaints. The Mormons had hoped that their show of force would gain the sympathy of the governor; instead, the Jackson County men rallied their own troops, and the governor refused to intervene. On advice of his attorneys, on June 25 Joseph disbanded Zion's Camp and headed back to Kirtland. As he had with so many other disasters, Joseph and other Mormons emerged with their backs stiffened. Nine of the twelve apostles called the next year were veterans of Zion's Camp. They had already sacrificed for Zion, and they later saw the camp as preparation for the challenges ahead.

The Mormons managed, with the help of their attorneys, to forge compromise in the Missouri legislature: the Mormons would be exclusively granted Caldwell County and be given access to Daviess County, largely empty tracts of land north of Clay County. The revelation seemed correct; the democratic processes had worked. It seemed justification not only of the revelation but of the Mormon claim to American identity; there was no reason Zion might not rise within the boundaries of the United States and coexist, albeit uncertainly, with the Missourians.

Even with this uneasy peace struck with their neighbors, the tensions within the Mormon community proved as powerful as those without. Joseph's bid for consecration always struggled. In the fall of 1831, Isaac Morley swallowed hard when he was asked to sell his farm and use the proceeds to move to Missouri and serve the United Firm there, but he did it. Levi Hancock complained that when he visited the Morley Family soon after Joseph proclaimed consecration, Heman Bassett (whom Hancock would later say acted like a baboon) took Hancock's watch "as tho it was his I thought he would soon return it soon but I was disapointed he sold it." When Hancock complained, Bassett said, "Oh he thought it was all in the family."[36] In Missouri and in Ohio, the wealthy Mormons who submitted to consecration like Morley were few. Others, such as Leman Copley, who claimed a thousand acres, balked; as Joseph Knight remembered, "Brother Copley would not Consecrate his property therefore he was Cut of[f] from the Church," though such enforcement was hardly standard.[37] Those Mormons who joined themselves to consecration tended to be those who needed it most; those who did not, did not, so the bishops were chronically short of supplies. After his storehouse in Jackson County was assaulted in the raids of 1833, Edward Partridge dissolved the United Firm in Missouri. Upon the collapse of Zion's Camp, Joseph dictated a revelation declaring that the Mormons "do not impart of their substance, as becometh Saints"; it blamed this recalcitrance for the failure of Zion.[38]

In Kirtland, the Mormon economy proved not much more successful. After the artificial bubble of temple building burst, Kirtland's economy collapsed. As with Jackson County, Joseph seemed rather dithering, trying solution after solution; a revelation took him to Salem, Massachusetts, on a convert's story of hidden treasure buried in a cellar, which proved elusive. Through gritted teeth he told missionaries that the Kirtland stake could no longer support poor converts. In late 1836, the Mormon leadership decided to open a bank to stabilize Kirtland's economy and attract capital. In 1830s America, small banks were popular business ventures; more than twenty had opened in Ohio in the previous few years. But the Mormons had little experience, particularly not Joseph Smith, whose interests ran along decidedly different paths.

The Ohio legislature, correctly identifying the implausibility of the Mormons' plan, refused to charter the bank. But Joseph, revealing the tenuous nature of his relationship with democratic government, refused to be stopped. He stamped the prefix "anti-" before the word "banking" on his Kirtland Safety Society notes and issued one hundred thousand dollars' worth, backed by his own heavy investments and those of his inner circle. On January 2, 1837, the Mormons began using them as currency, and all was well for three weeks. Then a few customers demanded to exchange their notes for other forms of capital, and the bank's feeble supplies could barely manage it. A panic began only two weeks after the bank opened, and on January 23 the bank ran out of capital, and the value of the notes crashed. Only months later, a similar crisis broke out for other banks across the country when New York's banks began refusing these sorts of local notes, and the American economy slipped into the Panic of 1837. All those who held the Safety Society notes lost virtually their entire worth and investors their entire investment. A carpenter named Jonathan Crosby once dutifully accepted the notes as payment for his labor but remembered that he "spent a day running about town trying to buy some food with Kirtland money, but could get nothing for it." The next day he threw himself on Emma's mercy and received a ham and some flour.[39]

The crisis shook not only the economic but also the spiritual foundations of the church. To many of his followers, Joseph Smith's blithe confidence that Zion would never need fear debt suddenly seemed naive. The gospel of salvation was one thing, but Joseph Smith's attempt to remake an entire society was quite another, and he suddenly seemed not quite up to the task. On top of that, his organization faltered. On two occasions in late spring Joseph attempted to claim payment of debt from the apostles Parley Pratt and Thomas Marsh. Neither encounter went well. Joseph exchanged harsh words with Pratt and blows with Marsh. Pratt later wrote an angry letter to Joseph declaring the whole business to be "of the devel," "which Has given rise to Lying deceiveing and takeing the advantage of ones Nabour."[40] In a council on May 29 Lyman Johnson and Parley's brother Orson accused Joseph of disrespect and lying; others loyal to Joseph accused five men, including Johnson, Parley Pratt, and David Whitmer, of causing damage to the church. The council tore itself apart, unable even to select someone to preside.

In August, a group of angry dissenters briefly disrupted services in the Kirtland temple with weapons. They sought an end to Joseph's economic and social experiments. The church they wanted was more along the lines of a Protestant denomination, which preached things spiritual and did no meddling with American life. By December, three members of the Quorum of the Twelve and twenty-eight other men had been excommunicated. Led by Joseph's former clerk Warren Parrish and the ex-apostles John Boynton and Luke Johnson, they declared themselves to be the Church of Christ. In rejecting the addition of the phrase "Latter-day Saints," they proclaimed themselves a restoration of the restoration and turned Joseph's claims against him.

Barely two years after Joseph's triumph at the Kirtland temple, he, Emma, and Sidney Rigdon fled into the cold of the Ohio night of January 12, 1838, headed for Missouri. Emma carried three children born in Kirtland with her—six-year-old Joseph III, the adopted Julia Murdock, and two-year-old Frederick, named after Joseph's friend Frederick Williams, who had recently been removed from the First Presidency for sympathizing with the dissenters. They were steps ahead of lawsuits, creditors, and perhaps a mob of angry apostates. Days after they left, a fire severely damaged the temple.

Nevertheless, the church survived. The Kirtland dissenters had reached out to the Whitmers and other Missouri Mormon leaders precisely because the stake in Missouri was thriving. The Mormon communities there did not depend on Joseph Smith's personal attention. David Whitmer, the Missouri state president, and the councils ran the Missouri communities well. In the summer of 1837 the fifteen hundred Mormons who lived in Caldwell County, Missouri, had broken ground for a new temple in the city of Far West, which they had surveyed and designed according to the plat of Zion, divided into equal blocks and centered on the temple lot. There were some two hundred homes, cleared streets, open roads. Far West was ready to receive the Kirtland Mormons. Joseph Smith had left word that he should be followed, and the second Mormon exodus began that spring. By summer 1838 there were some five thousand Mormons in Caldwell County.

The internal division that had destroyed Kirtland spread here too, and this time it was coupled with pressure from the outside. Sensitive to whispers of economic dissent, the Missouri high council assailed their own presidency, bringing David Whitmer and his brother John, W. W. Phelps, and Oliver Cowdery to trial under the accusation that they had abandoned Joseph Smith's vision and betrayed revelation. Perhaps increasingly suspicious of Joseph Smith's economic wisdom, they had sold their lands in Jackson County. Echoing Ezra Booth, the accused—even these accused, who had been with Joseph Smith since the beginning—declared that they "would not be controlled by an ecclesiastical power of revelation whatever in their temporal concerns."[41] Their protest reveals how tenuous and slippery the Mormon kingdom really was, how strong the grip of American ideas about liberty and capitalism could be, and how difficult was the balance between freedom and community, the language of revelation and the language of tyranny. The men were excommunicated, the council proclaiming its allegiance to Joseph Smith and the prophet himself accepting that even his dearest friends might be cast off. After all, the Mormon settlements were still expanding, across Caldwell County and into Daviess County.

It was the latter county that would cause trouble. Daviess was not solely reserved to Mormons, though it was the home of Joseph Smith's Eden; by August 1838 one of every three residents were followers of Joseph Smith. And again, as in Jackson County, local Missourians feared the intentions of the Mormons, particularly given the chaos surrounding the excommunications. That summer, Rigdon delivered a series of fiery sermons declaring hostility to those disloyal to Joseph Smith and warning, on the Fourth of July, that "to the mob that comes on us to disturb us; it shall be between us and them a war of extermination."[42] A man named Sampson Avard organized a shadowy fraternal society, possibly with the blessing of Joseph Smith, and called it the Danites, a name drawn from prophecies about Zion in the Book of Daniel. They swore to protect the church from dissenters with violence, if need be. None of these things were comforting to Missourians who feared Mormon power.

On election day that August, a fight broke out when a small group of Missourians attempted to stop a Mormon from voting in Gallatin, the county seat. Tensions rose and court hearings were called and postponed until October 1, when a mob burned the home of a Mormon family in a city outside Caldwell County's borders and the Mormons there were driven out. In response, Joseph Smith armed five hundred Mormons at Far West and declared the Mormons "had sought for redress through the medium of the law, but never could get it."[43] His old confidence in the Constitution, in civil liberties, in the calm strength of government had been dashed and he would never quite trust these things again. Led by the apostles David Patten and Lyman Wight, the Mormons raided into Daviess County, seeking to drive out the ringleaders of the vigilantes and burning some fifty buildings. Daviess became a war zone. Mormons clashed with vigilantes in several engagements, and Patten and three others were killed. Outraged, the new governor, Lilburn Boggs, issued an executive order to the state militia ordering that "the Mormons must be treated as enemies, and must be exterminated or driven from the state if necessary for the public peace."[44] On October 30, a group of vigilantes stormed the Mormon settlement of Haun's Mill, near Far West, and executed seventeen Mormons, including women and children.

The violence proved too much. That same day, several Mormon leaders surrendered to a friendly officer in the Missouri militia, and Joseph was taken into custody, saying that he preferred to go to prison than to have his people destroyed. The terms of the surrender required the Mormons to leave the state, and on November 1, Far West surrendered. The Mormons fled, once again, east, as religious refugees seeking sanctuary in the town of Quincy, Illinois. The exodus was under the direction of Brigham Young, who had replaced the slain Patten as head of the Quorum of the Twelve. Joseph Smith himself was taken to a prison called Liberty Jail.

THREE

CITY OF JOSEPH

1839–1846

In late 1838, Quincy, Illinois, became a refugee camp. The Mormons in flight from the Missouri militia turned to the citizens of Illinois, across the Mississippi River, who were appalled by the Missouri government. The largest city in the area on the river, Quincy, some 150 miles from Far West, threw its doors open. As the snow began to fall in November and December, the Mormons started to struggle across the frozen river on foot or in small rafts or canoes. Quincy citizens organized ad hoc patrols to rescue Mormons stymied on the opposite bank. As one Quincy woman wrote, the Mormons "were in such distressing condition when they arrived that the good people of the town took them in and gave them temporary relief."[1] A thirteen-year-old Mormon remembered that "everything was overrun, hundreds of men out of employ, wages very low."[2] Mormons took what odd jobs they could, boarded and rented in homes and inns, and by the end of the year, some five thousand had gathered in Quincy, with several thousand more scattered in settlements along the river.

Though Joseph Smith, his counselors, and several apostles were imprisoned in Missouri, the councils of the church slowly began to grind into motion. The Quorum of the Twelve, in particular, seized the initiative. The apostles Brigham Young, John Taylor, and Heber Kimball persuaded most of the Mormons remaining in Far West by January 1839 to pool their resources, sell abandoned property, and move east to Illinois. Refugee committees were dispatched to various points along the river to assist and direct the families trailing eastward. Though some veterans of Jackson County and Far West advocated dispersing the church to avoid renewed persecution, in March 1839 Young arrived in Quincy and summoned a meeting of the Saints. There he declared that the Mormons needed to be "nourished and fed by the shepherds," calling for them "to unite together as much as possible."[3] Mormon leaders were already negotiating with the land speculator Isaac Galland for a large tract of land some fifty miles north of Quincy surrounding a small village called Commerce. The bank failures and deflation that had plagued the western frontier since the Panic of 1837 produced a buyer's market for seekers of land, and the Mormons purchased it with little more than promise of payment over the next twenty years.

While the councils searched for a new Zion, Joseph Smith laid over with his brother Hyrum, Sidney Rigdon, Lyman Wight, and two others through the winter in a fourteen-foot-square unheated stone building lined with filthy straw called Liberty Jail. Emma and Sidney Rigdon's wife, Phebe, visited several times, bringing blankets and Joseph's children. Later, the Mormon scholar B. H. Roberts would call Liberty Jail a "prison-temple," a holy place that purified suffering, like the deserts of the Bible. There Joseph pondered the repeated failures of Zion. He believed unwaveringly in his vision. Why, he asked, had God allowed the work to fail? "Oh God, where art thou, and where is the pavilion that covereth thy hiding place? How long shall thy hand be stayed?" he pled. And the answer came: "Know thou my son that all these things shall give thee experience, and shall be for thy good. The son of man hath descended below them all; art thou greater than he?"[4] This answer invested Mormon suffering with meaning: rather than stymie God's will, tribulation revealed it. The histories that Mormons produced thereafter would dwell on the Missouri experience, on the assaults on Joseph's person, on the repeated flights to new Zions. These things brought them together, cultivated their strength, gave them character and built their faith. Through an act of imaginative will, suffering became deeply ingrained in the Mormon identity.

By April Missouri officials had begun to find the fact that they were holding Joseph Smith prisoner vaguely embarrassing. The Mormons' plea for religious liberty gained traction: the nation's newspapers blasted the Missouri mobs, and even Jonathan Turner, a Presbyterian minister whose damning *Mormonism in All Ages* became a popular exposé of Joseph Smith, wrote, "Mormonism is a monstrous evil; and the only place where it ever did or ever could shine this side of the world of despair, is by the side of the Missouri mob."[5] On April 6 the prisoners were taken from the jail to a hearing, where they were indicted for treason, arson, and several other charges. A few days later, on the way to trial, their guards allowed them to escape. Two weeks later they arrived in Quincy. Soon after that, Joseph Smith set eyes on Commerce, Illinois.

The location was good, but the land was not. It lay low and humid on an overgrown bend in the Mississippi River, making it a natural port for the steamships and riverboats that floated past in ever larger numbers. But because the "flats" of the town rose only a few feet above the water level before rising into hills a mile or so inland, when the Mormons arrived it was marshy, damp, a haven for mosquitoes. Only three buildings of log and stone stood on the banks of the Mississippi. In late spring, Mormons began to move onto the land, and the council bought another tract to the north, anticipating expansion. They began to dig trenches to drain the marsh, to clear streets, and to build homes. In July, unsurprisingly, malaria struck, and Joseph Smith himself caught it. Unlike in Zion's Camp, this time when he laid his hands on the sick many "leaped from their beds made whole by the power of God," as the new apostle Wilford Woodruff recorded in his journal.[6] It was a good omen.

Early the next year Joseph renamed Commerce "Nauvoo," a transliteration of a Hebrew word meaning "beautiful." He likely learned the word from Joshua Seixas, a professor at Oberlin College whom he had hired to teach Hebrew to several Mormon leaders in Kirtland for a few months in 1836. Despite the name, Joseph never invested Nauvoo with the same sort of metaphysical meaning that he had Missouri. Nonetheless he declared it was indeed a central stake of the coming New Jerusalem, from which a Zion society would expand across the American continent. Though he had surrendered Jackson County for a time, and been driven from Far West and Kirtland, his ambitions had not faded. By the fall of 1839, the conferences of the church were being held in Nauvoo. William Marks was selected stake president, a high council was organized, and bishops were assigned to see to the temporal needs of the Mormons. Though Joseph did not attempt to enforce the law of consecration again, he declared that henceforth, until the Mormons were ready to practice consecration, they would be asked to tithe 10 percent of their gain to the bishop's storehouse.

The disasters in Missouri had shaken the process of the Gathering somewhat; to many Mormons, Zion seemed lost, and the flight from Ohio to Missouri to Illinois in such a short span of years left them scattered across the nation. They organized in small congregations called "branches," outside the stakes of Zion and under the authority of the apostles, who visited when they could. Some two dozen branches remained in northeastern Ohio, around Kirtland. Many Mormon immigrants would stop in St. Louis, a cheaper fare than Far West or Nauvoo; in 1845, the apostle Heber Kimball reported some four hundred Mormons living in the city. Boston, Philadelphia, and Baltimore all had branches with many dozens of members, occasionally visited by a traveling apostle in the same way an itinerant Methodist minister might visit a congregation once a year to offer the sacraments. To reach these branches, church leadership directed that newspapers be published— *The Evening and the Morning Star* in Missouri and *Times and Seasons* in Nauvoo, among others. But as Mormonism evolved through the give-and-take between Joseph Smith and the Saints who surrounded him, the brands of the faith that developed in these more distant congregations often did not keep pace with that in the center. Because of this drift, and because they believed that the growth of Nauvoo would strengthen the city financially and politically, the Mormon leaders renewed the call of the Gathering, summoning Mormons from around the world to settle in Nauvoo. In August 1840 Joseph Smith sent a letter "To the Saints Scattered Abroad," calling on them to "unite our energies for the upbuilding of the Kingdom."[7]

And they came. The greatest source of converts in the late 1830s and early 1840s was Great Britain. In June 1837 and in April 1839, during the heart of the Kirtland bank crisis and the aftermath of the Far West collapse, respectively, Joseph Smith declared that revelation demanded he send some of the most trusted members of the Quorum of the Twelve to Great Britain. By the time the apostles Heber Kimball and Orson Hyde returned to the United States in April 1838, there were some fourteen hundred Mormons in Great Britain. When Kimball, Brigham Young, and six other apostles arrived in Liverpool in April 1840, they began proselytizing efforts that converted some sixteen thousand more by 1847. Unlike most American converts, many British Mormons were from the industrial working class of the urban centers of Manchester and Liverpool, which was suffering the effects of a late 1830s depression. The apostles offered them land, fresh air, and independence. The *Latter-day Saints' Millennial Star*, a newspaper the apostles ran in Britain, promised, "Millions upon millions of acres of land lie before them unoccupied, with a soil as rich as Eden."[8] Many of these converts were radical religionists. From April through December 1840, Woodruff converted some three hundred United Brethren, members of a charismatic, self-consciously lower-class branch of the British Methodist movement that stressed autonomous control of one's spiritual life, personal access to God, and ecclesiastical reform. Methodism in Britain was repeatedly wracked with schism, as groups such as the United Brethren called for more immediate spiritual experience, social reform, and the rejection of a priestly caste: the Mormon community in Nauvoo promised all of these things. On June 6, 1840, the apostles sent the first boatload of forty-one British converts to Nauvoo. Thousands would follow over the next few years.

The apostles ran the mission brilliantly, organizing an emigration fund to support transport back to Nauvoo, establishing a press infrastructure that became one of the most important public organs of Mormonism for decades, and by the mid-1840s establishing a church in Britain that rivaled the one in the United States in size. By virtue of his editorship of the *Millennial Star* and the publication of his two long tracts *A Voice of Warning and Instruction to All People* and *History of the Late Persecution Inflicted by the State of Missouri upon the Mormons*, Parley Pratt became the voice through which hundreds of converts encountered Mormon ideas. In his writings, Pratt presented Mormonism first of all as a restoration of the Biblical kingdom of God and of the prophetic leadership that kingdom had enjoyed, distinct from traditional Christianity primarily in organization rather than theology. He downplayed the distinctive doctrines that Joseph Smith's revelations were beginning to unfold, emphasizing instead persecution as a sign of the truthfulness of the work and the Mormons' ability to resist it as a sign of their character and chosen status.[9] This was the Mormonism that many converts, particularly in Britain, understood themselves to be embracing. Similarly, because of his direction of the mission effort, Brigham Young became the most respected and successful organizer in the church. To thousands of British converts, the apostles were their natural leaders, and indeed, in Nauvoo, they had become second only to Joseph Smith.

For their first eighteen months in Nauvoo, the Mormons were governed by the high council, which divided and sold parcels of land, established regulations for ferries and other public utilities, and erected a public school system. In 1840 Joseph and a new associate, John C. Bennett, sent the Illinois legislature a city charter. Bennett, a small, quick man trained as a physician but variously a soldier, an educator, and a politician, was a rare sort of Mormon convert: polished, educated, well-connected. He would also prove to be an opportunist. Bennett was never much interested in Mormonism as a religious movement. He knew that the Mormons were a powerful potential political base and saw himself as a power broker.

The Mormons had cultivated an uneasy relationship with American politics. In the wake of the Missouri disasters Joseph Smith had journeyed to Washington, D.C., to seek aid. He encountered a string of politicians interested in his growing bloc of voters, but the president, the Democrat Martin Van Buren, rejected Joseph's appeal for aid, saying that he could do nothing that would infringe on the rights of the state of Missouri. Infuriated, Joseph returned west, and he was not shy about his contempt for the president. In the elections of 1840 the

Mormons offered the Whig Party, the Democrats' major national opponent, an almost unified bloc of votes. That year the Whigs won 70 percent of the vote in Hancock County, where Nauvoo lay. Such reactionary voting, however, concealed deeper uneasiness. The Whigs believed in strict restrictions on emigration and evangelical Protestants exerted a great deal of power in the party, and the Mormons found both troubling. A Democratic state supreme court justice named Stephen Douglas saw opportunity: he befriended Joseph Smith, aided the passage of the Nauvoo charter, and brought the Mormons to the Democratic aisle. In 1841 Joseph Smith published a statement in *Times and Seasons* declaring that the Mormons "would be influenced by no party consideration." But it also endorsed Democratic candidates by name, stating that "we shall go for our friends."[10] The Mormons were never comfortable with American politics; rather, they tended to see the political process through the narrow lens of their self-interest and in basic conflict with their dreams for a community of universal brotherhood. Their numbers made them valuable to politicians, but their utopian religion made them difficult partners to keep.

Only four cities in Illinois were large enough for a formal charter when Nauvoo was settled, but Nauvoo was growing fast: by fall 1840 its 2,450 residents already made it larger than Quincy. Nauvoo's charter drew on rights given to other cities to maximize local authority. The city government had wide legal power: the authority to pass all laws not explicitly forbidden by the state or national constitution, and the right to establish a university and militia. Bennett's connections ensured that the charter sailed through the legislature with little debate, and Mormons hailed the passage as a sign that the American system was finally ready to protect their constitutional rights. Bennett was elected the city's first mayor. Though there were usually a few non-Mormons in city government, in practice members of the high council, apostles, and Joseph Smith himself almost always held top political positions. Joseph became mayor in 1842, serving in that capacity until his death in 1844. This interweaving of ecclesiastical and political government disturbed many of Nauvoo's neighbors; some of the suspicion Mormons encountered in Missouri followed them to Nauvoo.

Far West and the plat of Zion lingered in the Mormons' minds. As the plat of Zion directed, Nauvoo was laid out in four-acre blocks, each with four lots, divided by wide, straight streets. The church sold the lots to its members at varying prices, based upon the ability to pay. Though they were often subdivided, these large plots were meant to encourage an agrarian lifestyle within the town, and many residents indeed raised animals, small orchards, or vegetables on the land surrounding their homes. The city's farmers traveled to their lands outside the city boundaries each morning, while others, particularly British immigrants trained in industry, erected brickyards, smithies, potteries, and other small industries in their back lots. By 1844, there were some two hundred shops in the city, but there was also often little cash in circulation; many Mormons survived for long periods of time on a barter economy. The family of Alfred Cordon, for instance, arrived in Nauvoo from Britain on a steamship in April 1843. They had a single dollar, seventy-five cents of which they spent for wood to burn in the empty log cabin where they took initial shelter. In the absence of money, they began to trade their possessions for food. For several months Alfred worked as a laborer, seeking jobs that would pay in kind rather than in cash, before his family was able to purchase a home, and even then they continued to barter goods for furnishings.

The city grew quickly. Houses spread north and east from the bend in the riverbank where the original small cluster of cabins sat. For the entire duration of Joseph's church in Nauvoo, from 1839 to 1847, there was immigration, construction, expansion; log cabins gave way to brick homes, which in turn began to give way to frame houses. In 1844, the apostle John Taylor wrote, "In every direction may be heard the sound of the mason's trowel, the carpenter's hammer, the teamster's voice."[11] Joseph Smith lived on Water Street, which ran along the river only yards from its bank, first in a cabin and then in the two-story Mansion House, where he and Emma frequently took in boarders. Main Street ran north perpendicular from Water Street, and along its path a number of public and cultural institutions appeared: a two-story store Joseph Smith ran that also held a storehouse for the bishops and a large meeting hall on the upper floors, the printing offices of *Times and Seasons,* a library, and a public debating society called the Nauvoo Lyceum. In 1842 and 1845, respectively, the Masonic Hall and the Concert Hall were built; both were used regularly not merely by the associations that gave the buildings their names but for all sorts of public events. Above them all, on a ridge north of the city, the walls of a new temple began to rise.

Unlike many other separatist religious groups in early nineteenth-century America, the Mormons did not spurn dancing, secular music, or the theater; indeed, the Mormons today have a reputation for musical ability and interest in theater, and both of those traditions find their roots in Nauvoo. The Mormons regularly gathered for concerts and house parties, and Joseph Smith often hosted dances at the Mansion House that went deep into the night. The city supported a choral group and, eventually, a Nauvoo Music Association, which sponsored a number of musical groups and solicited annual memberships. An actor from New York City named Thomas Lyne operated a theatrical troupe called the Nauvoo Theater on the first floor of the Masonic Hall. Brigham Young and other Mormon leaders were occasionally known to take a role.

A few years before Nauvoo began rising on the river, Alexis de Tocqueville observed, "In no country in the world has the principle of association been more successfully used or applied to a greater multitude of objects than in America."[12] For Tocqueville, voluntary associations, public organizations such as the Freemasons, the Lyceum, or, of course, religion itself, were the blood and marrow of American democratic society, the means through which a national culture was created and individuals initiated into the common life. The early nineteenth century was the great age of the voluntary association, as the young republic built a public culture to match its democratic government. And in Nauvoo the Mormons built as enthusiastically as anyone. The quorums and meetings of the church itself were such associations, and powerful ones: men were expected to gather regularly with their respective priesthood quorum for worship and to work for the community and the church. But the Mormons understood their church to be more than simply another such organization; rather, it was itself a society, and they built associations to deepen and support its goals. The Nauvoo Lyceum regularly debated religious topics, fulfilling its occasionally enunciated purpose to train missionaries; the University of Nauvoo, which sponsored classes held throughout the city, offered classes on church history, and encouraged students to weave together their studies and their faith. Many Mormon men became Freemasons, finding in its fraternal rituals a mirror for the religious community of their church.

The most influential of these distinctively Mormon voluntary associations was the Relief Society. For a dozen years after the founding of Joseph Smith's church, women had no formal role in its organization. Other radical religious movements, such as the Quakers or some Methodist groups, encouraged women to serve as missionaries, but the Mormons did not. Several others, such as the Seventh-day Adventists, which grew from William Miller's apocalypticism, or the Shakers, had female leadership; again, the Mormons did not. The gendered particularities of Mormon organization were one thing the Mormons had in common with the mainstream of American society. American women in the 1840s had little access to government, little independence under the law, and few opportunities to gain power. But one route that stood open to them was the voluntary association. Common cultural assumptions credited women with superior moral delicacy and spiritual insights, but these blessings also bound women to the home, where they were to invest their sons with the morals necessary for self-government and their daughters with the talents to pass virtue on to the next generation. By the 1840s, however, this moral imperative had given birth to an ideology called civic housekeeping: citing their mandate to protect virtue, many women began to enter the public sphere as advocates for social reforms such as temperance, organizing programs such as Sunday schools, and calling for greater feminine influence in public life.

The Nauvoo Female Relief Society began very much like other civic housekeeping organizations. Sarah Granger Kimball, who lived in the north of Nauvoo with her husband, the non-Mormon Hiram Kimball, organized a small group of friends to make clothing for the workers building the Nauvoo temple. This was a task Sarah had been doing informally for several months; given that her husband was not a Mormon, she had no property to offer the church in tithing and found shirtmaking a way to contribute. Sarah and her friends went to

Eliza R. Snow for advice. Snow, then close to forty, was well educated and known as a poet from her teenage years. She had been baptized in 1835 in Kirtland, where she had worked as a schoolteacher and in the office of her father, who was a justice of the peace. She quickly became respected as a leader within the informal visiting and charity networks that women formed in the Mormon settlements. When Sarah Kimball wanted to form a society, Snow was an obvious person to recruit.

Eliza Snow produced a constitution for a "benevolent society," a common organization in Jacksonian America. Like other such women's organizations, it was designed primarily to coordinate charitable work. Then Joseph Smith intervened. As Sarah Kimball remembered, when the women took their plan to him for approval, he praised it but told them, "This is not what you want," and announced that this benevolent society would be more than a secular reform group. He told Snow and Kimball and the rest that God had "something better for them than a written constitution," making the distinction between those voluntary organizations governed by rules written by humans and the divine forces that ran his church. "I am glad to have the opportunity of organizing the women, as a part of the priesthood belongs to them," he said.[13]

On March 17, 1842, twenty women gathered in the large room above Joseph's store, where Joseph intended to organize their society "after a pattern of the priesthood."[14] He proposed that they elect a president and two counselors, the same leadership structure as the priesthood quorums, and stated he would "ordain them." Emma Smith was unanimously elected president, and Eliza R. Snow became secretary. Joseph then recalled the old revelation he had received for Emma more than ten years earlier, when she was still deliberating whether to join her husband's church, and declared that this revelation had charged her to teach the scriptures. It would be the women's responsibility to instruct and to look "to the wants of the poor—searching after objects of charity, and in administering to their wants—to assist; by correcting the morals and strengthening the virtues of the female community." Though Joseph Smith recommended the society be dubbed the "Benevolent Society," Emma preferred the title "Relief Society," to differentiate the Mormons from secular organizations; she did "not wish to have it call'd after other Societies in the world," and her proposal carried the day.[15] One British convert remembered the charge as being twofold: "To dispense goods to the poor was the Relief Society's temporal responsibility; to practice virtue and preach truth, its spiritual obligations."[16]

These the Relief Society did. The treasurer collected donations, and the society's leaders directed members to seek out those throughout the city who needed aid, both through informal conversations and through organized visitation committees. Membership rapidly increased; there were twenty-seven women on the rolls at the end of the first meeting in March 1842; two years later, there were 1,341. In addition to organizing charitable efforts and expounding scripture, at their meetings women worshipped together, shared impromptu testimonies, spoke in tongues, and administered to one another in ritual blessings in cases of pregnancy, disease, or misfortune.

Communal worship took place in other venues as well. Lucy Mack Smith, the child of a long tradition of Anglo-American Protestant piety, had regularly tried to gather her family for devotions, such as scripture reading, prayers, and hymn singing, and in Nauvoo many Mormons of similar cultural ancestry continued the tradition. Fathers, particularly holders of the priesthood, were expected to preside over their families, administering blessings and conducting family worship. Smaller prayer meetings in which Mormons would gather with friends and neighbors to testify to one another, to sing and pray together, and to lay hands on one another for blessings were also popular. Eliza R. Snow's journal frequently described such events; in December 1843, for instance, she visited the home of Isaac and Lucy Morley and received from Isaac a blessing "to speak wisdom and counsel in prudence."[17] Most Sunday afternoons, Mormons from throughout the city and surrounding areas would gather in what later records would call the groves, a lightly forested area at the base of the gentle rise a mile or so inland from the riverbank. There they would sit on benches hewn from tree branches and listen to Joseph Smith or Sidney Rigdon or others and sometimes receive the Lord's Supper. Biannually Joseph Smith called a conference of the church, where sermons were delivered and the church's authorities confirmed in their office by common consent. As in Kirtland, the Mormons built no meetinghouse in Nauvoo.

Again, though, Joseph Smith was determined to build a temple. As in Kirtland, he selected a site above the city, on the bluff that rose above the groves. The plan also somewhat resembled the Kirtland temple's mixture of New England meetinghouse and Gothic styles. In October 1840 Joseph Smith asked a General Conference of the church for a tithe of time: each man would work one day out of ten on the construction. It would be three times the size of the Kirtland temple, 128 feet long and 88 feet wide, but its basic design would be the same: a lower floor for large meetings, with pulpits designated for various priesthood quorums, a second floor with another assembly hall, and an upper floor with various smaller meeting rooms. The Nauvoo temple would take five years to complete, though as its walls began to go up and the main room became at least somewhat enclosed it hosted meetings and dances, as early as 1842.

Though it greatly resembled the Kirtland temple in floor plan and architecture, Joseph Smith had plans for the Nauvoo temple that far exceeded those for the earlier structure. While the Kirtland temple was used primarily as a meetinghouse, a schoolhouse, and a site for a few rituals, the Nauvoo temple was designed for much more extensive ritual worship. In January 1841 a revelation commanded, "Let this house be built unto my name, that I may reveal mine ordinances therein unto my people."[18] These ordinances, sacred rituals designed to gain that celestial kingdom that the Vision had described, pressed back against the uncertainty, confused loyalty, and constant fear of disorder and death that had plagued the Mormons in general and Joseph Smith in particular since the founding of the church. Through these rituals Mormons would not only gain individual salvation but also explicitly tie that salvation to membership in the strong community that the church had wrought.

One such ordinance was already under way when construction on the temple began. In August 1840 Joseph Smith, explaining an obscure reference in 1 Corinthians, taught that baptism by proper priesthood authority was essential for salvation and was available to the dead by proxy. In the October conference of the church, he announced the ordinance publicly, and Saints flocked to the banks of the river to be baptized for their parents and grandparents. For several months the river's edge was crowded. Vilate Kimball, wife of the apostle Heber Kimball, wrote to her husband that the announcement had caused "quite a revival in the church." "Since this order has been preached here the waters have been continually troubled," she wrote, "sometimes from eight to ten Elders in the river at a time baptizing."[19] Wilford Woodruff later said, "How did we feel when we first heard the living could be baptized for the dead? We all went to work at it as fast as we had an opportunity, and were baptized for everybody we could think of."[20] After a year of such activity, in October 1841 workers erected a font in the basement of the unfinished temple; it was dedicated with a prayer, and baptisms for the dead were thereafter restricted to that place. More than fifteen thousand were performed before the Mormons left Nauvoo.

Other rituals, more complex, soon followed. On May 4, 1842, Joseph Smith invited nine men—including his brother Hyrum; the apostles Brigham Young, Heber Kimball, and Willard Richards; William Marks, the Nauvoo stake president; and William Law, a member of the First Presidency—to the upper room of his store, where the Relief Society had been organized a few weeks before. There he administered to them what he called the "endowment," a word the revelations had invoked in association with the temples since the early 1830s. The endowment far expanded the washings and anointings of the Kirtland temple; indeed, those rites now became preparatory. The men were washed and anointed, then dressed in a white garment and a robe in imitation of the priests of the Hebrew Bible. Then the initiates watched a ritual drama depicting the creation and the fall of Adam and Eve from Eden, ending with the institution of priesthood authority as a means to regain that perfect state of divine communion. Along the way Adam and Eve—and the initiates, told to view this first couple as models for themselves—made covenants to follow God's commandments. Finally, they were ushered through a veil into the symbolic presence of God.

The attic of the Nauvoo temple was furnished to accommodate the endowment ritual, but the temples of the church have since been built to accommodate it more fully. They are not normally used for regular worship, but for the endowment, baptism for the dead, and marriages. Some have various rooms representing the Creation, the Garden, and the World; all are built with veils separating the final room from a Celestial Room, finely furnished and decorated to represent heaven. While in the temple, Mormons wear white clothes and the robes Joseph Smith introduced. They are also given the white garment upon beginning the endowment session, and are instructed to wear it beneath their clothes for the rest of their lives. When introduced in Nauvoo the garment looked like long woolen underwear, but it has since been shortened and separated into two parts, resembling boxer shorts and a white T-shirt. Intended to be reminiscent of the skins in which God clothed Adam and Eve after the expulsion from the Garden of Eden in the third chapter of Genesis, the garment, Mormons are told, is a constant reminder of their dependence on God and the covenants they make in the temple to obey him.

The endowment owed a great deal to Genesis and to Joseph's retellings of its creation story in his books of Moses and Abraham and to the descriptions of the rites of ancient Israel in the Biblical book of Leviticus. Joseph also introduced it only six weeks after Abraham Jonas, the grand master of the Great Lodge of Illinois, came to Nauvoo and inducted Joseph and several dozen other Mormons into Freemasonry. Joseph's ritual mirrored Masonry partly in form, particularly in the use of certain signs and grips, and in its construction of an initiation rite through elaboration of Biblical story and drama. Most of all the endowment used ritual to bind people together through oath and covenant. Freemasonry offered the same sense of an ordered world that Joseph was seeking to find in his faith; it is little surprise that he would find in the Masonic ritual the same inspiration that he found in Biblical texts. But unlike Freemasonry's drama, which focused on the shadowy Biblical figure Hiram Abiff and hence was restricted to men, the endowment, focused on the pair of Adam and Eve, was open to women. A year after the first endowments were given, the same group returned with their wives and a handful of others to pass through the ritual again. Many of these couples were also invited to participate in the final key ordinance Joseph Smith introduced in Nauvoo: sealing.

The idea of sealing lay at the heart of Joseph Smith's attempt to build a better world, one that overcame the turbulence of American life and the constant threat of death. Little brought Joseph more joy than when he baptized his father, or when he saw his dead brother Alvin in heaven, or when his other brother Hyrum was baptized for Alvin in the fall of 1840 in the Mississippi waters. He recalled the recitations of Moroni and Elijah, their invocation of the Hebrew prophet Malachi's injunction to turn the hearts of children and fathers toward each other, and he invoked Jesus's promise to Peter in the New Testament that whatever he bound or loosed on earth would be bound or loosed in heaven. The promise of sealing was that these familial relationships could become stronger than the whirlwinds of economy and society that tore them apart and would even, in the end, outlast death. Sealed relationships would last into the eternities, and indeed, none could enter the highest levels of heaven alone. Joseph taught that parents and children, brothers and sisters, ancestors and descendants should all be sealed together.

The ordinances that the Nauvoo temple offered were the ritual focus of the radical theological innovations Joseph Smith began to unveil in Nauvoo. In 1842, Joseph completed work on the translation of the Book of Abraham that he had begun in Kirtland and published it in *Times and Seasons*. Like Moses or Genesis or the endowment drama, Abraham presented another depiction of the creation of the world, a story Joseph Smith constantly told and retold. The vision of Abraham offered a long prologue, a precreation history, showing the primordial origins of humanity itself: "Now the Lord had shown unto me, Abraham, the intelligences that were organized before the world was . . . and he said unto me, Abraham, thou art one of them, thou wast chosen before thou wast born." These intelligences were human beings in a premortal state. Like Joseph's church itself, the creation was governed by council, presided over by "one among them that was like unto God," obviously but never identified as Jesus Christ, who "said unto those, who were with him, we will go down, for there is space there, and we will take of these materials, and we will make an Earth whereon these may dwell."[21]

Later, in April 1844, only weeks before his death, Joseph preached a funeral sermon in the grove at the foot of the temple for his friend King Follett, and gave further shape to these ideas. He said he had come to "refute the idea that God was God from all eternity." Rather, "God that sits enthroned is a man like one of yourselves." After all, Joseph said, Jesus had declared that he had done nothing but what he saw his father do. Likewise, he told his audience, "You have got to learn how to make yourselves God, king and priest, by going from a small capacity to a great capacity to the resurrection of the dead." God was God because he had attained glory and power, and now he sought to guide other intelligences along the same path. The traditional divide between the creator and the creation did not exist for Joseph Smith; both humanity and divinity were eternal beings, existing only in different states of progression: "God was a self existing being," he said, and "man exists upon the same principle."[22] This meant also that God the Father and Jesus Christ were possessed of bodies, while the Holy Spirit possessed a "tabernacle of spirit."[23] These three became the Holy Trinity through their perfect communion, and their task was to bring humanity through the perils of mortal life to participation in these divine relationships. This was a radical reframing of the traditional Christian narrative. In place of creation, fall, and redemption, Joseph offered a vision of eternal progress: the movement of these raw intelligences through mortality and to divinity, gained through the experience of mortal life and through entering into the sort of holy relationships that the ordinances created.

These doctrines illustrated more than anything else a strikingly optimistic view of human nature, one that reflected the expansive spirit of antebellum America. Other apostates from Puritanism such as the Unitarian William Ellery Channing and the Transcendentalists offered similarly exalted images of human potential, preaching, as Channing put it in his famous sermon "Likeness to God," that "true religion consists in proposing, as our great end, a growing likeness to the Supreme Being." He spurned warnings of "danger from too literal an interpretation," stating flatly that "man has kindred nature with God"—though while he and Transcendentalists like Ralph Waldo Emerson happily divinized humanity, they would have found baffling and vulgar Joseph Smith's humanization of God.[24] Nonetheless, the inexhaustible capacity for divinity all of them located in the human soul reflected the sentiments of the American romantic movement: a hunger for spiritual and emotional connection with the infinite beyond the self. Other Americans found connection through the sacramental community of Catholicism, savoring the metaphysical and spiritual bonds that joining a priestly church provided. As Orestes Brownson, who left Transcendentalism for Catholicism, wrote, "The church is defined by the blessed apostle to be the body of Christ, and must therefore be an organism like every living body, not a simple organization or association of individuals."[25] Those sympathies Joseph Smith understood, for he tried to create such relationships himself.

The most controversial of his relationships was the practice of plural marriage, which was intimately bound to sealing. The revelation that narrated the one also taught the other. Just as the Vision grew from questions raised during the translation of the New Testament, the idea of plural marriage most likely emerged from Joseph's encounter with the story of Abraham, who in the book of Genesis marries multiple wives. In 1843 Joseph dictated a revelation he said had originally come to him much earlier, probably around 1831. It declared that all human "bonds, obligations, oaths, vows" not "sealed by the Holy Spirit of Promise" would not persist into the afterlife. But if a marriage was so sealed, the couple "shall inherit thrones, kingdoms . . . exaltation and glory in all things." The revelation then asserted that God sanctioned Abraham's polygamy, that it was "the new and everlasting covenant" given by "the power of the priesthood, wherein I restore all things," and commanded Joseph to "do the works of Abraham; enter ye into my law and ye shall be saved."[26]

For some the notion was repugnant. In 1838, struggling for his membership in the church, Oliver Cowdery wrote a letter to his brother Warren, denouncing the "dirty, nasty, filthy affair" that he believed Joseph Smith had had with Fanny Alger, a teenage serving girl who had lived with the Smiths in Kirtland a few years before.[27] Cowdery had evidently been discussing his suspicions with others;

when he was tried by the Missouri church court that year, he was charged with making false accusations against the prophet. Cowdery, a man highly protective of his honor, angrily defended his honesty, while Joseph Smith insisted vehemently and specifically that he was not guilty of adultery. Fanny left Kirtland in 1836 with her family at the age of seventeen. Like the Alger case, the later plural marriages that Joseph Smith would enter into or oversee in Nauvoo are hard to recover. The historical evidence is elusive and sometimes contested, much derived from affidavits given long after the fact that nonetheless recall vividly the strain and confusion that the practice, variously called the "principle," the "new and everlasting covenant of marriage," or "celestial marriage," caused.

Plural marriage in Nauvoo began early, when Joseph Smith chose Louisa Beaman to be his first plural wife there. Louisa turned twenty-five in 1840. She and her family were from Avon, New York, a small town not too far from Palmyra. They had joined the church in 1835, after a party of Mormon missionaries, including Joseph Smith, stayed the night in their home. Louisa's parents both died before the Mormons settled in Nauvoo, so she moved in with her sister and brother-in-law, Joseph Noble. In the fall of 1840, Joseph approached Noble, explained to him that he wanted to marry Louisa, begged Noble to be silent, and asked him for help in approaching her. On April 5, 1841, Noble sealed Joseph and Louisa in a grove near Main Street in Nauvoo, repeating the words that Joseph had directed him to say.

Later that year Joseph would marry two sisters, Zina Huntington Jacobs and Presendia Huntington Buell. Both were married to other men, but in civil secular marriages, which Joseph believed held no power in eternity. He approached Zina before she married her husband Henry in March 1841 and told her about the principle. She turned him down. But later that year, she changed her mind, reporting later that "I searched the scripture & buy humble prayer to my Heavenly Father I obtained a testimony for my self that God had required that order be established in this church."[28] In October she was sealed to Joseph Smith. Presendia married Joseph on December 11, 1841. The next year Joseph married some eleven more women; the year following, 1843, he married perhaps seventeen. In total, his wives numbered perhaps thirty, perhaps thirty-two, though the fragmentary records make it difficult to say for certain. The age range was wide: He married Eliza R. Snow, two years older than him and never married, in July 1842. In November 1843, he married Brigham Young's widowed sister Fanny, who was fifty-six. In May of that year, he married Heber C. Kimball's daughter Helen, who was fourteen.

Despite the unique circumstances of each wife and marriage, some patterns emerged. Joseph would often have a conversation with a male relative first, as he did with Young and Kimball and Joseph Noble. He usually brought that person when he made the proposal. He urged the woman to seek spiritual confirmation, telling her that if she acceded celestial blessings would descend upon her family. And after he married the wives, they continued to live their lives mostly as they had before, in the homes of their fathers or brothers. At least ten of them were already married, six to Mormon men, who generally seem to have been aware of the ordinance. He did not associate with them with much frequency; he never said much about romantic love but rather stressed the doctrines of the revelation. Lucy Walker, who married Joseph at age seventeen, insisted that their marriage "was not a love matter . . . but simply giving up of myself as a sacrifice to that grand and glorious principle that God had revealed."[29] Later critics often accused him of sexual rapacity, and disentangling sexual interest from religious conviction remains a difficult problem. Perhaps a third of his wives left a clear record that he had indeed slept with them; Joseph Noble said as much about the night following Louisa's wedding. But for most of the others it is uncertain.

In the fall of 1840 the Quorum of the Twelve returned from England, and Joseph told them that the principle applied to them as well. For the most part they blanched. John Taylor remembered that the doctrine "made my flesh crawl."[30] Brigham Young said that "it was the first time in my life that I had desired the grave, and I could hardly get over it for a long time."[31] Both eventually overcame their distaste. Parley Pratt, though, was a widower remarried and was happy to discover that he could have both his wives in the hereafter. He rejoiced over "the eternal union of the sexes in those inexpressible endearing relationships . . . which are at the very foundation of everything worthy to be called happiness."[32] This alternation between distress and acceptance seemed typical for the twenty-nine men and an uncertain number of women who began practicing plural marriage before Joseph Smith was killed in 1844.

Zina Huntington Jacobs was neither the only woman to turn Joseph Smith down nor the only one to accept him after seeking her own spiritual confirmation. Nancy Rigdon, Sidney's daughter, was distressed when Joseph and the apostle Orson Hyde's wife attempted to convince her to marry Joseph; she left the Hyde home insisting that she would be married to one man or none at all. On the other hand, Lucy Walker wrote that when Joseph first approached her, "I was tempted and tortured beyond endurance until life was not desirable" for several days, until she had a spiritual experience: "It was near dawn after another sleepless night when my room was lighted up by a heavenly influence. . . . My soul was filled with a calm, sweet peace."[33] Helen Mar Kimball reported that when Joseph Smith told her father of polygamy and requested the hand of Heber's wife Vilate, it "worked upon his mind that his anxious and haggard looks betrayed him daily. . . . He would walk the floor till nearly morning, and sometimes the agony of his mind was so terrible that he would wring his hands and weep like a child." He prayed for relief at the same time her mother prayed for illumination on the matter that had so distressed her husband, and "as darkness flees before the morning sun, so did her sorrow and the groveling things of earth vanish away." She saw "the vast and boundless love and union which this order would bring about . . . the power and glory extending through the eternities, worlds without end." They returned to Joseph, only to have the prophet say he did not want Vilate's hand, merely confirmation of her faith. This echoed God's command to Abraham to lay his own son on the altar of obedience, and indeed, the story of Abraham entered frequently into the Mormons' struggle to make sense of this new order of marriage. As Helen Mar Kimball insisted, describing her own family's struggle, "When Abraham made his sacrifice, the Lord restored it, which ought be lesson enough for all of us."[34]

For the Kimballs, as for Joseph Smith, plural marriage ritualized and solemnized bonds of commitment: Joseph's marriage to Kimball's daughter and Brigham Young's sister and his proposal to Rigdon's daughter, members of the families of his closest associates, all look vaguely dynastic, and in a real sense they were. After her parents went to Joseph Smith and asked him to marry their daughter, Joseph promised Helen Mar Kimball that the marriage would "ensure your eternal salvation & exaltation and that of your father's household & all your kindred." Though secret, these marriages were not intended to be private communions but rather links in a great network of relationships that bound Joseph's people together to him, made them a family, and ensured that their bonds would never fade.[35] Indeed, in a real sense, those bonds themselves became the stuff of salvation; as Lucy Walker put it, they were "a chain that could never be broken."[36] The deep need for connection, belonging, and relationship that drove so much of Joseph Smith's religious passion found its greatest expression here.

But at the same time, Joseph Smith's experiments in plural marriage were capable of wreaking havoc in his Zion. Joseph knew this; it was why he begged Joseph Noble and others for secrecy. The vast majority of those excited British converts who disembarked onto the Nauvoo docks had heard nothing about polygamy, save for the occasional rumor—which Joseph in public staunchly disavowed. Their church was the church of the charismatic young prophet who preached in the grove, the church building a Zion with noisy streets on the sunny shores of the Mississippi. The evening rituals of polygamy and the endowment belonged to a select circle, a secret church within the church, and went on only behind closed doors.

The most prominent figure who vacillated between the two was Joseph's wife. She had stood by her husband since Palmyra; she believed absolutely in the Book of Mormon. But plural marriage shattered her world. Joseph's reach for more relationships did irrevocable harm to the one that had sustained him for so long. The pain and anger Joseph's relationship with Fanny Alger sparked never cooled, and in Nauvoo Joseph crept around Emma, concealing the true extent of his marriage activity from her. In the early meetings of the Relief Society she denounced rumors of plural marriage, perhaps unaware that some of Joseph's plural wives sat in the audience. In the spring of 1843 she gave her approval to several such marriages but seems to have immediately regretted it; one of those wives, Emily Partridge, remembered Emma calling her into a room where "Joseph was present, looking like a martyr. Emma said some very hard things—Joseph should give us up."[37] In June Joseph's scribe William Clayton recorded in his journal that Joseph's behavior continued to cause problems in his marriage, describing Joseph's worries that Emma "treated him coldly and very badly."[38]

In July, Hyrum suggested that showing Emma the revelation might help. For the first time, Joseph dictated it, and it contained harsh words for Emma. "I command mine handmaid, Emma Smith, to abide and cleave unto my servant Joseph," it said, warning her that she might be "destroyed" if she rejected the principle.[39] Fearful of his wife's anger, Joseph sent Hyrum, manuscript in hand, to his wife, "who said she did not believe a word of it and appeared very rebellious," Clayton noted. The next day Joseph and Emma spent hours together; Clayton remembered that "they both stated their feelings on many subjects & wept considerable."[40] Joseph told Clayton later that year that Emma had completely rejected the doctrine, and she once grew angry when she found letters from Eliza Snow in his pocket. But by that fall, the struggle between the two seemed to have burned itself out; Emma had fallen ill while tending Joseph's sick mother, and Joseph tended Emma in turn, and in September she received the endowment. Joseph took no more wives after that summer, and thirty years later Emma would tell her sons that her husband had never married any wife but her.[41]

Though Emma may have reached some degree of reconciliation with her husband, if not with the practice, polygamy rocked the rest of the church. The secret could not be kept. In 1842 John C. Bennett, whose competence and political savvy had gained him Joseph Smith's trust, was excommunicated when Smith caught him making overtures and sleeping with multiple women in Nauvoo. Like the Kirtland prophets, Bennett claimed to be following Joseph Smith's own path, though Joseph vehemently disagreed, saying that Bennett's practices had no sanction and were driven by lust. Once cast out, the opportunistic Bennett, who denied ever having been much of a believer in the first place, wrote a self-declared exposé, stirring up a number of traditional fears of Mormonism's authoritarian and anti-American nature. He reported that Joseph Smith planned to build a "Mormon empire" and warned, "If this Mormon villain is suffered to carry on his plans, I warn the people of the United States that less than twenty years will see them involved in a civil war [with] a numerous and ferocious enemy." He called on all citizens to meet "the Mormons with their own arms, crush the reptile before it has grown powerful."[42]

Throughout 1842 and 1843 a host of hostile figures rose up. Lilburn Boggs, still governor of Missouri, immediately suspected Mormon hostility when a gunshot flew through his window in May 1842, and Missouri's attempts to extradite their escaped prisoner Joseph Smith gathered intensity. Joseph several times had to flee Nauvoo to escape government agents, once slipping from the dinner table out the back door while Emma stalled a sheriff at the front door. In June 1843 Thomas Ford, governor of Illinois, agreed to an extradition, though under the supervision of Illinois officials. The prophet was arrested and carried toward the Mississippi River. But the lawmen were intercepted by a party from Nauvoo, who intimidated the Missouri officials to the point that they agreed to have the writs of habeas corpus they carried heard in the Nauvoo courts, which meant Joseph was functionally free.

To many Illinoisans, this was a blatant manipulation of the legal process—a suspicion only exacerbated when, immediately afterward, the Mormons began playing politics. In 1843 Joseph Smith negotiated both with various Whig officials, who sought to protect the Mormons, and with Ford, whose agents implied that the Mormons would be left alone should they vote Democratic. Joseph Smith tried to split the difference; he himself voted Whig while encouraging others to vote for the Democrats. Nauvoo went for the Democrats en masse, and the Whigs felt infuriated and betrayed. Thomas Sharp, a Whig and editor of the *Signal,* paper of record for the nearby town of Warsaw, seized on these events and on Bennett's book and began a shrill campaign calling for the end of Mormon corruption of the democratic process and American culture. He invoked the same principles of community self-defense that had animated the Missourians.

Joseph believed that Nauvoo would not remain secure. He quietly sent agents to Texas, California, and Oregon, looking for places where the Saints might go. But he still dreamed of remaking American public life according to the principles of relationship and sympathy. As he began to contemplate Mormons settled across the nation, he organized a final council, which he called the Council of the Fifty. It included the leaders of Mormonism, but in a gesture of reconciliation Joseph also invited several non-Mormons to participate. The council first oversaw westward exploration, but Joseph also saw in it the seed of a new human government, a "theodemocracy" in which "God and the people hold the power to conduct the affairs of men in righteousness, and where liberty, free trade, and sailor's right, and the protection of life and property shall be maintained." Theodemocracy would succeed only when human societies submitted to God's will. Joseph worried that "the world is governed too much," a curious complaint that invoked the sort of government he dreamed of. [43] He hoped to eliminate the rough-and-tumble of American politics, the electioneering and pandering that had so often betrayed the Mormons. Rather, Joseph looked to the righteous councils of God's priesthood and the principles of fellowship and community that lay behind his ordinances. It was a surprisingly hopeful dream, and perhaps a naive one. The men on the council were appointed, not elected; on April 11, 1844, they appointed Joseph Smith king of Israel. To Joseph Smith's opponents this would have seemed a breathtaking confirmation of their own worst fears. To him, it was a scriptural restoration that would repair all that was wrong with democracy.

His decision to run for president of the United States in 1844 reflected his persistent optimism that American politics could be perfected through righteousness. He likely had few expectations of winning the office, even though he had a large Mormon missionary force doubling as his campaign team. His campaign seemed primarily concerned with declaring to the nation that its politics had forgotten the blessings of brotherhood and egalitarianism that had once made it great, an amnesia manifested in its cruelty to minority groups. The Mormons were denied "the blessings and privileges of American citizens." The nation must "break off the shackles from the poor black man, and hire them to labor like other human beings." He hoped to annex Texas, Canada, and Mexico, all as "one great family; and let there be universal peace," and he seemed idealistically convinced that appeals to the generosity and common welfare of humanity could sweep all differences away. "The southern people are hospitable and noble," he said, explaining why they would embrace his plan for emancipation. The optimism about human nature that blossomed in his theology bled into his politics: his platform promises reflected faith that people of righteousness and goodwill would naturally form healthy communities when freed from the perversities so abundant in the world.[44]

Again, as he had in Kirtland, Joseph pushed his followers further than many were willing to go. When dissenters appeared, they sought less to abandon Mormonism than to restore it to the pristine faith that had existed before whatever corruption pained them had set in, be it the failure of the Kirtland Safety Society, the violence in Missouri, or, in Nauvoo, polygamy. Most prominent among the dissenters was William Law, a member of the First Presidency, one of the original nine to receive the endowment, and a man who deeply recoiled from polygamy. Late in 1843 Joseph approached Jane Law with a proposal, and Jane fled back to her husband. Hyrum showed them the revelation, but it made no difference. Law confronted Joseph in agony, and the two had several intense conversations. Stories later recalled them standing face-to-face intent in discussion, Law clutching Joseph's shoulders, a posture that simultaneously evokes frustration, intimacy, and desperation. But Joseph was unyielding, and the Laws could not bear it; they rejected polygamy, and in April 1844 William and Jane were excommunicated, along with William's brother Wilson. The three sorrowfully concluded that Joseph had become a fallen prophet, and they joined a small but growing group of dissenters.

Like the Kirtland dissenters, Law's group organized a church that claimed to practice "true Mormonism," and Law quickly rose to its head. They also secured a printing press. On June 7, a thousand copies of the reform church's broadside, the *Nauvoo Expositor,* appeared. On the front page an article, likely from Law's pen, declared that "abominations and whoredoms" demanded "reformation," a return to the religion "originally taught by Joseph Smith."[45] And it exposed polygamy to the world. On Monday, June 10, Joseph attended a six-and-a-half-hour meeting of the Nauvoo city council, where he argued forcefully that the paper was a threat to the public peace. The council passed an ordinance declaring the paper guilty of libel and by eight o'clock that evening the city marshal had destroyed the *Expositor*'s press and remaining copies.

An uproar broke out. The dissenters sought legal injunction. Thomas Sharp of the *Warsaw Signal* raged, demanding of readers "Can you *stand by*, and suffer such INFERNAL DEVILS! to ROB men of their property and RIGHTS" and calling for a solution of "POWDER AND BALL!!!"[46] Meanwhile, Thomas Ford, governor of Illinois, struggled to ensure that legal action unfolded as it should. On June 21 he arrived in the county seat of Carthage and encountered both an ad hoc militia assembled without command eager to stamp out the Mormons and John Taylor of the Quorum of the Twelve. Ford feared a reprise of the Missouri wars in Illinois and implored Taylor to convince Joseph to give himself up for a hearing. He then went to Nauvoo and, to his despair, found there the Mormon militia mobilized and nervous. Early in the morning of June 23 Joseph fled across the Mississippi with Hyrum and Willard Richards, but he returned in desperation when reports followed that "some were tryed almost to death to think Joseph should leave them in the hour of danger."[47] For Joseph Smith, who valued human bonds above all else, this was heartrending. He promised Ford he would give himself up if he would be protected, and Ford swore to it, but Joseph told his brother that he knew he rode to his death. Late in the evening of June 24, Joseph Smith left Nauvoo, riding for Carthage. Hyrum Smith, John Taylor, and the apostle Willard Richards rode with him.

They spent the next three days in the jail at Carthage, on the second floor above the jailor's living quarters. Visitors came and went, including the governor, various Mormons, and other messengers. They brought the captives a Book of Mormon, a bottle of wine, and a smuggled pistol. On Thursday, June 27, Ford went to Nauvoo to urge the Mormons to lay down their arms, promising them the rule of law. He left Joseph and his companions in the hands of the Carthage Greys, the city militia. Late in that hot afternoon Willard Richards looked out a bedroom window and saw the Greys gathering below. He turned to the three other men in the room as shots were fired and footsteps pounded up the stairs. The four Mormons threw themselves against the door to hold it closed, but bullets tore through the wood. Hyrum was hit in the face and toppled backward to the floor, dead. John Taylor fell with a bullet in his leg and dragged himself to safety under the bed. The door flew open, trapping Richards against the wall. Joseph emptied the pistol into the stairwell, then turned and sprinted for the window. As he reached it, bullets from inside and out hit him four times, and he cried out "O Lord, my God!" He crashed through the panes, landed near a well, struggled to a sitting position, and died.

Thomas Sharp swore that the death of the Smith brothers would incite a Mormon uprising, and that the governor would likely be assassinated. He hoped for it, looking for a war that would drive the Mormons from the state. Governor Ford denounced "the stupidity and baseness" of the crime but found it difficult to identify the men who stormed the jail; the mob appeared to have been a mixture of Greys, private citizens, and other members of the militia of Warsaw and other surrounding towns.[48] In the end he ordered Thomas Sharp and several militia leaders tried, but all were acquitted. The apostle Willard Richards urged his Saints to do nothing, but such pleas seemed unnecessary: the Mormons had been stunned into passivity. On June 28 several thousand silent mourners met the wagons bearing the bodies of the Smith brothers a mile from Nauvoo and trailed after the coffins to the Mansion House, where the prophet and his brother were buried. And the Mormons grieved, uncertain of what might happen next.

Many expected that the Mormon movement would collapse, like any number of sects and communes dependent upon the charismatic presence of a fallen leader. The *New York Herald* mused that "the death of the modern Mahomet will seal the fate of Mormonism. They cannot get another Joe Smith."[49] Certainly, Joseph's intentions about a successor were never clear. Both Oliver Cowdery, until his excommunication, and Hyrum Smith, until his death, had held the position of "assistant president" of the church; Hyrum had also been given the mantle of patriarch that had previously belonged to his father. Joseph had also occasionally spoken of his son Joseph III following him, but the boy was only eleven when his father died. But then, of course, there were the councils. The Mormons faced a choice at Joseph Smith's death—they could attempt to find another charismatic leader, somebody of the vision and magnetism that Joseph Smith had possessed, one capable of holding the church together through sheer force of will. Or they could follow the route of early Christianity and seek not charisma but institution, the stability of bishops, priests, and elders. That choice would transform their visionary and apocalyptic sect, once poised on the brink of the Second Coming and convinced that time would require no prophet after Joseph, into a church among churches, an institution of offices rather than leaders, whose very existence acknowledged the inevitability of history and time and change.

By August the paralysis in Nauvoo began to ease. On August 3 Sidney Rigdon, who still served in the First Presidency despite the tension that had developed ever since Joseph's unsuccessful proposal to his daughter, arrived in Nauvoo from his family home in Pittsburgh. Three days later, Brigham Young and most of the apostles returned from a mission to the East Coast. Among them were Joseph's brothers Samuel and William. And a struggle for control of the church began. Many sought to set themselves up as replacement Josephs, hoping to replicate the fallen prophet's charisma. That month, at a public meeting gathered in the groves, Rigdon declared that in a vision in Pittsburgh God had told him that he stood in the role of mouthpiece and "guardian." He said, "I have been consecrated a spokesman unto Joseph, and I was commanded to speak for him." He proposed that he continue to do so.[50] After Samuel Smith died of a fever in late July, Lucy Smith favored her son William. His Smith blood, she said, entitled him to the office of patriarch and perhaps the presidency until Joseph Smith III came of age. But lacking his brother's strength and depth of will, William attracted the allegiance of only a few. James J. Strang, a convert of only a few months, presented the most eerie case. Young, tall, and handsome, he possessed a letter he claimed to be from the hand of Joseph Smith naming him Joseph's prophetic successor. Strang wielded a seerstone, claimed visitation from angels, and issued new revelations. He appeared to be Joseph in miniature, and he attracted the allegiance of Martin Harris, William Marks, and eventually some few hundred other Mormons who followed him, at least for a time, to his Zion in Voree, Wisconsin.

Many Mormons in Nauvoo accepted one of these men. Many others simply remained in Nauvoo or elsewhere in Illinois, drifting from association with any particular Mormon church at all. Emma Smith was perhaps the most prominent of these. She seemed to have little interest in the battles to replace her husband. Rather, her concerns rested with her daughter and three sons and the child still unborn when Joseph died. Her well-known distaste for plural marriage grated on Brigham Young and other of Joseph's successors, but her insistence that her home and property belonged to her family rather than to the church annoyed them even more, because Joseph had been cavalier with such distinctions. As various Mormon groups left Nauvoo, Emma remained, even as the once-thriving port became a ghost town. In 1847, she married a non–Mormon, raised her children on the Bible and the Book of Mormon, hung a portrait of Joseph above her fireplace, and treasured the manuscripts of Joseph's translation of the Bible that were left to her.

However, the Smith family's association with Mormon religion was not done. On April 6, 1860, William Marks, disillusioned with Strang's church, gathered a conference of other Mormons at Amboy, Illinois, and founded the Reorganized Church of Jesus Christ of Latter-day Saints, proclaiming a version of Mormonism that closely resembled the church of the dissenters. They repudiated polygamy, throwing all such rumors in the lap of John C. Bennett, and ignored the endowment and the doctrines of preexistence and progression to godhood Joseph had taught in the last years of his life. Nonetheless Joseph Smith III, then twenty-seven, confessed that he came before the conference inspired "in obedience to a power not my own." He accepted the presidency of the church and began the reorganization.[51] He gained legal ownership of the Kirtland temple and sent missionaries across the Midwest, gathering in the scattered Saints, including his mother, who dutifully joined in 1872.

But the majority of the Mormons in Nauvoo in August 1844— about ten thousand—elected to follow the Quorum of the Twelve. Brigham Young, president of the Twelve, followed Rigdon to the pulpit at that August meeting and declared that he came to "speak of the organization of the Church"; accordingly, his argument was not one of charisma but of institution.[52] He stolidly declared that the Quorum of the Twelve held in collective all the priesthood authority Joseph Smith had possessed and that the quorum was thus the logical organizational successor to the dead prophet. The majority of Saints accepted his arguments over those of Rigdon, Strang, or even the surviving Smiths. Many reported later that as Brigham Young spoke, they saw the image of Joseph Smith descend upon him. But just as importantly they knew the strength of their councils, for many had served on one, and they trusted the quorum. The apostles had the loyalty of the British Saints. They were members of Joseph's inner core, the church within the church, the church that practiced polygamy and had been inducted into the endowment ceremony, the church that had begun making itself into an alternative society. They were determined that this version of Mormonism should carry on. Rigdon retreated to Pennsylvania.

Brigham and the Twelve decided that the Mormons should stay in Nauvoo at least through the completion of the temple. This was not an entirely safe decision. In January 1845 the city charter was revoked, removing much of the city government's power. Thomas Ford hoped that this would resolve the tensions, but the church's failure to collapse and continued rumors of plural marriage meant that many non-Mormons remained leery of Mormon power. The Twelve's concerted effort to summon Mormons from all over the country to come to Nauvoo and contribute to the building of the temple did not help. But for a year peace held; the Twelve concentrated on reorganizing the administration of the church, turning much of the temporal affairs over to the bishops of the various city wards and delegating responsibility for mission work to men ordained to the office of Seventy. They also considered places for resettlement, studying the reports of the Council of the Fifty's emissaries and the writings of explorers such as John C. Frémont.

In September 1845 riots broke out again. Vigilantes attacked Mormon settlements in the rural areas of Hancock County, hoping to drive the Mormons together into Nauvoo, and thence from the state. Brigham Young reached out to Illinois officials seeking help, promising that the Mormons would be gone by the next year. He made the vow with confidence, because by early October the temple was complete, and the apostles had selected a place for resettlement. Brigham called a General Conference of the church to meet in the temple's halls and informed the body of the church that they would be departing Nauvoo for the valley of the Great Salt Lake in the Rocky Mountains. He also announced that the endowment ceremony, previously secret, would be opened to all who wanted to participate in it. Beginning on December 10, 1845, a steady stream of Saints, about a hundred every night and every day for two months, passed through the ceremony.

The two announcements leaned upon each other, because Brigham Young believed that the experience of the endowment transformed the Mormons into a new Israel, a community bound by their covenants, set apart from the world in their relationship with God. Their move west would be their Exodus. Young received only one revelation that joined those of Joseph Smith in Mormon canon: titled "The Word and Will of the Lord concerning the Camp of Israel," it gave scriptural imprimatur to the metaphor, declaring in the voice of God that "I am he who led the children of Israel out of the land of Egypt; and my arm is stretched out in the last days, to save my people Israel." Young taught that "this shall be our covenant: that we will walk in all the ordinances of the Lord."[53] As a Mormon named George Alley wrote to relatives, when the Saints left Nauvoo, "We shall go as the Israelites, by the shadow of the tabernacle of the Lord."[54] John Taylor declared, "The power of Israel was lost, by disobedience and scattering; and his power will be regained by obedience and gathering."[55] The Nauvoo ordinances directed the Mormons inward, focused them on the spiritual community they had created, and pushed them even further from the American society that had decisively rejected them. Identification with the children of Israel completed their transformation: the Mormons would walk away from America gladly. A folk song began to circulate:

> *Early next spring we'll leave Nauvoo*
> *And on our journey we'll pursue*
> *We'll go and bid the mob farewell*
> *And let them go to heaven or hell.*[56]

By the fall of 1845, Young and the Twelve had divided the Mormons into companies of a hundred families each, directed by members of the Quorum of the Twelve or Council of Fifty. Parley Pratt reported that 3,285 families were organized by the end of the year; this made roughly sixteen thousand people. They began to sell their property to buy wagons, oxen, and supplies. On February 4, 1846, the first wagons rolled down Parley Street and across the Mississippi, out of Nauvoo and into the wilderness.

FOUR

COME, COME, YE SAINTS

1846–1877

If the Mormons saw themselves as a new Israel, the trek west was inevitably their Exodus. For generations of Mormons, including the one that walked across the prairies, what mattered more than the destination was the act of the journey. It was a collective rite of passage that thousands of Mormons endured, as they had learned to endure all suffering: the death of their prophet, their flight from Ohio and Missouri, and their march across the plains all were taken as divinely sent education, clarifying and refining, testing the bonds that the temple ordinances had created, and they saw God's hand in every bush of berries. Many Mormons were rebaptized upon reaching Utah; they had traveled not only from the United States to the Utah territory but also from the secular realm to God's promised land, reborn into a sacred world. The banks and courts still close in Utah on July 24, the day Brigham Young crossed into the Salt Lake Valley, and the Mormons there celebrate it still, though the number of those who have ancestors who walked across the plains is a fading minority. They have become an archetype.

The myth may sometimes obscure the daily wretchedness of life on the trail. In the spring of 1846 William Clayton, dutiful scribe to Joseph Smith and clerk to the Twelve, sat in a tent some hundred miles out of Nauvoo. Clayton bore heavy burdens, managing the records and public stores of the camp while at the same time struggling with his wagon, his arthritis, and two weary and sometimes sick wives; as he complained in May, Willard Richards "wants me to do his writing, although I have more writing to do as clerk of the camp than I can possibly do. Moreover I have to unpack the chest and wait on all of them with the public goods in my charge, which keeps me busy all of the time."[1] But only a month before, having just discovered that his third wife, who had remained in Nauvoo with her parents, had given birth to a son, he was full of the sort of melancholic confidence that kept many of the Mormons afloat. In his tent at Locust Creek, Iowa, he wrote a poem. "We'll find the place which God for us prepared / Far away, in the West," it promised, and its first verse ran:

> Come, come, ye Saints, no toil nor labor fear;
> But with joy wend your way.
> Though hard to you this journey may appear,
> Grace shall be as your day.
> 'Tis better far for us to strive
> Our useless cares from us to drive;
> Do this, and joy your hearts will swell—
> All is well! All is well!

When put to the melody of an old English folk tune, the song quickly became the anthem of the trail. It remains one of the great Mormon hymns. It evokes the myth of the Mormon trail for modern Latter-day Saints better than any relic or remembered story.

By mid-1845 the apostles had investigated possibilities for settlement in Texas, California, and even Vancouver, and some Mormons were anxious to leave Nauvoo. The apostle Lyman Wight, acting on discussions in the Council of Fifty shortly before Joseph Smith's death, led a small colony to the newly independent Republic of Texas. Similarly, a recent convert named Sam Brannan had left Nauvoo for New York with several other Mormon agents to seek federal aid for the Mormon settlers. He organized an emigrant company out of the New York branches and chartered a ship to carry them around South America to California, where a group of American settlers had invited the Mormons to join them in organizing an independent nation. Wight had gone against Brigham Young's wishes. Young, interested in California's potential, gave his blessing to Brannan's mission, but ultimately he decided against all these options. He desired for his people a place apart, and he was through attempting to build common cause with non-Mormons. The apostles studied carefully the reports of John C. Frémont, who had explored the Great Basin, and concluded that its eastern edge, the valley around the Great Salt Lake, would serve as their new Zion.

The first passages out of Nauvoo came in fits and starts, and many would remember that the trials of the first three hundred miles of the trail—the trek from Nauvoo across Iowa to the Missouri River—were the hardest. Every day or every other day for a month after a few advance scouts crossed the Mississippi into Iowa on February 4, 1846, a knot of Mormon men would gather at the end of Parley Street, where the road vanished into the river. There they grappled with wagons and oxen, loading chests and carts onto rafts and flatboats and steering them uneasily across the nearly mile-wide expanse of the Mississippi River, dodging ice floes and working through the chill of the February rain. After an ox lurched on one flatboat, ripping off the side and capsizing the boat, the Nauvoo police organized a regular ferry service that ran from dawn until after nightfall. On February 9, Joseph's widows Presendia and Zina Huntington crossed with their father, William, and their brothers. On February 12, Eliza R. Snow forded the river; two days later, Parley Pratt and his family followed. A day after that, Eliza's brother Lorenzo left, in the company of two more apostles, Willard Richards and George A. Smith, and, finally, on February 15, Brigham Young himself departed.

They headed for a place called Sugar Creek, seven miles into Iowa, where those who had crossed early gathered and waited for those that followed. A blinding storm began on February 19, and the Saints huddled in tents, while Eliza Snow composed a hymn: "Altho' in woods and tents we dwell / Shout, shout, O Camp of Israel."[2] Upon his arrival Brigham Young climbed on top of a wagon and gathered his people around him. He divided the perhaps five hundred who had crossed into tens, fifties, and hundreds, directed them to plot a trek for the Missouri River, on the other side of Iowa, organized a lost and found and feeding arrangements for the animals, warned those who had guns to be careful with them, and promised them that they would yet reach Zion. Then he headed back across the river to attend to the last matters of church business in Nauvoo. As he wound his way back, he passed more Mormons heading toward Sugar Creek, a steady flow leaving Nauvoo behind.

On March 1 the four hundred wagons of the camp of Israel gathered their strength and lurched into movement. They made five miles that day from Sugar Creek and had to scrape snow from the ground where they pitched their tents that night. Each river proved an obstacle. Men and women waded the chilly waters and hauled the wagons across with heavy ropes. To provide for those who would follow, Brigham left camps at Sugar Creek, at Richardson's Point, fifty-five miles west of Nauvoo, and at Garden Grove and Mount Pisgah, a hundred miles farther. The men left planted crops and built log cabins and dug wells and established way stations for the great stream of Mormon wagons that would continue to flow across Iowa that spring and summer, and beyond, for the continuing tide of immigrants following the Mormon trail would persist for another two decades, until the railroad reached Salt Lake City in 1869.

The chill and the rain seemed constant, and with them came whooping cough and fever, dysentery, malaria, typhoid, and diphtheria, the painful black canker. When the rain stopped, giving the travelers a chance to clean the mud from their tents, the sun-dried ground brought out swarms of rattlesnakes. A line of gravestones trailed backward to Nauvoo, and the damp and mud made the going hard. As Hosea Stout recalled, "It was up and down sloughs on spouty ridges and deep marshes, and raining all the while. The horses would sometimes sink to their bellies."[3] Wagons rarely made more than a few miles a day. There was never enough food, and when the camp halted for Sabbath worship, Brigham sometimes preached in aggravation against stealing from the local settlers and disciplined Saints who fell to fighting for resources. Both men Brigham Young left to preside at Garden Grove and Mount Pisgah, one of them Zina's father, William Huntington, would die before the year was out. Emily Partridge, another widow of Joseph Smith's, declared the huddle of small cabins on the dirty plains of Mount Pisgah "the most like nowhere" of any place she had ever seen.[4]

The road was so hard that by June, Brigham's camp had reached only the Missouri River, three hundred miles across Iowa from Nauvoo, and came to a stop on land belonging to the Potawatomi Indians. Brigham had hoped that this advance party would reach the Great Salt Lake before the winter, but progress was so slow that he called a halt. They would wait a year. They had to: the hard road across Iowa had been devastating, far harder than expected, and Brigham knew his people were simply not healthy enough to continue. So on either side of the Missouri, in Nebraska and in Iowa, the Mormons settled in what they called Winter Quarters, a sudden city erected on the plains, designed to outlast the winter and to gather in the ten thousand or more Mormons scattered across the Iowa prairies behind them. After the winter had passed, an advance party would be sent to the Great Salt Lake to mark the path and plant crops in preparation for those who would follow.

If the Mormons had experience in anything, it was city building, and as might be expected, the plat of Zion again rose. Eight hundred cabins, tents, and sod houses stood divided into squares with wide straight streets. But the people were sick and exhausted, underfed and tormented by the rain and mud. In the "sickly season" of late summer malaria raced through the camp; in the winter, pneumonia and famine. The food was mostly corn bread and salted bacon. Some six hundred died. In the late fall the last stragglers from Nauvoo, the poor camp of those who could not or would not leave earlier that year, arrived, many carted to Winter Quarters in wagons sent back for them. They brought with them news of the battle for Nauvoo. The growing tension between the remaining Mormons and roving vigilantes had erupted during the second week of September when shots were fired between rival militia encampments, leaving the Mormons with no option but flight. Nauvoo stood almost empty by October, and there was no turning back.

When spring finally came, Brigham Young recruited an advance camp—143 men, including six apostles, three women (Harriet Decker, whose asthma was exacerbated by the Missouri River air, and her daughter Clara, wives of the brothers Lorenzo and Brigham Young, respectively, and Ellen Sanders, a plural wife of Heber Kimball), and two children. Brigham was a shrewd leader, and he was determined not to repeat his mistakes. Though he agreed to take Harriet and her friends, he would otherwise limit this party to a relatively small group of selected men capable of traveling light and fast. He also timed their departure strategically. They left Winter Quarters on April 5. Brigham was determined to make the Salt Lake Valley by midsummer, to plant, build, and prepare the land for the thousands who were following more slowly. He organized his company into the familiar regimental tens, fifties, and hundreds commanded by the revelation naming them the Camp of Zion. Thomas Bullock, who provided some relief to William Clayton as camp clerk, recorded the orders: "At 5 AM the Horn should be blown & every man then arise & pray, attend to their cattle" so that the wagons could roll by seven. They would travel with a gun ready, for snakes and other vermin as much as for hostile Indians, and "halt for an hour to have dinner, which must be ready cooked." At night, the wagons would be organized in a circle with the horses and live-stock inside. Prayer was at eight-thirty, sleep at nine.[5] By the end of the month they had made two hundred miles, following the Platte River across Nebraska through a dry and chilly spring.

The Mormon migration was like few others that ventured into the American West. Though they had built Nauvoo, the Mormons were inexperienced in the rigors of cross-continental travel. Many were British immigrants for whom the American continent itself was a strange wonder. They were chronically undersupplied. But that they traveled believing themselves to be God's people gave their camp an uncommon character. Theirs was the exodus of a true community: men, women, and children, all bound to the body of the Saints by the mystical force of priesthood and covenant. Though men were often pulled from their families and sent ahead in advance companies or posted at Garden Grove or Mount Pisgah, their wives still traveled with wagons and oxen and children. Families were separated, but all experienced the trail. Eliza Snow and others organized female blessing meetings through the familial networks created by plural marriage in which they prayed and prophesied and laid hands on one another to bless.

The Mormons never forgot that they were the new Israel. This may be Brigham Young's greatest achievement. He bound even more closely than had Joseph Smith the Mormons' sense of themselves as a covenanted people, specially chosen by God, to the practical work of building a community on earth. The distance between the sacred and the secular on the trail was vanishingly small. The captains of the companies routinely celebrated the Lord's Supper as they prepared decisions about when to move and what trail to take. The Sabbath was always observed; Thomas Bullock described one as "a day of rest for meditation, prayer, & praise. All was harmony, peace & love, and a holy stillness prevailed."[6] On another such stop Brigham rebuked the camp for light-mindedness, cardplaying, and quarrelling, announcing, "I would rather risk myself among the savages with ten men that are men of faith, men of mighty prayer, men of God than to be with this whole camp when they forget God."[7]

And as they had in Nauvoo, the Mormons found refuge and identity in art: in music and song and dance, activities that gave their spiritual unity tangible form. Music, as ever, was as the Western historian Wallace Stegner later described it: "their gift and their blessing, an expression of their oneness in the hostile wilderness."[8] They would gather together around what fires they could maintain in the chill and rain and sing hymns—their own, such as W. W. Phelps's "Redeemer of Israel" and "Come, Come, Ye Saints," and traditional Protestant hymns such as "He Died! The Great Redeemer Died!" or "O God, Our Help in Ages Past." The Nauvoo band followed Brigham across Iowa, occasionally playing for money in towns, and across the Great Plains, offering accompaniment to the Saints at worship and at dance, which was a particular diversion from the bruising trail. Helen Mar Kimball, by then married to Horace Whitney, remembered how her company dealt with the chill of nights on the plains: "Everyone danced to amuse ourselves as well as to keep our blood in proper circulation."[9] Eliza Cheney wrote from Winter Quarters that "we have good meetings and good music, and we are all as brisk as larks."[10] And sometimes, at night,

Eliza Snow would write poems exhorting her fellow Saints to "mourn not" for those that had gone on to their eternal reward.

Their stubborn will to rejoice and refusal to be cowed reflected their providential orientation. The West the Mormons imagined themselves in was the wilderness of scripture, divinely prepared to test and reward them. But the West they settled was not empty and waiting to be tamed. Like every other group who sought to seize it, the Mormons found its spaces crowded, and they carved out their own claim less through the awesome proclamation of God than through negotiation, cooperation, and sometimes conflict. The Mormons struggled to bring their vision of a holy society into being, finding the task repeatedly complicated by the competing agendas of others: the federal government, Native Americans, and non-Mormon settlers who often proved obstacles to the fruition of the Mormons' dreams.

Like many others who sought to colonize the West, the Mormons sought aid from the federal government. They were eager for the money but ambivalent about the source. In June 1846, while Winter Quarters rose and Brigham Young pondered the possibility of sending an advance party forth that summer, James Allen of the U.S. Army rode into camp. A month earlier the Mormons had learned that the United States had declared war on Mexico. This caused some dismay, as many had hoped to flee the nation and now feared they might end up back within its territories. Nevertheless, Brigham had sent appeals for federal aid, and suddenly found it offered. Allen requested five hundred men, offering to pay each between seven and fifty dollars a month and an advance of forty-two dollars immediately. The subsidy was a happy exception in the near-constant train of disappointed expectations the Saints nursed toward the federal government. Brigham Young himself noted the irony: "It must ever remain a truth on the page of history, that while the flower of Israel's camp were sustaining the wings of the American eagle . . . their brothers, sisters, fathers, mothers and children were driven by mob violence from a free and independent state of the same national Republic."[11] The Mormons were not happy with Brigham's request for volunteers; they knew they could ill spare the men, and some grumbled. Nevertheless, Brigham knew the money was essential, and he could be firm when necessary. The Mormon Battalion set out for Mexico in July.[12] The federal funds went to supplies and transportation for five hundred Saints.

Even on the trail, the Mormons did not walk through an empty landscape. In Iowa the Mormons traded with local settlers, hiring themselves out as workers. The advance camp of 1847 for a long way followed the well-traveled Oregon Trail, on which they routinely encountered traders, settlers, and hunters, occasionally making a profit ferrying other migrants across rivers. They rested in June at Fort Laramie, in northwestern Wyoming, owned by the American Fur Company, and in early July at Fort Bridger, in the southwestern corner of the state. It was only after leaving Fort Bridger that the Mormons departed from the Oregon Trail, making their own way with advice from the mountaineers Miles Goodyear and Jim Bridger, founder of the fort. The former advised them on the best route into the Salt Lake Valley, and the latter warned them to avoid the "Utah tribe" of Native Americans who dwelt near Utah Lake; Bridger said the Utes were violent and fiercely protective of their land.

Brigham took that advice with equivocation. On July 21, a group of scouts led by Orson Pratt crossed into the Salt Lake Valley. They found a large valley along the eastern rim of the Great Basin divided by a jutting mountain and marked in the north by the Great Salt Lake and in the south by the smaller, freshwater Utah Lake. Connecting them ran a stream, which the Mormons named, with Biblical resonance, the river Jordan. The land's only drawback seemed to be the absence of timber, but when the main body of the camp arrived in late July they began building an adobe and log settlement in the northeastern corner of the valley, where Salt Lake City stands today. They also organized farming teams that worked in four-hour shifts from 4 A.M. to 8 P.M., hurriedly trying to get a crop in before the fall.

In the fall of 1847 the main camp of fifteen hundred Mormons followed Brigham's vanguard into the Salt Lake Valley, and late that year Brigham returned to Winter Quarters to lead a second company to the West. There, in February 1848, the church solemnly gave common consent to the selection of Brigham Young as their new president in name and not merely form. He returned to Salt Lake City in the early fall of 1848 and would never leave the Utah territory again. Initially, the Mormons relished their solitude. Brigham dismissed what he called the "Gentile" world, the Americans the camp of Israel had left behind. As he said, "I am determined to cut every thread of this kind and live free and independent, untrammeled by any of their detestable customs and practices."[13] He immediately selected a site for a new temple, and following the old plat of Zion he laid out the city around it, with wide roads dividing into a grid of ten-acre blocks, each subdivided into large lots. The streets were named according to their distance from the temple: 100 South, 200 South, and so on in every direction of the compass. These names were a constant reminder that Salt Lake City was oriented toward God's temple and that the settlement itself was never merely material. The moral, the economic, the political, the spiritual— all were the same in Brigham's eyes.

By early 1849, there were several thousand Mormons in Salt Lake City. The city sat in the western shadows of the Wasatch Range, between the mountains and the salty lake, on land well watered by a host of creeks that ran down the slopes of the mountains. The grass was high, and the land was fertile, though rockier and far less forested than the Mormon emigrants had expected. The large game had long since been hunted nearly to extinction by Native Americans and wandering trappers. The dry climate and high elevation were a welcome relief from the swampland of Nauvoo and the disease-ridden Missouri River lowlands of Winter Quarters. Set apart from the Gentiles and blessed with a salubrious environment, the Great Basin was truly the Mormons' promised land. One pioneer named the Mormons' valley "a little World of Blessings," noting that "the atmosphere is pure."[14] By 1849 the Mormons had spread from the original adobe-and-log compound Pratt's team had built into homes on the streets around the temple. Lots were distributed by lottery at first, but immigrants were also frequently assigned to settlements; sometimes they were allowed to purchase special cases from the church. As in Nauvoo, they would garden or plant orchards on their lots and farm outside the city.

Jim Bridger had warned the Mormons that the Native Americans were simultaneously a nuisance, a threat, and a trading partner, ultimately

disposable. To the Mormons, they possessed cosmological and apocalyptic significance, essential to the western Zion Brigham hoped to
build. The Mormons believed that the Native Americans were a remnant of Israel, the last descendents of the Book of Mormon peoples,
and that the restoration of their gospel and the Book of Mormon
would speak particularly to them. Joseph Smith's first declaration of
the New Jerusalem had foretold that it would be built with the aid of
these recovered lost sheep, and the Mormons believed sincerely that
their gospel would restore them to the glorious civilization that the
Book of Mormon described. Brigham promised that "the Lamanites
would become a White & delightsome people," that when they became righteous they would intermarry with Mormons, and together
"our descendents may live to the age of a tree & be visited & hold
communion with the Angels; & bring in the millennium."[15]

Brigham Young believed this, as had Joseph Smith, but the Mormons never found much success in preaching to the Indians. More
often the relations of the two groups were shaped by a curious combination of the Mormons' providential idealism and the brutal realities of
the struggle for food and space on the frontier. They did occasionally
baptize Indians, including some leaders of native bands, whom they
called "chiefs." Such conversions often seemed to reflect this particular
combination of spiritual and material motivation, as in the case of Sagwich, a Shoshone leader who turned to the Mormons for help after a
clash with the U.S. Army in 1863. The Mormons offered food and
supplies and also ordained Sagwich an elder. His people eventually
formed a Mormon congregation conducted entirely in their native
tongue. Somewhat surprisingly, Sagwich's people, apparently attracted
to the Mormons' visionary culture and ritualized religion, took to it
with gusto.

But such cooperation was not the rule. In Winter Quarters Mormons had struggled with local Native Americans for resources throughout the cold winter. Having as usual learned his lesson, in Utah
Brigham had carefully chosen the banks of the Great Salt Lake to avoid
both the Utah peoples in the south around Utah Lake and the Shosho-
nes farther north. He warned early settlers to avoid moving too far
south before the Mormons had a chance "to form an acquaintance

with the Utes," but Mormon settlement quickly spread.[16] For several years there were violent clashes between Mormons and Natives in the area around Utah Lake. In 1849 Mormon settlers killed a Ute named Old Bishop, either because he stole a shirt or because he caught three Mormon men killing game in Indian territory, depending on which party's reports are to be believed, and warfare broke out. Violence again erupted in 1853 when the Mormons attempted to choke off the Ute trade with Mexico by force. Having learned that the Utes were selling children as slaves to the Mexicans, they were determined to uplift the Lamanites by any means necessary. Both conflicts drifted to an inconclusive close, and relations later grew warmer, with one notable exception. Angered when Mormon leaders snubbed a Native American delegation's request for help, in 1865 a Ute named Black Hawk united factions of the Utes, Paiutes, and Navajo tribes and initiated raids on Mormon settlements. The Mormons appealed to a suspicious federal government for aid, and when none proved forthcoming began a sporadic war with Black Hawk's followers that lasted until 1872.

Though Brigham began using occasional force by the 1850s, he never gave up the dream of a converted Indian people. He hoped that the Mormons might be able to uplift and civilize the tribes, and he encouraged settlers to offer them trade. He distributed gifts, cultivated friendly relationships with Indian leaders—most famously, the Ute Walkara, an on-again, off-again opponent—and encouraged them to take up farming, which some did, with mixed success. He also encouraged Mormons to adopt Indian children, even doing so himself, in the hopes of providing a model for acculturation. For many Americans, the Mormons' attempts to cultivate a relatively cordial relationship with the Utes and other peoples were a source of suspicion. Many Native Americans in Utah distinguished between "Mormons" and "Americans," a distinction of which Brigham Young was proud. But gradually, as with other Native peoples and other white colonies, the continual influx of Mormon settlers pushed the Natives to the margins: Brigham tried to stamp out unauthorized trade and generally reacted with annoyance and aggression when he felt his colonies were being threatened. The Utah Territory would become Mormon country.

Emigrants continued to flow into the Salt Lake Valley. By 1852 virtually all of those who had left Nauvoo had reached the Great Basin, but
they were not the only ones. Thousands of converts from Britain and
eventually Scandinavia arrived in the years before the railroad reached
Salt Lake City in 1869. To aid them, in 1850 the Quorum of the
Twelve established the Perpetual Emigration Fund. Reliant on donations, the fund began in the fall of 1850 to provide means for converts
to travel to Salt Lake City. Once established in Utah, the immigrants
were asked to contribute to its replenishment. The fund was dissolved
in 1887; by that time it had helped many of the roughly eighty-five
thousand European converts to come to Zion.

In the mid-1850s, after a series of poor harvests in Utah, the Perpetual Emigration Fund ran shallow for several years, and for a time the
leaders of the fund, particularly Franklin D. Richards, an apostle who
presided over the British mission, encouraged emigrants to use handcarts instead of the more expensive wagons. These were boxy two-
wheeled carts, most seven feet long, four wide, and two deep. Families
piled their goods on the cart and pulled it behind them as they walked
across the plains. Richards declared that "it is only to those who have
traveled the plains with ox teams that the advantages of doing without
them will appear." He shook his head over the dullness of yoking and
feeding and chasing runaway cattle, lamenting their vulnerability to
disease and appeal to Indian raiders, and then noted that handcarts
would reduce the cost of migration by a third, sometimes even by
half.[17] Accordingly, for five years, from 1856 to 1860, several thousand
British immigrants in a half-dozen or so companies pulled handcarts
across the plains, carrying flour and clothing that they prayed would
last them along the trail.

Though only a few thousand took handcarts to Zion, the trials they
endured are nothing less than the distilled apotheosis of the Mormon
trail, an archetype of the holy suffering the immigrants endured and
the strength of community the Mormons built in their valley. The
handcart pioneers were dropped at the end of the rail line in Iowa City,
where they began walking, ten to twenty miles a day. Diarists recalled
Iowans gaping and laughing, but to the Mormons the handcarts were

the means ordained to reach Zion. They took pride in their journey, singing, "For some must push and some must pull / As we go marching up the hill / As merrily on the way we go / Until we reach the Valley, oh!" Brigham Young hoped that the constant walking would toughen these British immigrants unused to American humidity, rainfall, and wilderness. And for some it did. But for others, the ordeal was exhausting. Those who were sick added to the weight others pulled, and the flimsy boxes frequently broke down. As one man recalled, "Had to pull the carts through 6 miles of heavy sand. Some places the wheels were up to the boxes and I was so weak from thirst and hunger and being exhausted with the pain of the boils that I was obliged to lie down several times and many others had to do the same."[18] The handcart travelers were chronically undersupplied, for they had no livestock, no horses, nothing other than what they could carry. By the end of their nine weeks of walking, the first handcart expedition had only a few ounces of flour for each walker per day; of the initial five hundred, twenty-one had died. The leaders of the church routinely sent parties from Salt Lake City to meet the handcarts and bring them in, and the first companies relished the melons they were given when they rolled into the canyon.

The later companies were the greatest disaster of the two decades of the Mormon trail. In late June and early July 1856, two more wagon companies, led by James Willie and Edward Martin, arrived in Iowa City. They gathered supplies but were not ready to depart until August. Some experienced pioneers begged them to wait until the next year, which proved good advice. But their own leaders were confident, and Franklin Richards urged them on. The first week of October they lost supplies to a buffalo stampede. The nights grew colder and colder, and men—mostly men, those who labored the hardest and pulled the carts on which their children sat—began to die. The Willie handcart company ran out of supplies with Salt Lake City still three hundred miles distant. The Martin handcarts took the wrong path and had to wade the icy Platte River in falling snow. Patience Loader remembered that she and her sisters nearly drowned before "several of the breathren came down the bank of the river and pulled our cart up for us and we got up the best we could Mother was there to meet us her clothing was

dry but ours was wet and cold and very soon frozen."[19] Twelve died
that night, and there was snow the next morning to cover them. A
handful of scouts discovered the companies soon after, and their commander sent a message with a single rider back to Salt Lake City: "It is
not much use for me to attempt to give a description of the situation
of these people . . . men, women and children worn down by drawing
handcarts through snow and mud; fainting by the wayside; falling,
chilled by the cold, children crying, their limbs stiffened by cold, their
feet bleeding."[20]

On Saturday, October 4, Richards arrived in Salt Lake City and
informed Brigham Young that the Martin and Willie companies were
on the trail. The next day Brigham stood in a General Conference of
the church and announced that the doctrine preached in this meeting
would be the recovery of those lost on the plains. "That is my religion," he declared. "That is the dictation of the Holy Ghost that I
possess. It is to save the people . . . I shall not wait until tomorrow nor
the next day."[21] And the great mechanism of Mormon organization
whirred into action. Thirty-six hours later, twenty-seven men with
sixteen mule teams pulling sixteen wagonloads of food departed. They
reached the Willie company on October 20 and the Martin company,
huddled in the rock formation of Wyoming's Devil's Gate for meager
protection from the snow, ten days later. Two hundred had died.
Though Brigham continued to urge handcarts on emigrants, four years
later they were abandoned. To Mormons today, the self-created disaster
of the Willie and Martin companies is myth, the stuff of noble tragedy,
the dangerous naïveté of the migrants woven into a romanticized theology of suffering. But with the myth always comes a just pride in the
tough faith of Brigham Young and the capacities of those who followed him, in the strong reach of the community they built, and in its
determination to let none be lost.

Most immigrants rested in the Salt Lake Valley only briefly. Brigham
was determined that Mormons and Mormons alone would live wherever there was good land in his territory; he also wanted settlements
strategically placed so that settlers could extract the best possible natural resources with an eye to how they might fit into the larger eco-

nomic order he envisioned. Almost immediately on arrival in the valley Brigham sent an exploratory party to Cache Valley, eighty miles north of Salt Lake City in the heart of the Wasatch Mountains, and they eventually discovered extraordinarily rich farmland there. Two years later he sent another party south. In the late 1840s and early 1850s Mormon settlers followed. In Utah they founded Logan, Provo, Richfield, and Cedar City; they also founded cities like Las Vegas, Nevada, and distant San Bernardino, California.

Frequently, Brigham, his counselors, and the apostles made settlement decisions together, chose a leader to serve as the stake president or bishop of the new colony, and directed him to gather volunteers. Isaac Morley, for instance, was called to found the city of Manti in central Utah, and within a week he had recruited nearly a hundred volunteer families from his friends and neighbors in the Salt Lake City area to settle the desert. Less often, church authorities would assign particular families to move here and there across the Great Basin landscape, selecting Mormons of particular skills or backgrounds to go to certain colonies. Converts from the southern United States went to the area of southern Utah eventually called "Dixie" to grow cotton; British converts from the mining districts of Wales went to the hills of southwest Utah to extract iron. These efforts were often only marginally successful. The Mormons rarely had the expertise and equipment to erect fully functional industry, and Brigham often micromanaged too much, preventing these industries from developing their own consistency and rhythms.

The degree of authority Brigham Young and other Salt Lake City leaders wielded over these settlements varied widely. Often settlers approached Brigham for approval or simply to announce their intentions, as was the case in Provo, the second largest settlement after Salt Lake City, founded in 1849. Often Brigham and his counselors simply gave advice, usually that the men should go first and build a fort for protection, or encouragement that settlement parties combine British, American, and Scandinavian converts in order to encourage cultural intermixing. Some settlements became ethnically homogeneous: the Sanpete Valley, for instance, became a particular haven for Scandinavian converts.

From the beginning, the Mormon settlements were governed ecclesiastically. Though the law of consecration had failed in Kirtland and Missouri, the ethic of economic cooperation had sunk deep in the Mormons' bones. Brigham warned that "each man must keep his lot whole, for the Lord has given it to us without price."[22] They organized themselves in patterns familiar from Nauvoo and Far West: their settlements were divided into wards, geographical areas usually containing several hundred people, and a bishop was placed at the head of each, charged with overseeing and organizing its spiritual, economic, and social welfare. The towns were centered on public and ecclesiastical buildings: the bishop's storehouse, where tithing proceeds given in kind were kept, the meeting hall, the granary, and so on were laid out in wide streets oriented to the cardinal directions. These streets divided large lots that encouraged family orchards or gardens and hence a semiagrarian urban lifestyle. Houses were brick or stone or adobe, firm materials that would last. Farmland was outside the city, and farmers would travel there each day and back at night. This compact living encouraged residents to live close to one another, develop communal attachments, and support public institutions: libraries, theatres, and, of course, the church.

From the first months of settlement in Salt Lake City, the wards worked together to divert the creeks that ran down from the mountains and to ensure that every family drew a share of the water. They dug ditches, built bridges, and marked off farmland cooperatively. Wards also began to support the most poor among them; impoverished immigrants who arrived in Utah were assigned to wards capable of feeding and clothing them, and the central tithing office also frequently gave assistance to the poor. In exchange, poor residents were given work on public projects—an assembly hall, a storehouse, a sugar factory that processed the sugar beets that grew around the Great Salt Lake, and an endowment house in which temple ordinances were performed until the Salt Lake Temple was completed in 1893. The church administered a "tithing farm," a place where the livestock, crops, and other supplies donated by members were kept, and members occasionally worked there, rotating from their own labors on a regular basis.

The desire for a righteous society, ordered by commitment to the principles of the faith rather than by the democratic capitalism flourishing in the United States, made such sacrifices acceptable. As the economy of the Salt Lake Valley began to prosper in the 1850s, some leaders of the church began advocating a revival of the law of consecration. The Mormon settlements had been in place for several years and were beginning to feel the pressures of the outside world: in 1849, a tidal wave of gold seekers passed through the Salt Lake Valley on their way to the mines in California. Their money was welcomed, if a bit grudgingly, but Brigham was distressed at the numbers of Mormons who sold their lands and joined the caravans to California. Following the gold seekers came merchants who brought eastern goods to Salt Lake City at prices that undercut those for items the Mormons were producing at home. Many simply passed through, but a good many stayed. The Mormon leaders, confounded at how easily the economic strength of their communal commonwealth could be sapped, again began preaching consecration, asking the faithful to turn over all their property to the church, receive as stewards what was essential, and see the rest donated to the poor. In particular, the apostle Orson Pratt, a visionary and theologian always impatient with the world's failure to resemble heaven, railed against the "Gentile God of property" and urged Mormons to go to their bishops with deed forms that the church printed and provided.[23]

Pratt would be disappointed. By the end of the 1850s, after nearly a decade of urging, a majority of the families in Utah had not embraced consecration, preferring instead to pay the one-tenth tithe established in Nauvoo or to ignore the church's attempts to involve itself in their business at all. Instead, the growing numbers of merchants on the streets of Salt Lake City founded thriving businesses, and many Mormons were joining their ranks. Disgruntled, Brigham complained in one conference that "I would rather see every building and fence laid in ashes than to see a trader come in here with his goods."[24] He urged the Mormons to make the things they needed, to barter with friends, above all to cultivate self-sufficiency: anything but dependence on the capitalist marketplace. He castigated those who patronized the stores of Gentiles, and as Mormons themselves began to pursue trade with the outside world, he accused them of placing the acquisition of wealth above the cultivation of the kingdom. Finally, in the late 1860s, the leaders of the church became convinced that further steps were necessary.

In 1869, Zion's Cooperative Mercantile Institution, a wholesale store run by the church but owned collectively as a joint-stock corporation, opened its doors. It was designed to control prices in Utah, to discourage non-Mormon merchants from entering the Salt Lake Valley, and to serve as a distributor of goods to cooperative societies the leaders of the church hoped would be organized in other settlements. Many of the Mormon settlements caught the dream and experimented with more radical ways of resisting the encroachment of capitalism. In 1864 in Brigham City, sixty miles north of Salt Lake City, the apostle Lorenzo Snow, Eliza Snow's brother, organized the Brigham City Cooperative Association, a joint-stock company of which more than a hundred citizens of the small town had bought shares by the early 1870s. Collectively, they owned the entire economic life of the city: a general store, a woolens factory, livestock herds, a dairy, a leatherworking shop, a furniture manufacture, and more. The Brigham City Cooperative established a school, a "tramp department" to employ beggars at odd jobs, and a community center. And, most important to Brigham Young, the city was almost completely self-sufficient.

Buoyed by Brigham City's success, Brigham Young in 1874 traveled across southern Utah, calling for each town to restore "the Order of Enoch." In consultation with his counselors, Young prepared a proclamation that described the order as more than an economic system. Consecration, Brigham promised, would foster a culture, a society, and a community; it would make the Mormons self-sustaining and pious. As was true in the civilizations of the Book of Mormon and the Hebrew Bible, Brigham Young believed that the Mormons' prosperity was tied to their righteousness, and he sought a system that would promote both. Those who undertook the order pledged, among other things, to pray several times a day, to surrender private property, to work for the collective, and to avoid patronizing establishments outside the order. In several towns, "United Orders" appeared, to varying degrees of success. As in the Brigham City Cooperative they would sometimes gain partial ownership of the common means of production. A board made up of church leaders distributed cows, flour, homes, and so on, assigned men to jobs, and allotted wages at levels designed to promote social equality. The most radical of these communities, Orderville, was built from the ground up according to the principles of the Order of Enoch. In Orderville there was no private property, and families lived in dormitories and ate in a collective dining hall.

Many of the United Orders struggled to survive more than a few years. As before, though a majority of Mormons in any particular community generally agreed to participate, a large minority often declined, or if they joined protested the amount of property they were allotted. Nearly all wanted as much from the storehouse as they could get, and the boards struggled with Mormons who deeded their property but then changed their minds and sought to regain their farms. Yet they continued to spread across southern Utah and even into some northern parts of the state throughout the 1870s: arising, flaring, sputtering, and sometimes failing, only to appear again elsewhere. Brigham Young prayed for their success, and to the Mormons they remained the greatest symbol of their conviction to live a way apart.

When the Mormons arrived in the Great Basin, the land they settled was the northern wilderness of Mexico. Two years later, the Mexican-American War had ended, Mexico had ceded its territory north of the Rio Grande, and the Mormons found themselves again in the United States. Though that fact did not please some, Brigham Young sensed opportunity. The United States was, after all, made up of states, and the Constitution reserved to states many powers. With a state government in their hands, the Mormons might enjoy greater autonomy than they had ever before possessed. In consultation with Thomas Kane, a well-connected Philadelphia attorney, Brigham Young decided to seek statehood for a territory called "Deseret," a Book of Mormon word meaning "honeybee." With entirely typical confidence Brigham sent Wilford Woodruff and John Bernheisel to Washington, D.C., with a map that would have granted Deseret the entire Great Basin: present-day Utah, most of Nevada, half each of Colorado, Arizona, and New

Mexico, with a chunk of Idaho and the city of San Diego thrown in. Congress rejected the plan and the name (too much like "Desert") and pared down the borders to form the Utah Territory. Nevertheless, after some urging from Kane, President Millard Fillmore appointed Brigham Utah's first territorial governor.

The Mormons had always chafed under secular authority. Their apocalyptic communalism made them impatient with bureaucracy, and they nursed the wounds their repeated unsuccessful appeals to the government had left. In turn, politicians were often suspicious of Mormon loyalties. Brigham Young had essentially governed both the territory he called Deseret and his church as one entity for three years before he received formal appointment, and to the frustration of the agents and judges and clerks the Fillmore administration sent to Utah in 1851, he seemed to have no intention of changing his style. Brigham frequently snubbed federal officials, sought to gain control of their budgets, complained about receiving directives from the federal government—particularly in regard to Indian affairs—without sufficient funding, and, one by one, drove them from the territory. One judge who brought a mistress to Utah particularly scandalized the Mormons; he made it known that he took the sentiment with a grain of salt coming from a society of polygamists.

To many Mormons the territorial government Congress established seemed an awkward and rickety framework forced on an entirely suitable ecclesiastical government, and they frequently ignored the distinction. Those offices Brigham had appointment authority over and the elected legislature were generally filled with candidates the church councils selected. The legislature itself often functioned like a council; Brigham and the apostles would visit and contribute to its debates, and the laws it passed usually reflected the will of the church's leaders. But in other cases, Mormons ignored the territorial government entirely. Most were accustomed to using the church councils or consultations with bishops to resolve disputes rather than appeal to the court system, and federal judges watched in alarm as the Mormons went about their business as though they did not exist. When Indians killed Brigham Young's secretary Almon Babbitt, a Mormon of lukewarm commitment who seemed more interested in preserving the federal government's authority than the welfare of the church, non-Mormon officials murmured that the Danites who had defended the church with threats and violence in Missouri had returned.

In Washington, the Mormons became a useful political foil. Inspired by slavery, and later by the Civil War and Reconstruction, American politics was in the middle of the nineteenth century consumed with debates over majoritarianism, morality, and freedom. Politically, these debates were about the proper relationship between the federal government and the states; culturally, they were about whether the majority of the nation had the right to control practices it found morally abhorrent. The particular issue at hand was slavery, but Mormonism seemed to have more than a passing resemblance to the South's peculiar institution. The Mormon settlements in Utah, which like the South seemed to have a recalcitrant relationship with the rest of the nation, inadvertently found themselves near the center of the conflict. The leaders of the Democratic Party had developed a theory they called popular sovereignty, the notion that the inhabitants of any particular territory of the United States had the right to determine what policies would be in force there. In practice, Democrats such as the Mormons' erstwhile friend from Illinois Stephen Douglas, now a senator, used the theory to defend slavery. In the presidential election of 1856, the Republicans, whose evangelical base gave them a deep moralistic streak and a particular hostility toward slavery, linked it to the marital and political depredations of the Mormons, declaring both the unholy fruit of popular sovereignty.

When he assumed the presidency in 1857, Democrat James Buchanan was determined to prove that popular sovereignty did not require him to countenance the rebelliousness and moral degradation of the Mormons. Buchanan hoped that a crusade against Brigham Young would distract the nation from its battles over slavery. He decided to replace Brigham Young as governor with a non-Mormon, the mild and competent Alfred Cumming. Based on the reports of federal officials in Utah, he concluded that the Mormons would likely resist any attempt to replace their leader, and in late May 1857 he directed Colonel Albert Sidney Johnston to take twenty-five hundred soldiers to Utah to ensure Brigham would step down. In late May Johnston departed Kansas, where he had been imposing peace upon a state torn apart by disputes over slavery. Rumors began to drift toward Salt Lake City. On the eve of the tenth anniversary of his arrival in the valley, Brigham Young was leading a celebration in Big Cottonwood Canyon just south of Salt Lake City when he received word of the army's approach. It did not come from Buchanan but from several Mormons who had learned of the decision when the government canceled their postal delivery contract.

The Mormons immediately recalled Jackson County and Carthage Jail and Parley Pratt, murdered only a month earlier in Arkansas. Heber Kimball, Brigham's counselor in the First Presidency, flared that he had enough wives to defeat the U.S. Army. Brigham himself told a scribe, "Fixed my determination not to let any troops enter this territory. . . . I do not feel to be imposed on any more."[25] In early August he declared martial law in Utah, erected fortifications, ordered that no supplies should be sold to any non-Mormon passing through Utah, and called out the Nauvoo Legion, which had survived the plains to become the territorial militia. The apostle George A. Smith toured settlements in southern Utah warning of invasion, preaching self-defense, and appealing to local Paiute bands for assistance in fighting the Americans. Young met with Paiute leaders seeking the same. He sent several cavalry detachments under the command of a young pioneer named Lot Smith to destroy the army's supply chains and steal its cattle and posted the legion in Johnston's expected path. As the army approached the borders of the Utah Territory, Brigham sent them a message stating that he had seen armies profess peace and end up routing the Saints before. In any case, he had yet received no official communications from Washington and thus felt justified in labeling the army's approach "an act of usurpation and tyranny unprecedented in the history of the United States."[26]

In late September the army arrived at the boundaries of the Utah Territory and exchanged shots with Lot Smith's men, who harried it until it settled into winter camps around the ruins of Fort Bridger, which the Mormons had razed in anticipation of the standoff. On November 21 Alfred Cumming, who had traveled with the army, declared the Mormons to be in rebellion and ordered the indictment of

Brigham Young and sixty other Mormon leaders. The entire debacle was quickly labeled "Buchanan's Blunder," so the president was willing to listen when Thomas Kane arrived at the White House and requested appointment as a special envoy. Over the course of several months, meeting with Young and the federal envoys, Kane brokered a deal: if Cumming would enter the valley alone, if the army would not trespass Salt Lake City, Brigham would step down in his favor. Meanwhile, in Utah, the situation grew tense; Brigham ordered Salt Lake City evacuated for several months and threatened to burn the city to the ground. Eventually, however, Kane's efforts succeeded. Cumming agreed to the deal, and Kane took him to meet with Brigham Young. The army insisted on establishing a permanent base at Camp Floyd, fifty miles south of Salt Lake City, in western Utah, angering the Mormons, but in June, a blanket pardon for Mormon "seditions" arrived from Buchanan. The Mormons resented its implications; as one young missionary wrote, "It was so full of lies, and showed so much meanness, that it elicited three groans from the company," but they accepted it.[27]

The Mormons accepted the outcome of the Utah War, as it came to be called, because they had little choice. Young knew that despite his desires to set Zion apart, the Mormons could not ultimately avoid the power of the United States, and he still hoped to win statehood. The territorial legislature sent proposed state constitutions to Congress in 1856, 1862, and 1872; all were rejected. But Young still proved willing to cooperate when he must. In the 1860s he sponsored the construction of a telegraph line through the territory connecting California and the East Coast. In 1869 he grudgingly greeted the transcontinental railroad, which drove its final spike at Promontory Point, near Brigham City. The railroad marked the end of the Mormon trail, the handcarts, and the wagons—and more: it was the beginning of the slow death of the United Order, for with the railroad came capitalism and business in a tide too deep and fierce for the Mormons' fragile cooperatives to resist. The same year, the Utah Territory lost a vast swath of land on its western border to the state of Nevada because representatives of the silver mining industry convinced Congress that their ventures were far preferable to the Mormons' polygamy and communal farming.

Despite their loss of territory, the Mormons still only gradually abandoned their settlements in Nevada. They were not willing to surrender yet. The Utah War also began a forty-year-long struggle between the federal government and the power of a church that still claimed the right to shape the lives of its members in ways that defied all other authority. Cumming knew that Brigham Young remained the de facto leader of the territory he ostensibly governed, and he was careful to cultivate a good relationship with the Mormon hierarchy while continuing to insist on the authority of federal courts and other appointments. Others would not be so accommodating.

Patrick Connor, commander of the U.S. Army post in Utah during the Civil War, was convinced that the Mormons were plotting subversion, and moved his headquarters to a base three miles from Salt Lake City in order to keep a close eye on Brigham Young. He organized mining efforts in central Utah, hoping to attract non-Mormon settlers to dilute the Mormon voting base. Infuriated, Young insisted that Utah would remain loyal to the Constitution. But the Mormons were neither invited nor volunteered to participate in the Civil War on either side, and in sermons Young frequently expressed a certain degree of schadenfreude at the nation's insistence on tearing itself apart. Like Abraham Lincoln, he seemed to believe that the war was a divine judgment expressed upon the American people, though to the sin of slavery Brigham added the murder of Joseph Smith and the persecution of his people.

More ominous than Connor was John J. Cradlebaugh, a federal judge who gained appointment in Utah in 1859. In March of that year he opened an investigation in the Provo court of strange military reports coming from southern Utah: a field called Mountain Meadows where "women's hair . . . hung to the sagebrushes. Parts of little children's dresses and of female costume dangled from the shrubbery . . . for at least a mile in the direction of the road, by 2 miles east and west, there gleamed, bleached white by the weather, the skulls and other bones of those who had suffered."[28] The military had been sent to Mountain Meadows to investigate reports that the Fancher party, an emigrant wagon train headed for California, had fallen prey to Indians, but Major James Carleton quickly concluded that local Mormon settlers had been involved in their deaths. Cradlebaugh ordered the arrest of three local church leaders, who fled into the desert to evade capture, and attempted to indict Brigham Young himself, calling him an accessory before the fact. Unable to gain any of his indictments, Cradlebaugh left for Nevada soon after.

In 1871, Phillip Klingensmith, a blacksmith and former bishop in the town of Cedar City, some forty miles from Mountain Meadows, reawakened the affair. According to Klingensmith's confession to federal prosecutors, in early September 1857 a number of local church leaders, including himself, had conspired to destroy the Fancher party. In their capacity as officers of the militia, the stake presidents and bishops of Cedar City and the nearby town of Parowan mustered the men of their community to lay siege to the train. After several days of standoff, on September 11 the militia raised a flag of truce. When the members of the wagon train laid down their arms, the soldiers separated the men, women, and children and executed all who could speak, some 120 people. Klingensmith reported that he took seventeen children who could not yet talk back to the Mormon settlements, where they were adopted. On the strength of Klingensmith's testimony, warrants were issued for eight other Mormon leaders: the stake presidents of Parowan and Cedar City, several bishops, and John D. Lee, an adopted son of Brigham Young who, according to Klingensmith, was the ground commander of the militia in the siege.

These men vanished into the deserts of Utah, and the leadership of the church did little to assist federal officials in finding them, although Isaac Haight, the former stake president of Cedar City, and John D. Lee were eventually excommunicated. Brigham Young offered more aid in rhetoric than in fact. In 1874, Lee was finally arrested and brought to trial; three years later he was executed. The only man convicted of any crime related to the massacre, he bitterly complained that he was being made a scapegoat all the way to the firing squad. Many suspected Brigham Young of ordering the massacre or, more likely, covering it up. And indeed, though Lee was central to the execution of the massacre, the guilt hardly ended with him.

The massacre was the grisly conclusion of a terrible sequence of mistakes. When the Fancher party reached Cedar City in the first week of September 1857, they were entering a dangerously tense atmosphere. George A. Smith and Brigham Young had told local Mormons to sell no goods to wagon trains passing through, to be ready in case the U.S. Army invaded Utah, and that the Mormons would not flee persecution again. But the Fancher party had counted on purchasing supplies along the trail, and food was low; when they realized that no goods would be available to them in Cedar City, tempers boiled over. Some members of the party expressed a desire to join the federal troops marching toward Utah; one apparently claimed to possess one of the guns that had killed Joseph Smith. Alexander Fancher, captain of the train, attempted to soothe relations, but Isaac Haight, stake president in Cedar City, would have none of it. He wanted to summon the militia to arrest the offenders and confiscate cattle as a fine, but other militia and church leaders, requiring Brigham Young's permission, sent a letter to Salt Lake City and allowed the wagon train to depart. Nevertheless, Haight and John D. Lee persuaded local Paiutes to join a few members of the Cedar City militia in an informal raid on the party that would punish the worst offenders and steal some cattle for good measure. But it went awry. Lee led an early attack, and a Fancher scout saw white men leveling guns at the wagons.

This placed Haight in an impossible position, for he had hoped to hide behind the Paiutes, keeping Mormon involvement secret. If the Fancher party was allowed to travel to California bearing the knowledge that the Mormons had attacked them, Utah's impending encounter with the U.S. Army could quickly become disastrous. Haight went back to other officers in the local militia, confessed Lee's raid, and persuaded them that to preserve Zion the party must be eliminated. They summoned the militia. The day after the party was destroyed, Brigham Young's response arrived: "In regard to emigration trains passing through our settlements we must not interfere with them untill they are first notified to keep away. . . . While we should be on the alert, on hand and always ready we should also possess ourselves in patience, preserving ourselves and property ever remembering that God rules."[29] According to one of his associates, when Haight received the message he broke down into tears, stammering, "Too late, too late."[30]

For many Americans, the confused stories of the massacre and Brigham Young's reluctant cooperation with the investigation confirmed their consistent fears that the Mormons were dangerous, uncivilized, not fit to participate in American society. And the Mormons, in some measure, agreed: they believed that their faith called on them to live in ways higher than the rude capitalism and rampant immorality that they saw plaguing the United States. As Brigham Young had sensed, the Americans in the last half of the nineteenth century were a people convinced that they must bring civilization to the world. The Americans subdued the South and gained an empire overseas, sending missionaries to Africa and India and passing laws designed to uplift African Americans and Native Americans. It was only a matter of time before they turned their attention to the Mormons as well.

FIVE

THE RISE AND FALL
OF PLURAL MARRIAGE

1852–1896

The move west completed a transition not merely from the leadership of Joseph Smith to that of Brigham Young, but from the church Joseph Smith had founded to the new Israel that settled Utah. The apostles' determination to throw open the secret church of Joseph Smith, to initiate the membership into the rites of the temple and into the bonds of plural marriage, marked their desire to create a people, a nation, a new Israel from the church that Joseph Smith had founded. By the time the last Mormon wagons left Nauvoo in the fall of 1846, thousands had passed through the endowment, and 153 men had entered into plural marriage with 587 women. As the Mormons moved mile by mile away from American civilization, their confidence in their new way of life rose, and the need for secrecy faded. The church that settled in the Salt Lake Valley could, at long last, not merely worship as they wished but build the sort of society that matched the fullness of Joseph Smith's dreams. From the beginning, of course, it could not be done without interference; the Mormons challenged too many American norms to be left alone. But they persisted, and for more than forty years they insisted on the right to live as they believed God desired. George Q. Cannon, a longtime member of the First Presidency in the late nineteenth century, even declared that the doctrine of plural marriage was designed to bring God's people into conflict with the world around them. If this was his purpose, God had succeeded impressively.[1]

In the 1850s the Mormons were at the peak of their isolation but also their self-confidence. The initial struggles with the Native Americans had ceased, Brigham Young reigned as territorial governor, and the settlements were beginning to thrive. In 1851, the Iowa courts in Winter Quarters summoned a young Mormon named Frederick Cox, the son-in-law of old Isaac Morley of Kirtland, and commanded him to abandon his two youngest wives. Declaring that his grandfather had fought in the Revolutionary War to allow him the right to practice his religion, he refused and moved out of the court's jurisdiction. In that defiance was Mormon confidence in microcosm. That same year the Utah territorial legislature, dominated by Mormons, voted to incorporate the Church of Jesus Christ of Latter-day Saints and gave it authority to solemnize marriages in the territory. In 1876, church authorities added the revelation on plural marriage Joseph and Hyrum had shown Emma to the Doctrine and Covenants, a canonical collection of Joseph Smith's revelations. It remains there still.

On August 29, 1852, Brigham Young called a special conference of the church. He had asked the apostle Orson Pratt, the most theologically minded of the Twelve, to prepare an announcement of what was by then an open secret: the Mormons were practicing plural marriage. Pratt defended the practice not just theologically but as a better order of human life that would bring humanity closer to the state God imagined for it. In so doing, Pratt began the project of systematizing the often obscure theologies of Joseph Smith's scripture and sermons. The dead prophet had presented many concepts, but almost always in the form of conclusion rather than premise, a scattered and often confusing cornucopia of insight and ideas. Pratt's task, and that of other Mormon leaders like his brother Parley, the apostle John Taylor, and Brigham Young himself, was to sculpt Joseph Smith's ideas about polygamy and God, humanity and salvation, into a coherent narrative of the nature and purpose of human existence.

First, Pratt asserted that marriage was an integral part of human salvation. If all human beings existed in spirit before they were born, and if God's purpose was to guide them into his own likeness, then procreation was essential. These spirits needed a body, for God had a body. Embodiment sat at the center of divinity. Pratt declared, "The Lord ordained marriage between male and female as a law through which spirits should come here and take tabernacles, and enter into the second state of existence. The Lord Himself solemnized the first marriage pertaining to this globe."[2] And more, Pratt and Brigham Young declared that the procreative power that marriage legitimized persisted into the eternities, where glory was measured in the number of relations. Young taught that God was literally the father of humanity, progenitor of the spirits of the human race in the eternities that predated human existence on earth, and that he had created this earth as a place for his spirit children to experience mortality and grow morally and physically. Soon after Joseph Smith's death, the notion of a Mother in Heaven, a divine female and the mother of human spirits, began to circulate, most famously in one of Eliza Snow's poems, written in November 1845:

> I had learned to call thee Father, through thy Spirit from on high,
> But until the key of knowledge was restored, I knew not why.
> In the heavens are parents single? No, the thought makes reason stare!
> Truth is reason, truth eternal, tells me I've a mother there.[3]

Snow, Pratt, and others taught that the heavens were a great interlocking network of families of greater and lesser sizes and glories, each woman adding to the glory of her husband and each son subordinate to his father. As Orson Spencer, a British convert and tireless pamphleteer, wrote, "The family order which God established with Abraham and the Patriarchs, was the order observed among celestial beings in the celestial world. . . . It is of perpetual duration."[4] To gain this celestial glory was to enter into communion with God, to join his eternal family in exaltation, and while Pratt, Young, and the rest generally stopped just short of asserting that plural marriage was required to join this chain, they were comfortable stating that those who wished exaltation should be willing to practice it. This narrative, tracing human existence from a spiritual preexistence born of God to an eternal afterlife of glory and exaltation, pieced together the scattered ideas, revelations, and practices that Joseph Smith had introduced and proved a firm bedrock for the Mormon faithful for generations to come.

These were theological arguments with social implications: the family, and particularly the plural family, became the foundation of the social order God desired. In 1852 Pratt argued that plural marriage was the means through which "a numerous and faithful posterity can be raised up, and taught in the principles of righteousness and truth." Families that practiced plural marriage tended to be more committed to Mormonism, and Pratt believed that they also had more children than monogamous families; both characteristics strengthened God's kingdom on earth. For the Mormons, the great revolution of polygamy was not against Victorian morality; rather, it was against the lifestyle of Victorian monogamy. Plural marriage revealed that the sociality of heaven was far different from that which existed on earth.

That plural marriage was in fact a more moral system than monogamy was a common assertion among Mormons. Because polygamy was a social revolution, Pratt did not limit himself to theological arguments. He taught that since monogamous societies were not aware of God's true intentions for marriage, and particularly of plural marriage, they were disordered. They misdirected the love and passion of human beings inward, creating a weak and atomized society divided into isolated couples. These societies' families were fragile; they bred orphanages and runaways; their streets were filled with abandoned and forgotten women too often forced into prostitution; their men were dissolute and consumed with lust. Such societies lacked moral fiber. They did not encourage loyalty and faithfulness to community and family but instead fostered immorality and lack of self-control. "It would be considered an awful thing by them to raise up a posterity from more than one wife," Pratt sneered, but to "debauch themselves in the lowest haunts of degradation all the days of their lives, they consider only a trifling thing." On the other hand, because they had embraced plural marriage, Mormon societies were stable, their members committed to the health of the community, and they lacked the poor underclass that fostered crime and debauchery in the United States. Polygamy spread affection and sentiment across larger numbers of people and hence fostered a society of greater graciousness and love than that of the United States. Pratt wanted his listeners to believe that there were no lost young women in Salt Lake City, no orphanages, no brothels. "Do you find such haunts of prostitution, degradation, and misery here, in the cities of the mountains? No," the apostle declared.[5]

Helen Mar Kimball Whitney, Joseph Smith's widow, concurred. "It is no wonder that they of the world have so many domestic broils and law suits for divorce," she wrote, "nor that children born of such parents with the constant example before them should turn out prostitutes and fit subjects for a life of crime and debauchery."[6] The Mormons drew upon common mid-nineteenth-century American fears of urban decay, poverty, and corruption. The only difference was that the Mormons blamed these problems on the curse of monogamy from which American society suffered. Helen Mar Kimball Whitney cited with approval DeWitt Talmage, the Brooklyn pastor who denounced the sins of his city's red-light district and warned that such things would lead to the collapse of the United States. Though Talmage and other American Protestants recoiled from Mormon polygamy—Talmage once called Utah "the national stable," comparing Mormon women to breed cows—they shared a similar religious outlook shaped by a moralistic apocalypticism, and the Mormons were convinced that what they called "the principle" left them protected from such depredation.[7]

Given their affinity for Talmage's moralism despite his distaste for Mormonism, it is evident that Pratt and Whitney were improbable Victorians, committed to sexual morality and a certain degree of prudery despite their principle, and they practiced plural marriage with all the rectitude they could manage. And indeed, the practice of plural marriage was strictly governed by church regulation and social mores. Though the numbers vary from place to place and over the forty-year life of official plural marriage in territorial Utah, in general some 20 to 30 percent of Mormons belonged to a family that practiced the principle. This was more than Mormons acknowledged once polygamy came under withering fire, but also fewer than their opponents often stated. It still represented a stunningly large congregation; some tens of thousands of people, though of course far more women than men.

The demographics of the participants reflected the differing experiences each gender had with the practice. For men, there existed an intimate connection between the practice of the principle and their place both in the institution of the church and in the social world of territorial Utah. The higher priesthood office a man held, the more likely he was to participate in plural marriage; similarly, the higher the office, the more wives he was likely to have. As John Taylor, who succeeded Brigham Young as president of the church after Young's death in 1877, declared to a gathering of the apostles and stake presidents, "A man obeying a lower law is not qualified to preside over those who keep a higher law."[8] In the April 1884 General Conference of the church, Taylor's First Presidency issued a message more strongly binding the practice of polygamy to church authority. As one observer noted, the First Presidency stated that "Celestial Marriage . . . was binding on all Latter-day saints, and that no man was entitled to the right of presiding without abiding this law. They advised Presidents of Stakes who have not obeyed this law to do so; or resign."[9] The most married men of Mormonism—Brigham Young, who had fifty-five wives, and Heber C. Kimball, who had forty-three—were also its highest leaders, but their marriage rate far outstripped that of the vast majority of their followers. Local leaders, the bishops of ward congregations, the stake presidents who supervised them, and the members of high councils were generally also polygamist, but they almost always had far fewer wives than did Brigham or Heber. In Manti, Utah, for instance, one of the earliest Mormon settlements outside Salt Lake City, such leaders had an average of 3.4 wives in 1860. Twenty-three percent of Manti's polygamist men that year had four or more wives (and half of those had four); 20 percent had three, and 57 percent, the majority, had only two.

Men chose to become polygamists for one of two reasons. Sometimes a man might take a new wife due to personal inspiration, the sense that God desired it. But as frequently a more highly ranked officer of the church might take him aside and note that his leaders felt the time was right for him to take another wife. Even those who felt impressed on their own to marry again would seek the approval of the local bishop or stake president before they did so, because church leaders regulated access to the ritual of sealing, and they used it to enforce what they believed to be proper standards of marriage. Heber J. Grant, a polygamist who became president of the church in 1918, said that while serving as a stake president in the 1880s, he denied two applicants who asked for permission to marry a plural wife, one because he was an alcoholic and the other because, as Grant put it, "What is needed in your family is sufficient brains to take care of one wife and one family."[10] In this way, church leaders effectively regulated the marriage practices of their members and ensured that plural marriage was pursued with a certain sense of responsibility: men who became polygamists were expected to serve honorably in the church, to be community leaders, and, perhaps most of all, to support their large families economically. There was a positive correlation between wealth and plural marriage, and men who wished to gain respectability in the community felt pressure to seek out not only the first but also the second.

Women, of course, faced similar pressures to enter plural marriage but often paid higher costs. The demand for wives meant that almost all women married, and many married young. Slightly more than 97 percent of the women who turned eighteen in Manti, Utah, before the railroad arrived in 1869, in the period of the wagon trains and handcarts, were married by age twenty-four, and the average age of marriage was twenty. Less than 1 percent of those women never married, in contrast with 7 to 8 percent of women in the same age range in the United States more generally. Moreover, immigrant women from Europe in particular generally married within a year of arriving in Utah, nearly half of them as plural wives. In all, slightly more than a third of those women who came of age before 1869, 36.9 percent, became plural wives when they married. As time went on, and as federal pressure on the Mormons increased, the number declined; of women who turned eighteen after 1869, only 10.5 percent married into polygamous relationships. These demographic trends reflected the urgency of Utah's gender ratios: in all the censuses of the territory in the nineteenth century, men outnumbered women. The scarcity of potential wives meant that competition for them was fierce, driving both the practice of rapid marriage and the church leadership's strategies for regulation.

Particularly in the early years of plural marriage in Utah, the hard years of the 1840s and 1850s, when settlement was just beginning, polygamy often provided plural wives with economic resources. Plural wives tended to come from the poorer stratum of Utah society, particularly from the ranks of immigrant women who came to Utah, often alone, with few or no resources. Elizabeth Haydock, a fifty-five-year-old British widow converted in 1854, lost an eye while trapped in the Wyoming snow with the Martin handcart company. When she arrived in Manti, Utah, with her daughter she was destitute and soon became the third wife of the community's bishop. Her story was typical. Many single British and Scandinavian female converts found work or refuge in the homes of established Mormon men and eventually became their plural wives.

Such marriages immediately connected women to established kinship ties, gave them social status, and entitled them to economic support; this often replaced the absence of more traditional such networks. Women without a father in Utah were far more likely than other single women to enter plural marriage. Similarly, men frequently married along family lines, taking sisters-in-law, cousins, or nieces of earlier wives as subsequent plural wives; infrequently but occasionally, daughters of wives who had been married before would enter into plural marriage as well. Levirate marriages, in which a man would marry the widows of a male relative, were common and were often solemnized only "for time," providing women with temporal support while preserving their eternal bond to their first spouse. Some of these marriages were never consummated, nor would the new husband and wife live as such.

Mormon polygamy was a patriarchal system in a patriarchal time, and the language surrounding it reinforced male authority. In the sealing ceremony women were asked to give themselves to their husbands, who were asked to receive; men spoke of "taking" another wife, and the dynastic aspects of polygamy may recall medieval geopolitical strategies that used women as bartering chips. Even if women did not feel powerless, they often felt lonely. Though the principle had many vocal female defenders who believed ardently in its divine provenance, these women often had a profoundly ambivalent relationship with it. Helen Mar Kimball Whitney was one such defender, but even in the midst of her rhetorical salvos, her voice wavered slightly: "If I did not know my husband was actuated by the purest of motives and by religious principle, I could not have fortified myself against the demon Jealousy," she observed.[11] Ironically, the practice that in the imagination of Joseph Smith and Orson Pratt created familial relationships in heaven more glorious than any on earth tore apart many families in Utah.

Whitney was not alone. Many women who stoutly defended polygamy in public struggled silently. Whitney's invocation of Abraham's sacrifice of Isaac spoke to many who hoped, as did she, that "when Abraham made his sacrifice, the Lord restored it, which ought be lesson enough for all of us."[12] But often they were disappointed. When Patty Sessions was fifty-two, her husband took a second wife, Rosilla, with whom Patty had a troubled relationship. Patty's brief diary entries offer a sharp insight into the struggles a polygamous family could have. On October 4, 1846, soon after the marriage, Patty wrote, "I feel bad. I am in trouble." The two women did not get along; Patty complained to her husband that "if she came in I should be boss over the work and she must be carefull how she twited and flung at me, without more humility in her than I see than I could bear but little." By late October, Patty's entries had grown terse: "Wednesday 28 Ironed but little said between she and I. Thursday 29 I cook still she does not ofer to."[13] Patty was relieved when the marriage failed and Rosilla returned to the East.

Emmeline Wells, seventh wife of the apostle Daniel Wells, was one of the leading women in Mormonism, an intellectual and spiritual leader, but she had experiences similar to Patty Sessions's. "I believe in women, especially thinking women," she wrote.[14] But in her diary in September 1874 she wrote sentiments that many plural wives craving companionship and security shared: "Misery and darkness and I have no one to go to for comfort or shelter no strong arm to lean upon no bosom bared for me, no protection or comfort in my husband. . . . O if my husband could only love me even a little and not seem so perfectly indifferent to any sensation of that kind. He cannot know the craving of my nature."[15] The gap between a busy and fulfilling public life and a lonely private life was a nagging thorn in the side of many women.

Still, Mormon women were offended when Grover Cleveland, president of the United States, declared in his 1885 State of the Union address that "the mothers of our land, [each] within her pure and wholesome family circle . . . are not the cheerless, crushed, and un-womanly mothers of polygamy."[16] They were offended when Eliza-beth Cady Stanton and Susan B. Anthony, leaders in the woman's suffrage movement, visited Salt Lake City in 1871. The territorial leg-islature had recently extended to women the right to vote. Stanton gained permission to hold a meeting of Mormon women in the Salt Lake Tabernacle near the temple site, where the church's General Conferences were held. She congratulated her audience on their suf-frage, but also called on them to rise up and overturn "polyandry, po-lygamy, monogamy, and prostitution." The pair was cast from the Tabernacle and Stanton remembered that "the women who believed in polygamy had much to say in its favor."[17] The Mormons could not win. On the one hand, as Cleveland's complaints illustrated, they of-fended traditional Victorian gender standards, which declared women simultaneously the strong moral backbone of society responsible for the cultivation of a virtuous home but also too delicate to enter the public sphere of business and politics. On the other hand, that Mor-mon women stubbornly clung to their presumed enslavement earned them pity from reformers like Stanton. They bristled at both.

Mormon women were determined to demonstrate that these accu-sations were untrue; that in fact Mormonism and polygamy enabled the women of Utah to be truly virtuous and thus more capable than the reformers themselves of accomplishing social betterment. In 1871, Eliza R. Snow stood before a great gathering of women and declared, "We stand in a different position from the ladies of the world. We have made a covenant with God, we understand his order, and know that order requires submission on the part of woman."[18] For Eliza, this knowledge was actually a blessing because it meant that Mormon women were uniquely capable of understanding the will of God. But this did not mean that women were to be powerless or dominated. As Emmeline B. Wells wrote, "The world says polygamy makes women inferior to men—we think differently. Polygamy gives women more time for thought, for mental culture, more freedom of action, a broader field of labor [and] leads women more directly to God, the fountain of all truth."[19] Helen Mar Kimball Whitney concurred. She remembered visiting with a non-Mormon woman traveling through Salt Lake City who asked with curiosity about plural marriage. "I did not try to conceal the fact of it having been a trial, but confessed that it had been one of the severest of my life," Whitney remembered. But "I could truly say that it had done the most toward making me a saint and a free woman, in every sense of the word."[20]

Much of this work was done in the company of other women. In Winter Quarters polygamous families gradually, timidly, began to publicize their relationships, and the patterns of life in the principle began to emerge. Zina Huntington Jacobs, widow of Joseph Smith, married Brigham Young, who pushed her civilly married husband Henry aside as Smith had, sending him on a mission to England. Zina remembered that marrying Brigham brought her into "the President's family some six or seven of us in a tent." It was a remarkably positive experience: "Some of the Girls it was the first time they had ever left there parents but the Pres was so kind to us all, nothing but God could have taught him and others how to be so kindly." In her first months in Salt Lake City, Zina found that her interactions with her husband Brigham would be occasional and frequently ceremonial. She lived for a time with several other wives and then with her sister Presendia, a new wife of Heber C. Kimball's, and finally in a small cabin that she shared with her children. She frequently spent time visiting her siblings and other women for companionship and spiritual nourishment; as she recorded of one such meeting, "Sister Rockwood & Ellen, Martha and myself fasted & Prayed that we might be blest and be guided by the trew speret. . . . Spent the afternoon together very happily."[21] For most of the rest of her life in Utah, Zina lived with her children in small homes within a mile or so of Brigham's official residence, walking to visit with her husband or siblings or friends regularly and supporting herself with schoolteaching, sewing, and breadmaking.

Zina's life as a plural wife was similar in many respects to those of most of her sisters in the principle. Many second and later wives bore for their husbands the sort of affection, though generally not romantic love, that she had for Brigham Young because they conceived of their choice to marry as a religious duty. Love was a luxury often reserved for the first wife. Likewise, as her ad hoc living arrangements illustrated, there were no formal guidelines for housing a plural family. Some lived together under one roof; others, like Brigham Young's, had some wives in a main home and others scattered nearby, as Zina was. A few men had wives living across the Utah Territory. Nor were there standards for where husbands should spend their time or how the work of supporting the family would be divided. In general, however, the leaders of the church urged husbands to be considerate and fair, and wives to share burdens among themselves, both to lighten the load and to build community. Men were admonished to seek the advice and consent of their first wives as they sought a second, and occasionally a married couple would seek an additional wife together. Though social pressure and de facto patriarchal authority meant that this sort of cooperation did not always happen, Brigham Young also staunchly defended the right of plural wives to seek divorce for lack of affection, desertion, or economic neglect. As his secretary wrote to one inquirer, "As a rule, the Prest. never refuses to grant a bill on the application of the wife, and NEVER when she INSISTS on it."[22] To one woman who sought a divorce from a husband who had refused to come to Utah from Nauvoo, Young wrote:

Your letter of the 16th Inst is before me and I write again that you are at full liberty to marry again as soon as you choose and that you are perfectly free from all marriage obligations or ties to Brother Coolidge. In marrying again please try to get a saint who will take good care of you.

from your Brother in the Gospel
Signed Brigham Young[23]

Perhaps the most striking effect plural marriage had on Mormon society was the creation of a powerful, strongly bound female society.

The ideals of civic housekeeping that inspired many American women to march into the public sphere as protectors of the home were strong in Utah, and as the Relief Society and other civic organizations in Nauvoo followed the organization of the church, so did female activism in Utah. While the women lacked the formal authority of the priesthood and access to the bureaucratic power of the councils, Zina's "Girls," the informal community of wives connected through the network of plural marriages, became the primary emotional and social replacement for the often absent husbands in the lives of women. And it became a powerful mobilizing network as well. Among the wives of Mormonism's leaders, a group of "leading sisters" emerged—women such as Zina, Emmeline Wells, and Eliza Snow, for whom lack of fulfillment in the private sphere combined with some degree of economic security and independence to produce a strong commitment to public engagement.

Their main vehicle was the renewed Relief Society. After the catastrophes of the summer of 1844 and Emma Smith's alienation from the main body of her husband's church, the Relief Society slipped into inactivity. But Eliza Snow carried its minute book across the plains, and in Winter Quarters she, the Huntington sisters, and Patty Sessions—all elevated by their status as former wives of Joseph Smith—led prayer meetings with the women in the camp. In Salt Lake City, these meetings continued and gave rise to grass-roots, self-organized Relief Societies scattered throughout the settlement, designed to aid Indians and look after the poor. In 1867, Brigham Young asked Eliza Snow to unite the disparate, informal ward-level gatherings into an official churchwide institution—that is, to formally revive the Relief Society.

Eliza took up her task with vigor. She traveled across the territory, establishing local chapters in wards wherever she went, and as Emma Smith had before her, she selected two counselors, Zina D. H. Young and Elizabeth Ann Whitney. Primarily, Eliza and her counselors emphasized organization and self-sufficiency. She directed the local Relief Societies to raise their own funds to build meetinghouses and storehouses and encouraged them to aid the bishops of their wards in caring for the poor and tending to the sick. The Relief Societies organized visitation systems to ensure that none in the ward had unmet needs and sponsored regular meetings where women could receive instruction on topics ranging from doctrine to gardening to Shakespeare. In 1882, the central Relief Society had grown financially strong enough to open a free clinic in Salt Lake City called the Deseret Hospital. It was staffed with mostly female doctors and nurses whose education the Relief Society had largely sponsored. By the time Eliza Snow died in 1887, the Relief Society had some twenty-two thousand members across the Mormon settlements.

By the late nineteenth century, many civic housekeeping organizations in the United States had moved beyond social reform to political activism, and the Relief Society was no exception. Eliza preferred to focus on charitable organization, but other women, particularly the fiery Emmeline Wells, called for activism on behalf of women's rights. The newspaper she edited from 1877 to 1914, the *Women's Exponent,* was widely read; some 10 percent of Relief Society membership subscribed, and her editorials calling for women's suffrage and property rights were influential. The Relief Society also moved into political activism. In 1870 the organization stood strongly behind the legislature's bill to grant women the right to vote; that February, Mormon women became the first women in American territory to cast a ballot in an election. Under the leadership of Zina D. H. Young, who became general president of the Relief Society upon Eliza's death, the society shook off past offense and formally affiliated with Susan B. Anthony and Elizabeth Cady Stanton's National Woman Suffrage Organization. Wells, who served as president of the Relief Society in the last decade of her life, from 1910 to 1921, traveled across the country in the late nineteenth century refuting tales of Mormon enslavement of women before Congress and in public lectures. Other Mormon women traveled to the East to pursue training, especially in medicine and education, often with the funding of the Relief Society and the approval of Brigham Young.

The organizing capacity of these Mormon women deeply influenced the direction that the church took as it faced a particular challenge in the 1850s, 1860s, and 1870s. The first generation of Mormons, those who had known Joseph Smith, fled Kirtland or Missouri for Nauvoo, and walked across the plains, was growing old. As the Puritans had two hundred years before, Mormon parents faced the problem of how to bequeath the faith that had seized them with its apocalyptic vision and millennial community to their children. While sociologists call early Mormonism a sect, a self-consciously marginal society created exclusively of self-selected converts, thirty years after Joseph Smith produced the Book of Mormon it had become a church, expanding through reproduction as much as conversion, hoping for longevity, and as dependent on bureaucracy as on charisma.

In 1856, Utah had suffered several years of drought, and the hard work of settlement meant that many local church leaders had turned a blind eye to deviant behavior among younger Mormons. The combination of economic pressure and a sense that the younger generation was slipping away led the First Presidency to launch what came to be called the Mormon Reformation. Brigham Young sent his counselors and apostles on preaching tours across Utah, calling the Saints to repentance and increased devotion, warning of hellfire and judgment, and invoking sacrifice and obedience. Church authorities often directed that the Lord's Supper be withheld from members—and sometimes entire congregations—who refused to embrace penitence. The measure of sincerity was acts of worship that affirmed a recommitment to community; many Mormons were rebaptized, and many agreed to enter plural marriage. The immigrant Levi Savage, for instance, was told he must be rebaptized "for the remission of your sins; for the renewal of your covenants with God and your brethren, and for the observance of the rules that have been read in your hearing."[24]

Though the Reformation sought to revive the old utopian communalism of the church community, ironically it drew the Mormons closer to Protestant worship practices. Before the Reformation most Mormons within a fair distance would travel to the center of Salt Lake City on Sundays to hear Brigham Young and the apostles preach in the Tabernacle near the site where the Salt Lake Temple was slowly rising. On weeknights they would attend small prayer meetings or meetings of the Relief Society and the priesthood quorum. But the Reformation emphasized the importance of the wards. During the settlement of Utah, wards were primarily understood as social and economic organizations; the bishops had custody over aid to the poor, directed settlement efforts, and resolved disputes. They would meet to worship irregularly. The apostles who preached the Reformation, however, gathered the Mormons by wards and emphasized the importance of ward meetings. By the end of the Reformation many wards were building meetinghouses and holding regular Sunday meetings there— and looking more and more like the congregations of other American faiths.

The timing was apt. The late nineteenth century was the golden age of the American congregation. The institutional church movement emerged among Protestants in the 1870s, redefining the church as not merely a place of worship but a community engaged in any number of campaigns for personal, familial, and social improvement. Protestant churches founded youth clubs, charity organizations, and other outreach programs to the poor designed to both spread the gospel and help the needy. As Edward Judson, pastor of the Judson Memorial Church in New York City, explained in 1899, the institutional church was "a system of organized kindness, a congeries of institutions, which by touching people on physical, social, and intellectual sides, will conciliate them and draw them within reach of the Gospel."[25] The organized congregation in the late nineteenth century became the primary expression of Protestant mission work in the United States, both to the unchurched and to members of its own congregation, even as the task of evangelism was often redefined as the cultivation of character. In the broad strokes, if not in the particulars, Mormons were quite typical.

Women organized many of the efforts of the institutional church, and in Utah the Relief Society was the engine behind the rise of a number of auxiliaries that transformed the ward into the central hub of Mormon religious life: a Primary Association, later called simply Primary, that sponsored lessons, activities, and singing for young children; a Sunday school organization; a Young Ladies' Co-operative Retrenchment Society; and a Young Men's Mutual Improvement Association. Eliza R. Snow sponsored the creation of the Primary and the Young Ladies' groups, and women of the Relief Society often served as Sunday school teachers. All of these organizations held weekly meetings designed to better integrate the young generation of Mormons into the social mores and expectations of the church by offering instruction in doctrine and other moral behavior. The Young Ladies' Society of Salt Lake City's Eighth Ward resolved, "Inasmuch as order is the first law of heaven, we will endeavor to learn the law by making ourselves acquainted with the principles of life and salvation. . . . We will also study all literature that will qualify us to become ornaments in the kingdom of God, that we may merit the approbation of our brethren and sisters and of God."[26] The rise of a ward that served particular congregational functions facilitated the gradual decline of the utopian millenarianism that had conceived of Mormonism as an apocalyptic community set apart from the rest of society. Rather, by the late nineteenth century to be a Mormon increasingly meant meeting a set of standards in personal behavior, and as the nineteenth century wore on, the religious culture of Mormonism shifted to reflect priorities of socialization.

The most dramatic of these changes came in the 1870s, when in the last years of his life Brigham Young reorganized the priesthood, a generation-long process that transformed Mormon administration and religious culture in two ways. First, confirming the liturgical reorientation of the Reformation, the various priesthood quorums men belonged to were organized by ward and placed under the authority of the ward bishop. Henceforth, their meetings would be organized around the ward's weekly meetings. Second, Young directed that men would no longer serve in only one or two priesthood offices over the course of their entire lives; rather, they would move through priesthood office as they aged.

Beginning at twelve years of age, men would be ordained into the priesthood and would move through a progression of priesthood stations throughout their lives. Teenagers would progress through the offices of the Aaronic priesthood and be given the Melchizedek priesthood at adulthood. This was most significant, because the Aaronic priesthood held the scriptural mandate to administer the Lord's Supper. Brigham Young and other leaders hoped that entrusting this responsibility to the young men would encourage their faithfulness and dedication, and Salt Lake City bishop Angus Cannon applauded the result as "an excellent experience" that provided "a marked improvement" in the behavior of the boys.[27] Every Sunday since, Mormon wards have gathered for worship, and while hearing sermons and singing hymns, they receive the Lord's Supper, administered to them by the teenage boys of the congregation.

Despite their efforts to make of themselves a moral community and the Mormon women's angry rejection of rumors of enslavement and debauchery, the Mormons were unsuccessful in convincing the American public that Utah was not a hive of lasciviousness and tyranny. The parallels between the slaveholders of the South, conquered, subdued, and remade in the image of the North as a result of the Civil War, and the Mormons in Utah were irresistible. The crisis over slavery had taught the nation that, as one abolitionist declared, if some objectionable social institution, be it polygamy or slavery, were "tolerated as a local institution, it must be tolerated also as a national institution, and stamp its impress forever upon the national character."[28] This was dangerous. Just as slavery degraded southern civilization, so did polygamy destroy the character of those Americans who fell into its clutches. Historian Hubert Howe Bancroft called polygamy a "retrogression," warning, "When Greece and Rome were the foremost nations of the world they did not practise polygamy, nor has ever the highest civilization entertained it. Polygamy is to monogamy as Greece to China or as England to India."[29] Some scientists, in all seriousness, warned that polygamy was producing a corrupted and degenerate human race; as one team of doctors warned, "The yellow, sunken, cadaverous visage; the greenish colored eyes, the thick, protruberant lips, the low forehead . . . all constitute an appearance so characteristic of the new race, the production of polygamy."[30]

Bancroft and the physicians were defenders of a particular way of thinking about civilization. They believed that the freedom and self-government upon which American civilization rested were fragile and required certain intellectual capacities to flourish: curiosity, diligence, independence, will. They agreed that many societies simply lacked these gifts. Many northerners believed that white people in the South, seduced by wealth, hierarchy, and aristocracy, had abandoned their love for liberty. African Americans were often judged just as deficient, due either to racial characteristics or to their long period of enslavement. Therefore, Republican leaders in Congress believed that Reconstruction, the military occupation of the South that lasted from 1865 to 1877, was necessary to instill again in the South the virtues that self-government required. After Reconstruction, as Americans began to look overseas, they interpreted other civilizations in the same way: after a successful and brief war with Spain in 1898, President William McKinley announced that the United States would assume governance of Cuba and the Philippines and other territories the Spanish had controlled, saying, "There was nothing left for us to do but take them all, and to educate the Filipinos, and uplift and civilize and Christianize them."[31]

The Filipinos posed little direct threat to the United States, though they did mount a stiff guerrilla war against the U.S. Army. But the Mormons were within American territory, corrupting American citizens and presenting a real and direct threat to the very life of American self-government itself. As Josiah Strong, a prominent evangelical minister, warned, "The Mormon, in his mental make-up, is a distinct type. There are men in every community who were born for the Mormon church . . . they are credulous and superstitious, and are easily led in the direction of their inclinations, they love reasoning but hate reason; they are capable of blind devotion." Mormonism gathered such converts, clearly incapable of self-government, together and turned them into a force. Strong warned Americans not to be misled by the most lurid aspects of Mormonism. "Polygamy might be utterly destroyed without seriously weakening Mormonism," he said. "What is the real strength of Mormonism? It is ecclesiastical despotism."[32] To Strong, as to many other Protestants, Mormonism was a distinctly un–American church, like Catholicism, to which it was frequently compared. Its heresies and its offenses against democracy were one and the same: the presumption that the individual soul required guidance from ecclesiastical authority, the conviction that God had established a church through which salvation would be gained, and the belief in the need for priesthood ordinances. All of these things offended Protestants theologically, but they also seemed suspicious to Americans who believed in individual liberty and political democracy.

Americans had an example of a good version of Mormonism. In December 1869 David and Alexander Smith, sons of Joseph, confronted Brigham Young in his office in Salt Lake City. Their brother Joseph Smith III, in his capacity as president of the Reorganized Church of Jesus Christ of Latter-day Saints, had sent them to seek converts. The aging Young impatiently called Emma Smith a liar when David began to echo her·claim that his father had never practiced polygamy, and he dismissed their requests to speak in the Tabernacle. Despite Young's dismissiveness, in 1880 Joseph III won for his church clear legal title to the Kirtland temple and, moreover, a legal declaration that the Reorganized Church was the rightful successor to the church that Joseph Smith, Jr., had founded. Bolstered by his success, Joseph Smith III through the 1870s and 1880s made four tours of Utah, delivering across Mormon country an address denying that his father had conceived of the principle, assailing "Brighamite" Mormonism for corruption and theocracy, and proclaiming himself the true heir of his father's mantle. He also eagerly seized on popular distaste for polygamy, seeking to aid court cases against the Utah church, insisting that his version of Mormonism embraced the pure religion his father had taught, and gladly appearing in the national press. Though he gained only a few hundred converts among Brigham's followers, he placed the Utah church in an uncomfortable position—on the one hand, they faced suspicion and fear from many Americans because of their polygamy; on the other, to refute Joseph III required them to document its existence exhaustively.

Congress acted on these concerns as early as 1862, when the Republican senator Justin Morrill of Vermont successfully proposed the Morrill Anti-Bigamy Act, which effectively outlawed plural marriage in the territories of the United States. But neither the president at that time, Abraham Lincoln, nor his immediate successors had much interest in trying to enforce the law. Lincoln did not want a feud with Brigham Young on his hands at the same time that he was negotiating the Civil War. Those federal officials who did attempt to prosecute polygamists found that gaining convictions in front of a Mormon jury was remarkably difficult. Mormons blasted the law for failing to distinguish between the crime of bigamy—marrying a new spouse while already married to another, a crime against the first spouse as well as against the state—and their own plural marriage, which was a religious rite rather than a legal marriage, one to which all members of the union were willing parties.

In 1874, George Reynolds, Brigham Young's secretary, took a second wife and agreed to be a test case of the constitutionality of the Morrill Act. He gave himself up to prosecutors, and the attorneys began preparations to take the case to the Supreme Court. Reynolds's attorneys challenged the Morrill Act on a variety of technical arguments, but primarily on the First Amendment, arguing that Reynolds's plural marriage was protected as a free exercise of his faith. George Biddle, the renowned Philadelphia attorney who defended Reynolds, was aware of the broader cultural forces the Mormons faced and invoked the hated *Dred Scott* decision that had required territories to accept slaves brought onto their soil, helping to spark the Civil War. He blasted the federal government for treating the Mormons as "mere colonists, dependent upon the will" of the rest of the country rather than free to live as they chose.[33] *Reynolds v. U.S.* was the first Supreme Court case to consider the First Amendment, and the Court unanimously decided that the Constitution did not protect polygamy. The Mormons were free to believe in the principle, the Court stated, but not free to pursue actions deleterious to the public interest. This separation of belief and action reflected what most Americans of Protestant heritage believed: authentic religion was about belief, about faith, not about odd rituals or strange practices, and the esoteric rites and institutions that the Mormons had erected destroyed their ability to be truly pious.

At the news of the *Reynolds* decision, the Mormons reeled in disbelief but, as they had so many times before, also proved defiant. Wilford Woodruff, by then the president of the Quorum of the Twelve, asked a congregation meeting in the great Tabernacle, "Now, which shall we obey, God or Congress?" The crowd cried, "We will obey God."[34] And so they did. John Taylor, who had succeeded Brigham Young at the head of the church after Young died in 1877, repeatedly declared that polygamy could not be abandoned and that God would encourage and protect those who continued to practice it. He urged his people to, as he said, "put up our coat collars and wait till the storm subsides. . . . While the storm lasts it is useless to reason with the world."[35] There could be no compromise, only endurance. In 1882, Congress passed the Edmunds Act, designed to close the loopholes and increase the strength of the Morrill Act. Instead of bigamy, the Edmunds Act outlawed "unlawful cohabitation," wording designed to eliminate the need to prove that a marriage ceremony had occurred. In practice, as the Salt Lake City bishop Angus Cannon discovered when he challenged the law in court, cohabitation could be proven merely with records documenting that a man supported more than one woman financially. The Edmunds Act further denied polygamists the right to vote, the right to serve on a jury, and the right to hold office.

Soon after the Edmunds Act passed, federal marshals began to enter Utah in force, and the period the Mormons called "the Raid" began. The Mormon leadership scattered to avoid arrest, abandoning Salt Lake City. As high-ranking Mormons left political offices vacant, they were filled by federal appointees sympathetic to the Raid, and by 1886 every Mormon settlement in the Utah Territory had been visited and its people questioned. Citizens were asked on the street where polygamists might be hiding; federal agents followed suspected polygamists in the hopes of catching them meeting with secret wives. In one such case, the apostle Rudger Clawson was trailed to a boardinghouse, where marshals surprised him as he met his plural wife Lydia Spencer. When he appeared before the judge, Charles Zane, Clawson declared that he would always choose the law of God over the law of man; replying that polygamy was a reversion to an immoral and superstitious civilization, Zane sent Clawson to prison for four years.

Clawson was not the only important leader of the church to fall prey to the marshals. The apostle Lorenzo Snow was captured while hiding in a makeshift cubbyhole he had built under his living room floor, while George Q. Cannon of the First Presidency repeatedly posted bail and vanished before being captured for good in 1888. John Taylor himself traveled from house to house in northern Utah, staying with his followers and rarely sleeping in the same bed two nights in a row. He died in 1887 in hiding in Kaysville, Utah, just north of Salt Lake City. The General Conferences of the church in the middle 1880s were often presided over only by the handful of apostles with the confidence to appear in public. And less prominent Mormons suffered as well. In Manti, Utah, guards were posted outside the city to watch for marshals; when they approached, polygamous men fled into the mountains or hid in cellars. Men sent their plural wives back to the homes of their fathers in an attempt to evade charges of cohabitation; they fled on foreign missions, often evading arrest only for a time. One bishop, trapped in a department store, had himself boxed into an organ crate and carried out to safety. Plural wives learned the art of denial and forgetting, frustrating judges and prosecutors who found that the women they expected to be sympathetic and grateful met them with stone faces and terse words.

Despite all their evasions, more than a thousand Mormon men were convicted of a crime relating to plural marriage in the 1880s and early 1890s, with penalties ranging from fines to imprisonment. The federal marshals seized a territorial prison a few miles south of the temple site, and multiple high-ranking Mormons—Cannon, Clawson, Snow, and the apostle Francis Lyman among others—found themselves in black-and-white striped prison uniforms. Charles Card, husband to Zina Presendia Young, Brigham Young's daughter by Zina Huntington, leapt from a moving train to escape arrest and fled from the Utah Territory to avoid recapture, only occasionally sneaking home to the Salt Lake City area to visit his three wives and children. Like many Mormon men, he shaved his beard to avoid recognition, and in February 1887 he wrote in his journal that on a visit home his children, who had not seen him for six months, "stopped and looked at me with amazement. I did not wonder at this for when they saw me last I had a very heavy beard. . . . It made me feel sorrowful & I burst into tears." He mused that "no wonder the brethrens children who are permitted to visit them in prison do not know their fathers with shaven faces & striped clothes."[36]

Several apostles fled the Salt Lake Valley, hiding in southern Utah, California, or Idaho. Others went to Canada or Mexico. In 1885, the apostles Erastus Snow and Moses Thatcher visited Porfirio Diaz, the president of Mexico, and gained his approval for several settlements Mormon refugees had already established in northern Mexico. While Mexican officials were wary of polygamy, they hoped to spur economic development in the arid regions where the Mormons settled, and they welcomed the settlers as long as they kept their marital practices quiet. Accordingly, Anthony Ivins, who served as the first stake president in Mexico, remained a monogamist. Two years later, John Taylor sent Charles Card to Canada to found a similar settlement there. Card and his associates met with Sir John Macdonald, the Canadian prime minister, who asked if polygamy was the same as bigamy; when the Mormons denied it, Macdonald, who desired similar things for his frontier that the Mexicans wanted for theirs, extended to the Mormons a welcome so long as they embraced the laws of Canada. To the Mormons, this meant that plural marriage might be practiced in a circumspect fashion, though the attentiveness of Canadian officials meant that polygamy was somewhat attenuated in the colony Mormons founded in Alberta called Cardston.

In Utah, despite the tide of arrests, federal marshals were growing impatient. The Mormons seemed to be constantly slipping through their fingers. They would arrest one, only to have two others escape; the man arrested would serve six months and return to his wives and ward a martyr. In the face of such resistance Congress was increasingly inclined to impose harsher sanctions. In 1887, it bolstered the Edmunds Act with the Edmunds-Tucker Act. While the Edmunds Act sought to destroy the social institution of polygamy, the Edmunds-Tucker Act was aimed at the church itself. In addition to strengthening the tools prosecutors held strictly to combat unlawful cohabitation—for instance, ending spousal privilege that allowed legal wives to refuse to testify against their husbands—it contained provisions that seemed designed to ensure that the Church of Jesus Christ of Latter-day Saints would not survive the Raid in the form it had taken to that point. The Edmunds-Tucker Act legally abolished the incorporation of the church, and the property the church was no longer able legally to possess reverted to the ownership of the federal government, which agreed only that the church might retain control of chapels and cemeteries. It revoked the women's suffrage that the Utah legislature had passed in 1870. It required that marriages in Utah be regulated by state government. It declared all children of polygamous relationships to be illegitimate and unable to inherit. It required all voters in the Utah Territory to swear that they would uphold the Edmunds-Tucker Act before they would be allowed to cast ballots. In 1887, the prosecutors returned to Salt Lake City, armed anew.

The Mormons were weakening, but they still put up a fight. Again they retained attorneys and challenged the Edmunds-Tucker Act in court, but in 1890 the Supreme Court ruled the act constitutional. That same year it approved of a state law in Idaho that disenfranchised all those who believed in plural marriage, whether or not they practiced it. The Mormon leadership despaired. Wilford Woodruff had succeeded Taylor as president of the church, and he was faced with legitimate concern for the survival of his faith. There were astute politicians and legal thinkers among the leadership of the church; Woodruff was not one of them. But he was a visionary, a man of unshakable faith whose eyes seemed sometimes to gaze through the veil dividing heaven from earth. He spent much time in the summer of 1890 pondering the fate of his church and later claimed that God had granted him visions in which the Raid destroyed it altogether. As he said, "All ordinances would be stopped throughout the land of Zion. Confusion would reign throughout Israel, and many men would be made prisoners. This trouble would have come upon the whole Church."[37] He particularly stressed the danger facing the church's temples. In St. George, Logan, and Manti, Utah, temples had already been dedicated, and the great Salt Lake City temple, under construction for some forty years, was nearing completion. Under the Edmunds-Tucker Act, these temples lay vulnerable to seizure at the hands of the federal government, and the ordinances—endowment, sealing, baptism for the dead— therefore stood threatened. For Woodruff, the relationships with past generations sealed in the temple came to trump those that plural marriage had created.

On Monday, September 24, 1890, Woodruff met with three apostles and presented to them a declaration scratched out in his own precise handwriting and rough diction. In a few paragraphs Woodruff denied rumors that the church leaders were seeking to circumvent the law in order to perform plural marriages and announced that, since the Supreme Court had repeatedly upheld anti-polygamy legislation, "I hereby declare my intention to submit to those laws, and to use my influence with the members of the Church over which I preside to have them do likewise."[38]

Those of the Quorum of the Twelve who could meet, some eight or nine apostles, did so several times over the next two weeks to intensely discuss Woodruff's declaration, which appears to have surprised most of them. Eventually, they agreed to support it, though not without some reservations. B. H. Roberts, a president of the Quorum of the Seventy and immediately below the apostles in rank, shared a train ride with the apostles Abraham Cannon, Francis Lyman, John Henry Smith, and John W. Taylor (the former church president's son) on September 25, the day local newspapers announced Woodruff's "Manifesto." Roberts was taken by surprise and reported that Taylor and Smith seemed sympathetic to his own distress. Abraham Cannon's diary mentions both Taylor and Smith raising reservations to the Manifesto in meetings of the Twelve.[39]

Less than two weeks after the Manifesto's publication, the apostle Lorenzo Snow proposed in the General Conference of the church that it be accepted as binding and asked the congregation assembled to raise their right hands in support. Woodruff was entirely convinced of the Manifesto's necessity, but it was a bitter cup for a people who had suffered and sacrificed so much. Never before had they acquiesced to such a glaring compromise; never before had their dream of a new society been so ruthlessly dashed. Joseph Dean, who sat in the Tabernacle when Snow called for the raising of hands, wrote, "A great many of the sisters weeped silently, and seemed to feel worse than the brethren."[40] Many observers remembered that a great number of people abstained from raising their hands, and John Whittaker remembered seeing on the faces of the crowd "great sadness and sorrow in the hearts of many."[41]

The profound ambivalence toward the Manifesto among the leaders of the church and the thousands of Mormons who practiced polygamy seems mirrored in its careful wording: it says merely that Woodruff urged his flock to obey the law. It does not renounce polygamy as a doctrine, nor does it appear to be in any sense the voice of God or a revelation, though when Woodruff discussed the document in later years he said that it reflected the will of God. In 1893 the First Presidency and the apostles accepted a presidential amnesty for their past polygamy on condition that they take an oath to obey the Edmunds Act, but for some Mormons the Manifesto was less a renunciation of the practice of polygamy than a signal that the practice must enter a period of secrecy and concealment. Some church leaders ceased cohabitation with plural wives, but most quietly did not. Woodruff sometimes publicly declared that they should live as monogamists, and sometimes in private he insisted that it would be base cruelty to abandon the families that were theirs for time and all eternity. The mixed signals left men often confused and women sometimes petrified.

Further complicating the Mormons' new relationship with polygamy, some Mormons continued to marry into the principle. The apostle John W. Taylor, who was uncomfortable with the Manifesto in the first place, took a third wife only four days after the General Conference in which the Manifesto was announced, and several other apostles followed in the next few years, including Woodruff's own son Abraham. The First Presidency and the apostles gave approval to several such marriages among lay Mormons, and some men traveled to Mexico precisely for that reason. Some marriages occurred in the United States as well. The Arizona Mormon Margaret Cullen, for instance, married William Geddes as a plural wife in 1884, and after his death in 1891 the apostle Marriner W. Merrill sealed her as a plural wife to Geddes's employer, David Eccles. When Margaret got pregnant in 1899, her bishop threatened her with excommunication for adultery, and Margaret refused to say a word until Lorenzo Snow, the president of the church, intervened and directed local leaders to pursue the case no further. Eventually, after Eccles died, Margaret confessed all to a court in order to secure for her son an inheritance from his father. Such marriages, though authorized, were never numerous; at most a few dozen were performed per year over the fifteen years after the Manifesto was issued, after which point the tides among the church's leaders turned against them, and the principle withered entirely.

Many Americans, unaware of the slow trickle of secret marriages, were impressed with the Manifesto. Arthur Thomas, the federally appointed governor of Utah, reported to Congress in 1891 that he believed the Mormons had taken it as a revelation. Senator George Hoar declared the Manifesto a victory over "sectionalism," celebrating the successful imposition of American Christian civilization upon the recalcitrant kingdom of the Mormons.[42] With the support of these men, statehood for Utah seemed virtually assured, and in 1894 Congress declared that so long as polygamy would be forever banned, an application for statehood would be taken favorably. In 1895, the Utah legislature called for a constitutional convention. Thirty polygamists were elected among the 107 delegates, and all of them committed their signatures to a constitution that specifically declared, in Article 3, "No inhabitant of this State shall ever be molested in person or property on account of his or her mode of religious worship; but polygamous or plural marriages are forever prohibited."

On January 4, 1896, Utah became a state of the Union. In celebration, a year later, on the fiftieth anniversary of Brigham Young's entry into the Salt Lake Valley, July 24, 1897, the freshly completed Salt Lake temple and the interior of the Tabernacle where Young had preached were draped in American flags. If the Mormons had lost their struggle, they would make the best of it; if they had to become Americans, they would do so on their own terms. Though polygamy had ended, the power of Joseph Smith's God and Brigham Young's Israel had not, and the Mormons would continue to seek ways to make themselves a peculiar people. Though the temple stood covered in the stars and stripes, the endowment ceremony, baptisms for the dead, and the sealing of married couples continued within, and as Wilford Woodruff prayed to God when he dedicated the temple in 1893, the Mormons approached the new century with "increased faith and renewed hope . . . with regard to Thy great work in gathering Thine Israel and building up Thy kingdom on earth in the last days."[43]

SIX

ETERNAL PROGRESSION

1890–1945

The end of polygamy was more than simply the end of a marriage system; it was an admission that, in large measure, the Mormons' attempt to make of themselves an independent civilization had failed. The dream of Zion seemed scattered. Polygamy lay in ruins, consecration had ended, and the theocracy of Utah was defeated. The year 1890 is a convenient turning point, but it was only one moment in a long season of slippage. Equally important were gradual changes in Utah's demographics. The coming of the railroad had brought an onslaught of American capitalism, and successful mining enterprises founded by non-Mormons in central Utah attracted a host of non-Mormon prospectors and laborers, who eventually became a significant political force in the state.

But at the same time, by the late nineteenth century few Mormons desired separation with the fervor their parents had. The Mormons of Joseph Smith's generation had seen their leader's ambivalence toward the United States, the repeated disappointments that tainted his idealism, and to some degree their patriotism curdled at his death. One hymn describing Smith proclaimed for several decades, "Long shall his blood, which was shed by assassins / Stain Illinois, while the earth lauds his fame," and through the late nineteenth century participants in the

temple endowment prayed for vengeance for the blood of the prophets. Given all this, it is perhaps surprising that the Mormons did not
enter the Union more grudgingly. Despite their long standoff with the
federal government, they began the new century with tremendous
confidence that the stuff of early twentieth-century American life—its
values, ideas, habits—was eminently suited to the pursuit of their religion. Their task became assimilation, finding ways to translate the
things America demanded of them into the language and imperatives
of their own faith. If Joseph Smith's Zion community had faded, its
values were not destroyed, and the Mormons were confident that other
paths to them must lay open. Eighty years after Joseph's death, many
Mormons seemed willing to forgive, or at least to engage again, and
the call for revenge was quietly removed from the temple liturgy. The
wording of the hymn now claims Joseph's blood will "Cry unto
heaven, while the earth lauds his fame."

The Mormons found the temper of American public life at the turn
of the century congenial. Many Americans in the thirty or so years
before the First World War broke out in 1914 were extraordinarily
optimistic about the capacity of American civilization to improve itself. They believed in rationality, science, and political reform. They
believed that human organization could take on and defeat any social
problem so long as it had access to the right expertise and dedicated
bureaucrats. They believed that American democracy, American business, and American reform movements were well on their way to making the United States the most perfect country in human history. The
most dedicated called themselves Progressives. As Theodore Roosevelt, one of their great tribunes, declared, Progressives were those who
"with fervor and broad sympathy and imagination stand for the forward movement, the men who stand for the uplift and betterment of
mankind, and who have faith in the people."[1] His fervent platitudes
demonstrate the extent to which Progressivism was as much a mood
and attitude as it was a particular reform agenda. Progressives, more
than anything, were profound optimists.

Venturing into American society in the late nineteenth and early
twentieth centuries, many Mormons found with pleasure that theirs
seemed a faith tailor-made for the era. Joseph Smith's vision of human

potential and Brigham Young's fusion of faith and community building wove nicely into Progressivism's confidence in human effort. Even
its conviction that organization, rationalization, and commitment to
moral virtue could accomplish breathtakingly utopian goals echoed the
· old dream of a Zion society. Many Mormon leaders at the turn of the
century found in Progressive ideas the way to harmonize their faith
with their nation. They came from a wide range of professions and
interests. Among them were students of philosophy, science, history,
and scripture who read widely in American scholarship and found
there tools to help them explain their own faith to themselves, to
Americans still skeptical of them, and, with luck, to the rest of the
world. Others were businessmen and politicians, eager to find success
in a nation that seemed increasingly enamored of bureaucracy, efficiency, and expertise. Many found that as they cultivated success in
areas quite apart from their faith, they could gain the respectful attention of their nation.

In seeking common ground with Progressive America, Mormons
drained from their faith the apocalyptic utopianism of the dusty Great
Basin frontier and made of it a church more American, but also no less
Mormon. They did not understand themselves to be compromising or
assimilating their faith; rather, they believed that what they found in
America gave them new ways to express its possibilities. That they became in the fifty years after the Manifesto a model American minority
was a happy side effect. During the Utah War of the 1850s Brigham
Young appeared in newspaper cartoons across the nation as a tyrant
atop his throne in the mountains, surrounded by a harem of bound
plural wives. In 1930, Heber J. Grant, Young's successor five presidents
removed, appeared on the cover of *Time* magazine, praised for his acumen as a businessman and for his church's rectitude and frugality. The
difference in the two images is striking—and telling.

Mormons were not entirely accustomed to participating in democracy,
and the first problem its leaders faced was integration into the national
political community. While many Americans seemed, at least initially,
happily convinced by the Manifesto, the problem of politics in Utah
remained a thorny point even after 1890. For many years in territorial

Utah, there were no political parties; candidates were generally selected by church councils and usually won with overwhelming support. But in 1870, a faction of Mormons dissatisfied with Brigham Young's efforts to promote consecration founded the Liberal Party, which quickly became the vehicle for the non-Mormons of Utah. In response, the Mormon leadership organized the People's Party, which essentially served as the church's party, and it won an overwhelming number of elections until the early 1890s. Hoping to promote the cause of statehood, the church dissolved the People's Party in 1891, but even before that point, the Liberals, bolstered by increasing numbers of non-Mormons in the state, were beginning to find success: they carried Salt Lake City in 1890 and won a third of the territorial legislature in 1891.

When the People's Party was dissolved, church leaders—rather hamfistedly—urged members to get involved in the Democratic and Republican parties, in the hope that the Liberal Party would likewise collapse and Utahans would seamlessly join the broader national political spectrum. Eager to further this assimilation, these leaders routinely visited wards to urge members to vote for one party or the other. Which party often mattered less than the simple act of casting a ballot; anecdotes from the time describe bishops dividing their wards down the middle of the chapel aisle and assigning a party to the congregants on either side.

However, such aggressiveness signaled to many Americans that their fears of Mormon ecclesiastical power were not entirely without merit. As partisan divides began to appear within the Mormon community, the problem became particularly pointed. A large number of rank-and-file Mormons tended toward the Democrats, generally seen as the party of farmers and the rural West. However, the Republican leadership in Congress, hoping to make allies of the Mormon leadership, proved stronger advocates of statehood for Utah. The stratagem worked. By the 1890s many Mormon elites had entered the demographic of Republican supporters across the nation: middle-class, well-to-do, educated, and urban, interested in business, possessed of a streak of moral paternalism and wary of the populism that fueled the Democrats.

Throughout the two decades after statehood, a partisan divide ran through the middle of the Mormon leadership; the few Democrats among the authorities of the church bridled at the clear Republican sympathies of the majority, and occasionally disputes broke out. The apostle and Democrat Moses Thatcher, for instance, lost his place in the Quorum of the Twelve when he protested both the First Presidency's directive that he end his 1895 campaign for the Senate and their subsequent announcement that no Mormon leader would be allowed to seek office without approval. Thatcher saw these acts as a partisan attempt to stop his campaign, and he may have been correct: the First Presidency feared that if a Democrat were elected, Republican support for Utah statehood would cool.

Thatcher's conundrum recalled an old Mormon paradox: the struggle between loyalty to the church and the expectation for civil and political freedoms bred into the bones of any American of any religion. Thatcher complained that the First Presidency was trying to have it both ways. On the one hand, the Mormons had made the decision to join the American political community; they had surrendered their bid for a separate Zion and their leaders urged cooperation with the various political parties. On the other hand, Thatcher suspected that the church president still wanted to dictate acceptable candidates. Many believed the tension was unavoidable and should simply be acknowledged, because the church's presence in Utah was overwhelming. As the apostle John Henry Smith said, the question was not whether the church would use its influence, but how.[2]

Despite the Republican sympathies of the Mormon leadership, Utah tended to elect Progressive Republicans or Democrats, even electing a Jewish Democrat, Simon Bamberger, governor in 1916. But Joseph F. Smith, son of Hyrum and nephew of Joseph Smith, who became president of the church in 1901, campaigned against Bamberger and publicly endorsed the Republican William Howard Taft for president in 1908 and 1912, commending Taft for his moderation, caution, and sound economic policies. Other apostles, particularly Francis Lyman and John Henry Smith, also worked for the election of Republicans, while the apostle Heber J. Grant, a successful businessman, vigorously supported the national Prohibition movement. In the 1920s, such activity declined somewhat, though during the Great Depression Grant, who had succeeded Joseph F. Smith as president of the church in 1918, had scathing words for Franklin Roosevelt and repeatedly endorsed his Republican opponents. To Grant's frustration, Utah gave the Democratic president large majorities four times in a row, from 1932 to 1944. Utah's rejection of the church president's election counsel made church leaders wary: by the middle of the twentieth century, they began to avoid blatant political involvement.

The church leadership's inability and perhaps lack of desire to extricate itself from politics meant that Americans' fears of Mormon tyranny did not fade quickly, and neither did suspicions about the persistence of polygamy. In 1898, Utah's citizens elected B. H. Roberts to Congress as a Democrat. An ally of Moses Thatcher, Roberts was likewise a general authority of the church, one of the seven general presidents of the Quorum of the Seventy. Roberts was British, converted with his family while a child. He walked across the plains of the Midwest with his sister when he was nine years old. Twenty years later in 1889 he served five months in prison for practicing polygamy, and his stubborn loyalty to his faith was made clear when upon his release he promptly married a third wife. Congress refused to seat him because of his marriages, and the American public seemed uneasy that eight years after the Manifesto they were forced again to confront Mormon polygamy. Rumors that it had never died out began to stir and soon found public hearing. In 1903 the Utah State Legislature sent Reed Smoot, an ambitious and conservative Republican, to Washington to assume duties as a senator from Utah. Smoot was a monogamist, but he was also an apostle and member of the Quorum of the Twelve. The Senate immediately received a deluge of protests and requests that Smoot, like Roberts, be denied his seat. In early 1904 the Senate impaneled a fourteen-member committee to investigate Smoot's fitness to serve, and a four-year ordeal began.

The Smoot hearings consummated the controversies evident since the beginning of the Raid. Smoot's arrival in Washington attracted an uproar not seen since the 1880s. Though Smoot was a monogamist, his position as an apostle made up the difference between him and Roberts. Progressives harbored deep suspicion of monopolies, organizations that appeared to deny American citizens freedom of choice, be it political, moral, or economic. Their most famous crusades were waged against the great business trusts, but they saw in Mormonism (as they did in Catholicism) a religious monopoly. To Progressives, that the Mormon prophet Joseph F. Smith and the other apostles quietly discouraged Mormon Democrats from opposing Smoot seemed to confirm that Mormons still sought to govern through their autocratic hierarchy. That they had sent Smoot, an apostle himself, as Smith's viceroy seemed to add insult to injury. Given these issues, Smoot's monogamy seemed largely irrelevant, though when on the eve of the hearings the non-Mormon newspaper *The Salt Lake Tribune* claimed to have documented proof that plural marriages continued, it seemed doubly clear that the Mormon menace continued unabated.

Ironically, Joseph F. Smith had hoped that sending Smoot to Washington as an ambassador of sorts would cool rather than stoke apprehension of Mormons. But he found himself—along with dozens of other Mormons, from B. H. Roberts to Moses Thatcher—called before the Senate to defend his faith's capacity to participate in American society. For four years the Senate investigated polygamy and its persistence, the content of the endowment ceremony (many senators were troubled at the prayer for vengeance for "the blood of the prophets"), Brigham Young's attempts to establish economic communalism, and most centrally the authority of those men Mormons revered as prophets. Smoot's opponents contended that the president of the church, Joseph Smith's prophetic successor, ruled his followers by fiat, his word taken as divine proclamation and hence given far more weight in Utah than the Constitution or any law Congress might pass. Smoot, for his part, declared that the leaders of the church claimed no power "either divinely sanctioned or otherwise, to shape the belief or control the conduct of those under them in all or any matters, civil or temporal."[3]

But many were doubtful. George Hoar, a venerable Republican senator from Massachusetts who had been an active abolitionist, found claims to prophecy and direct revelation implausible despite being sympathetic to Smoot's cause. "Which, as a matter of obligation is the prevalent authority, the law of the land or the revelation?" he inquired of Joseph F. Smith, who was forced to concede, "Well, perhaps the revelation would be paramount." Incredulous, Hoar demanded, "Perhaps?"[4] Despite the exchange, Smith spent much of his time before the committee seeking to defuse the fears of Congress and to present a Mormonism compatible with American life. He insisted to Hoar that he had approved no new plural marriage. He said the specter of a Mormon prophet claiming revelation to govern his people in all matters was incorrect; indeed, he said of himself that though he was specially entitled to receive such revelations that God might give, "I never said I had a revelation except so far as God has shown to me that so called Mormonism is God's divine truth; that is all."[5] More important, Smith sought to present to Congress a Mormonism that looked much like the Protestantism that functioned essentially as the civic religion of the Progressive era: a church that venerated and upheld individual liberty and freedom of conscience, that persuaded through appeal to mind and virtue rather than through coercion. He appealed less to revelation than to the divine influence of the Holy Spirit, which guided him and all other Mormons who sought it. When Hoar asked whether a Mormon might refuse to accept the content of a particular revelation if he remained in good standing with the church otherwise, Smith delivered an impassioned speech defending his claim that "members of the Mormon Church are among the freest and most independent people of all the Christian denominations. They are not all united on every principle. Every man is entitled to his own opinion and his own views."[6]

Though this argument may have assuaged the Senate's fears, back in Utah Smith faced a more complicated dilemma. His willingness to downplay the nature of prophecy before the Senate and to back off from polygamy raised protests from some at home. The publicity and rigor of the Smoot hearings had convinced Smith that further action to distance the church from polygamy was necessary, and, by this point, the weight of the church itself was with him. Two apostles, John W. Taylor and Matthias Cowley, refused to appear before Congress. They had been among the most active defenders of continued plural marriage, and by 1904 they were almost entirely isolated. That April, in the church's General Conference, Smith announced a second Manifesto: henceforth, he declared, plural marriage would be entirely prohibited, and any Mormon who officiated at or entered into such a

marriage would be excommunicated. When Taylor and Cowley reacted with displeasure, Smith quietly requested and received their res-
ignations from the Quorum of the Twelve. When Taylor nonetheless
continued to perform plural marriages, Smith confirmed his seriousness and ordered Taylor excommunicated.

Smith's determination to see his people at peace with America won
him some battles. Smoot was confirmed a senator in 1907, and Smith's
second Manifesto ended a period of uncertainty and disagreement. It
remained, however, to ensure that this altered Mormonism could still
provide a satisfying spiritual life to its believers. It was one thing to state
officially that plural marriage was at an end, but in the tangible world
of families, feelings, and hopes for a particularly imagined afterlife, the
process was far messier. The cases of Cowley and Taylor proved that the
divergence between officially stated policy and the continued practice
of secretly authorized plural marriages left many members of the church
with some degree of cognitive dissonance. Some believed Woodruff's
Manifesto was God's will and should become the policy of the church
in practice as in word, others saw it as a feint designed to pacify the federal government, and uneven enforcement left many Mormons firmly
attached to their principle well into the twentieth century.

Polygamy had long been a marker of Mormonism to observers
throughout the world, and even within the faith it lay near the center
of Mormon identity. Even those who did not practice plural marriage
had been told that they must accept it, if only in theory. It shaped how
they imagined the afterlife, how they understood their familial relationships, even how they chose their homes and designed their living
arrangements. For Mormon identity to survive, the principle could
not simply be abandoned. Rather, it had to be translated, and a way to
make its promises true and valid even in the world of the Manifesto
found.

The process of reconceptualization had begun in the fires of the
Raid. Institutionally, the break was dramatic. The 1890 Manifesto became sudden, even shocking, policy in the fall of that year. The brutal
whiplash thousands of Mormons suffered bore testimony to that. But
the trailing handful of secret plural marriages over the next decade

demonstrated that the evolution from plural to monogamous marriage was far more organic than policy might imply. In the 1880s, a linguistic shift began to emerge. For two generations of Mormons, following the close association of the phrases in the revelation Joseph Smith dictated for Emma in July 1843, the "new and everlasting covenant of marriage" was "celestial marriage," the work of Abraham, the principle of plural wives, the order of marriage that existed in the celestial kingdoms of heaven. During the Raid many Mormons insisted particularly on this definition, even rejecting what the apostle Franklin D. Richards called "Gentile" words like "plural marriage" or "polygamy" that implied that the Mormon practice had base motives. Richards insisted that the Mormons followed "patriarchal or Celestial marriage," not polygamy.[7] As late as 1898, another leader of the church used the same definition, arguing that Mormons "believed in and practiced plurality of wives—more properly, celestial marriage."[8]

But at the same time, other Mormons were beginning to emphasize different ways of interpreting the language of Joseph Smith's revelations, finding ways to preserve their celestial inheritance should plural marriage be lost. Ironically, Franklin S. Richards, the son of Franklin D. Richards, made the most critical distinction with the greatest clarity. Franklin S., an attorney, became the general counsel for the church in 1879 at the age of thirty. He quickly embarked on a line of argument that eventually became official. As he testified before Congress in 1888 of his fellow believers, "It has been made plain to this committee that celestial marriage means to them marriage for all eternity and that it does not necessarily involve plural marriage, that is, polygamy."[9]

The vast numbers of Mormons who found plural marriage closed to them after the Manifesto embraced Richards's argument, and it gained increasing support and visibility. The most prominent advocate of this new way of understanding "celestial marriage" was James Talmage, the son of British converts who rode the railways to Utah in 1876. He was the first Mormon to earn a PhD (from Illinois Wesleyan University, in the sciences), one of the leading Mormon intellectuals in an age full of them, and, perhaps critically, a monogamist. Talmage became an apostle in 1911. In 1899, he published a series of lectures he had delivered in Salt Lake City under the title *Articles of Faith*. There Talmage emphasized that celestial marriage was celestial not because of plurality but because it was sealed to eternity, "the system of holy matrimony, involving covenants to time and eternity." He later insisted that "plural marriage was an incident—never an essential" to the eternities.[10] In 1933, Talmage's argument received formal imprimatur when Heber J. Grant, president of the church, issued an official statement declaring that "celestial marriage—that is, marriage for time and eternity—and polygamous marriage are not synonymous terms." Rather, Grant wrote, "Monogamous marriages solemnized in our temples are celestial marriages."[11]

The application of plural marriage's motifs to monogamous marriage made the Mormons as passionate defenders of the American family patterns they began to adopt as they had ever been of polygamy. Mormons began to echo the same defenses of monogamy that their own critics had leveled at them during the Raid. Talmage declared that "the stability of society" depends on "the divinely established institution of marriage" and laid out its ideal arrangements. He endorsed as "the birthright of every worthy man the privilege and duty of standing at the head of a household, the companion of a virtuous wife, both imbued with the hope of posterity." A properly ordered household, he declared, was "God's beneficent plan of uplift and development" for both individuals and society and made it possible for humans to create on earth in microcosm the social order of heaven and cultivate their lives in anticipation of that ultimate reward: celestial marriage, recast as virtuous monogamy and the bedrock of a righteous society.[12] These were goals any Progressive might endorse, but Talmage and other Mormons found in their faith uniquely powerful resources that gave them the means to make the crusade for monogamy truly their own.

This renewed focus on traditional family penetrated even into the rituals and sacraments of Mormonism. A few years after his Manifesto, Wilford Woodruff called for the creation of the Genealogical Society of Utah, a church-sponsored institution that offered aid and resources to Mormons seeking records of their ancestors. The great sealed networks that polygamy created had been for many Mormons reduced and narrowed. Woodruff reminded them of other directions in which links could be forged. "We want the Latter-day Saints from this time to trace their genealogies as far as they can, and to be sealed to their fathers and mothers," he said, "and run this chain as far as you can get it."[13] Just as the Mormons could be baptized for their dead by proxy, Woodruff urged his people to begin performing the other ordinances for them in earnest: to be sealed for their deceased ancestors by proxy, to go through the temple endowment in their stead, and most of all to seek the names and identities of their ancestors so that families could be bound together through the sealing power. Mormons today often quote the verses of Malachi that Joseph Smith reported the angel Moroni reciting at his bedside that New York September night: "He shall turn the heart of the fathers to the children, and the heart of the children to their fathers." The sentimental, emotional power of the passage took hold among the Mormons with force. The bonds that polygamy had created across space would now reach with renewed vigor across time; the old dream of a human race bound together link by link would survive polygamy with renewed strength.

The rhetorical, religious, and institutional recalibrations over marriage and politics demanded a great deal of intellectual work. Mormons sought reassurances of the sort Talmage and other thinkers could give: ways to explain and assimilate their adoption of new and abandonment of old practices into the promises Mormonism had always offered. The struggle to meet these demands has led to the christening of the late nineteenth and early twentieth centuries as the golden age of Mormon theology: many ideas Mormons today take for granted blossomed at this time. The three most prominent contributors to the effort were Talmage, the Seventy B. H. Roberts, and another apostle, John Widtsoe. They were all European immigrants—Talmage and Roberts from Britain, Widtsoe from Norway—who converted as children with their families. Talmage and Widtsoe were both highly educated, with PhDs in the sciences; Roberts was a brilliant autodidact.

Further, these men were taken as authorities both inside and outside their faith. All served among the highest leadership of the church, and their work gained exposure and credibility because of it. Roberts and Widtsoe wrote official manuals of study for the priesthood quorums that incorporated their ideas, and Talmage's writings on Jesus Christ, temples, and other topics were often issued with official approval. They were sent into the public eye as curiosity about Mormonism rose in the aftermath of the Manifesto and the firestorm of the Smoot hearings. All three men regularly booked speaking engagements across the nation and represented their church at various conferences and gatherings. Talmage and Roberts wrote serialized books about Mormonism published in national periodicals. When a publicist obtained unauthorized photos of the interior of the Salt Lake Temple—like all Mormon temples, closed to non-Mormons—Talmage coolly suggested that the church issue official, quality pictures and wrote a book explaining temple worship to accompany them.

All three men were in many ways typical of the Progressive era. Their education bequeathed to them a very Progressive faith in the capacities of human reason, education, and effort along with their particular subjects of study. Their optimism was perhaps most readily apparent in their faith that science, scholarship, and philosophy could help them better understand their religion. Many Protestant Progressives dealt with the challenges scholarship on the Bible, evolution, and the origins of the earth posed to faith by arguing that God's will could be encountered through the study of the natural world. Moreover, they believed that God's benevolent hand was evident in human progress: in the scientific advances that brought medicine, sanitation, and the comforts of technology; in the rise of democratic government, education, and justice; in the spread of charitable organizations, temperance, and piety. To these Protestants, science revealed divine truths.

Widtsoe, Talmage, and Roberts believed the same. John Widtsoe, for instance, argued in a volume titled *Joseph Smith as Scientist* that "there is no real difference between science and religion. The great, fundamental laws of the Universe are foundation stones in religion as in science."[14] The roots of this idea lay in Joseph Smith's assertion that human beings were of the same type of being that God is, only vast eons behind in their divine progression. If this was indeed the case, the principles that governed the creation must be comprehensible to humans, and Widtsoe was convinced that science had begun to take the first steps toward grasping them. *Joseph Smith as Scientist* cites numerous passages from Joseph Smith's revelations asserting that the universe functions according to "law, irrevocably decreed before the foundation of the world" or describing spirit as "matter, more fine or pure," no different at its base than the stuff that makes up the visible world.[15] Working from these notions, Widtsoe, Roberts, and Talmage used the raw material of scripture, and the thoughts of Joseph Smith, Brigham Young, and other nineteenth-century thinkers to fashion a new comprehensive history of the plan of salvation, the story of humanity's existence from the eternities past to the eternities yet to come. It was now shorn of polygamy and based instead on Joseph Smith's profound optimism in human potential. With a few alterations, the achievement of Talmage, Widtsoe, Roberts, and Smith remains the Mormonism believed by most Latter-day Saints today.

Their theology was focused on two principles: the comprehensible nature of the universe and humanity's godly ability to act on that comprehension. They first emphasized that God was a God of laws, subject in some capacity to the deep principles of the universe, and that God's divinity derived from his perfect understanding and manipulation of them—the same way, a Progressive might argue, that a scientist or economist might so perfectly understand their discipline as to apply it to profound results. Drawing on the ideas of Joseph Smith, Widtsoe, Roberts, and Talmage all taught that the universe was not created ex nihilo, out of nothing, but rather that God's work was that of a great craftsman, organizing previously inchoate matter. Talmage's magnum opus, the 1915 biography *Jesus the Christ,* explained that Christ's suffering and death satisfied apparently universal laws of justice, which bound even God's desire to forgive sin should they not be satisfied.[16] For these men, God did not function in mysterious or supernatural ways; the creation and sustenance of the universe and humanity's redemption within it were all accessible to rational investigation.

Secondly, their theology emphasized the similarity between God and man. Like many Progressive Protestants, Mormons since Joseph Smith's time had rejected the doctrine of original sin. Smith had written, in a letter canonized in Mormon scripture, "We believe that men will be punished for their own sins, not for Adam's transgression."[17] This meant that human beings had a profound capacity to achieve righteousness. B. H. Roberts in particular wove together the ideas of

Joseph Smith and Brigham Young to formulate the radically optimistic understanding of human identity most Mormons accept today. He taught that humans were both uncreated, eternal beings of the same divine nature as God himself and the literal children of God. Their identities and intelligence were clothed in bodies spiritual and physical through God's creative powers, destined, ultimately, to achieve the same degree of divinity and glory that their heavenly father enjoyed, though always, as children are always the children of their father, in a position of subordination and respect.

The two points of their theology led these thinkers to a new emphasis on personal character, self-discipline, and morality as the primary pathway to salvation. The ability to learn the laws of creation and also to abide by them became critical. Mormons had once imagined salvation gained through participation in society transformed and sanctified by consecration, by the righteous government of the church councils, and particularly by sealed relationships. While these sacraments remained essential, Mormons cast about for a way to speak about what salvation and the afterlife looked like. Moral rectitude and the cultivation of personal character, the refinement of the divine qualities of the soul, replaced polygamous marriage as the image of heaven. The phrase "eternal progression" moved to the center in the Mormon lexicon in the early twentieth century. It came particularly to describe the refinement of the soul's capacity to participate in divinity through the exercise of Christ-like virtues. B. H. Roberts perhaps articulated these ideas most eloquently when he wrote that "I believe it consistent with right reason to say that some of the lowliest walks in life, the paths which lead into the deepest valleys of sorrow and up to the most rugged steeps of adversity, are the ones which, if a man travel in, will best accomplish the object of his existence in this world."[18]

Mormons believed that they were of the family of God himself, that his divine attributes, theirs by inheritance, could be developed through right choices. Talmage's *Jesus the Christ* lauded "the humble offer of Jesus the Firstborn—to assume mortality and live among men as their Exemplar and Teacher, observing the sanctity of man's agency but teaching them to use aright that divine heritage."[19] The issue of this relationship was important enough that Joseph F. Smith's First Presidency issued a proclamation in 1916 clarifying the relationship not only between the Father and the Son but also between them and humanity. The First Presidency, following Talmage's ideas in *Articles of Faith,* identified Jehovah, or Yahweh, the God of the Hebrew Bible, as the premortal Jesus Christ, acting as the agent of his father. Insisting on this distinction was critical, according to the First Presidency, because "Jesus Christ is not the Father of the spirits who have taken or yet shall take bodies upon this earth, for He is one of them. He is The Son, as they are sons or daughters of Elohim." Furthermore, the Holy Spirit or Holy Ghost was also a distinct person of identity and self-awareness. As Roberts asserted, these relationships meant that Mormons must "think as Christ did, that it is no robbery to be equal to God," for they could claim the same inheritance as he.[20]

These ideas spread among the Mormons not merely in scholarly writings, textbooks, and formal discourses. The first hugely popular Mormon novel, Nephi Anderson's *Added Upon* (1898), traced the story of two lovers from their preexistent state through life as late nineteenth-century Mormons and into the Millennium. Anderson described their journey explicitly in terms of learning, progress, and knowledge and mastery over the world; as God informed the two spirits as they prepared for birth on earth, "Your experiences have been wholly within the compass of spiritual life, and there is a whole world of matter, about which ye know nothing. . . . If, then, ye ever become creators and rulers, ye must first become acquainted with the existence of properties, laws, and organization of matter other than that which surround you in this estate."[21]

Anderson's novel was the crowning jewel of a movement called "home literature," work produced by and for Mormons, self-conscious and eagerly didactic, instructional, and moralistic. Despite its frequent clumsiness, Mormons were delighted to have art of their own: the apostle Orson Whitney declared, "We will yet have Miltons and Shakespeares of our own. . . . In God's name and by his help we will build up a literature whose top shall touch heaven."[22] Whitney contributed to the effort in a magisterial poem called *Elias* that likewise celebrated human potential, while in 1890 the church sent many of its most promising young visual artists on an "art mission" to study in

Paris in preparation to beautify the interior of the Salt Lake Temple. The most gifted Mormon painter of this generation, the post-impressionist Minerva Teichert, studied in Chicago and New York under the famous realist Robert Henri in the 1910s. She covered the walls of the Manti Temple with her work, a series of murals depicting scenes from the Book of Mormon and the trek west from her ranch in Wyoming.

Their new theology gave Mormons a language common with the Progressive Americans around them and a robust and satisfying theology that emphasized character, self-discipline, and righteous action. It allowed Mormons to recenter the boundaries of their sacred world from the community of Zion to the strict codes that governed their own lives and undergirded the continuing development of a distinctively Mormon devotional life that emphasized worship as a form of education and stressed adherence to a strict behavioral code. The administrations of Joseph F. Smith and Heber J. Grant, who between them served as president of the church for the first four decades of the twentieth century, implemented a number of policy reforms to promote the modern Mormon way of life.

Joseph F. Smith's reforms focused particularly on the youth. He circulated a letter to local leaders of the church encouraging members to begin a weekly "Family Home Evening," one night a week set apart for family hymn singing, prayer, and scripture study. He also pursued a formal affiliation between the church and the Boy Scouts of America, which he considered a repository of the Progressive values the Mormons had come to honor. The church's Primary for young children began consciously to implement Progressive theories of education, which maintained that education of character and spirit comes through activity and practice rather than memorization and recitation. The Primary began to implement group songs, games, and stories as means to teach important values like honesty and kindness to small children. Similarly, Smith and his successors transformed the Church Educational System, narrowing its focus from common subjects like reading or mathematics to rather a sort of youth ministry, designed to promote faith and educate young people of high school and college age about religious subjects, in "seminaries" for high schoolers and "institutes" for college students.

Joseph F. Smith also mounted a massive effort to promote participation in the various, and formerly voluntary, auxiliaries of the church. All young men and women were urged to participate in the young men's and young women's programs, all parents were asked to take their children to Primary activities, all women were automatically enrolled in the Relief Society, all men were assigned to particular priesthood quorums; increasingly, such participation was expected of all who wanted to be considered practicing members of the church. All these organizations were given standardized meeting schedules, duties, and curricula. The terms "active" and "inactive" entered the Mormon lexicon to describe practicing and nonpracticing members of the faith, and they bore with them particularly Progressive implications about duty, exertion, and effort. ·

When Heber J. Grant became president of the church after the death of Joseph F. Smith in 1918, he implemented a set of similar reforms centered on the temple. As Wilford Woodruff had, he encouraged the Mormons to include regular participation in proxy temple rites as part of their regular practices of worship. Previously, most Mormons would attend the temple only for their own rites, and rarely afterward. Reed Smoot, an apostle, testified before Congress that he had not participated in temple worship in the years since his marriage. But Grant urged all Latter-day Saints to "start the battle of life under the inspiration of the living God and with the blessings of the authority of the priesthood of God held by His servants who administer in the Temple."[23] He saw the sealing ceremony and the endowment not merely as a single rite of passage but as regular practice that would bolster Mormon spirituality through its very repetition. Grant himself went weekly and made wide note of the fact. Such exhortations found their mark: over the first few years of Grant's administration, from 1918 to 1922, attendance at the temple in Salt Lake City increased more than three-hundred-fold; some four hundred thousand endowments were administered in 1922—more than the population of the state of Utah.

To this increased pressure to attend Grant also affixed increased expectations. In 1921 he directed that "temple recommends"—certifications of good standing given to Mormons who wished to participate in temple rituals—should be withheld from those who did not follow the Word of Wisdom. The common name for a revelation to Joseph Smith canonized in the Doctrine and Covenants, it advised Mormons that "hot drinks," tobacco, and alcohol were not healthy, recommended a diet of vegetables and little meat, and promised strength to those who obeyed. For the previous hundred years most Mormons had understood it as a "word of wisdom"—sound advice, but Grant elevated it to a code, identifying "hot drinks" as tea and coffee.

Ever since, the Word of Wisdom has become perhaps the most recognizable social marker for Mormons in America, a boundary that sets them apart perhaps not in ways so scandalous as polygamy but certainly in ways that reflected the emphases on right behavior and moral rectitude that Grant and other Progressive Mormon leaders desired. After wrestling with adherence to the Word of Wisdom as a youth, Grant became a staunch advocate of the American temperance movement; he cited approvingly evangelical and Progressive reformers who argued that alcohol was as detrimental to society as it was to the individual. In particular, Grant believed that abstention from alcohol and tobacco was an essential and virtuous way to build character. As he said when he endorsed the Word of Wisdom to the young men and women of the church, "We, the youth of Israel, if we shall accomplish anything for the reformation of the world, must accomplish a reformation first in ourselves."[24]

Grant brought to his administration another aspect of Progressivism: its fascination with efficiency and expertise, its confidence in organization. He became president of the church in 1919 at the age of sixty-two, after a long career spent juggling the demands of an extremely successful career in business with thirty-seven years of service as an apostle. At fifteen he was working in an insurance agency; at nineteen he bought out his partners, and diversified his investments. By his early twenties he was wealthy. John Taylor appointed Grant an apostle when he was twenty-five. Initially Grant worried that his financial entanglements might render him unfit to serve, but his success in navigating the new economic order equipped him well to guide the church through transition from the collectivist aspirations of his parents' generation into the increasingly nationalized capitalist economy of the Progressive era. Grant struggled to balance the two, to preserve the distinctive idealism of the Mormon community but also to ensure that the church would flourish in the new economic order. He firmly believed that both were possible, because he believed that Mormon values and Progressive values were congruent: the diligence, sobriety, and self-reliance that had made the settlement of Utah possible and had made his own fortune would guide his people.

Grant took over a church in somewhat shaky financial circumstances. The Raid, an enormous blow to Utah's economy, had destroyed most of the church-owned cooperatives. By the late nineteenth century, the church found itself deeply in debt. During his brief presidency (1898–1901), Lorenzo Snow divested the church of sole control of several low-yield businesses and repeatedly stressed the importance of paying the 10 percent tithing expected since Nauvoo. by the early twentieth century, these strategies had saved the church from a large and nagging debt. However, after World War I ended, European crop markets regained normalcy, leading to a collapse in American crop prices. Utah's agricultural economy sagged throughout the 1920s. Additionally, Progressives in the federal government suspicious of the church's involvement in business had spent much of the previous decade investigating church-owned sugar-beet processing industries for antitrust violations. In the 1920s prosecutors handed down several indictments.

Despite these setbacks, the church was still deeply invested in Utah's economy, and Grant still held to Brigham Young's dream of "home industry" that would make the Mormon community largely self-sufficient. He spent much of his presidency struggling to save the sugar companies to keep Utah's floundering agricultural economy afloat, using his business contacts and financial talents to secure loans and balance their books. At the same time, Grant sought to find firmer footing for the church's resources in newer financial and service industries like banking, life insurance, and, most famously, the opulent Hotel Utah. In 1923, he organized the Corporation of the President of the Church to manage the various properties and interests of the church. His efforts reflected his desire to allow capitalism to flourish in Utah while at the same time maintaining the rather paternal sense of responsibility church leaders held for the state's economic and social health.

Perhaps the most impressive achievement of Grant's administration was the Church Welfare Program. Utah, so dependent on mining and manufacturing, suffered tremendously as the Great Depression dragged onward. By 1933, the state's unemployment rate had reached 33 percent. Each individual ward and Relief Society had its own means for coping with unemployment or poverty, but as the numbers of destitute families, young men drifting from job to job, abandoned mothers, and struggling elderly swelled, the bishop's storehouses emptied and the efforts of the Relief Society slowly succumbed to the sheer pressure of need. In the Pioneer Stake in Salt Lake City, where fully half of the men were unemployed, the stake president, Harold B. Lee, began experimenting with cooperatively owned farms, providing a share of the goods produced to people who volunteered to work either in the fields or in storehouses and canneries. The remainder was distributed to bishops across the stake to help those who could not work. In 1935, Grant asked Lee to present his program to the First Presidency, and the next year the program was implemented on a churchwide scale. In 1941 Lee joined the Quorum of the Twelve Apostles. He and Grant noted with satisfaction that the Church Welfare Program provided work as well as relief. Like many other men who had gained their success in the Progressive era, Grant was a Democrat horrified by Franklin Roosevelt and the New Deal. To him, the technocratic, powerful state that Roosevelt created seemed entirely to lack the moral values that the Progressives sought to incorporate into their reform efforts. Many Progressives found the New Deal's suggestion that the sort of voluntary reforms and disciplined uplift the Progressives believed in could not solve the problem of poverty insulting. Grant spoke frequently against Roosevelt in his later years as church president, touting the Church Welfare Program as a virtuous alternative to the president's policies.

To the leaders of the church, the syncretic cooperation between their faith and Progressivism was immensely useful and satisfying. It not only opened participation in the American community but also offered ways of interpreting their faith that seemed consonant with their needs and values. The adaptation, however, was neither complete nor painless. While many Mormons believed that Progressive ideas and methods strengthened or reemphasized their own distinctiveness, others recoiled from their implementation. The scientistic theology of Roberts and Widtsoe and the corporatist reorganizations of Grant and Smith did violence to the Mormonism they believed in, and they rebelled. Their dissent colored the progress of reform at the time and foreshadowed the development of Mormonism later in the twentieth century.

For many Mormons, the most troubling aspect of bureaucratic innovation was the slow decline of the charismatic and dramatic presence of the supernatural in the spiritual life of Mormonism. Through the end of the nineteenth century, when Mormons gathered in priesthood quorums or in Relief Society or in the small prayer meetings held many weeknights, they regularly participated in speaking in tongues, inspired prophecy, weeping, and impromptu laying on of hands. Heber J. Grant himself remembered weeping, feeling overwhelmed with the presence of the Holy Spirit during a small gathering in the 1890s when the apostle John W. Taylor stood to offer a revelation that financial difficulties Grant suffered at the time would soon be relieved. But in the early twentieth century leaders in the church began to discourage such practices through public letters and instructions to local leaders, and by the 1920s these spiritual experiences were in full retreat. In 1923 the First Presidency wrote to a stake president in Idaho about a woman who rose in Relief Society to prophesy in an unknown language, after which her Relief Society president offered an interpretation. The First Presidency urged her to "let speaking in tongues alone and to confine her speech to her own language," stating that it "was not the sister's place to pronounce a revelation."[25]

The motivation behind this impulse appears to be twofold. First, by the early twentieth century most Americans associated such charismatic experiences with the Pentecostal movement, a frequently interracial religious revival that most Americans found disreputable, lower-class, and rude. Pentecostals preached in tongues, shrieked, fainted, and practiced faith healing, all of which disturbed many aspiring middle-class Americans. The Mormon leadership, by contrast, was bidding for cultural respectability and believed that their religion was one of progress, education, and uplift. In the South, in particular, Mormon missionaries sometimes encountered accusations of Pentecostalism and strained to disassociate themselves from it. In 1901 one missionary in Virginia reflected on visiting such a service: "At night we went over to hear a Sanctified Methodist preach. His performance would have done grace to a Negroe revivalest, but for a white man, who took for his text the light of the gospel was truly a disgrace."[26] The emotional, unpredictable, and unreliable nature of such religious experience coexisted uneasily with the rational theology of men like Roberts and Widtsoe, for whom true religious experience enlightened the mind and character and could be explained rationally.

But as important, Smith, Grant, and other leaders wanted to redirect spiritual experience in the church along appropriate administrative lines. This was not a new impulse; it was not so different from Joseph Smith's reactions to the Kirtland visionaries a hundred years before. Mormons did not stop believing in miraculous healing or divine revelation, but increasingly the leaders of the church stressed that such gifts should be accessed through the priesthood hierarchy. Blessings of healing should come from men ordained to priesthood office and be pronounced by the authority of the priesthood. Institutional forms of spiritual expression replaced charismatic experience, impromptu administration, or sudden spiritual intervention. Joseph F. Smith himself, only weeks before he died, experienced a vision of Christ preaching to the spirits of the dead, as described in 1 Peter 3:18–20. It was added to the Doctrine and Covenants, but not before being approved by the general authorities of the church and presented to the church itself assembled in conference. Indeed, that it was Smith himself who received a vision affirmed the new order of things: as president of the church, he was the man entitled to receive revelation for it.

Restriction of spiritual gifts was particularly troubling to Mormon women. From the earliest days of the church, women had routinely administered to one another, as well as to men. The "blessing meetings" frequently held by Eliza Snow and other women in frontier Utah had featured such rites. Further, there existed a set of rituals that women performed upon other women, particularly surrounding pregnancy and birth. Many nineteenth-century Mormons associated miraculous healing and the right to prophecy with faith rather than with possession of priesthood authority. Margaret Gordon remembered fondly a blessing of comfort that Zina Card had given her, "not in the authority of the Priesthood but in the simple faith of a good true Woman Saint."[27] Through the 1920s and 1930s, the First Presidency and the Quorum of the Twelve slowly chipped away at the practice, arguing that healing and blessing were the prerogative of the priesthood alone. In 1921 Charles Penrose of the First Presidency observed that though there were "occasions when perhaps it would be wise for a woman to lay her hands upon a child, or upon one another. . . . But when women go around and declare they have been set apart to administer to the sick . . . that is an assumption of authority."[28]

Loss of control over such rites to the male priesthood was painful. Louise Robison, president of the Relief Society from 1928 to 1939, received a letter in 1935 from Martha Hickman, who lived in Logan, Utah. Hickman asked, "Is it orthodox and sanctioned by the Church today to perform 'washing' and 'anointings' for the sick [sisters] especially in preparation for confinement in childbirth? . . . We have officiated in this capacity some ten years, have enjoyed our calling, and have been appreciated." But Martha, having heard of stake presidents and other officials forbidding the Relief Society from performing these rituals, wanted, as she said, "to be in harmony." Robison replied, "It is our earnest hope that we may continue to have that privilege," but "where a definite stand against it has been taken by the Priesthood Authorities, and where such is the case we cannot do anything but accept their will in the matter." She told Hickman that if her local priesthood authorities were not opposed, Hickman's group could perform their ceremony, but "we wish it done very quietly." Further, Robison advised Hickman that "we do not advocate the appointment of any committees to have this in charge, but any worthy good sister is eligible to perform this service if she has faith."[29] The exchange reflects the great pathos and frustration behind the process Max Weber called the routinization of charisma, the eventual subordination of impromptu, charismatic authority to the institutional, bureaucratic authority that emerges inevitably as a religion ages.

A woman named Jane Manning James suffered perhaps the most at the hands of the Progressive impulse toward systematization and order. She was an African American convert who arrived in Nauvoo in time to meet Joseph and Emma Smith. Jane lived in the Mansion House with them for a few months before Joseph Smith died and she walked across the plains with her husband and children. Her husband abandoned the family in 1869, and Jane asked the First Presidency if she might attend the temple, receive her endowments, and be sealed by proxy to Walker Lewis, an African American man since dead who had been ordained to the priesthood in Massachusetts. She claimed also that Emma Smith had promised that Jane could be sealed to her and Joseph as a child.

She was refused. In the years since the death of Joseph Smith, the leaders of Mormonism had grown increasingly uncomfortable with the place of African Americans in Mormonism. In Winter Quarters a black man named William McCary was baptized and ordained and almost immediately began to challenge Brigham Young's authority, claiming prophecy and aggressively pursuing polygamy with white women. He was quickly excommunicated, and soon afterward Brigham Young and Parley Pratt began to teach that Africans were the descendents of Cain, the first murderer, and subject to the curse God had levied in punishment for the crime. Young declared publicly in 1852 that Africans could neither hold the priesthood nor participate in temple ordinances, thus denying them the endowment and the possibility of exaltation. Further, though Young specifically rejected the doctrine, other Mormon leaders, particularly Orson Pratt, began to teach that Africans, though spirit children of God, were less valiant than the spirits of other races in the premortal realm and thus received a lesser inheritance when they came to earth. In 1877, the Book of Abraham, in which an Egyptian pharaoh seeks the priesthood but is denied it due to his lineage, became canon, adding more scriptural weight to these ideas.

In large measure Young's declarations were symbolic, for the number of African Mormons in territorial Utah was vanishingly low. The two most prominent black priesthood holders, Walker Lewis and Elijah Abel, died before they could press very hard to attend a temple. But Jane was persistent: repeatedly in the 1880s and 1890s she petitioned to receive her endowment and to be sealed, even by proxy, to Lewis. Her persistence caused some dissension among the leaders of the church. While the apostles and the First Presidency knew what Brigham Young and the Pratt brothers had said on the subject, much surrounding the issue was hazy: how precisely to translate Brigham Young's statements into policy, how to determine what Joseph Smith had believed, and how to reconcile all these things with the evident experience of Walker Lewis and Elijah Abel. An elderly Seventy named Zebedee Coltrin claimed to recall Joseph Smith telling him that ordaining Elijah Abel was a mistake; others, like Joseph F. Smith, vigorously disagreed with Coltrin's memory.

The contest refracted into microcosm a struggle going on in American culture. Many African American activists seized on Progressivism to press for equal rights, arguing, as did W. E. B. DuBois, that African Americans must take equal advantage of the opportunities for education and political participation that Progressivism made available. But many white Progressives, uncertain about African Americans' capacity to participate in the community of expertise and civic engagement they were creating, used the very processes of systematization and bureaucratization then being invented to ensure that African Americans would be excluded. Many devoted evangelicals believed in the same Biblical racial theories that the Mormons had also absorbed. In the South, the same Progressives who advocated for laws banning child labor and enforcing workplace safety instituted the Jim Crow laws, designed to restrict African Americans from participation in political, economic, and public life.

Likewise, the tragic irony of Jane James's petition was that it transformed ambiguity into formal barrier. John Taylor and Joseph F. Smith ruled against Jane's petitions and formalized Brigham Young's proclamations into policy. Joseph F. Smith directed that the decision applied to anyone with even a drop of African blood in their veins—similar to common American genealogical practice during slavery, encoded into law in the South—and discouraged missionary work in Africa and in the American South. By the time Heber J. Grant ascended to the presidency, the doctrine of the curse of Cain and the formal barriers to African participation in the church were firmly erected. Jane James died in 1908, never having been endowed, though her wish was partly granted: in 1904 Joseph F. Smith agreed to have her sealed to the Smith family, though by proxy even though she was still alive, a measure instituted in order to prevent her from entering the temple. She was sealed to Joseph and Emma as a servant.

Louise Robison, other women of the Relief Society, and most painfully Jane James prized their membership in the church enough to subordinate their frustrations to loyalty. But others were willing to sacrifice their institutional affiliation to preserve that charismatic authority they believed essential. The most dramatic example was the loose collective of men and women who surrounded a man named Lorin C. Woolley, who was in his seventies when he became an unlikely prophet in the 1920s. Woolley was a dairy farmer from Centerville, Utah, a few miles north of Salt Lake City. In 1912 he wrote and signed an affidavit claiming that in 1886 the president of the church, John Taylor, while hiding from federal marshals in the home of Woolley's father, had seen and conversed with the resurrected Joseph Smith and had sworn to the dead prophet that he would never allow the church to cease the practice of polygamy. While there remains a fair amount of evidence that Taylor had indeed reported such a vision, a few years later Woolley made a more controversial claim: that Taylor had given Woolley and a handful of other men the priesthood authority to solemnize plural marriages along with the charge to keep the practice alive. Both Woolley and his father were excommunicated for rejecting the Manifesto, and by the 1920s Lorin Woolley began to attract the attention of a host of Mormons who had never been comfortable with Woodruff's proclamation. Some had been excommunicated for practicing polygamy after 1904, some had managed to conceal their continued practice of the principle, and some merely sympathized. Woolley's claims to authority, however, became a rallying point, and gradually his story spread.

In 1934 Woolley and three other men formed an organization they called the Council of Friends. Contrary to the church's close identification between priesthood authority and church organization, a trend that grew stronger with the reforms of Smith and Grant, the Council of Friends taught that in fact the priesthood was separate from, and higher than, the organization of the church. While the LDS church was in apostasy for rejecting polygamy, true priesthood could be preserved by a remnant dedicated to preserving true order of marriage. The Council of Friends immediately began to publish long theological tracts taking on the LDS church's claims to authority and refuting the validity of the Manifesto.

In response, the First Presidency issued a final statement denouncing plural marriage and denying even that the authority to perform such marriages remained on earth. J. Reuben Clark, just called from the State Department to serve in Grant's First Presidency, began a systematic investigation and prosecution of remaining polygamists, excommunicating dozens and driving hundreds more to Short Creek, Arizona (today called Colorado City), just south of the Utah state line. There, in long Mormon tradition, they hoped they could practice their faith in privacy. They found some success; with the exception of a raid in 1953 by the coordinated governments of Utah and Arizona that received heavy and negative publicity, the defiant polygamists were generally left alone. However, their movement has since been riddled with schism. While several thousand remain in Colorado City as the Fundamentalist Church of Jesus Christ of Latter-day Saints, multiple other factions rejected the move south in the first place, rejected the decisions of leadership succession made in Colorado City, or simply desired to return to urban Utah. While the FLDS church remains the largest organized Mormon fundamentalist group, the second largest, the Apostolic United Brethren, is headquartered in suburban Salt Lake City, and many hundreds, or perhaps even thousands, of independent polygamists quietly continue to reject the accommodations that Joseph F. Smith and other Mormon leaders made in the Progressive era, choosing instead to remain loyal to the defiantly unassimilated faith of their ancestors.

The most influential resistance to the Progressive project within the church came from theological conservatives who rejected the work of Roberts, Widtsoe, and Talmage. Their loudest and most effective voice was Joseph Fielding Smith, son of Joseph F. Smith, grandson of Hyrum Smith, and an apostle from the age of thirty-four. Like B. H. Roberts, he was largely self-educated and possessed a powerful and encyclopedic mind; unlike Roberts (or any of Roberts's associates), Fielding Smith consciously rejected Progressive philosophy and the influence of liberal Protestantism. Rather, he hewed to theological conservatism, rejecting enthusiasm for science and reason in favor of a strict emphasis on scripture. His sense that Progressivism's confidence was, in the end, slightly naive was ahead of its time, but in practice, Fielding Smith found mentors instead within Protestant fundamentalism.

A vocal presence in American culture in the 1910s and 1920s, fundamentalists argued for Biblical inerrancy, a strictly literal interpretation of the creation story of Genesis, and, more generally, the authority of scripture over human reason. Fielding Smith corresponded with fundamentalist thinkers like George McCready Price, who developed the theory of creationism. As men like his father, Roberts, and Widtsoe created a dynamic, Progressive form of Mormonism, so did Fielding Smith begin in the 1920s and 1930s to formulate a version of the faith that exalted revelation and downplayed reason, that rejected engagement with the world in favor of emphasis on Mormon exceptionalism, and tended toward a pessimistic view of the progress of human civilization. It would gain ascendency in the middle of the twentieth century. Fielding Smith was a generation younger than Roberts, Talmage, and Widtsoe, and the rise of his influence in the Quorum of the Twelve and the church more generally also marked their decline.

In particular, a confrontation between Fielding Smith and Roberts in 1931 symbolized the passing of Roberts's rational version of the faith. Roberts was in his mid-seventies by then, having served a long career as a general authority of the church, and had spent much of the 1920s on his magnum opus, a comprehensive theology of Mormonism he called "The Truth, The Way, The Life." He sought approval from the First Presidency, given so many times before, to publish it and was taken aback when Joseph Fielding Smith objected to certain passages that discussed what Roberts called "pre-Adamites." In an attempt to reconcile the creation story of Genesis (and the many other places in Mormon scripture where Adam and Eve are described) with geology and the theory of evolution, Roberts posited that generations of human, or human-like, beings had lived and died long before God sent Adam and Eve to earth.

It is important to recognize how conservative even Mormons like Roberts, Widtsoe, and Talmage really were. Their liberal Protestant contemporaries, such as the famous preacher Harry Emerson Fosdick, claimed vehemently that they were Christian even though they were entirely prepared to give up the literal nature of miracles like the resurrection of Christ, let alone the veracity of the creation story. To paraphrase Fosdick, he and other liberal Protestants believed they faced a choice between faith in religion as metaphor or no faith at all. Mormonism existed on a much narrower theological scale. This is not to say that Mormons were not aware of the challenges Fosdick and others faced. They were aware of modern Biblical scholarship, which posited, among other things, that the Five Books of Moses were a composite of a number of different authors and that the various gospels possessed a variety of theological and political perspectives. But they understood religion in a somewhat different way.

Though they were confident that the universe could be understood through reason and therefore believed that such scholarship might produce useful insights, they also believed that there were truths about God that could only be learned through revelation. This was a particular inheritance of their Mormonism, the legacy of Joseph Smith, and it kept these Mormon thinkers firmly bound to a fairly literalist interpretation of scripture. Since Adam and Eve were mentioned in Joseph Smith's revelations, most Mormons were quite unwilling to speculate that they might not have been real people. Talmage's biography of Jesus relied on conservative scholarship and sought to harmonize the gospel narratives, a feat most scholars believed (and still believe) to be not only impossible but also a hindrance to properly understanding them. Upon hearing the liberal Protestant Henry Ward Beecher's Biblical mantra "It cannot be history—it may be poetry," Roberts sneered at "the views of the late Henry Ward Beecher, and in fact all of his school, which I am sorry to say is rapidly increasing in number."[30] Though they had absorbed the method and mood of liberal Protestants, these Mormons were far from it theologically.

Still, Roberts's notion of pre-Adamites offended Fielding Smith and several other apostles. The old man was recalcitrant and refused any suggestion of edits to the manuscript, whereupon Fielding Smith, convinced that Roberts was promulgating false doctrine and suspicious that he was secretly promoting evolution, accused Roberts in a public lecture of desiring "to square the teachings in the Bible with the teachings of modern science and philosophy with regard to the age of the earth and life on it." He then instructed his audience, "If you hear anyone talking this way you may answer them by saying that the doctrine of pre-adamites is not a doctrine of the Church and is not advocated or countenanced in the Church." Fielding Smith implied that the doctrine of the church rather was creation in seven days and that belief in evolution was heretical.[31]

These accusations greatly upset Roberts. He protested to the First Presidency, and in early January 1931 both he and Fielding Smith were invited to present their views to the Quorum of the Twelve. In meetings following these presentations, James Talmage, a trained geologist, took exception to Smith's reliance on George McCready Price and determined to state his views in his own public lecture. In "The Earth and Man," delivered several months after Roberts and Smith clashed, Talmage argued that plants and animals "lived and died, age after age, while the earth was yet unfit for human habitation" and that Adam—though a real person—bore little relationship to Neanderthals and other early hominids.[32]

Under Heber J. Grant, however, the First Presidency had little appetite for such debate. After the presentations were concluded, Grant wrote in his diary that the dispute seemed to be over "the finest kind of things to be left alone entirely. I think no good can be accomplished by dealing in mysteries, and that is what I feel in my heart of hearts these brethren are both doing."[33] He instructed both sides to let the matter drop, stating that the argument would only divide the leaders and members of the church further, instilling controversy and rancor, and stated that henceforth Mormons should "leave geology, biology, archaeology and anthropology, no one of which has to do with the salvation of the souls of mankind, to scientific research, while we magnify our calling in the realm of the Church."[34] No longer would church authorities debate matters of doctrine in public. Roberts and Talmage both died in 1933. Their passing—and the decision that preceded it—marked a particular moment of evolution in twentieth-century Mormonism; the conviction Roberts, Talmage, and Widtsoe shared that rational inquiry and scientific ways of understanding the world in fact contributed to the progress of the faith and were one means by which humankind's divine potential could be realized no longer held sway. This form of intellectually progressive Mormonism fell to another form it helped foster: Grant's diligent, dutiful, pragmatic religion was concerned less with faith than works and far less with theology than character building. The optimism born of Widtsoe's and Roberts's metaphysics Grant took as a matter of course; it seemed entirely unsurprising to him that application of will and discipline could transform human character, and he was little aware of how revolutionary an assumption this seemed to historic Christianity.

Both forms of the faith could claim a Mormon inheritance: while Roberts and Widtsoe intently studied Joseph Smith's more elliptical passages and marveled at the prophet's visions, Grant stood solidly in the lineage of Brigham Young at his kingdom-building best. And neither, of course, really won or lost. Roberts's mark on Mormonism was indelible despite what Joseph Fielding Smith might have wished. Though Roberts's scientific premises struck Fielding Smith as heretical and would seem to later generations overly optimistic, the conclusions he and his fellow thinkers had come to about the nature of God, humanity, and eternal progression remain as deeply embedded within the faith as the words themselves; indeed, they formed assumptions that continue to guide the ways Mormons live today.

SEVEN

CORRELATION

1945–1978

I n 1940 Twentieth Century–Fox released *Brigham Young,* an epic
retelling of the Mormon exodus from Nauvoo and settlement in
the Great Basin. Produced by Darryl F. Zanuck, one of the last
great Hollywood moguls, it featured well-known actors like Vincent
Price (as Joseph Smith), John Carradine (as Porter Rockwell, one of
Joseph's and later Brigham's bodyguards), and Dean Jagger, who bore
an uncanny resemblance to the eponymous Mormon prophet he por-
trayed. Heber J. Grant, always concerned about his church's respectability, asked John Widtsoe to give the screenwriter a tour of Salt Lake
City and tactfully seek information on the production's treatment of
Mormonism, but he needn't have worried. Zanuck himself wanted no
part of polygamy or conspiracy. Rather, he believed the Mormon story
embodied the very essence of American virtue: courage, independence, heroism. Indeed, in an effort to downplay any sense of difference in some markets, he added the subtitle *Frontiersman.* For Zanuck,
a Jew very conscious of the gathering storms in Nazi Germany, the
mobs terrified of Mormon subversion were the intolerant villains, and
the Mormons themselves, of all people, exemplified America's promise of religious freedom and tolerance.

Grant was delighted. In the church's October 1940 conference he said, "I am thankful beyond expression for the very wonderful and splendid moving picture that has been made of Brigham Young. . . . It is a very marvelous and wonderful thing, considering how people generally have treated us and what they have thought of us."[1] *Brigham Young* was a smash hit in Utah, opening in a single theater and eventually expanding to seven more to meet the demand. It captured much of the essence that Mormons of the 1940s imagined of themselves. Young's struggle with his faith is resolved through his commitment to focus on the work necessary to better the lives of his followers. Though polygamy is glancingly mentioned, Young seems to have only one wife, and a fair portion of the story is given over to a definitively monogamous romance between a young Mormon man and a non-Mormon woman tentatively investigating the new faith. The Mormons are tempted by the quick and unearned wealth of the California gold rush but eventually find prosperity of their own in the Salt Lake Valley, thanks to a fortuitous combination of divine intervention and their own diligence. They were all that Americans wanted to believe of themselves: freedom seekers, hard workers, settlers of the West.

Hollywood's embrace seemed the definitive sign of inclusion in American culture, and the Mormons accepted it gladly. David O. McKay, who served as president of the church from 1951 to 1970, embraced Hollywood back, making his relationship with celebrities symbolic of what it meant to be Mormon in the mid-twentieth century. He eagerly seized the opportunity to consult with Cecil B. De-Mille while DeMille was making the epic 1955 movie *The Ten Commandments* and cultivated a lasting friendship with the director. This was characteristic: McKay traveled widely, welcomed publicity, and maintained relationships with Lyndon Johnson, president of the United States from 1963 to 1969, and Charlton Heston, who played Moses in DeMille's movie, among many other well-known Americans. *Time* magazine declared, "McKay was an affable new image of Mormonism to a world that had previously seen the Mormon leaders as dour, dark suited figures."[2] He led a public life to show that his church welcomed the public eye. A tall, robust, and charismatic man with a thick and flowing head of white hair, the first president of the church since Joseph Smith himself who did not wear a beard, McKay intentionally cultivated an image as the embodiment of his faith: benevolent, fashionable, hardworking, and public-spirited.

McKay's image-making owed something to those who came before him. He combined the broad-mindedness of Talmage and Roberts with Grant's emphasis on diligence and effort, adding to these qualities personal warmth. He was not merely optimistic; he was upbeat. Neither Grant nor Roberts would have named a book *Secrets of a Happy Life,* as McKay did. But in this, he was characteristic of his time: the Christian West in the 1950s was enjoying an age of particular prosperity. John XXIII, pope during McKay's own administration, was similarly famed for his ecumenical impulses, his joy in his ministry, and his beneficence. For both men, the world was to be embraced rather than feared. In the United States, the optimism of the Progressive era had borne fruit. Americans in the 1950s had triumphed over fascism, built a prosperous society, and were extraordinarily confident in the goodness of their nation. For culturally marginal faiths in America, accommodation was irresistible, and the Mormons were not alone in becoming a model minority. The Catholic archbishop Fulton J. Sheen hosted radio and television shows throughout the middle decades of the century, showing Americans still suspicious of Catholicism that his religion taught virtues they could embrace. He published more than fifty books, most famously a five-volume series whose title echoed McKay's: *Life Is Worth Living.* Most famously, the Protestant preacher Norman Vincent Peale, never pictured without a beaming smile, in 1952 published *The Power of Positive Thinking,* which made religion as much a means to a successful and fulfilling life as to salvation. It was no mistake that all these men wrote books with basically interchangeable titles.

To his cheer and clean-cut optimism, McKay added a resolute confidence in hard work, competence, respect—all virtues he believed Mormonism taught and America prized. He was a teacher of literature, and as such was given to aphorism. Over his nineteen years at the head of his church, his followers became familiar with many: "Whate'er thou art, act well thy part" or "No other success can compensate for failure in the home." He emphasized the importance of character and virtue, those things that had moved close to the heart of what it meant to be a Mormon. These ideals also made McKay seem an exemplary American to many. He was particularly insistent that the rituals of Mormonism, the worship services that had grown increasingly quiet and orderly over the previous five decades, be used as tools for teaching these values. While early Mormons had celebrated the effusions of spirit, the ecstasy and joy that flowed through their meetings, for McKay and other church leaders in the mid-twentieth century, the appropriate emotion for the Sunday sacrament meeting in which the Lord's Supper was served was reverence. McKay was particularly fond of the term. For him it meant not simply awe before God but rectitude, self-discipline, and the ability to sit still. He said in 1966, "The greatest manifestation of spirituality is reverence; indeed, reverence is spirituality."[3]

In the 1940s, McKay and J. Reuben Clark, as counselors in the First Presidency, initiated a reform of the music in sacrament meetings, the primary Mormon worship service, named because the Lord's Supper is administered there. Seeking to eliminate anything too ornate, too luxurious, too secular, they removed classical music from Mormon services and likewise eliminated many especially energetic or emotional gospel tunes from Mormon hymnbooks. Though for many decades in most sacrament meetings an organist quietly played Bach or Brahms while the young men of the Aaronic priesthood administered the Lord's Supper, in 1946 the First Presidency directed that silence was more appropriate. McKay was also the first high leader of the church to argue that the young men should be required to wear white shirts and ties while they administered the ordinance. He found white clothing to be appropriate because it was both symbolic and formal. Today, white shirts are the standard uniform of Aaronic priesthood holders.[4]

McKay's concern for the youth of the church went further. "Children should be impressed with the inappropriateness of confusion and disorder in a worshiping congregation," McKay said. "We must surround this sacred ordinance with more reverence."[5] McKay endorsed the administration of the elements to children too young for formal membership in the church on the grounds that it was a teaching measure. In the children's Primary, President LaVern W. Parmley, who served from 1951 to 1974, placed the concept of reverence near the center of her administration, seeing it as a means to introduce children to LDS doctrine. Parmley sought to teach children to use scripture, commissioning editions of the Bible produced especially for young people and distributing them among her charges. She also focused on music, overseeing the compilation of two songbooks that encouraged both self-discipline and education. As one Primary song, "Reverently, Quietly," put it: "Reverently, quietly / Humbly now we pray / Let thy Holy Spirit dwell / In our hearts today." Another song, "I Am a Child of God," was introduced in 1957 and has since become as well known among Mormons as "Come, Come, Ye Saints." In 1985 it migrated from the children's songbook to the official LDS hymnal. The chorus runs, "Lead me, guide me, walk beside me / Help me find the way / Teach me all that I must do / To live with Him someday," encapsulating in a handful of lines mid-twentieth-century Mormonism's devotion to the importance of right behavior and the church's responsibility to teach it.[6]

At the same time that McKay was working to guide Mormonism toward a particular way of being American, the faith was beginning its first serious expansion around the globe. When McKay became president of the church in 1951, its numbers had already swelled from some four hundred thousand at the turn of the twentieth century to 1.1 million. When McKay died in 1970, that number had surged to 2.8 million. Mormonism was not only growing quickly; its rate of growth was speeding up. This was in part due to a high birthrate. Ever since Brigham Young and Orson Pratt had described the countless spirits in heaven waiting to be given bodies, the Mormon leadership had discouraged birth control. Thus Mormon birthrates were rather higher than those of Americans around them. Most of the growth, though, came from conversion.

Despite the pressures of the Raid, the church's missionary efforts remained vigorous through the late nineteenth century. By the early twentieth century, church leaders generally extended calls to serve to young unmarried men, who were asked to fund themselves in a year or two's service in any number of places across the world. Heber J. Grant had spent 1901 to 1903 supervising a platoon of missionaries in Japan attempting to root the church there. Others went to South America, the Polynesian islands, and especially Europe, which had been the most fruitful region since Brigham Young and Heber Kimball had gone to England in the 1830s. McKay himself had spent two years in Scotland and presided over the European mission in the 1920s. In these years growth was steady, though not spectacular. In Europe missionaries often had to wrestle with stories of polygamy; in South America and elsewhere they were confronted with language and cultural barriers. McKay was determined to revise and modernize the program, so early in his presidency, he reorganized the top leadership of the missions program and instituted a number of reforms.

The first was an increased emphasis on missionary training and professionalism. In 1959 the age for service was standardized at nineteen, and McKay's administration also formalized a number of other procedures and policies, mandating, for instance, that missionaries travel in pairs and wear standard American formal dress. At the same time, McKay and several apostles began stressing that all young Mormon men were under the obligation to serve. As a result, the number of missionaries rose steadily throughout McKay's administration, and the church worked to provide more systematic instruction. In 1925 the Mission Home in Salt Lake City opened, providing missionaries with a few days of informal advice before they ventured out of the Salt Lake Valley. In the 1950s, many missionaries waiting for visas before they headed overseas began taking language classes at Brigham Young University, passing the time in preparation for imminent immersion in a foreign tongue. Gradually, these efforts formalized, and by the 1960s these missionaries were staying on campus at Brigham Young University for several weeks of intensive language training. Mission officials reported that these missionaries, unsurprisingly, seemed much better prepared. In 1968, the Language Training Mission, dedicated to the preparation of overseas missionaries, opened on the university campus. In addition to language training it offered courses in pedagogy, leadership, and scripture, and all missionaries leaving the United States could expect to spend time there before departing the Salt Lake Valley.

Another of McKay's aphorisms ran, "Every member a missionary."

He meant that missionary work was far more than merely the full-time missionaries' task of dogged knocking on doors. Rather, he believed that every member of the church should attempt to project a positive image of Mormonism, and he began with himself. On McKay's death, *Time* magazine put its finger on the Mormon leader's intentions when it marveled, "He was perhaps the first Mormon president to treat non-Mormons as generously as members of his own faith. . . . If he had not completely destroyed Mormon exclusivism, he had certainly tempered it with his own remarkable vision of a much wider, friendlier world."[7] McKay spent four months in Europe in his first five years as president of the church. He opened or planned temples in Switzerland, England, and New Zealand as well as in Washington, D.C., and Los Angeles, and he began the custom of inviting the public to tour the buildings before they were dedicated. In 1954 he traveled across South America and Africa. In all of these tours he met with local dignitaries and the media, generating a great deal of favorable publicity.

McKay's presence was only one portion of a broader campaign of outreach, and he may not even have been its brightest light. In 1955, the 360-member Mormon Tabernacle Choir toured Europe to rapturous reviews. The choir had roots in Nauvoo and the Utah territorial period and had slowly gained attention in the United States, having sung at the funeral of Franklin Roosevelt. In the 1950s and 1960s, the choir became something of an American institution. In 1959 it won a Grammy for its recording of the *Battle Hymn of the Republic*, and sales of its albums began to skyrocket. By 1962, 330 television stations worldwide regularly broadcast the choir's weekly Sunday morning devotional service. By the same year, the church's broadcasting company, KSL, had gained affiliates nationwide; in April 1962 fifty-two stations carried the church's General Conference from coast to coast.

Three parallel trends followed the mid-twentieth-century successes of Mormon mission work. The first was the increasing strength and importance of the church, both within and outside the United States. The second and third seem in part consequences of the first. They are, respectively, an increased emphasis on strong, centralized institutional authority (universally known as "correlation") and a growing suspicion of theological innovation in favor of an emphasis on correct behavior. Correlation was more than merely an administrative effort. As it identified authority in the church closely with the priesthood hierarchy and sought to discourage the possibility of schismatic groups or misinterpretation of important Mormon doctrine across a variety of cultures, it also produced a culture that some scholars have called "retrenchment Mormonism." This version emphasized Mormonism's claims to unique authority and truth and the incapacities of the rest of Christianity. It stressed the authority and revelatory power of the general leadership of the church. Because it sought to avoid the possibility of theological controversy it downplayed theology in favor of a strict moral code and conservative doctrinal beliefs about scripture, the supernatural, and the creation of the earth. It was also, therefore, skeptical about academia and philosophy and the sort of intellectual work that earlier Mormon thinkers had pursued. Correlation made it possible for Mormonism to become a global religion, but it also wrought its own changes on the faith in the process.

The church grew at an extraordinarily rapid pace from the 1950s through the 1990s, particularly outside the United States. From 1950 to 1960, the church expanded by nearly 50 percent; over the same span, the percentage of members residing outside the United States grew from 7.7 to 10.4 percent.[8] In 1960, the first stake outside the United States was organized in Manchester, England, and McKay's aggressive policy of building temples in foreign countries made it more desirable for many converts to remain in Europe or Polynesia rather than to move to Utah so they could be sealed or endowed there. McKay told a reporter in England, "We aim to keep our adherents here instead of encouraging them to immigrate to Utah."[9] This decision marked the end of the Gathering of Zion as Brigham Young had imagined it. Instead, McKay explained, the Zion of Mormon scripture was not merely defined as a literal community in a literal place but as "the pure in heart," the true believers, the invisible kingdom of God. This decision and redefinition reflected McKay's optimism. The world, he believed, was ready for the leaven of the Saints.

This growth—and particularly the presumption that from then on, the church would be an international organization—first seemed to pose a challenge of organization. Though by the 1950s the church had commissioned translations of the Book of Mormon into foreign languages for more than a century, little other material—hymnbooks, church magazines, seminal books like those of Talmage—existed in any language other than English. Even if translations existed, much of this material was shot through with American culture, sentiments, and values. It was routine, for instance, to sing patriotic anthems like "America" or "America the Beautiful" in General Conferences of the church, and Sunday school lessons frequently dealt with American issues like dating, frugal shopping, and proper dress. Further, finding local leadership proved difficult; most of the men who presided over missions were American, solidly middle-class, and well educated. In Central or South America, or even in Europe, many converts were none of these, and the American authorities of the church were often reluctant to turn the reins of authority over to them. Local men who remained faithful long enough to receive their endowments and who exhibited leadership skills were in short supply. Thus, many local leadership posts were filled by visiting missionaries. In 1958 McKay was embarrassed when a British journalist asked a pointed question about the London mission: "Mr. McKay, the London President is an American. Is there no Englishman or man in Great Britain who could become the London President?"[10]

The problem was particularly pressing in Brazil, where missionaries were finding great success but generations of intermarriage had made it difficult to tell who had African blood and who did not. Finding leaders in Africa was even more difficult. Outside of Africans of European descent in South or East Africa, where virtually all Mormon mission work had taken place, no native-born African member of the church could hold the priesthood and hence could not serve in a position of leadership. However, as early as 1946, letters from two Nigerians, O. J. Umordak and Honesty John Ekong, had begun to arrive in Salt Lake City, requesting that missionaries be sent.

Further investigation revealed that a group of Nigerians had discovered copies of the Book of Mormon and other church materials through the media and other routes and had begun to use them in worship. They organized congregations that routinely had one or two hundred members; in total it appears that several thousand Nigerians embraced a faith they learned about from the wrinkled, weathered tracts passed from hand to hand. They seemed particularly interested in Mormon ritual worship and in doctrines of prophecy and continuing revelation. One Nigerian's letter to Salt Lake City described reading about the faith in *Reader's Digest* and spoke of prophetic "dreams of various degrees about the Mormon church. I have even worshiped in the Great Temple with thousands of other brethren."[11] These people were largely second- and third-generation Christians who, typical of African Christians, tended to adapt the faith they received from Europeans according to their own interests and spiritual inclinations. Elements of Mormonism seemed to them particularly appealing.

The First Presidency and the Quorum of the Twelve were torn; they felt deeply the imperative to preach the gospel but also feared creating congregations among a people who would require a constant foreign presence to administer the ordinances because they could not hold the priesthood. After several years of vacillation, in the early 1960s McKay decided to send missionaries to Nigeria but was almost immediately stymied. The Nigerian government had gained independence only in 1960 and was sensitive to any hint of domination by another white nation. Offended at learning that Mormon converts in their country would not be allowed to serve as leaders in this new church, the Nigerians refused to grant visas to Mormon missionaries. McKay resigned himself to several years of negotiation, and in the meantime he began to consider how best to administer a church whose growth across the globe presented convoluted challenges: how to preserve doctrinal integrity, the authority of the priesthood hierarchy, and the emphasis on right behavior that had become so important to Mormonism, while at the same time embracing the opportunity to become a global faith.

The solution McKay and other general authorities of the church developed came to be called correlation. While the reforms of Grant and Smith had firmly established the priesthood hierarchy—from the general authorities, the First Presidency and the Quorum of the Twelve at the top to stake presidents at mid-level to bishops at the head of individual congregations—as the central backbone of Mormon organization, the auxiliaries of the church had a great deal of independence and power. The Relief Society, the children's Primary, the Young

Men's and Young Women's associations, and the Sunday school program each technically reported to the president of the church, but in most areas they were functionally independent. They wrote their own curricula, published their own journals (some sold advertising space, others felt that a bit too secular), pursued their own initiatives and programs, selected most of their own leadership (with the exception of presidents, who were selected by the president of the church), and in some cases had their own budgets and raised their own funds. Both Grant and Smith had made weak attempts to bring auxiliary curricula into sync with little success.

By the early 1950s, fragmentation, overlap, and dysfunction had grown almost unmanageable. The curricula of the various auxiliaries overlapped and sometimes contradicted one another; they claimed different influences and priorities, and bureaucratic turf battles were common. At one point some advocates of the Sunday school program wanted to consolidate all teaching in that department. The other auxiliaries understood the proposal to be a power grab and successfully defeated it, but the problem remained: if they attended all their meetings, church members would be instructed from three or four different curricula, each at best vaguely aware of the others. As McKay and the Quorum of the Twelve began considering the problems of exporting this patchwork quilt of the church overseas, it became clear that, as the apostles Delbert Stapley and Adam Bennion put it in a memorandum to McKay, it was necessary to "correlate the courses of study given by the Quorums and auxiliaries of the Church."[12] In 1960 a Correlation Committee was organized, and McKay placed the apostle Harold B. Lee in charge.

Lee was a formidable personality. He was significantly younger than McKay and many other of his superiors, barely past sixty, vigorous, intense, and dedicated to his vision. By 1960 he had been an apostle for twenty years, and his talent for organization was unquestioned. He had first come to the attention of Heber J. Grant after constructing what became the Church Welfare Program in his Salt Lake City stake. His committee consulted with the auxiliaries, requesting curriculum materials, organization charts, and statements of purpose. Its next step was to commission an Education Committee, which reviewed the various curricula and recommended that a new All-Church Coordinating Council be created to coordinate the activities and education of three age groups—children, youth, and adults—across the various auxiliaries. Lee took the reins of this council as well and began to replace the auxiliaries' old curricula with, as the jargon went, "correlated" teaching manuals. From then on, all the Sunday schools in the church would teach from the same manual. The Primary's lessons would be coordinated with those of the Young Men's and Young Women's organizations to ensure continuity, and the experience of being a Mormon from ward to ward and country to country became increasingly uniform.

Though his committee was commissioned primarily to draw the various curricula of the auxiliaries into harmony, Lee envisioned much more. He wanted to restructure the organization of the church, centralizing authority in the priesthood quorums, particularly in the Quorum of the Twelve. By the late 1960s, he had succeeded in establishing a series of committees among the Quorum of the Twelve—a Missionary Committee, a Temple Committee, an Education Committee, and so on. Declaring the need for uniformity and a clear power structure, Lee gradually drew the relevant departments and auxiliaries of the church under the authority of the appropriate committee. The reorganization drained some power from the First Presidency itself and undeniably from the various departments and auxiliaries of the church. Some resisted as best they could; LaVern Parmley, president of the Primary since 1951, retained her position and through sheer force of personality a good deal of independent authority until she stepped down in 1974. But the tide was inevitable. By the 1970s the auxiliaries' independent property and budgets were absorbed into general church funds, their independent printing offices had been shut down in favor of curricula issued from the All-Church Coordinating Council, their periodicals subsumed into three churchwide monthlies (the *Friend* for children, the *New Era* for youth, and the *Ensign* for adults), and their once substantial freedom and authority now supervised by a committee of apostles.

Correlation accomplished important successes. The model for Lee's reorganization of his faith's bureaucracy was the American corporation, which stood astride the world in the 1950s and 1960s with a confidence rarely seen before or since. Lee's confidence in standardization and simplification, administration through committee, and meticulous documentation of everything from attendance totals at Sunday meetings to the number of manuals church headquarters sent each ward drew on the success of American corporations, and his reorganization succeeded tremendously at solving the sorts of problems any large and growing organzation might face. The church's budget, for instance, had since the time of Joseph Smith frequently—almost cyclically—found itself in precarious situations. Another budget crisis emerged in the 1950s, when the church building committee, seized with optimism, built too many chapels that were too large, commissioning expensive architects, purchasing costly land, and building extensively overseas in anticipation of future growth. Though these facilities would later become useful, at the time they pushed the church into a financial crisis. Correlation's close supervision slowly drew the church back into financial health and has ensured it since. Correlation eliminated a great deal of overlapping effort, relieved the growing administrative demands placed on the president of the church, created a strong support structure, and streamlined programs that aided Mormons in other nations as they sought to root the church in their own communities.

Lee implemented correlation with one eye on an international church with a growing population of first- and second-generation converts. Correlation's curriculum is designed for accessibility, to speak to the newest convert as well as those raised in the church. Correlation produced a set of common practices shared by Mormons in Utah and Uganda, Arizona and Austria. In 1980, church leaders announced the creation of the "three-hour block," which moved meetings of Sunday schools, priesthood quorums and auxiliaries, and the sacrament meeting for the Lord's Supper into a single three-hour sequence on Sundays. Coupled with the new standard curriculum, a single universal hymnbook published in 1985, and regularized procedures for the sacrament meetings (a handful of short sermons from members of the ward, bracketed by hymns), the experience of church-going across the Mormon world became quite similar. David O. McKay had announced that Zion could be anywhere, and the correlated Sabbath offered a vision of what it might look like.

But to many critics, correlation's administrative triumphs came at the cost of a certain degree of cultural vitality. Standardization and simplification sounded the final death knell of the charismatic spirituality of nineteenth-century Mormonism. Though the curriculum produced under correlation has grown steadily simpler and shorter, these manuals have come with consistent admonitions not to venture beyond their content or use other sources in lesson preparation. In 2010, the priesthood quorums and the Relief Society used the same manual. Entitled *Gospel Principles,* it contains forty-seven lessons on topics like "The Sabbath Day," "The Creation," and "Praying to Our Heavenly Father." Most lessons consist of a few pages of exposition on various themes about the topic, studded with scriptural citations and quotations from leaders of the church. These are followed by points for discussion like, "Think about what you can do to keep the purpose of the Sabbath in mind as you prepare for the day each week." *Gospel Principles* instructs teachers not to "substitute outside materials, however interesting they may be."[13] In practice, this ensures that a common set of ideas are taught in all Mormon chapels every Sunday. That these ideas are the basic principles of the faith mean that Mormon Sunday schools and other church lessons function, quite intentionally, as devotional exercises rather than instruction in new concepts. The curriculum encourages teachers to ask questions that encourage catechistic reaffirmation of core beliefs. Further, lessons focus to a great extent on the importance of basic practices like prayer, paying tithing, and reading scripture rather than on doctrinal content. In one sense, correlation is the child of the reforms of Joseph F. Smith and Heber J. Grant. Correlated materials are designed not to promote theological reflection but to produce Mormons dedicated to living the tenets of their faith.

Other challenges in the new era of mission work seemed to demonstrate the importance of correlation's theological emphasis on strict moral behavior and adherence to authority and not on theological innovation. Many of the men McKay initially appointed to run the missions sought to innovate, to find new ways of gaining conversion. For decades missionaries had been taught to provide evidence to their potential converts, just as Harvey Wheelock and David Whitmer had presented the Book of Mormon as evidence of Joseph Smith's divine calling to William McLellin and offered arguments for the necessity of the restoration of Christ's church. B. H. Roberts had written a manual that instructed young missionaries in precisely these points. Alvin Dyer, who had made a fortune in air-conditioning before he was placed first in charge of the missions in the central United States and then the missions of Europe in the 1950s, conceived of a different approach. With friends on the Quorum of the Twelve and able subordinates, Dyer wielded a great amount of influence over the concept and execution of Mormon missions in the 1950s and 1960s.

Dyer's way of thinking about religion was a throwback to the charismatic, emotional Mormonism that grew from its Kirtland roots and had found expression in those spiritual practices that Heber J. Grant had sought to discourage. He taught the missionaries who served under him that "the gospel of Jesus Christ is not knowledge. . . . The gospel is a feeling. It is controlled and governed by the power of the Holy Ghost."[14] Dyer chastised missionaries who believed that they could convince potential converts of Mormonism's truth through education or persuasion or argument. In fact, Dyer insisted that this methodical process probably lost missionaries potential converts in the aggregate. He wielded survey numbers declaring that 70 percent of converts were ready to join the church after their first contact with the missionaries. Dyer instead emphasized the Holy Spirit's authority as the source of faith and urged missionaries to promote spiritual encounters in their investigators. Dyer quoted a Book of Mormon passage long popular among Mormon missionaries, from Moroni, chapter 10:3–5:

And when ye shall receive these things I would exhort you that ye would ask God, the Eternal Father, in the name of Christ if these things are not true; and if ye shall ask with sincere heart, with real intent, having faith in Christ, He will manifest truth of it unto you by the power the Holy Ghost.

For Dyer, this confirmation was all that was necessary for one to become a Mormon. He declared that his missionaries would be "challenging and testifying missionaries," not teaching or persuading missionaries. The missionaries under him were seized by his confidence, and conversion rates erupted. In the European missions Dyer presided over in 1959 and 1960, baptisms rose 300 percent; in the British Isles alone, 4,904 were baptized in 1959, compared to 1,404 the year previous. Other missions saw increases as well, though not quite as dramatic as those in Dyer's own domain.

Dyer's emphasis on spiritual rather than intellectual conversion represented, in its way, an attempt to shift Mormonism away from the highly disciplined, demanding faith of the Progressive era. Though missionaries regularly directed the attention of their prospects to chapter 10 in Moroni and asked them to seek divine confirmation of the Book of Mormon's origins, Dyer's rhetoric went further than most. Instead of optimism about the potential of human reason to understand God, Dyer emphasized human dependence on the divine. In this way he echoed the evangelical revivalists of the period, preachers like Billy Graham and Charles Fuller, who taught that human effort at doing good or learning about Jesus paled against the power of a spiritual encounter with Christ. Billy Graham taught that "there have been thousands of people who have been intellectually converted to Christ . . . but they have never been really converted to him."[15] Dyer mourned those "not able to sustain their conversion, which more than likely has been a doctrinal and not a spiritual conversion."[16]

Though Dyer gained great initial successes, eventually problems began to emerge. They were not problems symptomatic only to Mormons; evangelicals had encountered them as well, and the German theologian Dietrich Bonhoeffer a decade earlier had labeled them "cheap grace." While evangelicals struggled with insincere converts who believed that a proclamation of faith in Christ immediately absolved them of sin, many Mormon missionaries seemed confident that baptizing on any pretext was worthwhile. In Europe and South America, some missionaries and mission officials adopted a strategy called "baseball baptisms," invitations to local youth to join a small baseball league. The initial plan was to gain the interest of families, but many missionaries dispensed with the follow-up work that required and simply made baptism a prerequisite to play. Other missions established baptism quotas, first as a form of encouragement and later as requirements to enjoy perks like visits to temples or attendance at speeches of church leaders. In 1961 several mission leaders told missionaries that they should try to double or triple baptism numbers that year as a "birthday present" for McKay.

By the mid-1960s it was becoming increasingly apparent that thousands of people on church rolls either had no idea they were considered Mormons or were unhappy with the fact. McKay and other top leaders of the church, now suspicious of Dyer's strategies, greatly curtailed his influence. Though baseball baptisms and other such strategies sometimes reemerged in various missions, church leaders reasserted the primacy of traditional policies that required prospective converts to sit through a short series of lessons and testify belief in certain truths before they would be allowed baptism.

Rejection of Dyer's theology of quick conversion and programs like the baseball baptisms derived from the conviction that local Mormon communities required a firm foundation of converts with reliable faith and experience in the church in order to thrive. But it also reasserted older Mormon theologies of the importance of effort and character and sought to simplify and harden the boundaries of orthodox Mormon belief. One of Dyer's primary opponents in church leadership was Joseph Fielding Smith, the apostle and great conservative theologian who had taken on B. H. Roberts and James Talmage three decades before and was suspicious of what he saw as Dyer's irresponsible theological innovations.

In the years after World War II, Fielding Smith became Mormonism's most respected religious thinker. He was tremendously prolific, producing a steady stream of books and articles. Two decades after the controversy over evolution, he published his most prominent book. Entitled *Man: His Origin and Destiny*, it denounced evolution as a veiled repudiation of Jesus Christ's atonement and chastised science in general for seeking to usurp those areas of knowledge over which revelation held sway. Fielding Smith also maintained for fifteen years a column called "Answers to Gospel Questions" in the church periodical *The Improvement Era* and eventually published his collected answers in a popular five-volume set.

Fielding Smith's prominence prepared the church for a new conservative version of Mormon theology, enunciated primarily by Fielding Smith himself and his son-in-law, Bruce R. McConkie, an attorney who became an apostle in 1972. Unlike Roberts or Widtsoe or other thinkers of an earlier generation who consciously sought to use the tools of Progressive thought to enunciate what was particularly valuable about Mormonism, the work of both Smith and McConkie is characterized by an exclusive focus on the canon of Mormon scripture. They sought to grant it as much authority as possible and to take its claims as literally as possible. This style of argument gave their pronouncements, if only by implication, an aura of timelessness, a sense that it was not merely the intellectual project of a particular writer but rather the restatement of truths found in scripture. This made their work congenial to correlation's tendency toward simplicity and its emphasis on the theological basics.

Of course, Smith and McConkie interpreted scripture as much as Roberts or Widtsoe or any other Mormon thinker did, though the voice in their writings (particularly in McConkie's work), stentorian and authoritative, seems to brook no disagreement. In this way their thought was characteristic of much of conservative American Protestant Christianity, which for centuries has maintained that God's truth is accessible to anyone with reasonable common sense and hence rejects the need for education, interpretation, or ecclesiastical authority to explain theology or doctrine. This is one reason Mormons, like other conservative Christians, are suspicious of the academic study of scripture. Smith may have picked up this populist streak in part from his study of evangelical writings, though certainly such confidence in human ability to comprehend God is present in the Mormon tradition.

Despite these influences, neither man is a fundamentalist Protestant in Mormon clothing. The authoritarian tone that McConkie in particular employed can be read as an attempt to reclaim the charismatic authority of men like Brigham Young and Joseph Smith within the institutional boundaries of correlation. McConkie's declaration to a Mormon academic who disagreed with him on a point of doctrine is instructive: "God has given apostles and prophets. . . . It is my province to teach to the church what the doctrine is. It is your province to repeat what I say or to remain silent."[17] Such assertions of authority would be anathema to any Protestant fundamentalist, but they would not have sounded out of place coming from Brigham Young. Both McConkie and Fielding Smith were important participants in the great ongoing dialogue about Christianity, scripture, revelation, and humanity that Joseph Smith inaugurated. Their theology and the religious culture it produced dominated Mormonism for two generations and remained influential at the end of the twentieth century.

While most of Fielding Smith's important work was done in the 1950s, Bruce R. McConkie was prolific through the 1980s, producing a three-volume commentary on the New Testament, a six-volume biography of Jesus Christ, and headings for every chapter of scripture in an entirely cross-referenced edition of the four works of Mormon scripture issued in 1981. However, his most influential work appeared in 1958, when he was forty-three years old, fifteen years before he became an apostle. He was then a president of the Seventy, below the apostles in authority, the same office that B. H. Roberts had held. The book was called *Mormon Doctrine: A Compendium of the Gospel*. McConkie called it "the first attempt to publish an encyclopedic commentary covering the whole field of revealed religion."[18] Its doctrine was a distillation of that of his father-in-law and nineteenth-century thinkers like Orson Pratt and to some extent Brigham Young. It strongly dissented from the rational theology of B. H. Roberts, John Widtsoe, and other thinkers of the Progressive age, particularly their willingness to draw upon non-Mormon thinkers, though its organization in the form of an encyclopedia, with entries from "Adam" to "Zion," mirrored Progressive belief in the use, if not the authority, of reason. McConkie declared that God's truths could be discerned only through the revelation received in scripture and the statements of prophets since Joseph Smith, not through rational investigation or logical deduction. McConkie's positions were stark and uncompromising: "When the Lord speaks he has spoken. His word is to be obeyed if men expect to receive salvation."[19] Though McConkie's tone was stern, it is important to recognize that he was neither power hungry nor devoid of humanity; on the contrary, when he served as president of the Australian mission in the 1960s he was beloved by the men he supervised, and he was known for his graciousness, sincerity, and lack of pretense. He simply took Mormonism's premises with particular seriousness, and imparted them with a certain form and rigor characteristic of his influences and age.

For instance, though Heber J. Grant's First Presidency had left the question of pre-Adamites and evolution unresolved, McConkie's ten-page entry on evolution in *Mormon Doctrine* drew heavily on Fielding Smith's *Man: His Origin and Destiny* to warn that the theory was inspired by Satan to destroy belief in the atonement. McConkie declared, "There is no harmony between the truths of revealed religion and the theories of organic evolution." He labeled attempts to reconcile science with the creation stories of scripture "scrubby and groveling."[20] McConkie also forcefully asserted traditional Mormon views about the apostasy of the rest of Christianity, claiming that Roman Catholicism was the "great and abominable" church of Satan described in the Book of Mormon prophet Nephi's vision of the last days, and maintained that among the signs of the impending Second Coming was the "apostate darkness" he saw spreading across the earth.[21] The book echoed Orson Pratt's theory that Africans' unrighteousness in premortal life cost them the priesthood while on earth. Finally, it strongly endorsed the Victorian moral code of Progressive-era church leaders, particularly Joseph F. Smith's suspicion of face cards, dance houses, and much of public entertainment. McConkie had particular fondness for absolute language; he repudiated the sin of gossip—"a wicked, evil practice, hated by God and loved by Satan"—with the same summary judgment as "the evil practice of infant baptism," which was not terribly different from his description of war, "the most satanic and evil state of affairs that can or does exist on earth."[22]

More than a boldly asserted compilation of conservative theology, *Mormon Doctrine* embodied a particular worldview, a comprehensive theology, and a way of being Mormon. It preserved certain beliefs from the previous generation of Mormon thinkers, particularly their emphasis on the importance of human effort and building character, and connected these things to the achievement of salvation. Like many other Mormon theologians, McConkie distinguished between salvation, defined as resurrection to immortality that all humanity would receive because of Christ's death and resurrection, and what he called "salvation in its true and full meaning," which was "synonymous with *exaltation* or *eternal life*," inheriting an eternal family and ascendency to participation in divinity. Despite the unearned gift of the resurrection, McConkie emphasized that all human beings would be judged according to their works, their "obedience to the laws and ordinances of the gospel," and rewarded accordingly. Mormonism had always been a sacramental religion, tying salvation to its ordinances and rituals and departing from Protestant doctrine that redemption comes through grace alone. But Mormon thinkers in the Progressive era began also to stress the work of righteous living, self-discipline, and ethical behavior, and McConkie wholeheartedly embraced this position. Despite his sternness and moralism, he was as ardent a rejecter of original sin as any Mormon before him; as far as McConkie was concerned, obedience to the commandments was a matter of will. As he declared in *Mormon Doctrine*, "Justification is available because of the atoning sacrifice of Jesus Christ, but it becomes operative in the life of the individual only on conditions of personal righteousness."[23]

The retrenchment Mormonism of McConkie and Fielding Smith was quite different from that of Progressive-era Mormons and even from that of David O. McKay. It did not share their expansiveness, optimism, and interest in the world around them. In part this was the effect of correlation, but it also reflected growing discomfort with the turbulence of American society in the 1960s. Mormon leaders vigorously condemned the counterculture movement sweeping American youth for its sexual permissiveness, drug use, and even casual dress. In 1965 the church distributed a pamphlet entitled *For the Strength of Youth* to its teenage members, urging conservative dress, manners, and chastity and warning that abandoning these standards would lead society into decay.[24] In 1971, in reaction to student mobilization on other campuses, Brigham Young University added a dress code to its honor code, making conservative haircuts for men and skirts for women a condition for enrollment in good standing. In 1964, the First Presidency issued a proclamation in support of the civil rights movement, but some church leaders continued to worry that it would lead to political instability and moral decay.

Under the leadership of David O. McKay, the Mormons seemed finally to have achieved consonance with American society. But suddenly the nation seemed to be slipping away from them again. While McKay and earlier leaders of the church had spoken expansively about the growth of Zion and the progress of humanity, Fielding Smith and McConkie emphasized instead the moral decline of the world in which the Mormons found themselves. In 1946 Joseph Fielding Smith published a book called *Signs of the Times,* which drew on a particular branch of fundamentalist theology called dispensationalism. Fundamentalism's project involved mining certain books of the Bible—Revelation, Daniel, Isaiah, Ezekiel, and certain passages in the Gospels—to patch together a history of the future, the events to happen before Christ's Second Coming. It was profoundly pessimistic. Dispensationalists believed that because of human wickedness, the world was doomed to decay and degeneration before Christ's return to save it; for them, the Bible taught of war, famine, conspiracy, disease. *Signs of the Times* interwove references to Mormon scripture into the narrative the dispensationalists had laid out, and McConkie recounted much the same story in *Mormon Doctrine.* These expectations of the Second Coming brought to Mormonism suspicion of the world, trepidation about the progress of human efforts in science, government, and culture, and a tendency to see in America burgeoning signs of inevitable and immoral decay.

Through the 1960s and 1970s, a number of factors made retrenchment Mormonism widely popular within the church. One was the growing amount of literature that supported its ideas. *For the Strength of Youth* continues to be edited and distributed among the youth of the church every few years. Further, although McConkie was largely unknown when he published *Mormon Doctrine,* the work became remarkably popular. McKay had asked a few apostles to review it, and though they expressed general admiration for the project, one apostle produced a list of over a thousand errors, while another expressed discomfort with its aggressive and authoritative tone. Concerned for McConkie's reputation, McKay asked him to quietly allow it to go out of print, even though the first print run was selling briskly. Initially McConkie agreed, but in 1966 a second edition with significant revisions reflecting the criticisms he received from the apostles appeared. The book remained in print until 2010, when its publisher announced that it would not be reprinted again. For most of those forty-four years it was a perennial bestseller at the church's vendor, Deseret Book. In the 1960s and 1970s it began appearing in citations in the official Sunday school curriculum and was also quoted in addresses by leaders of the church.

The Church Educational System was another vehicle for the spread of retrenchment Mormonism. In 1953 Ernest Wilkinson became "Administrator-Chancellor of the Unified Church School System," a title no one since has held. Wilkinson served simultaneously as president of Brigham Young University and as director of the Church Educational System, which operated seminaries and institutes that provided religious education to Mormon youth of high school and college age. With the backing of Joseph Fielding Smith and Harold B. Lee, Wilkinson began aggressive efforts to transform BYU into a national university, strengthening its faculty, expanding course offerings, recruiting students from all over the country, and eventually growing its student body from five thousand to twenty-five thousand.

Wilkinson was also part of an effort to transform the church's religious education. The Department of Religious Education at BYU in large measure set the tone for the seminaries and institutes, and in the 1930s and 1940s, many faculty there had studied at a wide range of American universities, where they received training in Biblical studies and theology. However, in the early 1950s the apostles J. Reuben Clark, Joseph Fielding Smith, and Harold B. Lee began efforts to reform the department and CES as a whole, eliminating outside influence in favor of faculty trained in education rather than in religion, a move that Wilkinson supported. Lee pushed for the use of Smith's writings, particularly *Man: His Origin and Destiny*. Gradually, education at BYU and in CES as a whole drifted toward theological conservatism, and teachers sought to exhort their students to live the moral code of their faith rather than to encourage intellectual inquiry.

A comparison of two surveys of BYU students, one done in 1935 and the other in 1973, illustrates the success of these developments. While in 1973 at least 98 percent of BYU students affirmed the three statements "Joseph Smith was a true prophet," "Mormon authorities get revelation today," and "The Mormon church is more divine than others," in 1935 those statements received the support of 88, 76, and 81 percent of students, respectively. In 1935, only 36 percent of students felt that "creation did not involve evolution"; in 1973 81 percent felt that way. In 1935 only 41 percent of students agreed that "obedience to authority comes above one's own personal preferences"; by 1973, that number had risen to 88 percent.[25] These numbers indicate two developments: growing uniformity in doctrine, but also in BYU's student body, which became almost entirely Mormon over the course of Wilkinson's presidency.

Much of mid-century Mormon popular culture also reflected the same theological developments. *Saturday's Warrior*, a 1973 musical originally produced in California, is probably the most significant product of these years. Its first production drew on a long Mormon tradition of amateur musical theater, but its unexpected popularity encouraged the makers to fine-tune it, form a production company, and tour Utah and other western states with strong Mormon populations. It lasted through multiple productions in the 1970s and led to a filmed version in the 1980s (released on DVD in 2000, to strong sales) and a stage revival in the 1990s. Unabashedly sentimental and celebratory of its Mormon faith, *Saturday's Warrior* is full of reasonably catchy 1970s-style light pop music.

The musical's plot derives from a combination of a surprisingly dense and speculative reading of Mormon theology and a sense of confrontation with an increasingly corrupt secular culture. Even the title references popular belief that the 1970s were "Saturday," one of the last days, and that Mormons had to struggle against the world to preserve their righteousness. The plot leans heavily on the narrative structure of Nephi Anderson's turn-of-the-century novel *Added Upon*, tracing the fortunes of a group of premortal spirits from before the creation of the world through their mortal lives. The musical adds a major subplot about a young Morman man tempted by peer pressure to discard his strange and abidingly conservative faith in order to fit in, to enjoy the fruits of secular American society, to be, in a word, cool. Mormon parents raising children in the countercultural fires of the 1960s and early 1970s found these stories compelling; youth found in them models for their own struggles.

The vehicle for these confrontations seems particularly dated from the vantage point of the early twenty-first century: the young hero's friends taunt him because his parents are expecting their eighth child. In one memorable song, "Zero Population," his villainous teenage friends improbably praise birth control. Meanwhile, his Mormon family expresses joy at the privilege of bringing another of God's children to earth. Before this song, the audience sees premortal spirits selecting the families they will join and premortal lovers plotting out where and when they will meet on earth. All of this was speculation on the part of the musical's creators, but it became folk doctrine appealing to Mormons seeking assurance that divine intentions were deeply woven into their lives and that though these beliefs set them apart from the world they were indeed fulfilling God's plan.

The suspicion of American culture manifest in *Saturday's Warrior* appeared as well in the growing strength of various forms of conservatism in the church's ranks. Though Utah gave its electoral votes to the Democrat Lyndon Johnson for president in 1964, it has supported only Republican candidates since, growing more and more politically conservative through the 1980s and 1990s. But as with national conservative politics, Mormon conservatism derives from a number of sources: some overtly political, some cultural, some religious. In particular, hostility to large government derived from the anticommunist movement and growing support for traditional moral values drew many Mormons into conservative politics in the middle twentieth century.

Like many other American churches, Mormonism cultivated a deep suspicion of the Soviet Union's communism and official atheism and hence also became wary of American liberalism's confidence in large government. To some Mormons, communism appeared to violate the principle of free agency, human beings' right to choose their own destinies that derived from their divine heritage. McKay had warned against communism since the Russian Revolution for these reasons, but the most visible and vocal Mormon advocate of political conservatism was Ezra Taft Benson, an apostle whom President Dwight Eisenhower appointed secretary of agriculture in 1953. Benson served through Eisenhower's two terms of office. Benson's appointment was ironic because he opposed on political grounds much of the mandate of the department he had been appointed to administer; he believed that the system of subsidies and price controls entrusted to the Department of Agriculture under Franklin Roosevelt was socialism in embryo, and he worked to dismantle what of it he could.

His political profile, however, only grew after he left office. In 1961 Benson met Robert Welch, founder of the John Birch Society, an anticommunist organization that had settled onto the far right wing of American politics. Welch wrote long tracts uncovering and denouncing communist infiltration of the United Nations, the American political parties, and the government itself, at one point accusing Benson's former employer Dwight Eisenhower of being a communist agent. Nevertheless, in meetings of the Twelve, Benson lobbied for church support of the organization, and though McKay considered himself a Republican and an opponent of communism, he repeatedly curtailed Benson's efforts. McKay struck down Benson's requests to invite Welch to speak in the church's General Conference, to gain McKay's endorsement of the Birch Society, and to run for the vice presidency in 1968 on a third-party ticket with George Wallace, the conservative governor of Alabama.

Still, with McKay's blessing, Benson spoke frequently in many venues about communism's threat to the United States. When he addressed Mormons, Benson used theology to explain his opposition to communism in particular and large government in general. Invoking the premortal existence, Benson and other advocates of political conservatism argued that God's plan for his children required that their ability to choose good or evil remain inviolate in order to preserve the possibility of moral growth. Communism and other political systems that seemed to restrict this freedom were therefore not only unworkable or cruel but also hostile to God's will and therefore a moral evil.

Though Joseph Fielding Smith and Harold B. Lee, McKay's immediate successors as president of the church, restricted Benson's political advocacy more than the gentle McKay had, by the 1970s Benson's moralistic libertarianism had gained a vocal following in the church. Ernest Wilkinson, the president of BYU, worked to ferret out communist sympathizers at the university. Cleon Skousen, who taught at BYU for a time in the 1950s and later served as police chief of Salt Lake City, published a series of books detailing the communist threat to American society and arguing that American government was particularly blessed because of its adherence to divine principles that maximized freedom and protected democratic government. This particular blend of theology and politics was especially appealing to Mormons of the twentieth century. The tensions that had plagued their relationship with the American nation in the nineteenth century—polygamy, theocracy, the impulse to build a separatist Zion—had largely faded, and what remained were those things that had drawn the earliest Mormons toward the nation in the first place: the Book of Mormon's sacralization of the American continent; the early Mormons' conviction that the Constitution had been divinely conceived to protect freedom of conscience, ensuring that the restoration of Christ's church could occur in the United States; and a theology that exalted the individual and freedom of choice.

As influential in the 1970s and 1980s was the willingness of church leadership to reenter American politics in defense of what church leaders called "moral issues." Though regularly since the 1940s the authorities of the church reaffirmed their commitment to partisan neutrality, in the 1970s church leaders began exerting influence in debates over particular issues rather than in electoral politics. Like many other religious organizations, many Mormons were disturbed by *Roe v. Wade,* the 1973 Supreme Court decision that ruled abortion legal. The importance of sealing, doctrines of premortal existence, and even the popularity of *Saturday's Warrior* signal the dense connections among reproduction, gender, and Mormon theology, and it was not uncommon in the 1970s for Mormon leaders to warn against birth control (though more recent official statements have declared the issue a personal matter). Though the church has taken no political position on abortion, it has addressed it as a moral issue, leaving the faithful to draw their own conclusions. Soon after *Roe,* the First Presidency issued a statement addressing abortion quoting Doctrine and Covenants 59:6: "Thou shalt not steal; neither commit adultery, nor kill, or anything like unto it." The church's official position on abortion, reaffirmed in 1973 and again in 1991, calls the practice an "evil" and declares, "The Church of Jesus Christ of Latter-day Saints has consistently opposed elective abortion," though "there may be rare cases in which abortion may be justified," namely rape, incest, to preserve the life of the mother, or if the child would not survive birth anyway. Even then the church urges couples to seek guidance by "consulting with each other, and their bishop, and receiving divine confirmation through prayer."[26] Since *Roe,* Mormons, like other conservative Christians, have considered abortion a political issue; seven in ten Mormons told the Pew Forum in 2008 that abortion should be illegal in most or all circumstances.[27]

The Equal Rights Amendment, which passed Congress in 1972, proved more controversial. Stating that neither Congress nor the states could pass any law that denied equality of rights based on sex, the amendment seemed widely popular; by 1974 thirty-three of the thirty-eight states needed for ratification had passed it. Early in 1975 an unsigned editorial appeared in the church-owned *Deseret News* opposing the amendment on the grounds that it was too vaguely worded, that it might harm longstanding benefits to women like maternity leave and government aid to single mothers, and finally that its consequent breadth would harm traditional gender roles. "Men and women are different, made so by a Divine Creator. Each has his or her role," the editorial declared.[28] Barbara B. Smith, the new president of the Relief Society, delivered a speech declaring her public stand against the ERA, and by late 1975 the tide in Utah, which had initially trended toward ratification, turned, and the Utah legislature rejected the amendment. Two years later, the Relief Society organized a national letter-writing and fund-raising campaign and recruited delegates to pack the house at the International Women's Year meeting and vote down support for the ERA. Ultimately, the church's intervention swayed the fate of the amendment, revealing that the vast organizing potential and social capital of the Relief Society had not vanished under correlation, though many Americans who favored the ERA voiced the old fears of Mormon lockstep obedience, and some Mormon women voiced feelings of betrayal.

Mormon conservatism sometimes took surprising turns; though it often manifested politically, its religious bent gave it a particular cast that sometimes put it at odds with the national movement. In 1980 Utah had given Ronald Reagan more than 70 percent of the popular vote, and the next year the Reagan administration announced the construction of the MX missile system in the south of the state. But almost immediately, Spencer W. Kimball, the short, unassuming, gravelly voiced president of the church since 1974, announced that the church officially opposed the construction of the missile site. Kimball, who had previously led the fight against the ERA, took the administration completely by surprise. But he had long been a vigorous critic of what he believed was the dangerous militarism of the Cold War. As he had declared several years earlier in his widely reprinted speech "The False Gods We Worship," "When threatened, we become anti-enemy instead of pro-kingdom of God; we train a man in the art of war and call him a patriot, thus, in the manner of Satan's counterfeit of true patriotism, perverting the Savior's teaching: 'Love your enemies.'"[29] Kimball's declaration reminded his people and the nation of the countercultural potential of Mormonism—that it still possessed the capacity to defy the national mood in pursuit of what it deemed higher laws. The announcement turned the opinion of Utah's state lawmakers, and the Reagan administration eventually backed down.

Kimball was also instrumental in the single most profound transformation of the Mormon community since the end of polygamy. Throughout the 1950s and 1960s, as church growth climbed in Africa and South America, David O. McKay and other leaders of the church wrestled with the problem of the restriction of priesthood and temple worship from Mormons of African descent. African congregations required white leadership, normally young missionaries, to administer the ordinances, while in Brazil missionaries and local authorities spent hours researching genealogical records to determine who might be ordained and who might not. Some members of the Quorum of the Twelve pressed as early as the 1950s to remove it; others, like Joseph Fielding Smith, insisted that absent a clear revelation from God, it must remain. McKay spent many hours in prayer wrestling with the possibility of a change; though he concluded that he did not have divine mandate to remove the ban, he did direct that potential priesthood holders whose ancestors were under scrutiny be given the benefit of the doubt and ordained unless African ancestry were certain, a reversal of previous policy. He told a friend in private that he believed the ban was merely policy, rather than doctrine, and hence could be altered.

Throughout the 1950s and 1960s, as the civil rights movement swept away various forms of racial discrimination across America, the restriction remained. It became an ever more visible sore on the public face of Mormonism, a clear sign to many that Mormonism was institutionally racist. The few African American members of the church during the civil rights era felt the sting particularly hard. Darius Gray, an African American convert, discovered that he would not be given the priesthood the night before he joined the church in 1964. He immediately recalled his mother's warnings that the Mormon church was racist, which he had ignored while meeting with the missionaries. "I just thought how foolish I'd been," Gray said. But he had had spiritual experiences with God that he felt he could not deny; he had a testimony of Mormonism. "I was a proud black man; I was proud of my race and I was proud of my faith," he recalled, still remembering decades later the tension he felt.[30] He elected to be baptized, but when he went to Provo to go to BYU he was acutely aware of the divide that separated him from his white classmates and the school's administration, suffering discrimination both formal and informal.

Many college athletic programs began to drop BYU from their schedules. Civil rights leaders called for pressure to be applied to the church. For the growing number of white Mormons uncomfortable with or embarrassed by the restriction, it was the result of racism in the

Mormon past that God for inscrutable reasons had allowed to stand, and which called for humility and repentance on the church's part. The leaders of the church, however, dug in their heels, insisting that it would take a revelation from God to reverse the policy. For them, the issue was not primarily racial equality but the authority and continuity of church procedure. If the church was indeed directed by God, then God's intentions must be followed.

On June 9, 1978, well after the great age of the civil rights movement had wound down, Spencer W. Kimball abruptly announced that the restriction had been revoked. In a short letter directed to the local leaders of the church (now canonized as Official Declaration 2) he declared that God "has heard our prayers, and by revelation has confirmed that the long promised day has come when every faithful, worthy man in the Church may receive the holy priesthood."[31] Kimball was flushed with joy; he had regularly prayed and fasted for two years for the restriction to be revoked. In April and May 1978 he felt that the time might be approaching and visited a small room in the Salt Lake Temple every day to continue his prayers. On June 1 he invited the Twelve Apostles to a special meeting and asked them to consider the issue again. Those present reported a powerful spiritual manifestation and came to the unanimous conclusion that revocation of the restriction was indeed God's will. Two months after the announcement, Bruce R. McConkie, who had once asserted firmly that Africans could not hold the priesthood, declared, "Forget everything that I have said, or what President Brigham Young or President George Q. Cannon or whomsoever has said in days past that is contrary to the present revelation. We spoke with a limited understanding and without the light and knowledge that now has come into the world."[32]

Of course, many Mormons did not forget. As late as April 2006, Gordon B. Hinckley, who had been one of the apostles present at the meeting in the temple and was then serving as president of the church, admonished the members of his church for racism among them, which, he mourned, "still lifts its ugly head." "I remind you that no man who makes disparaging remarks concerning those of another race can consider himself a true disciple of Christ," Hinckley said.[33] But the old stories about the lineage of Cain and speculation about righteousness in premortal life McConkie had disowned remained in the volumes of *Mormon Doctrine* that sat on the shelves of so many Mormons, and Hinckley's chastisement is the closest the church has ever come to a repudiation of such doctrines.

In June 1978, however, celebrations among American Mormons were widespread and joyful. For Kimball, though, the meaning of the revocation of the restriction meant more. The final paragraph of Official Declaration 2 declares, "The Lord has now made known his will for the blessing of all his children throughout the earth." It meant not only that men like Darius Gray in the United States might hold the priesthood but also that the church's scope and ambitions were broadening. Through the middle decades of the twentieth century, the Mormons had struggled with the first challenges of expansion overseas, but after 1978 the goal of becoming a truly global church suddenly seemed within reach.

EIGHT

TOWARD A GLOBAL CHURCH

1978–2011

In the early twenty-first century, a typical Sunday for an active,
committed Mormon family means three hours of ward meetings: a
sacrament meeting lasting slightly more than an hour featuring sermons delivered by ward members, hymns, and the administration of
the Lord's Supper followed by separate Sunday school meetings for
adults and youth and meetings of the various priesthood quorums and
the Relief Society. Small children attend Primary activities. But this
Sunday experience is only the beginning of their church involvement.
One night a week, Mormon parents send their teenage children to
Young Men's and Young Women's activities. If this family lives in an
area with a high Mormon population, these children might attend a
seminary five times a day in a building owned and staffed by the Church
Educational System near their local high school; if they live in the
South or on the East Coast or outside the country, they might get up
early to attend an hour of seminary in a local church building.

Everyone in this hypothetical family likely holds a calling, some assignment in their ward, varying in responsibility from teaching Sunday
school to conducting the ward choir. Even teenagers help to run the
Young Men's and Young Women's programs. The most demanding
callings are those of the bishop and his two counselors and the presi-

dents of the various auxiliaries in the ward. It is not uncommon for these people to spend fifteen to twenty hours a week attending to their duties, and most hold a full-time job as well. Periodically, entire wards might commit themselves to a group project of some sort: volunteering at a local church welfare farm or cannery or holding holiday parties to which the extended community might be invited (with missionaries conspicuously present). Many wards in America sponsor a Boy Scout troop for their young men. The faith demands a great deal of its members' time and resources, but the ward community they build is often strong and tightly knit. Mormons often describe their wards as a sort of extended family, and families fighting disease, celebrating childbirth, or preparing for a move routinely find ready hands and casseroles. The practices of "home teaching" and "visiting teaching," vestiges of the theocratic community of early Utah, assign to each Mormon household visitors from the ward's priesthood quorums and Relief Society, who are supposed to visit at least once a month.

This Mormon family also likely has a strong private devotional life. Monday nights are reserved for Family Home Evening, and the parents might attend the temple to worship in an endowment session once a month or so. Church leaders regularly exhort members to cultivate a personal relationship with God and seek familiarity with the Bible, the Book of Mormon, and other Mormon scripture, and according to recent surveys they have succeeded in doing so. Eight in ten American Mormons pray at least once a day, while three-fourths spend time every week reading scripture. Nine in ten of those Mormons with children share these activities as a family. These statistics make Mormons among the most devout of American religious believers.[1]

By the late twentieth century, correlation and the culture it created had largely succeeded in standardizing this experience for Mormons across the United States. But curiously, at the same time as its forms grew regular, Mormonism's adherents grew more diverse. At some point in the late 1990s, the combination of conversion and natural increase shifted the balance of the Mormon population: by the end of that decade more than half the eleven million Mormons or so in the world lived outside the United States, and nearly half of those within the United States lived outside of Utah. This success brought diversity to the church, and correlation was instituted in part to manage it. As Mormonism took root outside the American West and became more fully integrated into American life, correlation allowed the faith to maintain internal consistency and preserve strong hierarchical authority. But growing diversity also wrought growing tensions, and correlation in some cases succeeded too well, creating rigidity and conformity as well as uniformity. The thirty years after the revocation of the racial restriction on the priesthood saw Mormonism fully confronting these challenges and proving, as ever, adaptable.

In 1984 the non-Mormon sociologist Rodney Stark predicted that there could be some 265 million Mormons in the world within a hundred years. He based his prediction on the church's spectacular growth rate in the forty years after World War II, when church membership had increased more than 50 percent every decade, much from conversions outside the United States.[2] Stark's predictions—that Mormonism would be the next "world religion"—were probably always overly optimistic, and Mormonism's growth rate began to slow soon after his projection. In 1989, according to the sociologist Roger Loomis, the church grew from 7.3 million members to 7.7 million, including about 319,000 converts. In 2004, the number of converts declined to 241,000.[3] By 2010, the church claimed some 14 million members, reflecting a growth rate slower than the exponential increase of the mid-twentieth century. Less than half of those were American.

It may be possible to blame the shift on larger demographic trends, but as important was the church's desire to cultivate a sleeker and better prepared missionary force. In 2002 M. Russell Ballard of the Quorum of the Twelve announced that the church would henceforth be "raising the bar" on standards for new missionaries. Screening for emotional and health problems, once rather cursory, grew more rigorous; similarly, missionaries guilty of certain past sins—primarily involving substance abuse or sexual indiscretions—would now be excluded. From 2002 to 2004 the number of missionaries in service declined from sixty-two thousand to forty-one thousand. Around a third of eligible young Mormon men from North America serve. In 2005 the church introduced a new missionary manual, *Preach My Gospel: A*

Guide for Missionary Service, which replaced uniform guides produced during correlation that missionaries often memorized and recited word for word. *Preach My Gospel,* on the other hand, replaces lessons with an outline of central doctrine and requires missionaries to read the needs of every investigator and alter the structure and progress of their lessons under the guidance of the Holy Spirit.[4]

Though regimented instruction has been discarded, the missionary experience itself remains remarkably disciplined. Each year some twenty thousand missionaries enter the Missionary Training Center in Provo, Utah. Eighty percent are young men between the ages of nineteen and twenty-six. Nearly all the rest are young women, who are allowed to serve after the age of twenty-one. Though only a handful of women had served missions before the advent of correlation in the 1960s, the number is rising. The church has generally stressed that though women are welcome, they are not subject to the expectation to serve that men are. Marriage is a preferable alternative, and female missionaries, despite being slightly older, serve under the supervision of men who hold the priesthood. They serve eighteen months, the young men two years. Regardless, all undergo a rigorous several weeks at the MTC before spending ten hours a day, six days a week with a partner visiting potential converts, passing out tracts, wearing the mandated white shirt and tie or skirt, trying to master a foreign language. They are forbidden to indulge in television, music, video games, or most of the other things that typical American youths enjoy. They can call home twice a year. Some will convert dozens, others none.

As the church has spread across the world, the Missionary Training Center, successor to the Language Training Mission, began in 1977 to open branches in South America, Europe, and Asia to accommodate missionaries from those areas. In 1977, a center opened in São Paulo, Brazil; in 2002, fifty-four African missionaries began preparations at a center in Accra, Ghana. Fourteen such centers now exist, an illustration of the profound internationalization of the church that has occurred since the revocation of the priesthood restriction. For instance, in 1999, three years after Mormonism's membership became majority non-American, 38 percent of the church's membership, some 3.5 million, were Latin American. In 2010 there was a temple and nearly a hundred thousand Mormons in Nigeria, the heirs of O. J. Umordak and Honesty John Ekong. In 1980, Spencer W. Kimball dedicated a temple in Tokyo; in 2010 there were some 125,000 Mormons in Japan, half a million in the Philippines, and another hundred thousand scattered across the rest of Asia.[5]

Despite these impressive numbers, retention rates for new converts in most countries outside the United States are low. In 2000, the Mexican census included "Mormon" as a category for the first time, and about 205,000 Mexicans designated themselves as such, even though church records counted 850,000. Attendance at Sunday meetings in Latin America and Asia hovers at around 25 percent of the members on the rolls.[6] Strategies of quick conversion have something to do with these problems, and *Preach My Gospel* represented a conscious attempt to refocus mission work away from quick baptism and toward a more lasting conversion. Gordon B. Hinckley, president of the church from 1995 to 2008, emphasized that new converts needed three things: a calling in their ward to give them responsibility and an incentive to return, a friend, and regular nourishment from "the good word of God."[7] In recent years, missionaries have been instructed to seek greater cooperation with local congregations, integrating their potential converts well in advance of baptism.

But conversion strategies are not the only reason that convert retention rates are weak. In Africa, for instance, Mormonism seems an attractive package: its emphasis on prophecy, priesthood, the ritual worship of temples, and genealogy fits nicely into the contours of indigenous African religion. It seems a surprise, then, that Mormon growth in Africa is behind that of many other Christian churches.[8] But the firm hand of correlation ensures that the same curriculum is used in Mormon congregations the world over; the western formal uniform of white shirts and ties for men is expected at the temples and in the meetinghouses of Japan, Nigeria, and Chile, though women have slightly more latitude in their dress. Mormon chapels in Africa are built using one of the handful of standardized plans used everywhere else in the world. They are equipped with pianos and organs, European instruments, and the hymns are often the same used in the United States. American missionaries and church officials instruct African worshippers to avoid the clapping, stomping of feet, and swaying common in most other African churches. Drums, traditionally the sacred instrument of Africa, are not used. As one African convert instructed his congregation, "No more dancing and no more clapping, since our brothers in America don't do it."[9]

Correlation's success at promoting uniformity seems also to have ingrained within Mormonism the particular austere piety of the American Protestant middle class. The church continues to have a difficult time disentangling the cultural experience of American Mormonism from those elements that lie at the heart of Mormonism as a religion. Dallin Oaks, an apostle since 1984, has warned that "the traditions or culture or way of life of a people inevitably include some practices that must be changed by those who wish to qualify for God's choicest blessings," calling for converts to embrace the Sabbath practices of American Mormonism, adherence to the Word of Wisdom over ethnic dietary habits, and rejection of a "culture of dependency."[10] In South America some groups perceive Mormons as, essentially, agents of American assimilation, and Mormon missionaries and chapels have been assaulted multiple times since the 1980s. Some missionaries have been killed.

In part this investment in American culture may be due to the makeup of the church's highest leadership: that the First Presidency and the Quorum of the Twelve serve for life means that nearly all the men currently in those positions were born in the western United States into the church of Heber J. Grant. The church has not yet had a president born after World War II and likely will not for some years to come. The current president, Thomas S. Monson, was born in 1929, and as of 2011 only two members of the Quorum of the Twelve were born after 1950. Only one, Dieter Uchtdorf of Germany, was born outside the United States. Because the church leadership functions according to the principle of seniority, it will take time for members of the international church to climb the ranks. While Mormonism may be a global religion—it is present on every continent, the Book of Mormon is available in fifty-one languages, and the church's semiannual General Conference can be seen via satellite, translated into forty-three languages—it is not yet a world religion, one that, like Islam or

Catholicism, has found a way to adapt its forms to share its meaning in a panoply of cultures. There are, however, signs of change: Dallin Oaks and his fellow apostle Jeffrey Holland each spent several years in the early 2000s living in the Philippines and Chile, respectively, seeking to understand the challenges expansion into those nations posed to the church. Additionally, recent reforms in church administration have granted more power to local leaders, with a mandate to adapt select practices—albeit few—to local conditions.

Correlation has, however, managed to prevent large-scale schism and fragmentation. The Nigerian Christians who began to worship with Mormon materials in the 1940s and 1950s are the strongest independent community derived from the church's work overseas, and they willingly surrendered their independence upon the arrival of missionaries. A number of small schismatic groups claiming rival prophets and rival scripture exist, most scattered across Utah or the West and populated by former members of the Church of Jesus Christ of Latter-day Saints. One, the Latter Day Church of Jesus Christ, based in England, is headed by Matthew Philip Gill, who claims to be the true successor of Joseph Smith and has produced a work of scripture that mirrors the Book of Mormon in plot while locating the promised land in the British Isles rather than the Americas. None, including Gill's church, have more than a few dozen members.

The LDS church's strongest Mormon competitor, the Community of Christ (the name the Reorganized Church took in 2001), is growing at a faster rate than the LDS church in Africa. Like the LDS church, its membership of 250,000 is less than half American, though in the United States its population is aging rapidly. Unlike the LDS church, it has pursued policies of theological liberalization, choosing to ordain women to the priesthood in 1984 and strongly committing itself to social justice and peace. Other Mormon churches lag far behind. None of the fundamentalist Mormon churches have a strong presence outside the American continent.

Mormonism is expanding in the United States as well. Mormons have been leaving Utah to study and live elsewhere in the United States since the time of Brigham Young, who sent both men and women to eastern schools to study medicine or law. In the early twentieth century, many Church Educational System employees went to the University of Chicago and other schools to study religion. In the nineteenth and early twentieth centuries, most of them returned. By the mid-twentieth century the rate of return slowed, creating Mormon communities scattered across the United States. Most were centered on certain large university cities like New York, Chicago, Los Angeles, and Washington, D.C. Many of these Mormon emigrants were young and single, seeking education or jobs increasingly available in a professionalizing, urbanizing America. In the early years Mormon infrastructure was often weak in these places, and Mormons would worship in homes or in rented facilities or simply prove unable to gather enough critical mass to worship communally at all. Many slipped into inactivity in the church.

Others, however, did not. Many single Mormons moved, married, and settled in the city of their education or elsewhere where they might find employment. Gradually these communities accrued enough local strength to put down the roots of Mormon institutions. The most important ingredient was sufficient numbers of married men of some worldly success who could assume local leadership positions. This leadership then would seek permanent worship facilities, cultivate relationships with other community institutions, and build up a Mormon infrastructure: seminaries for high school youth, institutes for college youth, strong auxiliaries in the wards, and eventually perhaps a temple built nearby. These institutions encourage Mormon families to stay in the area and further strengthen the Mormon community there, though in a last faint echo of the pioneer dream of the Gathering of Zion, many Mormons outside Utah send their children to Brigham Young University to experience life, at least for a season, in a community dominated by their faith.

The great success of the outmigration is the further integration of Mormons into the texture of American life. By the 1950s and 1960s, Mormons had attained success across the United States in a number of professions: politics, business, academia, and law, among others. A particular hub of migrants was Washington, D.C. Reed Smoot, J. Reuben Clark, Ezra Taft Benson, and a number of other Mormons had held high positions in American government, and other Mormons had followed, taking lower-level bureaucratic positions or working in law or trade. In 1927, J. Willard Marriott, son of a farmer from Ogden, Utah, opened a root beer stand in Washington, having picked the city after a visit on his way home to Utah from his mission. Thirty years later he opened his first hotel in the Washington suburb of Arlington, Virginia, and ten years after that he owned a chain of hotels across the nation. By 1968 there were enough Mormons in Washington that the city was chosen to host the first temple built east of the Mississippi River, a spectacular building that has become a landmark for local drivers.

By the 1980s a number of other Mormons had become prominent outside Utah: Steve Young, a descendant of Brigham Young's and graduate of BYU, played quarterback for the San Francisco 49ers in the 1980s and 1990s and won the Most Valuable Player award in the National Football League in 1992 and 1994. In 1989, Stephen R. Covey, a graduate of BYU and Harvard Business School, published *The Seven Habits of Highly Effective People,* a self-help book that drew upon his experiences as a missionary and lay leader in the church; by the mid–1990s, the book had proved monumentally successful, and Covey had formed FranklinCovey, a globally successful business con- sulting and services firm. Orson Scott Card, born in Utah and edu- cated, like Covey and Young, at BYU, moved to Indiana to attend graduate school at Notre Dame in the early 1980s but dropped out to work for a computer magazine in North Carolina. By 1986 he had become the first author to win both the prestigious Hugo and Nebula awards in consecutive years for his novels *Ender's Game* and *Speaker for the Dead,* both now considered science fiction classics. Many observers have noted that Mormon themes of agency, freedom, and creation echo through his works.

The successes and challenges of one particular Mormon family ex- emplify the effects of the outmigration as well as any other. In 1929 George Romney, the grandson of polygamists who had fled to Mexico to preserve their marriages, was twenty-two years old. He had studied briefly at the University of Utah and served a mission in Scotland but was not much interested in his studies. Instead he followed the family of his high school sweetheart to Washington, D.C., and upon marrying her secured a series of jobs as a lobbyist. After ten years in Washington he moved to Detroit to take a job with the Automobile Manufacturers Association. By 1954 he was president of American Motors, and over the next ten years he gained national attention for his part in making the company a national success. At the same time as Romney's fame was growing, he was serving as an anchor in Michigan's Mormon community. During his tenure at American Motors he was stake president of the Detroit stake, supervising twenty-seven hundred Mormons in the region encompassing Detroit, Ann Arbor, and sections of Ontario, Canada. In 1962 he fasted and prayed for two days before deciding to run for governor of Michigan. He was elected, and in 1968 he mounted an unsuccessful but credible bid for the presidency. Remarkably, his faith was rarely mentioned in any of his political campaigns, for Mormonism by the 1960s had become unexceptional to most Americans, and Romney believed that it had taught him the very values that had made him a successful businessman. As he told *Time,* "My religion is my most precious possession. Except for it, I could easily have become excessively occupied with industry. Sharing responsibility for church work has been a vital counterbalance in my life."[11]

In recent years, however, the outmigration and the cultural assimilation that comes with it have contributed to tensions within the United States similar to those without: suspicion from non-Mormons for reasons political and religious, as well as irritation at the standardization and uniformity correlation wrought, and these have manifested in American politics. As America's foremost Mormon political family, the Romneys have naturally been caught up in these battles. In 2001 Gordon B. Hinckley, president of the church, dedicated a temple in Belmont, Massachusetts, just outside Boston. Near him sat the local stake president, Mitt Romney, George's son, a successful Boston businessman. It was the end of a long and painful struggle with the Belmont community. Most Mormons greet the announcement of a new temple with excitement and anticipation; this is particularly true for Mormons outside Utah, who often have to travel great distances if they wish to participate in temple worship or have their weddings sealed. But because the church prefers to build temples in quiet and scenic residential areas, the buildings are often not popular among non-Mormon locals who dislike the prospect of a large and heavily lit edifice attracting streams of Mormons to their neighborhoods.

These complaints proved particularly powerful in Belmont. The church, having searched for land in Boston for many years, finally decided to place the temple on a portion of a lot in a Belmont neighborhood originally purchased for a single meetinghouse, invoking an old Massachusetts state law permitting religions wide latitude in the construction of religious buildings even in areas zoned for residences. Feeling rudely surprised, the residents of the neighborhood sued to overturn the law, charging that it violated the First Amendment's prohibition against a government establishment of religion. They particularly complained about the height of the steeple bearing the statue of the angel Moroni, which is placed on every Mormon temple. The acrimonious legal battles dragged on for five years, until the residents lost appeals in the Massachusetts and the U.S. Supreme Courts. All hope of reconciliation seemed lost; Chuck Counselman, a Belmont resident who lived near the temple site, later expressed resentment at "the Justices' apparent disinterest in the facts and the law, and their sympathetic acceptance of the Church's key argument, which was not a legal argument at all. It was that 'God wants the Church to have this steeple.'"[12]

In Counselman's complaints the old tensions between Mormonism and American culture echo from across the decades: wariness of Mormon claims to be directed by revelation, discomfort with the temple's aggressive assertion of the rituals and practices that set Mormons apart, and ultimately fear of the intervention of Mormon religious power in American politics. Mitt Romney, a wealthy businessman who ran unsuccessfully for the Senate in 1994, helped to orchestrate the church's defense. Later, evidence emerged that Romney and Utah senator (and Mormon) Orrin Hatch had sought the help of Massachusetts senator Ted Kennedy, hoping that Kennedy's powerful influence in Massachusetts politics might help clear away legal challenges. Even years after the fact, when Hatch told the story at Kennedy's memorial service in 2009, for many like Counselman who resented what they saw as a Mormon willingness to manipulate the processes of American politics to their own ends, the sting remained.

These suspicions roared to the center of the public square in 2007 and 2008, when Mitt Romney, having served a term as governor of Massachusetts, made a bid for the American presidency. He made more headway than his father. George's 1968 bid peaked before he made his formal announcement in the fall of 1967, and he steadily lost ground in the polls to Richard Nixon until withdrawing before primaries began in early 1968. The younger Romney proved a legitimate contender well into primary season, ultimately finishing with wins in eleven states and in a dead heat with former Arkansas governor Mike Huckabee for second place to Arizona senator John McCain. Nevertheless, Mormonism weighed Mitt Romney down more than it had his father. Profiles of George tended to emphasize Mormonism's contribution to his strong family life, his work ethic, and his diligence. In 2008, even some Mormons were surprised when polls indicated that about a quarter of Americans believed that Romney's Mormonism disqualified him for the presidency. In June 2011, as Romney began preparations for another campaign, Gallup declared the number to be 22 percent.[13]

The difference indicates the changing dynamics between American religion and American politics. Romney's faith attracted criticism from both the political right and the left. The left-leaning periodical *The New Republic* voiced traditional fear of Mormon ecclesiastical authority, worrying that a potential Mormon president would be a puppet of the prophet, and other Americans voiced similar fears. But Romney's strongest critics were theologically and politically conservative Christians. In the late 1970s and early 1980s a broad coalition of socially conservative American Christians, who had largely been alienated from politics since the failures of the fundamentalist movement in the 1920s, began again to organize politically, discomfited with many of the same social issues that had driven Mormons to embrace political conservatism. In 1979 the Baptist minister Jerry Falwell organized the Moral Majority, which protested abortion, homosexuality, and the Equal Rights Amendment. The Moral Majority rapidly gained strength, and in 1980 its support for Ronald Reagan proved decisive. Though the Moral Majority dissolved in 1989, its legacy persists; conservative evangelicals in the early twenty-first century remain deeply involved in politics, particularly in the Republican Party.

Though the Moral Majority's political agenda seemed remarkably similar to the inclinations of many Mormons, Mormons were not allowed to participate in its events and organization. Conservative evangelicals remain very suspicious of a religion that many believe is not Christian but rather a cult whose beliefs are a lurid, even Satanic, parody of traditional Christianity. This is hardly true of all—or even most—evangelicals in America, but to a vocal minority Mormonism has been a dangerous heresy since its founding. In the 1970s and 1980s the efforts of the anti-cult movement intensified: Mormons, along with Jehovah's Witnesses, Muslims, and other dangerous heretics and apostates have received a great deal of attention. Most well known is the evangelical ex-Mormon Ed Decker, whose 1984 book (later turned into a film) *The God Makers: A Shocking Exposé of What Mormons Really Believe* selectively quotes Mormon scripture and the words of nineteenth-century Mormon leaders to paint an unflattering picture of the faith; it was designed to equip evangelicals to ask Mormons disturbing questions. In late 2007 the well-known Florida evangelist Bill Keller sent an email to the 2.4 million Americans on his mailing list warning that a vote for Mitt Romney was a vote for Satan.

The theological differences between Mormonism and traditional Christianity are real, though there are more overlaps than many might suppose. Frustrating to many traditional Christians who seek to engage Mormons in dialogue or even debate is the seeming lack of interest or education most Mormons—even the First Presidency or the Quorum of the Twelve—have in theological discussion. There is no trained Mormon clergy. The Church Educational System today espouses not only the conservative theology of Bruce R. McConkie but also his lack of interest in scholarship outside his own tradition. CES's work resembles a youth ministry more closely than it does the seminaries of other faiths. Similarly, leaders of the church today, unlike James Talmage or John Widtsoe or McConkie, avoid writing books about theology in favor of devotional or homiletic texts. This trend is likely intentional. After the public disputes over evolution in the 1930s and after correlation (a preemptive strike against potential doctrinal schism) the leaders of the church have decided to leave theological dispute alone. They conceive of their task largely in terms of ministry and pastoral work, consonant with modern Mormons' conception of their faith as a way of life and a system of ethical behavior rather than a theological argument.

It is thus difficult to pin down what precisely orthodox Mormon belief is. Mormons who wish to enter the temples must affirm their belief in Jesus Christ's divine sonship and atonement, in the truth of Joseph Smith's divine mission to restore Christ's church, and in the priesthood authority of the present leaders of the church. That is all, and particular key terms in those beliefs remain intentionally undefined. Through the church's 180-year existence, Orson Pratt, B. H. Roberts, McConkie, and many other authors have each offered up versions of Mormonism, and though ideas from many Mormon writers have seeped into the common discourse of the church, none is considered a final authority on what Mormons must believe. In an interview with *Time* in 1997, a journalist asked Gordon B. Hinckley about the doctrine that God was once a man, which Joseph Smith seemed to advocate. "I don't know that we teach it. I don't know that we emphasize it," he said.[14] The reply was less an evasion than a recognition of the modern place of theology in the church: the focus of Mormonism is very much not on the particulars of belief but whether a member is in the pews every week, holds a calling, and can be relied on if a bishop is looking for somebody to drive an elderly widow to the hospital.

The doctrine discussed in Sunday schools, in official church publications, and in the church's General Conference rarely moves beyond these points. Mormons today believe that God, Jesus, and the Holy Spirit are three separate individuals, that the first two have bodies and that they form the Trinity, or Godhead, by virtue of their unity of purpose and agreement with one another. They believe that they are the spirit children of God the Father (and perhaps a Heavenly Mother, though she receives little attention in official venues), sent to earth to gain bodies and to learn to obey God's commandments and develop their characters. They believe that this effort was made possible by the atoning death of Jesus Christ and that the restoration of Jesus's true church, the vehicle of the priesthood, rests at the heart of human salvation. And, though the doctrine has begun to drift out of casual Mormon discourse in recent years, Mormons still commonly believe that after death, should they have proven themselves worthy and been sealed into the great family of God's children, they will inherit godhood of their own.

Much of this doctrine is objectionable to traditional Christians. And on many issues, little in the way of reconciliation can likely be done. Mormons take immediate and universal exception to the notion that they are not Christian. Gordon B. Hinckley declared in 1997 that "no one believes more literally in the redemption wrought by the Lord Jesus Christ. No one believes more fundamentally that He was the Son of God, that He died for the sins of mankind, that He rose from the grave, and that He is the living resurrected Son of the living Father."[15] And yet many other Christians disagree. To many Mormons uninterested in theological niceties, this is a sign of bigotry, and indeed, it may often be such. But there are also theological issues at stake.

Mormons believe that God has a body and that embodiment is an essential aspect of divinity, but this runs counter to the basic presuppositions of the Nicene and Chalcedonian creeds, on which centuries of Western Christianity rest. According to these creeds the divine and the human are impassibly different, the one existing in spirit and the other in materiality. Jesus Christ, described in the Bible as the Word of God made flesh, is the bridge across the gap, the reconciler between God and humanity. For traditional Christians, the universe God created separate from himself has been corrupted by the fall of Adam and Eve. Therefore, Jesus Christ must be fully one with God the Father in order to avoid that corruption, but at the same time fully human in order to atone for the world's sins. This is the formulation of the creeds. To most Mormons, consonant with their general lack of interest in theological consistencies, this argument is abstruse and irrelevant to their claim to Christianity. The creeds rest on a supposition they do not share: that the gap between the nature of God and the nature of the creation yawns wide enough that only God himself can bridge it. For Mormons that gap does not exist, and thus there is no contradiction between the claim that Jesus Christ is the eldest son of God the Father and a separate being from him, and the claim that he nonetheless remains divine enough to work out the atonement.

Other theological differences are less distinct. Evangelical Protestants in particular find the Mormon emphasis on effort and the development of character as the route to salvation disturbing. They also object to Mormonism's insistence that ordinances administered by the authority of the priesthood, like baptism and the temple endowment, are essential means in the journey back to God's presence. Both disagreements rest on the Protestant doctrine of salvation by grace alone: the notion that God extends mercy and redemption entirely due to his own decision to do so, irrespective of human effort. Mormon theology, emphasizing sacrament and priesthood and the church's role as a mediator of grace, resembles Catholic more than Protestant teaching and tradition.

In recent decades, however, Mormonism has moved toward at least some slight rapprochement with the rest of Christianity, particularly with Protestantism. Correlation itself is one reason: the simplification and standardization of the Mormon curriculum tended to emphasize the mission of Jesus Christ. Another reason is church leaders' increased focus on devotional exhortation. In 1985, Ezra Taft Benson became president of the church, and many observers feared that he would continue his aggressive advocacy of ultraconservative politics. But instead, Benson's concerns as president were largely spiritual and homiletic. His best-remembered sermons warned against the deleterious effects of pride and, most famously, admonished his flock to attend to the Book of Mormon. Benson asked, "How are we to use it? We are to get a testimony of it, we are to teach from it, we are to hold it up as a standard. . . . Have we been doing this? Not as we should, nor as we must."[16] Benson stressed that the book was particularly intended for the "latter days" and as such holds particular relevance to modern times, and he was successful in encouraging its wider use. Since the 1980s that book has been quoted more often and read more frequently than was true before, and it moved to the center of Mormon religious life as a source of doctrine and also as a devotional object. In 2006 Gordon B. Hinckley invited all Mormons to read the Book of Mormon in its entirety that year, and though this was a unique circumstance, it reflects the prominence of the book in Mormon devotional life. Mormons today tend to be more familiar with the Book of Mor-

mon than with their other three volumes of scripture: the Doctrine
and Covenants, the Pearl of Great Price, and even the Bible.

Perhaps counterintuitively, this new emphasis on the content of the
Book of Mormon drew Mormons toward the basic Christian message
that lay at the base of their faith. Mormons have often pointed to the
Book of Mormon as an object, evidence of Joseph Smith's divine calling and gift of revelation. As a sign it serves to emphasize Mormon
distinctiveness. The content of the book, though, is profoundly Christian, and it often resonates with Protestant themes. Its verses emphasize
the depravity of what it calls "the natural man" who is an "enemy to
God" and therefore dependent on the atonement of Jesus Christ, who
"cometh unto his own, that salvation might come unto the children of
men even through faith on his name." In 1982 the church added the
subtitle "Another Testament of Jesus Christ" to the Book of Mormon.
In 1995, it redesigned the church logo to foreground the name of
"Jesus Christ," which now appears larger than the phrase "of Latter-
day Saints," and in 2000 the First Presidency and the Quorum of the
Twelve issued an official proclamation entitled "The Living Christ,"
which declared, "He gave His life to atone for the sins of all mankind.
His was a great vicarious gift in behalf of all who would ever live upon
the earth."[17] Mormons had not before ignored Jesus Christ in their
sermons or study, but the 1980s and 1990s saw greater emphasis on the
Book of Mormon as a source of doctrine about Christ and a de-
emphasis on its use as a sign of Joseph Smith's divine call. The sociologists Gordon and Gary Shepherd noted that as correlation began to
take hold upon the church's theological discourses, language about
Jesus Christ's mission and atonement began to appear more frequently
in the church's General Conference.[18]

In addition to these shifts in pastoral emphasis, by the 1990s a number of Mormon writers were seeking engagement with Protestant
ideas. In 1992 Stephen Robinson, a professor at BYU, published *Believing Christ: The Parable of the Bicycle and Other Good News*. Robinson
described many of his students at BYU who "know a surprising
amount about tithing, the Word of Wisdom, genealogy, LDS dating,
food storage, and so forth" but who "did not understand scriptural
doctrines such as salvation by grace, justification through faith in

Christ, sanctification, atonement." He told the story of his own wife, who, overwhelmed with the torrent of demands that the church placed on her, told her husband, "I can't get up at 5:30 in the morning to bake bread and help my kids with their homework and do my own homework. I can't do my Relief Society stuff and get my genealogy done and sew and go to the PTA meetings and write the missionaries" and so on and so forth.[19] Robinson diagnosed Mormonism with a case of collective anxiety. He warned that Mormonism's combination of B. H. Roberts and Bruce R. McConkie, its blend of optimism about human potential and stern commandments, had obscured the basically Christian nature of the faith. Robinson, essentially, despaired that Mormons failed to understand grace and did not really believe that God would extend mercy if humans failed to meet all the expectations placed upon them. Instead, Robinson called Mormons back to "believing Christ," to trusting in Jesus's promises that through his atonement all Mormons could be redeemed despite their consistent and constant—and profoundly human—failure to live up to their own high expectations.

Robinson's book was massively popular. He received invitations to speak to Mormon congregations across the nation, and the book remains in print nearly twenty years later. Inspired by its success, Robinson and other faculty at BYU have pursued more explicit attempts to find common ground between their own faith and Protestantism. Robinson has coauthored two books with Protestant theologians seeking to find common ground on which the two faiths might pursue similar purposes and enrich each other's understandings of religion. More recently Robert Millet, another BYU professor, has written a series of books explaining how Mormon doctrine, which extends immortality and resurrection to all humanity through Christ's sacrifice but which also teaches that the highest rewards available in the afterlife are contingent upon accepting Christ and following his teachings, might be understood in the Protestant language of grace and redemption. Both Millet and Robinson have engaged in a series of dialogues with evangelical Protestants.

Engagement with Protestantism, still the dominant form of Christianity in the United States, was more or less forced by Mormon outmigration as Mormons moved into the South, southern California, and other areas of evangelical strength. But the outmigration caused internal stresses as well, because as Mormon participation in American society grew more sustained and regular, the church found that its ways of teaching and thinking about the world increasingly came into conflict with the norms and values Mormons absorbed from the world around them. The struggle over the Equal Rights Amendment was a case in point. Strong factions of Mormon women, particularly in northern Virginia near Washington, D.C., opposed the apostles' decision to mobilize the Relief Society to defeat the amendment.

Sonia Johnson, a fifth-generation Mormon from southern Idaho, was part of the outmigration. After attending college in Utah she moved to the East Coast with her husband, earned a doctorate from Rutgers, and taught college part-time in Washington, D.C., where her husband worked. In 1977 she and several other women in northern Virginia organized Mormons for ERA and began an increasingly radical protest campaign. At one point they hired a plane to fly over the Tabernacle in Salt Lake City streaming a banner declaring "Mother in Heaven Supports the ERA" to the thousands of Mormons attending the General Conference below. In 1979 Johnson delivered an address to the American Psychological Association called "Patriarchal Politics: Sexual Panic in the LDS Church," arguing that the campaign against the ERA had its roots in the Mormon leadership's fear of female empowerment. Citing what he claimed was her espousal of false doctrine, the damage she had inflicted on the church's missionary efforts, and her slander of the Mormon leadership, Johnson's bishop excommunicated her. Nonetheless, she and the Mormons for ERA continued their campaign well into the 1980s; at one point some two dozen handcuffed themselves to the gates of the temple in Seattle, Washington, and waited for arrest.

The struggle over the ERA galvanized a nascent Mormon feminist movement. The key issues Mormon feminists gravitate to have generally been the existence of a Mother in Heaven, correlation's effective termination of the independence of the Relief Society and the consequent marginalization of female authority in the church under a male priesthood, and the positions the general authorities of the church have taken on broader cultural and political issues like the ERA, birth control, and women seeking jobs outside the home. In 1974, a group of academic Mormon women in Boston founded *Exponent II,* a periodical named after the journal Emmeline Wells edited in the late nineteenth century, focused particularly on confronting women's issues in the church. In 1992 Maxine Hanks published her edited collection *Women and Authority: Re-emerging Mormon Feminism.* Its articles addressed issues from the old practices of female ritual healing to the proposition that Mormon women be given the priesthood.

Though many women are troubled by one or more of these issues, and though Johnson's protests and high-profile excommunication attracted a great deal of media attention, she never represented more than the radical edge of Mormon feminism. Most Mormon feminists from the 1980s to today do not share Johnson's willingness to lose her church membership or her demand for radical structural reforms of the church leadership. The large majority of Mormon women who practice their faith find few of these issues challenging and feel little, if any, marginalization in Sunday meetings. The Relief Society, though it functionally exists today as a one-hour meeting on Sundays and an organized system of visitation, remains active and provides many women opportunities for leadership and teaching. The leaders of the Relief Society now serve for three to five years, far shorter terms than did their earlier counterparts like Eliza Snow and Emmeline Wells, who generally served for decades. Nonetheless, many Mormon women today profess particular admiration for strong members of the Relief Society's general leadership, such as Sheri Dew, unmarried but professionally successful as an author and CEO of the church's publishing company, Deseret Book, and the current president of the Relief Society, Julie Beck, who has called for both greater awareness of the society's activist past and for greater respect to be paid to the work of homemaking in the same vigorous and assertive tone. The sociologists David Campbell and Robert Putnam have reported that only 10 percent of American Mormon women claim to desire the priesthood.[20]

The generally conservative tone church leadership takes on issues of gender relationships troubles more Mormon women than does the leadership structure of the church. It is common for Mormon men to praise women for their superior spirituality, graciousness, and refinement, language strongly reminiscent of old Victorian ideas about the inherent differences between the sexes. Though undoubtedly uttered with genuine sincerity and all good intentions, some Mormon women find these paeans condescending and in fact disempowering. Such arguments extend even to the shadowy figure of Heavenly Mother, whom officially no Mormon is to worship. That policy officially derives from a lack of scriptural mandate to do so—indeed, from a lack of much canonized information about her at all—but it is often bolstered with arguments about Heavenly Mother's feminine qualities and the importance of preserving her privacy. In 1978, in the face of feminist demands for further discussion and that ritual respect be paid to her, Spencer W. Kimball pled for respect for "the ultimate in maternal modesty . . . the restrained, queenly elegance of our Heavenly Mother."[21]

Victorians believed that women's pristine nature suited them for life in the home, away from the brawling world, where they could nurture and raise the next generation. Mormons have often taken a similar tack. Through the 1970s and 1980s, leaders like Kimball and Ezra Taft Benson warned that taking a job outside the home defied women's essential nature and denied them the opportunity to raise children, their highest possible task. More recently, the line has been softened; in 2011 the apostle Quentin L. Cook encouraged women to focus on their children but also warned that "we should all be careful not to be judgmental or assume that sisters are less valiant if the decision is made to work outside the home."[22] Exhortations to women to stay at home and to avoid birth control have generally faded in favor of admonitions that such choices are private, between a couple and God. Nonetheless, since the 1970s, praise for, defense of, and emphasis on the traditional nuclear family has become perhaps the most common theme in public discourse of Mormonism.

In 1995 the First Presidency and the Quorum of the Twelve issued a statement called "The Family: A Proclamation to the World." It has since gained extraordinary prominence in the church: it is frequently quoted in the church's General Conferences, it is referred to in curriculum manuals, and various church-owned outlets sell nicely formatted editions suitable for framing and display on living room walls. The proclamation encapsulates in a few paragraphs the current state of Mormon belief about gender and the family but also demonstrates how intimately Mormons connect those issues to salvation, God, and the ultimate purposes of life. It relies on scripture and the ideas of Joseph Smith but also reflects the ongoing molding of that inheritance: just as Orson Pratt and John Taylor developed certain aspects of Joseph's thought to explain the divine nature and salvific qualities of polygamy, the proclamation on the family draws on similar language, themes, and ideas to sacralize monogamy. It defines the family as a "husband and wife" with "solemn responsibility to love and care for each other and for their children."

Gender distinctions receive particular attention in the proclamation, for two reasons. First, the proclamation insists that marriage exists in large part for the purposes of procreation, that "God's commandment for His children to multiply and replenish the earth remains in force." It also specifies that "gender is an essential characteristic of individual premortal, mortal, and eternal identity and purpose" and that therefore men and women are each suited to take particular roles in a family: men are to "preside" in the home and provide for their families, while women hold primary responsibility for "the nurture of their children." The two are to consider themselves "equal partners," but the proclamation is certain that the differences between the genders are as essential as that equality. Marriage fits these interlocking pieces into a complete whole, and, so the proclamation declares, it "is ordained of God. Marriage between man and woman is essential to His eternal plan." The sealing ordinances that bind those relationships into eternity "make it possible for individuals to return to the presence of God."[23] The proclamation binds Joseph Smith's impulses toward family and relationship, his introduction of ordinances that redefined heaven as an extension of the best of human life on earth, to the particular context of the late twentieth century. If the task of theology is to bring general religious principles into conversation with a particular time and place, the proclamation's powerful, if conservative, reading of Joseph Smith succinctly systematizes what his theology has come to mean to the church he founded.

Most recently, advocacy on behalf of the principles of the proclamation drew the church into extraordinarily controversial national debates over homosexuality. In 1959, David O. McKay asked Spencer W. Kimball, then an apostle, to find ways to counsel gay men in the church. Kimball thus became the church's leading voice on the issue for a generation. While many Americans in the mid-twentieth century believed that homosexuality was a mental disorder, Kimball defined homosexual acts as a heinous sin, the result of temptation and wrong choices. He also believed homosexuality might be resisted and overcome, just as the desire to steal or lie could be. Accordingly, much mid-twentieth-century church policy on homosexuality was designed to promote resistance and reversion to heterosexual impulses. Bishops were instructed to counsel those who came to them confessing homosexual impulses to pray and fast and seek opportunities to cultivate heterosexual desire by dating or sometimes even marriage. Kimball counseled gay Mormons that "the glorious thing to remember is that it is curable and forgivable."[24] It was not until the mid-1990s that Mormon leaders, following the findings of scientific investigation, began to acknowledge that homosexuality was not merely another temptation. The apostle Dallin H. Oaks offered a statement in 1995 that remains perhaps the closest thing to an explication of the church's official position:

> Some kinds of feelings seem to be inborn. Others are traceable to mortal experiences. Still other feelings seem to be acquired from a complex interaction of "nature and nurture." . . . Regardless of our different susceptibilities or vulnerabilities . . . we remain responsible for the exercise of our agency in the thoughts we entertain and the behavior we choose.[25]

Since Oaks's statement, the church has embraced the distinction he makes between action and orientation, gradually discarding Kimball's hope that homosexual orientation might be overcome while at the same time maintaining the rigorous moral code that requires celibacy outside marriage for all Mormons, homosexual or heterosexual. Gay and lesbian members of the church are, strictly speaking, welcome to participate fully in Mormon life as long as they remain chaste. No longer are bishops urged to attempt to "cure" gay members of their flock.

At the same time, the church has struggled to convince its gay and lesbian members that their outreach is sincere, because language associating homosexuality with sinfulness and weak moral character remains common among Mormons. In February 2000, Stuart Matis, a returned missionary, a graduate of BYU, and a believing member of the church took his own life on the steps of a Mormon chapel in Los Altos, California. In the days before his death he wrote a note despairing that he could not reconcile his faith and his orientation, describing the homophobia he encountered at BYU and pleading, "We have the same needs as you. We desire to love and be loved. . . . We are your sons, daughters, brothers, sisters, neighbors, co-workers and friends, and most importantly we are all children of God." His former bishop, Robert Rees, conducted his funeral, and the chapel was full.[26]

In 2008, after coordination with Roman Catholic leaders, the church threw its organizational weight behind California's Proposition 8 to establish a state law outlawing marriage between gay couples. Fearing the subtle shift of government toward support of gay marriage in adoption agencies and schools, the church had already been involved in similar campaigns in Alaska and Hawaii. However, its intervention into Proposition 8 drew negative publicity on a scale the church likely did not foresee. Leaders of the church asked members to volunteer their time and money for phone banks, leaflet campaigns, and voter mobilization efforts. The proposition passed, but with much pain. Many members of the church were disturbed with the campaign and some, like former San Francisco 49ers quarterback Steve Young, publicly refused to participate. Within the wards of California a great deal of frightening and misleading information circulated: an anonymous leaflet, "Six Consequences If Proposition 8 Fails," warned, with exaggeration and slippery slope argumentation, that religious leaders who taught that homosexual acts were sinful might be prosecuted, that churches would be forced to solemnize gay marriages in their sanctuaries, and that BYU would be required to provide housing for married same-sex couples. In many Mormon wards, the campaign was presented in martial terms, and there were reports that some members who refused to participate faced ostracism.[27]

At the same time the church encountered a vicious backlash. Mormon temples in California and elsewhere attracted protestors, and outside the temple in Denver one activist burned a Book of Mormon. Opponents of the proposition called for revocation of the church's tax-exempt status and ran commercials portraying Mormon missionaries destroying the home of a gay couple. Some organized a short-lived boycott of Mormon-owned businesses. In response, church leadership has recalled arguments over polygamy, insisting that the reaction to their involvement reflects a growing threat to religious liberty in America for all believers, not merely Mormons. The First Presidency issued a statement soon after the temple protests warning, "These are not actions that are worthy of the democratic ideals of our nation. The end of a free and fair election should not be the beginning of a hostile response in America."[28] The apostle Dallin H. Oaks, formerly a law professor at the University of Chicago and member of the Utah Supreme Court, has been particularly vocal since 2008 in defending what he believes to be the right of religious believers to participate as believers in the public square.

Though they were never as numerous as those who left Utah to work for the government or attend business school, some participants in the outmigration were Latter-day Saints who sought education in the humanities, and in the 1950s and 1960s began to emerge as a new breed of Mormon intellectuals, bringing their academic training back to Utah and the faith of their childhoods. There were no general authorities like a Talmage or a Widtsoe in their ranks, but they were as interested as those men were in the application of the academic disciplines to the ideas of their faith. In 1966, a group of Mormon graduate students at Stanford University in California founded *Dialogue: A Journal of Mormon Thought,* the first scholarly periodical dedicated, as the founding editor Eugene England put it, to the notion that "the Christ I have come to know through my Mormon faith affirms the world as good and each of its people as eternally precious. . . . My faith in him encourages me to enter into dialogue."[29] Like the thinkers of the Progressive era, Mormons involved in *Dialogue* were excited about the possibilities that the engagement of their faith with the world might offer. The journal published—and still publishes—essays, professional history, poetry, and fiction, all explorations of Mormonism and its place in the modern world. For several years it published most of the work of the Mormon History Association, organized in 1965 as a subset of the American Historical Association. But the MHA soon founded a journal of its own, and in 1975 another journal, *Sunstone,* intended to target a more popular audience than *Dialogue,* sent out its first issue. By the 1980s, both the MHA and *Sunstone* were sponsoring annual meetings, the first scholarly, the second often more raucous and sometimes intentionally provocative.

Until the 1980s, church leadership viewed these intellectual efforts with a mixture of wariness and enthusiasm. Some scholars found their efforts embraced and celebrated. Eugene England became known as an essayist of exceptional grace and poignancy; his essays, though they sometimes challenged the status quo, were suffused with his love for his faith and his yearning for the consummation of its ideals. He eventually secured work at Brigham Young University and served as a bishop. Other Mormon scholars found similar support. Hugh Nibley, a linguistic savant, received his PhD from Berkeley in ancient languages and taught languages, history, religion, and ancient studies at BYU for nearly fifty years, from 1946 to 1994. Familiar with a staggering amount of material and sources in the ancient world, Nibley generated a massive corpus of scholarship devoted to demonstrating the ancient provenance of the Book of Mormon, the endowment ceremony, baptism for the dead, and other Mormon rites. He also served as something of an in-house theological critic, blasting Mormon culture for its ready embrace of capitalism and war and environmental degradation. Leonard Arrington, one of the organizers of the MHA and a PhD in economics from the University of North Carolina, published his dissertation in 1958 as *Great Basin Kingdom: An Economic History of the Latter-day Saints, 1830–1900.* In 1972 he was appointed church historian, an office that until that point had been held by untrained general authorities. He began a rush of reforms, hiring many young PhDs, commissioning a series of academic publications on Mormon history, and seeking further to modernize the archival holdings of the church. Some historians of Mormonism, looking in wonderment at Arrington's efforts, dubbed the period "Camelot."

At the same time, church leaders were wary of other scholars. Juanita Brooks, a generation older than Arrington, had received a master's degree from Columbia University in the 1920s. Like many Mormons who left Utah for education in the early twentieth century, she returned to Utah, settling in the southern portion of the state to teach school. In 1950 she published *The Mountain Meadows Massacre,* the first scholarly study of the event. She concluded that Brigham Young had not ordered the massacre but had created the climate of fear that provoked it. Brooks was barred from publishing in church-owned periodicals, and one apostle—restrained by David O. McKay—sought her excommunication. A more serious case was that of Fawn Brodie, McKay's niece, who soon after finishing a master's degree at the University of Chicago published *No Man Knows My History: The Life of Joseph Smith, the Mormon Prophet* in 1945. Brodie frankly admitted lack of belief in Joseph Smith's divine calling, describing him as a brilliant improviser, a man with a life overrun by his own stories who came to believe in his fictions. The book is brilliantly written, and it still attracts praise from many historians for taking Joseph Smith seriously as a religious thinker. But while Brooks's work was tolerable, if uncomfortable, Brodie went right to the heart of the faith, and was excommunicated for apostasy in May 1946.

The ghost of Fawn Brodie hung over much of the church's interactions with its intellectuals in the 1970s and 1980s. At the turn of the twentieth century, Protestants had wrestled with scholarship that cast doubt on the legitimacy of Biblical narrative, and Catholics with a group of scholars who insisted that the history of their faith must be understood as a process of change over time rather than a pristine and timeless advance. As the Mormons began to grapple with their past they confronted similar challenges. Though non-Mormon scholars like the sociologist Mark Leone and the religious scholar Jan Shipps published important theoretical studies of Mormonism, within the church, the discipline of history attracted the most attention and controversy, precisely because the narrative of Joseph Smith lies at the heart of the faith's legitimacy. Several apostles, particularly Ezra Taft Benson and Boyd K. Packer, were protective of the founding stories of their past, and more, of the way they understood how history worked. Packer and certain other apostles complained about some of the work emerging from Arrington's department. As Packer insisted, "There is no such thing as an accurate, objective history of the Church without consideration of the spiritual powers that attend this work." For Packer—as for most Mormons today—God has guided the growth of the church, and academic history, which brackets consideration of the supernatural, cannot therefore explain it.[30] This puts Packer into good company with innumerable other religious leaders, but not with professional historians.

In 1973 *Dialogue* published an article documenting that Joseph Smith had ordained African Americans to the priesthood. Other works soon followed, the vast majority of them uncontroversial history that brought the study of the Mormon past into the conversations of professional historians. A small amount was controversial: books and articles that explored Joseph Smith's involvement in folk magic, the nature of polygamous marriages, the controversy over Brigham Young's succession to leadership. The journals *Sunstone* and *Dialogue* and a Salt Lake City publisher called Signature Books were generally willing to publish this material. Meanwhile, in 1979 admirers of Hugh Nibley organized the Foundation for Ancient Research and Mormon Studies in Provo, Utah. Initially intended to coordinate scholarship defending the authenticity of the Book of Mormon, FARMS quickly expanded and has become a ready and often aggressive center for Mormon apologetics, frequently publishing both scholarly defenses of Mormon belief and sometimes-biting rebuttals to work considered unfriendly.

In 1982 Arrington was removed from his post as church historian, inaugurating a period of tension between the ecclesiastical hierarchy and some Mormon intellectuals. Over the next decade leaders of the church and many scholars, amateur and trained, unleashed rhetorical salvos at one another. Church leaders like Packer warned of historians who seemed to delight in uncovering stories that complicated the official histories in the church curriculum; historians claimed the right of free inquiry and bristled at the implication of ecclesiastical control. At the same time, the Mormon feminist movement was coming into its own. Local church leaders received letters from Salt Lake City warning them not to invite Valeen Avery and Linda Newell, authors of a biography of Emma Smith that frankly discussed Joseph Smith's polygamy, to speak at informal congregational events. The pages of *Dialogue* and *Sunstone* grew increasingly and perhaps intentionally provocative, as did *Sunstone*'s annual symposium, which in 1991 hosted sessions that frankly and critically discussed temple worship and problems facing missionary work, much to the stated alarm of some leaders of the church. In General Conference, Dallin H. Oaks warned of "alternative voices" that might undermine faith or take sacred things lightly.[31]

In September 1993 a sudden wave of excommunications shocked the intellectual community. Six well-known Mormon intellectuals were tried in church courts. Five were excommunicated, one disfellowshipped, a punishment that stopped just short of deletion from the church's rolls. They included D. Michael Quinn, a BYU historian who had published on polygamy after the Manifesto and Joseph Smith's involvement in folk magic; Lavina Fielding Anderson, a writer and editor who had compiled and published in *Dialogue* cases of "ecclesiastical abuse"; and Paul Toscano, a lawyer who with his wife, Margaret, had written a work of feminist theology and who roundly criticized what he believed to be the spiritual destructiveness of correlation. These excommunications, which seemed coordinated and heavy-handed, emotionally devastated several (though not all) of the excommunicants. They stunned much of the Mormon intellectual community and provoked some outlets, particularly *Sunstone,* to consciously assume a skeptical and critical stance toward the leadership of the church.

The struggle was at its heart about control over the Mormon past, and who possessed the authority to tell it. In the early twenty-first century, there emerged signs that church leadership had come to recognize that it could no longer maintain the sort of authority over that past it once held. In 2009 the church opened a large new Church History Library. Marlin Jensen and Richard Turley, the church historian and assistant historian since 2005, revitalized the department, seeking active engagement with the Mormon History Association and greater involvement with the broader scholarly community. Turley, with two coauthors, wrote a new history of the Mountain Meadows Massacre published to wide acclaim by Oxford University Press, and the church itself in 2001 took on the ambitious goal of publishing a critical edition of the collected papers of Joseph Smith.

This new openness seems to have derived from a number of sources. The Internet provided ready access to many facts that had been new and disquieting in the 1970s and 1980s. In the late 1990s there had been something of a lull in Mormon scholarship, but by the new millennium a new generation of Mormons who lacked the combative stance of the 1980s and early 1990s were beginning to think and to write about their faith. They lacked the sense that seemed pervasive in those years that honest intellectual inquiry and faithful participation in the church were necessarily in conflict. They founded new venues like the blog *Juvenile Instructor* (named for a nineteenth-century Mormon periodical) and *The Claremont Journal of Mormon Studies,* edited by graduate students. New and important works of scholarship began to appear, the most prominent of which was the eminent Columbia historian and faithful Mormon Richard Bushman's exhaustive 2005 biography, *Joseph Smith: Rough Stone Rolling,* but there was also work by non-Mormon historians, who began to take interest in the ways Mormon history might illuminate larger narratives about American history or the history of Christianity. Serious interest in the Mormon past from scholars with no investment in the faith marks perhaps better than anything else the maturation of Mormon intellectual life.

This greater openness in intellectual life reflects much of what the Church of Jesus Christ of Latter-day Saints wishes itself to be at the beginning of the twenty-first century. In 1995, Gordon B. Hinckley became president of the church. He was already eighty-four years old, and his life had long been intimately bound to the church he now led. In 1935 he began working in public affairs for the church, in 1961 he became an apostle, and in 1981 he joined the First Presidency. His vigor belying his age, Hinckley proved to be dynamic and media-savvy, the architect of a subtle revolution in the church.

Hinckley made it his mission to make his people more comfortable in the world, preserving the moral values and commitment to faith that made Mormons distinctive but discarding clannishness and suspicion. Hinckley was perhaps the most visible Mormon leader since David O. McKay; he traveled to 161 countries, and personally dedicated 95 of the church's 130 temples across the world. He often took meetings with national leaders and media personalities. A sunny and genial man,

Hinckley was much like David O. McKay, though known less for his charisma than for his warmth and ease with people—from Bill Clinton to Mike Wallace to Bishop Desmond Tutu. In April 1995, at the General Conference in which he was sustained as the president of the church, he told his people, "There is so great a need for civility and mutual respect among those of differing beliefs and philosophies. . . . We can and must be respectful toward those with whose teachings we may not agree. We must be willing to defend the rights of others who may become the victims of bigotry."[32] In 2004 he received the Presidential Medal of Freedom.

The transformation Hinckley wrought in the church had to do less with policy than with rhetoric; it was less institutional than cultural. Though he stood unswervingly behind the truth of Mormonism, he was uncomfortable with the proposition that this truth necessarily made all others wrong and benighted. One of his favorites of Joseph Smith's revelations was Doctrine and Covenants 50:24: "That which is of God is light; and he that receiveth light, and continueth in God, receiveth more light; and that light groweth brighter and brighter until the perfect day." For Hinckley, this was a metaphor for how to think of missionary work. In a statement often repeated by Mormons today, Hinckley told a group of BYU students, "We say this to people: you bring all the good that you have and let us see if we can add to it."[33] He later repeated the line on CNN's *Larry King Live*. He admonished his people to be kinder, more open, more humble, urging them to seek opportunities to serve others in a variety of capacities and to seek friendship and participation wherever such opportunities might be found.

The great commercial success of Mormon culture in the Hinckley era was a series of novels by a seminary teacher named Gerald N. Lund. Called *The Work and the Glory* and published by the church-owned Deseret Book, they traced the history of the church from 1820s Palmyra through the settlement of Utah, told through the eyes of the fictional Steed family. Their soft-focus and devotional style made them unlikely to succeed outside of Mormondom itself. And yet early in the new millennium Utah filmmakers raised several million dollars, hoping to turn the novels into an epic series of films. Three eventually were made, and they showed not only in Utah but also in California, Arizona, Massachusetts, and several other states. The *Work and the Glory* films were just a few of several dozen Mormon-themed movies Utah filmmakers produced in the early 2000s, and though few proved capable of reaching beyond a Mormon audience, all had aspirations of doing so. The most talented of the Utah filmmakers, Richard Dutcher, produced a series of movies deftly combining humor and serious investigation of Mormon life: the missionary drama *God's Army* and its ambitious sequel *States of Grace* and a murder mystery called *Brigham City*. Dutcher took his art seriously and was frustrated at Mormon film's inability to attract non-Mormon audiences.

Dutcher's work illustrated a shift in Mormon culture: while an earlier generation of Mormons had created their own entertainment, through amateur road shows, *Saturday's Warrior,* the Mormon Tabernacle Choir, and oddities like "The Mormon Rap," a Deseret Book–produced cassette tape popular among Utah youth in the early 1980s, by the new millennium, the height of the Hinckley era, Mormons sought to produce crossover entertainment, mastering secular forms and turning them to their own ends. Though Dutcher's work and the *Work and the Glory* films failed to catch on, Mormons in other areas proved quite capable. Heirs to a long tradition of music and singing, Mormon contestants did disproportionately well on television talent search contests like *American Idol,* which produced three Mormon stars in under a decade. Similarly, BYU basketball star Jimmer Fredette became a phenomenon during the 2010–11 NCAA season, dominating a sport in which Mormons have not normally been known for excelling. The *Twilight* series by Stephenie Meyer, perhaps the most successful young adult author of the new millennium, is shot through with Mormon themes. Depicting a romance between a vampire and a mortal teenage girl, Meyer's series draws vast amounts of tension from the vampire Edward's refusal to sleep with his girlfriend, Bella, because to be unchaste would lead to their destruction. Rather, the two must be wed and Bella converted to vampirism before they can consummate their love. Emblematic of the Hinckley era, Meyer and Fredette both proved adept at translating their Mormonism into forms the rest of America could embrace, earning fame among their own people for doing so.

In 2010, a few years after Gordon B. Hinckley's death, the church launched a new ad campaign built around its website: mormon.org. Once designed as a series of questions and answers for the curious, the site began to feature a variety of Latter-day Saints: a New York City skateboarder, a single African American schoolteacher, a Spanish news anchor, a whole host of quirky and distinctive people brought together by nothing but their faith. None are the white, western American stereotype in a conservative white shirt and tie. If American Mormonism before Gordon B. Hinckley embraced that stereotype, setting itself apart from the world, Hinckley taught the church of the benefits of defying it. Though Mormonism still embraces personal self-discipline and a certain degree of conformity, the great strategy of mormon.org is instead to project a wholesome diversity, to reflect back to a pluralistic America itself revitalized by the fruits of Joseph Smith's revelations. Though it lacks the drama and confrontation of earlier years, the ongoing negotiation between the Mormon vision and American culture remains as dynamic as ever.

CONCLUSION

"Hello! My name is Elder Price, and I would like to share with you a most amazing book!" sang the actor Andrew Rannells to the audience of the Eugene O'Neill Theater in New York City. In March 2011 a tart musical satire called *The Book of Mormon* opened on Broadway to largely rapturous reviews and sellout crowds. It would receive fourteen Tony nominations and nine wins. By the early twenty-first century, many Mormons believed that a gulf again stood between themselves and American culture. After spending much of the twentieth century finding ways to make America's virtues their own, they discovered by the end of the century that propriety, rectitude, and dogged cheerfulness seemed not to gain them the admiration they once had. Those qualities had earned Heber J. Grant the cover of *Time* magazine and Mormons in general grudging respect that gradually became genuine. But in *The Book of Mormon*, the fresh-scrubbed diligence of Mormon missionaries is a mark of naïveté, repression, and foolish optimism. The childish buoyancy and faith of a pair of Mormon missionaries sent to war-torn, disease-ridden Uganda blinds them to how monumental the challenges they face really are, and their solution—the religion of the "all-American prophet" Joseph Smith, as one song labels him—seems hopelessly, even hilariously, inadequate.

Many reviews credited the musical with an underlying fondness for

Mormonism. *Sweetness* was often the word of choice. And indeed, the musical's Mormons are genuine, entirely without guile, thoroughly and unbelievably committed to the preposterous notion that their bizarre faith can make people's lives better. When the bumbling Elder Cunningham inadvertently produces a wildly bowdlerized version of Mormonism, the musical's African characters embrace it wholeheartedly because it directly addresses—though can hardly hope to solve—the problems of AIDS, poverty, and war. Mormons' ludicrous innocence, the musical's scribes appear to be saying, is perhaps slightly mitigated by the fact that it makes them extremely, almost impossibly, nice.

In light of the history of the relationship between Mormonism and the American nation, the transformations that produced the Mormons of *The Book of Mormon* seem rather staggering. From a looming threat to the American republic, a religion that Americans feared would inculcate the perversity of polygamy, the death of democracy, and raving heresy, Mormons have become at the dawn of the twenty-first century the living image of bland, middle-American tedium, so wed to awkward cultural conventionality that their strange beliefs seem a curious accessory rather than a serious challenge to American assumptions. To some Americans who still find Mormonism's claims about miracles and golden plates and prophecy scandalous for reasons of orthodoxy or skepticism, this stereotype is in fact frustrating. John Lahr of *The New Yorker* complained that the musical gave Mormon doctrine too much of a pass, lamenting that its creators "ultimately lack the courage of their non-conviction," and failed to pillory Mormons for the "surrealistic godsend for comic writers" that constitutes their theology.[1] To Mormons themselves, always sensitive to mockery or slight, the musical's version of Mormonism is, at the least, an improvement. The church's official response to the musical consisted of a single sentence, so dry and understated as to make one wonder if the Mormons, finally, might be in on the joke: "The production may attempt to entertain audiences for an evening, but the Book of Mormon as a volume of scripture will change people's lives forever by bringing them closer to Christ."

It is too easy, however, to mark off the history of Mormons in binary: now and then, polygamous visionaries and monogamous Puritans, social revolutionaries and dour Republicans, 1840s Nauvoo and present-day Provo, Utah. The Mormon embrace of American virtues was real because it emerged as much from the processes of their own beliefs as it did from outside pressure, and as such it was always directed to their own purposes first and to those of the nation second. At the heart of the faith a radical and transformative vision still lurks, and the Mormons made America their own as much as they made themselves Americans.

Tony Kushner's 1991 Pulitzer Prize–winning play *Angels in America,* sensing these discontinuities, consequently uses Mormonism as a symbol to explore what America might have been and what it is struggling toward. Kushner's Mormon characters fill the borders of the stereotype that *The Book of Mormon* skewers, but on closer investigation, they are the musical's bright-eyed missionaries in negative, afflicted with the same conventions but lacking any sense of naive idealism. A dull, conventionally ambitious, right-wing attorney and his detached and bored housewife, these Mormons have no sense that America might be anything other than a cold, cutthroat world of 1980s capitalism, cultural conservatism, and self-repression and certainly no inkling that their faith might offer any alternative. For Kushner, Mormonism's radical mythology is distinct from the dreary way of life slowly smothering his heroes, and it proves an astoundingly revitalizing force. Angels, the descendents of Moroni, crash through roofs into bedrooms, Mormons converse with suddenly conscious animatronics of their pioneer ancestors who remind them of the devastating sacrifices of the Mormon trail, and gradually, gradually, Kushner's characters become aware that there is a life of pain and intensity and passion beyond the world they know, though few may ever reach it.

Both the riotous musical and Kushner's brooding black comedy present faith defanged, Mormonism shorn of its revolution. The Mormons of *The Book of Mormon* offer no challenge to modern American life. Their beliefs are patently ridiculous, amplified and exaggerated in the song "I Believe" to emphasize Mormons' apparent utter detachment from reason and rationality. These Mormons are a national entertainment, an amusing foil to a satisfied modern and secular society; they seem hardly capable of keeping their own church running, let alone staking any ambitions upon the nation. Kushner's contemporary Mormons are the grim storm troopers of American capitalism, unthinking servants of all that is wrong with the status quo, barely conscious of their own once marginal heritage. To some evangelicals, they are dangerous heretics; to Republicans, they are merely reliable voters. All capture a part of what it may mean to be Mormon in America today, but none quite grasp the multifaceted ways in which Mormons currently define themselves and the strength with which their religion still creates for them a profoundly radical world.

Mormons still cling to a determined supernaturalism. Like few other Christian groups, Mormons' participation rates rise with their level of education. Though thoroughly integrated into the mores and functions of contemporary American life, they remain committed to at least the proposition that their prophet, inevitably these days a benevolent elderly man neatly dressed in a conservative suit, may indeed receive divine revelation that could uproot their lives in an instant. They believe that one day they may yet be asked to give up American capitalism and return to Joseph Smith's vision of economic consecration. Some fear that they may one day be asked again to practice polygamy. Nearly all believe that Joseph Smith truly was visited by an angel in upstate New York nearly two hundred years ago and that the priesthood of God held by the great figures of the Bible stands available to them, thoroughly average dentists and attorneys and businessmen today. Mormon fathers go home from these stolidly conservative occupations, consonant with Mormon men's general commitment first to be good economic providers, and lay their hands on the heads of their children and invoke the power of God to seal blessings upon their heads.

Their faith in the existence of the metaphysical world that empowers their blessings and seals their eternal relationships with their wives and husbands, parents, and grandparents drives the Mormons to devote hours a week to making that world real in the congregations of their church, to pay to spend eighteen or twenty-four months of their lives determinedly carrying copies of the Book of Mormon to any of hundreds of places across the globe, to devote weekends each month to attend the temple and perform proxy ordinances for their seventeenth-century ancestors. Their devotion to families, though it may be functionally deeply conservative in contemporary American politics and culture, in fact gestures toward the profound and radical vision of community that draws them toward salvation. While the story of Mormonism in America is in many ways the story of the Americanization of a radical religious movement, it is also the story of the preservation of a dream and the still-beating heart of Joseph Smith's vision of Zion.

APPENDIX 1

THE MORMON HIERARCHY

The General Authorities govern the church as a whole. They are the only full-time clergy in the Church of Jesus Christ of Latter-day Saints. Members of the local leadership serve for a few years on a rotating and unpaid basis. Most hold jobs in addition to their church work.

GENERAL AUTHORITIES

PRESIDENT AND FIRST PRESIDENCY
The official title of the leader of the church is "president." The president is assisted by two counselors, usually selected from the Quorum of the Twelve Apostles. Together, these three men constitute the First Presidency.

QUORUM OF THE TWELVE APOSTLES
Immediately under the First Presidency is the Quorum of the Twelve Apostles, often referred to as "the Twelve" or "the Quorum of the Twelve." They are organized by seniority in office; the longest-serving is the president of the quorum. When the president of the church dies, he is succeeded by the president of the quorum. New apostles are chosen by the president and his counselors.

QUORUM OF THE SEVENTY
Below the Quorum of the Twelve is the Quorum of the Seventy; despite its name it has for most of the history of the church not had seventy members. Primarily responsible for mission work and mediating between the Twelve and the First Presidency and local leaders, it is led by seven presidents of the Seventy.

AUXILIARIES

The church administers a series of auxiliaries: the Relief Society, a women's association; the Young Men's program; the Young Women's program; the Sunday school program; and the Primary, a program for children under the age of twelve. Each auxiliary is administered at the churchwide level by a president and two counselors. The Relief Society, Young Women's, and Primary associations are run by women, the others by men.

LOCAL LEADERSHIP

STAKE PRESIDENT

A stake president, with two counselors and a high council, administers a stake, which is composed of several congregations, called wards.

BISHOP

A bishop, with two counselors, governs a ward.

AUXILIARIES

Each auxiliary is administered at the stake and ward levels by a president and two counselors.

PRIESTHOOD

There are two orders of priesthood: the Aaronic, or lower, and the Melchizedek, or higher. Each order has three offices: deacon, teacher, and priest in the Aaronic priesthood and elder, Seventy, and high priest in the Melchizedek. Each office has particular functions. Young men are ordained deacons at the age of twelve and progress through the offices of the Aaronic priesthood until adulthood, when they receive the Melchizedek priesthood, usually at nineteen. All male missionaries of the church are ordained elders, and all men who serve in a leadership capacity are ordained high priests. All the holders of each office in a ward constitute a quorum.

APPENDIX 2

MORMON SCRIPTURE

Mormons include four volumes of scripture in what they call the "standard works."

THE BIBLE

Mormons use the King James Version, in part because its archaic Jacobean language, with its *thees* and *thys,* is imitated in all other works of Mormon scripture. Joseph Smith produced what Mormons call the "Joseph Smith Translation," adding emendations and commentary and revisions to the King James Version; this is not considered official scripture by Latter-day Saints but appears in footnotes in LDS editions of the Bible.

THE BOOK OF MORMON

Published in 1830 by Joseph Smith, who claimed to have translated it from golden plates an angel revealed to him. The Book of Mormon presents itself as the collected writings of a series of ancient prophets whose first ancestors God guided from Israel to the American continent around 600 BC. Consisting of fifteen books and nearly six hundred pages long in the current edition, it describes the rise and fall of two ancient American civilizations whose prosperity ebbs and flows with their righteousness and obedience to God. The climax describes the visit of the resurrected Jesus Christ to the American continent soon after his ascension to heaven described in the Acts of the Apostles.

THE DOCTRINE AND COVENANTS

Consisting primarily of more than a hundred revelations Joseph Smith dictated in the voice of God, the Doctrine and Covenants includes both long theological discussions about such topics as priesthood, the organization of the afterlife, and the nature of truth, and a number of shorter revelations offering directions to particular individuals in particular situations. A few revelations given to Smith's successors, such as Brigham Young's revelation on the organization of the wagon trains west, and a number of excerpts from letters and sermons of Joseph Smith are also included.

THE PEARL OF GREAT PRICE

A miscellany of documents largely produced by Joseph Smith. Some are longer excerpts from the Joseph Smith translation of the Bible, including "Selections from the Book of Moses" and "Joseph Smith—Matthew." Also included are the "Book of Abraham," which Joseph Smith produced from ancient Egyptian papyri he acquired while in Kirtland; "Joseph Smith—History," a description of Joseph Smith's divine encounters before the organization of the church; and "The Articles of Faith," thirteen statements summarizing Mormon beliefs Joseph Smith wrote in 1842. The Pearl of Great Price also includes a few documents not produced by Joseph Smith, including Official Declaration 1, Wilford Woodruff's 1890 Manifesto repudiating polygamy, and Official Declaration 2, which revoked the restriction on men of African descent holding the priesthood.

APPENDIX 3

CAST OF CHARACTERS

PRESIDENTS OF THE CHURCH

JOSEPH SMITH, JR. (1805–1844; PRESIDENT 1830–1844)
Born in Vermont, grew up in Palmyra, New York; translated and published the Book of Mormon; organized church on April 6, 1830; received revelations compiled in Doctrine and Covenants and the Pearl of Great Price; moved headquarters of church to Kirtland, Ohio, in 1831, to Far West, Missouri, in 1838, and to Nauvoo, Illinois, in 1839; introduced a number of new practices in Nauvoo, including plural marriage, baptism for the dead, the endowment ceremony, and the sealing of relationships; killed by a mob while held in prison at Carthage, Illinois.

BRIGHAM YOUNG (1801–1877; PRESIDENT 1847–1877)
Born in Vermont; converted to Mormonism in 1832 after receiving a copy of the Book of Mormon from his sister; ordained an original member of the Quorum of the Twelve Apostles, organized in 1835; gained the loyalty of most Mormons after Joseph Smith's death by arguing that the Quorum of the Twelve held the necessary priesthood authority to lead the church; selected president of the church in 1847; organized trek west from Nauvoo to Salt Lake Valley; governor of Utah Territory, 1851–58; colonized Great Basin; reorganized the priesthood into its modern structure.

JOHN TAYLOR (1808–1887; PRESIDENT 1880–1887)
Born in Milnthorpe, England; became a Methodist preacher while a teenager; moved to Canada in 1832; baptized into Mormonism in 1836; ordained an apos-

tle in 1838; with Joseph Smith, Hyrum Smith, and Willard Richards when the Smiths were killed at Carthage Jail in June 1844; directed Mormon missions in Europe in 1850s; became president of the church in 1880, after Brigham Young's death; staunch defender of polygamy.

WILFORD WOODRUFF (1807–1898; PRESIDENT 1889–1898)
Born in Connecticut; baptized after hearing a Mormon missionary preach in 1833; served six missions for the church, most famously in England; ordained an apostle in 1839; served as church historian, 1856–83; famous for his detailed, meticulous diary; issued the Manifesto, now known as Official Declaration 1, announcing his official counsel to the church to abandon polygamy in 1890; urged the Mormons to do more genealogical work.

LORENZO SNOW (1814–1901; PRESIDENT 1898–1901)
Born in Ohio; converted by his sisters—including Eliza Snow—while a student at Oberlin College in 1836; abandoned his education in favor of missions; became an apostle in 1849; founded Brigham City, Utah, the most successful of the cities functioning under the United Order in 1853; served time in prison for practicing polygamy in 1885; while president, took measures to leverage the church out of debt.

JOSEPH F. SMITH (1838–1918; PRESIDENT 1901–1918)
Born in Far West, Missouri; son of Hyrum Smith and nephew of Joseph Smith, Jr.; first president of the LDS church born into membership; served a mission to Hawaii, 1852–57; ordained an apostle in 1863; sought to integrate Mormonism into national politics, though personally a Republican; testified before Congress during Smoot hearings about Mormonism's compatibility with American political culture; directed the beginning of Family Home Evening; initiated reorganization of church bureaucracy; received a revelation of Christ teaching the spirits of the dead, later added to the Doctrine and Covenants; died in global influenza outbreak of 1918.

HEBER J. GRANT (1856–1945; PRESIDENT 1918–1945)
Born in Utah; the first president of the church who did not know Joseph Smith, Jr.; an extremely successful businessman wealthy by his early twenties; ordained an apostle in 1881; served as mission president in Japan, 1901–03; sought the modernization of church bureaucracy and business holdings; emphasized importance of the Word of Wisdom and respectability and modern nature of the church, discouraging charismatic forms of worship.

GEORGE ALBERT SMITH (1870–1951; PRESIDENT 1945–1951)
Born in Utah; son of John Henry Smith and grandson of George A. Smith, both apostles and cousins to the family of Joseph Smith, Jr.; ordained an apostle in 1903; deeply involved in such American fraternal organizations as the Sons of the American Revolution and the Boy Scouts of America; committed to Church Welfare Program, particularly in providing relief in Europe after World War II.

DAVID O. MCKAY (1873–1970; PRESIDENT 1951–1970)
Born in Utah; served a mission to Scotland; teacher; ordained an apostle in 1905; joined the First Presidency as a counselor to Heber J. Grant in 1934; known for his charisma, style, friendliness, and grace when representing the church in the public eye; traveled to Europe multiple times while president of the church; friend to politicians and celebrities; established regularized policies for the missionary program; opened the Missionary Training Center; dedicated first temples outside the United States; emphasized importance of reverence and character as defining traits of Mormons.

JOSEPH FIELDING SMITH, JR. (1876–1972; PRESIDENT 1970–1972)
Born in Utah; son of Joseph F. Smith, grandson of Hyrum Smith; ordained an apostle in 1910; served as church historian; known for his attentiveness to and knowledge of the scriptures and for his conservative theology, reliant in some particulars on the writings of conservative evangelicals; opposed B. H. Roberts and James Talmage in debates over the existence of pre-Adamites in 1930s; directed the evacuation of Mormon missionaries from Europe in 1939; published a number of books, including *Man: His Origin and Destiny,* an attack on evolution as inconsistent with the atonement of Christ.

HAROLD B. LEE (1899–1973; PRESIDENT 1972–1973)
Born in Idaho; became stake president in downtown Salt Lake City in 1930, where he developed the system of storehouses and farms eventually adopted as the churchwide welfare program; ordained an apostle in 1941; became head of the Correlation Committee in 1960 and directed the reorganization of the church, the standardization of its curriculum, and the consolidation of authority in the hands of the priesthood leadership, particularly the Quorum of the Twelve.

SPENCER W. KIMBALL (1895–1985; PRESIDENT 1974–1985)
Born in Utah; grandson of Heber C. Kimball, apostle and counselor to Heber C. Kimball; ordained an apostle in 1943; issued some of the first official statements on homosexuality; an unexpected president of the church, due to his consistent poor health and Harold B. Lee's comparative youth; particularly concerned about

racial relations in the church; strong supporter of the Indian Placement Program, which housed Indian children with white Mormon families; in 1978 announced the revocation of the restriction on African Americans holding the priesthood; his opposition to the Reagan administration's plans to build an MX missile base killed the project.

Ezra Taft Benson (1899–1994; president 1985–1994)

Born in Idaho; successful farmer; ordained an apostle in 1943; served in the cabinet of President Dwight D. Eisenhower, 1953–61, as secretary of agriculture; in the 1960s vocally espoused conservative politics, including the far-right John Birch Society; as president of the church, advocated greater attention be paid to the Book of Mormon, thereby drawing Mormons toward the theology of grace and emphasis on Christ's atonement taught in that book.

Howard W. Hunter (1907–1995; president 1994–1995)

Born in Idaho; attorney; ordained an apostle in 1959, despite having served in no church office higher than stake president; church historian, 1970–94; urged increased temple worship as president of the church.

Gordon B. Hinckley (1910–2008; president 1995–2008)

Born in Utah; journalist and public affairs professional; joined the Quorum of the Twelve in 1961 and the First Presidency in 1981; as church president, expanded and improved the public image of the church, touring 161 countries and meeting freely with officials and media; dedicated 95 temples, more than all his predecessors combined; encouraged Mormons to discard clannishness and to seek to be more neighborly and open; under his leadership, the general authorities issued the proclamations "The Living Christ" and "The Family."

Thomas S. Monson (1927– ; president, 2008–)

Born in Utah; newspaper publisher; ordained an apostle in 1963 (the youngest in fifty-six years); known for emphasis on humanitarian work and care for the poor.

OTHER EMINENT MORMONS

Elijah Abel (1808–1885)

An escaped slave and the first African American ordained to the priesthood under the hand of Joseph Smith in 1836; served missions to Canada, New York, and Maryland; ordained a Seventy in 1839; moved to Utah in 1853; was denied requests to attend the temple due to his race.

LEONARD ARRINGTON (1917–1999)
Born in Idaho; received a PhD in economics from the University of North Carolina in 1952; wrote a dissertation published as *Great Basin Kingdom: An Economic History of the Latter-day Saints, 1830–1900;* helped establish the Mormon History Association in 1965; appointed church historian in 1972; sought to sponsor a great expansion of professional history writing on the Mormon past; removed as church historian in 1982.

JOHN C. BENNETT (1804–1867)
Trained as a physician and alternately a soldier, entrepreneur, and politician in Illinois; arrived in Nauvoo in 1840 and aided in writing and securing passage of the Nauvoo city charter; baptized and served as assistant president of the church, 1841–42; elected mayor of Nauvoo; discovered seducing Mormon women, removed and disfellowshipped; wrote lurid exposé of Mormonism.

FAWN BRODIE (1915–1981)
Born in Utah; attended graduate school in English at the University of Chicago and lost her faith; married a non-Mormon in 1936; began work on a biography of Joseph Smith in 1939; published *No Man Knows My History: The Life of Joseph Smith* in 1945, at the age of thirty—the book remained the definitive scholarly study of early Mormonism for decades; excommunicated in 1946; continued to publish scholarly biographies throughout her career; niece of David O. McKay.

JUANITA BROOKS (1898–1989)
Born in Nevada to a Mormon family; educated at Brigham Young University and Columbia University; worked as a teacher in St. George, in southern Utah; collected the diaries and personal records of local residents, which sparked her interest in the Mountain Meadows Massacre; published *The Mountain Meadows Massacre* in 1950 to mixed reactions from other Mormons; later wrote several other historical works; one of the leading figures in modern Mormon history writing.

ORSON SCOTT CARD (1951–)
Born to a Mormon family in Washington State and raised in California and Utah; graduate of Brigham Young University; served two years as a missionary in Brazil; worked as a playwright for a university acting troupe and spent a year in graduate school at Notre Dame; began publishing science fiction and fantasy short stories while working as a copywriter for the church's official magazine, *Ensign;* novels *Ender's Game* and *Speaker for the Dead* have become genre classics; author of many other science fiction and fantasy novels.

J. Reuben Clark (1871–1961)

Born in Utah to a Mormon family; received a law degree from Columbia University and entered the civil service; worked as an attorney in Utah and for the State Department; called to the First Presidency by Heber J. Grant in 1933, despite not being an apostle; rose to first counselor under Grant and George Albert Smith and exerted a great deal of power in the 1940s while both presidents suffered health problems; promoted conservative worship practices and theology; demoted to second counselor under David O. McKay, a rare occurrence.

William Clayton (1814–1879)

Born in Lancashire, England; joined Mormonism in 1836 and emigrated to Nauvoo in 1840; became secretary to Joseph Smith and later to Brigham Young; produced *The Latter-day Saints' Emigrants' Guide* after serving as a recorder on the first pioneer wagon train west; wrote "Come, Come, Ye Saints," one of the most popular Mormon hymns.

Oliver Cowdery (1806–1850)

A schoolteacher from Vermont who rented rooms from the Smith family; became Joseph Smith's primary scribe during the translation of the Book of Mormon; one of the Three Witnesses to the golden plates; received priesthood in the company of Joseph Smith from various angels; Second Elder at the organization of the church in April 1830; in 1838 excommunicated for disagreements over the dispersal of property in Missouri and his accusations that Joseph Smith was having an affair with Fanny Alger, a likely early plural wife; journeyed to Winter Quarters in 1848 and requested rebaptism from Brigham Young.

Stephen Covey (1932–)

Born in Utah; attended the University of Utah, Harvard, and Brigham Young University; worked for a time as a teacher and management consultant; published *The Seven Habits of Highly Effective People* in 1989, which became an international bestseller, selling fifteen million copies; organized FranklinCovey in 1997.

Sheri Dew (1953–)

The first unmarried woman to serve in the General Presidency of the Relief Society, from 1997 to 2002 as counselor to president Mary Ellen Smoot; author of biographies of several prominent Mormons and an executive in the church-owned publishing company Deseret Book; known and admired for her forceful speaking style and strong leadership.

ALVIN DYER (1903–1977)

A businessman and heating and air-conditioning executive; placed over the missionaries in the central United States in 1954 and the European mission in 1960; ordained an apostle in 1967; radically reformed Mormon mission practices, emphasizing that missionaries should seek to inspire spiritual experiences in converts rather than teaching them doctrine; his strategies led to large numbers of unprepared or uninterested converts.

EUGENE ENGLAND (1933–2001)

Born in Logan, Utah, and raised on a farm in Idaho in a Mormon family; served a mission to Samoa with his wife, Charlotte, in their early twenties; entered graduate school in English at Stanford University in the 1960s; cofounded *Dialogue: A Journal of Mormon Thought* in 1966; lost his first job at St. Olaf's Lutheran College in Minnesota when parents complained about students showing interest in Mormonism; taught in the Church Educational System before securing a job teaching at Brigham Young University in 1977; became one of Mormonism's leading literary voices, particularly known for his skill at the personal essay and his eloquent explorations of faith and doubt; retired from BYU under pressure in 1998.

MARTIN HARRIS (1783–1875)

A wealthy farmer in Palmyra, New York; frequently employed the Smith men as laborers; prone to spiritual experiences; bore a transcript from Joseph Smith's golden plates to Charles Anthon, a professor of ancient languages, and returned claiming Anthon had asserted their genuine status but refused to endorse the plates afterward; served as Joseph Smith's first scribe in the translation of the Book of Mormon but lost the first 116 pages and was replaced by Oliver Cowdery; one of the Three Witnesses to the plates; underwrote the publication of the Book of Mormon; joined various schismatic movements after the death of Joseph Smith; went to Utah in 1870 and joined Brigham Young's church.

ZINA D. HUNTINGTON (1821–1901)

Born in Watertown, New York; converted to Mormonism with her family in 1836; married Henry Jacobs in March 1841 and Joseph Smith, Jr., as a polygamous wife in October 1841; married Brigham Young as a polygamous wife in 1846; worked as a schoolteacher and midwife in Utah and became a leader among Mormon women; counselor to Eliza R. Snow in Relief Society presidency, 1880; president of Relief Society, 1888–1901.

JANE MANNING JAMES (1822–1908)

An African American woman who joined Mormonism in the Nauvoo period; lived for a time with Joseph and Emma Smith in Nauvoo; walked across the plains with her family; in 1891 requested permission to receive her endowment and sealings in the temple, but her request was denied due to her race; sealed by proxy to Joseph and Emma Smith as a servant.

SONIA JOHNSON (1936–)

Born to a Mormon family in Idaho; educated at Utah State University and Rutgers; in 1978 organized Mormons for ERA and began a series of public protests of the church's campaign to defeat the Equal Rights Amendment; excommunicated for publicly opposing church doctrine and slandering the church in 1979.

HEBER C. KIMBALL (1801–1868)

A Vermont blacksmith and potter; converted to Mormonism in 1832; an original member of the Quorum of the Twelve Apostles, organized in 1835; served two successful missions in England; emotionally distressed on first hearing of polygamy but agreed to give his wife, Vilate, to Joseph Smith, a request that Smith then claimed to be a test of faith; counselor to church president Brigham Young, 1847–68; eventually took forty-three wives, making him the second most married Mormon polygamist after Young.

WILLIAM LAW (1809–1892)

Born in Ireland; immigrated to the United States in 1820 and converted to Mormonism in 1836 by John Taylor; led a band of converts to Nauvoo in 1839; joined the First Presidency in 1841; disturbed when Joseph Smith proposed plural marriage to his wife, Jane, in 1843; had a number of intense conversations with Joseph Smith and concluded that he had become a fallen prophet; excommunicated in April 1844 and joined a reform church; as its leader, wrote an editorial for its periodical *The Nauvoo Expositor* exposing polygamy; eventually moved to Wisconsin.

JOHN D. LEE (1812–1877)

Born in Illinois; converted to Mormonism in 1838; member of the Danites, a secret society sworn to protect the church in Missouri; sealed to Brigham Young as an adopted son; settled in southern Utah and worked as an Indian agent and a ferry operator; helped to organize the Mountain Meadows Massacre in 1857, leading Indian and Mormon troops on the ground; in 1877 became the only Mormon convicted and executed for the massacre; claimed before his execution that he had been made a scapegoat.

BRUCE R. McCONKIE (1915–1985)

Born into a Mormon family in Salt Lake City; an attorney and member of the Quorum of the Seventy; ordained an apostle in 1972; author of *Mormon Doctrine,* an encyclopedia of theological explication, in 1958, and numerous other doctrinal works; known for his systematic, comprehensive, and conservative approach to theology and for his authoritative tone; the most influential Mormon theologian of the late twentieth century.

WILLIAM MCLELLIN (1806–1883)

A schoolteacher in Paris, Tennessee; converted to Mormonism by Peter Whitmer and Harvey Wheelock in 1831; an original member of the Quorum of the Twelve Apostles, organized in 1835; among those disillusioned by the failure of the Kirtland Safety Society bank Joseph Smith organized in early 1838; after clashes with Joseph Smith, excommunicated in 1838; supported Sidney Rigdon's claims to leadership after Joseph Smith's death.

ISAAC MORLEY (1786–1865)

Born in Massachusetts; established a thriving farm in Kirtland, Ohio, in the 1820s; became a follower of Sidney Rigdon; with Rigdon's aid, established the Morley Family, an economic cooperative settlement on his farmland; converted to Mormonism by Oliver Cowdery and Parley Pratt in 1830; served as a stake president near Nauvoo; emigrated to Utah in 1848; directed by Brigham Young to found the town of Manti, Utah.

LAVERN PARMLEY (1900–1980)

Born in Utah to a Mormon family; became in 1951 the president of the Primary Association, the official church auxiliary for children between the ages of three and twelve; integrated the Boy Scouts of America program into the Primary; edited the Primary journal *The Children's Friend* and redirected its content to encourage children to read it; reorganized Primary curricula to focus on teaching church doctrine and moral habits, particularly reverence, through songs and games.

PARLEY AND ORSON PRATT (1807–1857; 1811–1881)

Brothers from upstate New York who joined Mormonism within days of each other in September 1830; both original members of the Quorum of the Twelve Apostles, organized in 1835; served missions in Europe, South America, and the Pacific; known for their voluminous writings defending and explicating the doctrines of Mormonism; both entered into polygamy; Parley Pratt murdered in 1857 by the ex-husband of one of his plural wives; Orson Pratt became a leading theologian in Utah and the main theological defender of polygamy.

SIDNEY RIGDON (1793–1876)

A Restorationist Baptist minister in Kirtland, Ohio; converted to Mormonism after reading a Book of Mormon given him by Parley Pratt; became the major public voice of Mormonism through the 1830s; a counselor in Joseph Smith's First Presidency, 1832–44; worked with Joseph Smith on the translation of the Bible; his relationship with Joseph Smith deteriorated in Nauvoo due to Rigdon's opposition to polygamy; spent much of 1840–44 in Pittsburgh presiding over a local congregation; sought to claim leadership of the church upon Joseph Smith's death in 1844; led a schismatic Mormon faith in Pennsylvania until his death in 1876.

B. H. ROBERTS (1857–1933)

Born in Lancashire, England; joined Mormonism with his family as a boy; walked across the plains in 1866 to Salt Lake City; attended the University of Deseret but was largely self-educated; became a president of the Seventy in 1888; wrote a number of important works of theology, history, and biography, including an edited six-volume *History of the Church of Jesus Christ of Latter-day Saints*, based on the production of official church historians since the time of Joseph Smith; also wrote theological curricula for several priesthood quorums, studies of the Mormon doctrine of God and of the Book of Mormon, and an unpublished systematic theology of Mormonism called *The Truth, the Way, the Life;* elected to Congress as a Democrat in 1898 but was denied his seat because of his polygamist practices; late in life, came into conflict with the apostle Joseph Fielding Smith over Roberts's theory that Adam was preceded on earth by "pre-Adamite" human beings.

STEPHEN ROBINSON (1947–)

Born to a Mormon family in California; received a PhD in the New Testament from Duke Divinity School and joined the faculty of Brigham Young University in 1986; author of *Believing Christ,* an enormously popular devotional work that helped spread ideas about grace and atonement in Mormon religious culture, in 1991; participated in a number of interfaith dialogues with Protestant evangelicals.

GEORGE AND WILLARD MITT ROMNEY (1907–1995; 1947–)

Father and son, served as governors of Michigan (1963–69) and Massachusetts (2003–07), respectively; descendents of Parley Pratt; George born in Mexico to Mormon migrants who fled there to preserve the practice of polygamy, though his parents were monogamists; among the most successful Mormon families of the outmigration from Utah in the mid-twentieth century, the Romneys became successful businessmen and politicians; each ran for president, George in 1968 and Mitt in 2008 and again in 2012; George faced few questions about his faith, but Mitt encountered opposition from some evangelicals and curiosity from others.

EMMA SMITH (1804–1879)

Born in Harmony, Pennsylvania, to Isaac and Elizabeth Hale, a middle-class farming family; met Joseph Smith, a worker hired by neighbor Josiah Stowall in 1825 and eloped with him in 1827; present when Joseph Smith recovered the golden plates in September 1827; worked briefly as Joseph's scribe during translation in 1829; baptized a Mormon by Oliver Cowdery in June 1830; received a revelation through Joseph directing her to compile a hymnbook and to expound scripture and teach; first president of the Relief Society; deeply hurt by polygamy, successfully demanded that Joseph stop marrying other wives in 1843; clashed with Brigham Young over ownership of her home after Joseph's death; stayed in Nauvoo as other Mormons began to leave; married the non-Mormon Lewis Bidamon in 1847; joined the Reorganized Church of Jesus Christ of Latter-day Saints, organized in part by her oldest son, Joseph III, in 1860.

JOSEPH SMITH, SR. (1771–1840)

Born in Massachusetts to an old Puritan family; the son of Asael Smith, a religious skeptic and Universalist; moved to Vermont in young adulthood and married Lucy Mack in 1796; failed in business and moved his family across New England and eventually to Palmyra, New York, in 1816, seeking economic opportunity; skeptical of organized religion, but regularly had symbolic and prophetic dreams; joined his son's church in 1830 and ordained patriarch in 1833, charged with giving blessings of counsel to members; one of the Eight Witnesses to the golden plates; died in Nauvoo.

LUCY MACK SMITH (1775–1856)

Born in New Hampshire to a veteran of the American Revolution and a deeply pious mother who ingrained in her habits of scripture reading and prayer; married Joseph Smith, Sr., in 1796 and raised her children in the same piety, teaching them loyalty to family; joined the Presbyterian church in Palmyra, New York, after the Smith family moved there in 1816; celebrated her son's prophetic calling and joined his church in 1830; remained in Nauvoo with Emma Smith and her grandchildren after the deaths of Joseph Jr. and Hyrum Smith, refusing to go to Utah with Brigham Young; dictated a family memoir in her old age.

SMITH BROTHERS

Alvin (1798–1823) became the main financial support of his family in his early twenties; died of appendicitis or of accidental calomel poisoning; later seen by his brother Joseph Jr. in a vision in heaven. ·

Hyrum (1800–1844) was his brother Joseph Jr.'s closest confidant and friend; succeeded his father as patriarch of the church in 1840; an apostle and assistant president of the church in 1841; died with Joseph Jr. at Carthage Jail.

Samuel (1808–1844) was one of the Eight Witnesses to the golden plates; celebrated as the first missionary of the church; considered a successor to his brother Joseph Jr. but died in July 1844 of a fever.

William (1811–1893) was the youngest of the Smith brothers; one of the Eight Witnesses to the golden plates; an original member of the Quorum of the Twelve Apostles, organized in 1835; emotionally erratic, his claims to succeed Joseph Jr. were rejected by the church; later joined the Reorganized Church.

JOSEPH SMITH III (1832–1914)

Oldest son of Joseph Smith, Jr., to survive to adulthood; according to some accounts received a blessing from his father in 1838 promising him that he would one day lead the church; became an attorney in 1856; approached by a number of Mormons who had not followed Brigham Young west and asked to lead a reorganization of his father's church in 1860; initially reluctant, but felt spiritually impressed to do so; became first president of the Reorganized Church of Jesus Christ of Latter Day Saints; rejected much of what many RLDS Mormons felt were excesses, misinterpretations, or inventions of Brigham Young in Utah Mormonism: polygamy, baptism for the dead, and other temple worship and much of Joseph Smith's Nauvoo theology; gained legal title to the Kirtland Temple in 1880; made tours of Utah in the 1870s and 1880s, coming into conflict with Utah Mormons.

REED SMOOT (1862–1941)

Born to a Mormon family in Utah; ordained an apostle in 1900; from a political family, as his father served as mayor of Salt Lake City; received permission from Joseph F. Smith to run for the Senate in 1902 and was elected as a Republican; though Smoot was a monogamist, the Senate proved reluctant to seat him due to his office in the church, and held four years of hearings to determine whether a Mormon could be trusted with such high office; confirmed to the Senate in 1907, served until 1933.

ELIZA R. SNOW (1804–1887)

Born in Massachusetts and raised in Ohio; her intelligence and literary gifts were apparent from childhood and she spent her youth working in her father's legal affairs and writing poetry; her family converted from Restorationism to Mormonism in 1835; worked as a schoolteacher in Kirtland and Nauvoo; became a plural wife of Joseph Smith in 1842; helped to organize the Relief Society and served as its first secretary; popularized the doctrine of a Mother in Heaven in the poem "Invocation," which later becomes a hymn, "O My Father"; at Brigham Young's request, reorganized the Relief Society in Utah in 1867 and served as president until her death.

JAMES TALMAGE (1862–1933)

Born in Hungerford, Berkshire, England; joined Mormonism with his family in 1872 and moved to Utah in 1877; studied science at Brigham Young Academy, Lehigh University, and Johns Hopkins University, eventually receiving a PhD from Illinois Wesleyan University; taught in Utah and composed several important works of theology, particularly *Articles of Faith* (1899) and *Jesus the Christ* (1911); became an apostle in 1911; one of the leading Mormon intellectuals of the early twentieth century; clarified Mormon ideas about the Trinity, Christology, and the Great Apostasy.

JOHN W. TAYLOR (1858–1916)

Born in Utah; son of the apostle and later church president John Taylor; ordained an apostle at age twenty-six by his father; rejected the 1890 Manifesto advising church members to cease the practice of plural marriage and continued to marry plural wives after 1890; refused a summons to testify before Congress in the Smoot hearings in 1905 and rejected Joseph F. Smith's 1905 proclamation that plural marriage was now grounds for excommunication; resigned from the Quorum of the Twelve at Smith's request in 1906; excommunicated in 1911.

MINERVA TEICHERT (1888–1976)

Born to a Mormon family in Ogden, Utah; trained at the Art Institute of Chicago and the Art Students League of New York under the noted painter Robert Henri; began painting while raising five children on a ranch in Wyoming; favored western scenes and scenes from the Book of Mormon; decorated temple interiors; work widely reprinted inside and outside of Mormonism, particularly *Christ in a Red Robe*.

EMMELINE B. WELLS (1828–1921)

Born in Massachusetts, joined Mormonism at fourteen; abandoned by her husband while living in Nauvoo; became a schoolteacher and later the plural wife of Daniel Wells, mayor of Salt Lake City; edited the journal *Woman's Exponent* from 1877 to 1914; a strong advocate of women's rights and women's suffrage; involved in the national women's suffrage movement, frequently traveling to Washington, D.C., and other East Coast cities to advocate on behalf of Mormon women; though a staunch public advocate of polygamy, wrote privately of the loneliness it caused her.

DAVID WHITMER (1805–1888)

Born in Pennsylvania; a friend of Oliver Cowdery's, and with the rest of his family hosted Joseph Smith and Cowdery at the Whitmer farm in Pennsylvania during the translation of the Book of Mormon; one of the Three Witnesses to the golden plates; made president of the church in the Missouri settlements in 1834; excommunicated with several other leaders of the Missouri church by the Missouri high council in 1838 for disloyalty to Joseph Smith; occasionally involved in small Mormon churches after the death of Joseph Smith.

JOHN WIDTSOE (1872–1952)

Born in Norway; converted with his family to Mormonism in 1883; studied at Harvard University and the University of Göttingen, Germany, receiving a PhD in the sciences in 1899; a professor of agriculture at Brigham Young University and president of Utah State University; became an apostle in 1921; writings on Mormon theology and priesthood emphasize the scientific nature of the universe, the ability of human reason to understand the workings of God, and the possibility of reconciling science and religion.

LYMAN WIGHT (1796–1858)

Born in Fairfield, New York; in late 1820s became a follower of Sidney Rigdon in Kirtland, Ohio, and joined an economic commune called the Morley Family; converted to Mormonism in 1830 by Parley Pratt and Oliver Cowdery; went to Jackson County, Missouri, and returned to Kirtland to request aid when Mormon settlements were attacked; one of the leaders of Zion's Camp; led Mormon militia during 1838 Mormon War in Missouri; ordained an apostle in 1841; sent by the Council of the Fifty to find possible places for settlement in Texas; founded a Mormon settlement in Texas soon after Joseph Smith's death in 1844, against the wishes of Brigham Young; excommunicated in 1848.

ERNEST WILKINSON (1899–1978)

Born in Utah to a Mormon family; worked as a teacher in early life; received a law degree from George Washington University and a doctorate in law from Harvard; became president of Brigham Young University in 1951 and appointed administrator-chancellor of the Unified Church School System, giving him authority over the Church Educational System of seminaries and institutes for young people as well as BYU; greatly expanded BYU, quintupling the student body to twenty-five thousand by the end of his tenure, recruiting new faculty, and inaugurating a large building program; sympathetic to the conservative politics of apostle Ezra Taft Benson; aggressively sought to root out communist sympathizers at BYU; the Republican nominee for U.S. senator from Utah in 1964, lost to incumbent senator Frank Moss.

LORIN C. WOOLLEY (1856–1934)

Born to a Mormon family in Salt Lake City, Utah; served as a courier for Mormon leaders hiding from federal officials during the polygamy raids; later claimed that while church president John Taylor stayed at his father's home in 1886, Taylor swore to a vision of Joseph Smith never to allow polygamy to leave the earth, and that Taylor gave several of the men present, including Woolley, the authority to seal plural marriages; in the 1920s became the focus of a burgeoning polygamist movement and ordained the members of the Council of Friends, the leaders of what became Mormon fundamentalism.

STEVE YOUNG (1961–)

Descendant of Brigham Young; raised in Connecticut; attended Brigham Young University; played professionally in the National Football League from 1984 to 1999; won Super Bowl XXIX with the San Francisco 49ers in 1994; one of the greatest quarterbacks in pro football history; opposed the church's involvement in the campaign over California's Proposition 8.

APPENDIX 4

THE FAMILY

A Proclamation to the World

THE FIRST PRESIDENCY AND COUNCIL OF THE TWELVE APOSTLES OF
THE CHURCH OF JESUS CHRIST OF LATTER-DAY SAINTS

We, the First Presidency and the Council of the Twelve Apostles of the Church of Jesus Christ of Latter-day Saints, solemnly proclaim that marriage between a man and a woman is ordained of God and that the family is central to the Creator's plan for the eternal destiny of His children.

All human beings—male and female—are created in the image of God. Each is a beloved spirit son or daughter of heavenly parents, and, as such, each has a divine nature and destiny. Gender is an essential characteristic of individual premortal, mortal, and eternal identity and purpose.

In the premortal realm, spirit sons and daughters knew and worshiped God as their Eternal Father and accepted His plan by which His children could obtain a physical body and gain earthly experience to progress toward perfection and ultimately realize his or her divine destiny as an heir of eternal life. The divine plan of happiness enables family relationships to be perpetuated beyond the grave. Sacred ordinances and covenants available in holy temples make it possible for individuals to return to the presence of God and for families to be united eternally.

The first commandment that God gave to Adam and Eve pertained to their potential for parenthood as husband and wife. We declare that God's commandment for His children to multiply and replenish the earth remains in force. We further declare that God has commanded that the sacred powers of procreation are to be employed only between man and woman, lawfully wedded as husband and wife.

We declare the means by which mortal life is created to be divinely appointed. We affirm the sanctity of life and of its importance in God's eternal plan.

Husband and wife have a solemn responsibility to love and care for each other and for their children. "Children are an heritage of the Lord" (Psalms 127:3). Parents have a sacred duty to rear their children in love and righteousness, to provide for their physical and spiritual needs, to teach them to love and serve one another, to observe the commandments of God and to be law-abiding citizens wherever they live. Husbands and wives—mothers and fathers—will be held accountable before God for the discharge of these obligations.

The family is ordained of God. Marriage between man and woman is essential to His eternal plan. Children are entitled to birth within the bonds of matrimony, and to be reared by a father and a mother who honor marital vows with complete fidelity. Happiness in family life is most likely to be achieved when founded upon the teachings of the Lord Jesus Christ. Successful marriages and families are established and maintained on principles of faith, prayer, repentance, forgiveness, respect, love, compassion, work, and wholesome recreational activities. By divine design, fathers are to preside over their families in love and righteousness and are responsible to provide the necessities of life and protection for their families. Mothers are primarily responsible for the nurture of their children. In these sacred responsibilities, fathers and mothers are obligated to help one another as equal partners. Disability, death, or other circumstances may necessitate individual adaptation. Extended families should lend support when needed.

We warn that individuals who violate covenants of chastity, who abuse spouse or offspring, or who fail to fulfill family responsibilities will one day stand accountable before God. Further, we warn that the disintegration of the family will bring upon individuals, communities, and nations the calamities foretold by ancient and modern prophets.

We call upon responsible citizens and officers of government everywhere to promote those measures designed to maintain and strengthen the family as the fundamental unit of society.

This proclamation was read by President Gordon B. Hinckley as part of his message at the General Relief Society Meeting held on September 23, 1995, in Salt Lake City, Utah.

BIBLIOGRAPHIC ESSAY

Mormons have been their own historians since the beginning. In March 1831 Joseph Smith issued a revelation to John Whitmer, one of the Eight Witnesses to the golden plates, directing that "it shall be appointed unto him to keep the church record and history continually."[1] The office of church historian has been occupied with varying degrees of vigor since Whitmer's time but has never been left unattended. Mormons are routinely exhorted to keep diaries and probe their own family pasts. The theology of genealogy and the elevation of Joseph Smith's experiences to sacred narrative have made them enthusiastic amateur historians. Though the 1980s and 1990s saw collisions between the keepers of the sacred past and historians adhering to the conventions of the academy, there is no shortage of historians of Mormonism, nor material for them to mine.

For decades the essential source for any historian interested in nineteenth-century Mormon history was *The History of the Church of Jesus Christ of Latter-day Saints,* commonly called the *Documentary History of the Church.* Produced between 1838 and 1856, its several volumes cover the life and career of Joseph Smith. Though written largely in the first person and though some portions do appear to be dictated by Smith, the bulk was produced by scribes and editors who transcribed letters, revelations, diary entries, and other sources and altered pronouns to produce Smith's own voice. The earliest extract, written in 1838 and describing Joseph's First Vision and recovery of the golden plates, has been canonized under the title "Joseph Smith—History" in the Pearl of Great Price. In 1902 Joseph F. Smith asked B. H. Roberts to edit the work, and he corrected errors, added material, and smoothed out the narrative. The church's official vendor, Deseret Book, still prints Roberts's version today, and it is frequently cited in official church publications, including Roberts's own *Comprehensive History of the Church,* the first major effort to write a history of Mormonism. As a historian, the modern scholar Davis Bitton has described Roberts as clearly partisan though also willing to acknowledge mistakes and disdainful of attempts to mythologize or massage the church's history to promote faith.[2] Roberts thus may be considered the founder of modern Mormon historiography, though his silent edits on the *Documentary History of the Church* render the work suspect to most historians today.

There exist several recent attempts to tell the same story as this volume. The most important is Bitton and Leonard Arrington's *The Mormon Experience: A History of the Latter-day Saints* (Knopf, 1979; 2nd ed. 1992). Combining a thematic and a chronological approach, it aimed both to tell the story of the Mormons and to introduce the reader to the paramount issues and ideas at the center of Mormon history within a scholarly framework. It still stands useful today, though as one of the definitive works of the wave of Mormon scholarship that began in the 1970s, it could not benefit from much of the work it inspired, and its treatment of the twentieth century is necessarily cursory. In 1976 James Allen and Glen Leonard published *The Story of the Latter-day Saints* (Deseret Book, 1976), though it was intended for Mormon audiences rather than a general readership. More recently Richard and Claudia Bushman produced *Building the Kingdom: A History of Mormons in America* (Oxford University Press, 2001), a very brief history focusing on the nineteenth century. Most of these works follow the church's own emphasis on the life of Joseph Smith and the trek west. Other works, like Richard Ostling and Joan Ostling's journalistic study *Mormon America: The Power and the Promise* (HarperSanFrancisco, 1999) and Terryl Givens's academic analysis in *The Latter-day Saint Experience in America* (Greenwood Press, 2004), offer less historical narrative than topical analysis. I have learned from all of them and have particularly attempted to show the narrative patterns present in twentieth-century Mormonism.

ONE. JOSEPH SMITH AND THE FIRST MORMONS: TO 1831

Though several biographies of Joseph Smith, Jr., exist—Donna Hill's *Joseph Smith: The First Mormon* (Doubleday, 1977) and Robert Remini's *Joseph Smith* (Penguin, 2002) are particularly useful—two essential efforts dominate the field: Fawn Brodie's *No Man Knows My History* (Knopf, 1946) and Richard Bushman's *Joseph Smith: Rough Stone Rolling* (Knopf, 2005). Brodie's gracefully written book defined the central issues of Joseph Smith's life and rescued the prophet from earlier interpretations as Sidney Rigdon's shallow front man or a schizophrenic with delusions of grandeur. Brodie offered instead a genuinely brilliant Joseph who earned his place as a central figure in American religious history. Bushman built on Brodie in many ways, richly contextualizing Joseph Smith's revelations and struggles in the visionary world of the early American republic and exhaustively plumbing sources that Brodie did not have.

I have, as in particular Remini did, interpreted early Mormonism in the context of the early American republic, when new patterns of economy, politics, and culture tore apart traditional social and familial structures, and confidence in rationality and individual efficacy altered but hardly destroyed the ways Americans thought about the supernatural. I relied on Charles Sellers, *The Market Revolution: Jacksonian America, 1815–1846* (Oxford University Press, 1991); Daniel Walker Howe, *What Hath God Wrought: The Transformation of America, 1815–1848* (Oxford University Press, 2009); Gordon Wood, *The Radicalism of the American Revolution* (Knopf, 1992); and Sean Wilentz, *The Rise of American Democracy: Jefferson to Lincoln* (Norton, 2005), as well as Wood's classic article "Evangelical America and Early Mormonism," *New York History* 61 (October 1980): 359–86. For religious responses to these changes, particularly that of evangelicalism, Nathan Hatch, *The Democratization of American Christianity* (Yale University Press, 1989) remains essential, as does Mark Noll, *America's God: Edwards to Lincoln* (Oxford University Press, 2005). All explore the way democratic culture altered American religion, infusing it with egalitarianism, suspicion of authority, and confidence in personal experience. Whitney Cross, *The Burned-Over District: The Social and Intellectual History of Enthusiastic Religion in Western New York, 1800–1850* (Cornell University Press, 1950) is the basic study of that area. On the various prophets and revivalists in the Smith family's world, see Susan Juster's *Doomsayers: Anglo-American Prophecy in the Age of Revolution* (University of Pennsylvania Press, 2003); Paul Johnson's flawed but worthwhile *A Shopkeeper's Millennium: Society and Revivals in Rochester, New York, 1813–1837* (Hill and Wang, 1978); and Leigh Eric Schmidt's provocative exploration of religion and language, *Hearing Things: Religion, Illusion, and the American Enlightenment* (Harvard University Press, 2000). Jon Butler's *Awash in a Sea of Faith: Christianizing the American People* (Harvard University Press, 1991) emphasizes the confusing diversity of the early American religious marketplace. Marvin Hill's *Quest for Refuge: The Mormon Flight from American Pluralism* (Signature, 1989) provides the classic argument placing Mormonism against that bewildering American religious landscape.

I have relied on a number of works to explore the various influences on the early Mormon movement. Dan Vogel's work on the Smith family in *Joseph Smith: The Making of a Prophet* (Signature, 2004) and *Religious Seekers and the Advent of Mormonism* (Signature, 1988) remains useful, as does his edited collection *Early Mormon Documents* (Signature, 1996–2003). Christopher C. Jones, "The Power and Form of Godliness: Methodist Conversion Narratives and Joseph Smith's First Vision," *Journal of Mormon History* 37 (Spring 2011): 88–114, offers a detailed analysis of Smith's visionary experiences in the light of evangelical revivalism.

D. Michael Quinn's *Early Mormonism and the Magic World View,* 2nd ed. (Signature, 1998), and Alan Taylor's "Rediscovering the Context of Joseph Smith's Treasure Seeking," *Dialogue: A Journal of Mormon Thought* 19 (Winter 1986): 18–28, exhaustively discuss the presence of folk magic in the early American republic, while John Brooke's *The Refiner's Fire: The Making of Mormon Cosmology, 1644–1844* (Cambridge University Press, 1996) is a wildly inventive and insightful, though often speculative, attempt to root early Mormonism in the European esoteric tradition. Val Rust's *Radical Origins: Early Mormon Converts and Their Colonial Ancestors* (University of Illinois Press, 2004) seeks to trace the heritage of early Mormons to radical colonial religious groups.

On the Book of Mormon, Philip Barlow's *Mormons and the Bible: The Place of the Latter-day Saints in American Religion* (Oxford University Press, 1991) explores the ways Mormons have thought about scripture more generally. Terryl Givens's *By the Hand of Mormon: The American Scripture That Launched a New World Religion* (Oxford University Press, 2002) is an essential reception history of the book, documenting its use as a sign of Joseph Smith's calling among the earliest Mormons. Grant Hardy's *Understanding the Book of Mormon: A Reader's Guide* (Oxford University Press, 2010) is the best and most penetrating examination of the text's content, voice, and theology to date.

Robert Matthews receives the treatment he deserves in Sean Wilentz and Paul Johnson, *The Kingdom of Matthias: A Story of Sex and Salvation in Nineteenth-Century America* (Oxford University Press, 1995).

TWO. LITTLE ZIONS: 1831–1839

I emphasize the idea of Zion as the central organizing principle of Joseph Smith's vision of Mormonism. This interpretation derives from some of the work already mentioned, particularly Bushman's biography, but from several other works as well. Grant Underwood, in *The Millenarian World of Early Mormonism* (University of Illinois Press, 1993), develops the eschatological aspects of the Mormon idea of Zion, stressing the millenarian aspects of the doctrines of the Gathering, the production of new scripture, and Joseph Smith's literal location of the place for Christ's kingdom. Samuel Brown's *In Heaven as It Is on Earth: Joseph Smith and the Early Mormon Conquest of Death* (Oxford University Press, 2011) discusses early Mormons' struggle with death, but more profoundly with the familial and social devastation death wrought, and reimagines the Zion community as a stand against the loss of human bonds. Stephen C. Taysom's *Shakers, Mormons, and Religious Worlds: Conflicting Visions, Contested Boundaries* (Indiana University Press, 2011) offers a highly theoretical and comparative analysis that is particularly useful for positioning Mormonism in relation to American culture.

Laurie Maffly-Kipp's "Tracking the Sincere Believer: Authentic Religion and the Enduring Legacy of Joseph Smith, Jr.," in *Joseph Smith, Jr.: Reappraisals after Two Centuries,* ed. Reid L. Neilson and Terryl Givens (Oxford University Press, 2009), 175–189, advocates an interpretation of Mormonism that downplays Joseph's charismatic leadership and looks instead to the influence of those around him. Terryl Givens and Matthew Grow, *Parley Pratt: The Apostle Paul of Mormonism* (Oxford University Press, 2011) presses this interpretation forward, arguing for Pratt's essential role as an expositor and interpreter of early Mormonism.

David Holland's *Sacred Borders: Continuing Revelation and Canonical Restraint in Early America* (Oxford University Press, 2011); Mark Noll and Nathan Hatch's edited collection *The Bible in America: Essays in Cultural History* (Oxford University Press, 1982); and the relevant portions of Noll's *America's God* provide essential context for the Mormons' lively experiments in scripture making, and Holland in particular shows the ways in which new scripture may function as a form of social criticism, offering a divinely sanctioned new way to access the society God might imagine.

Early Mormon converts have recently received a great deal of attention. Stephen J. Fleming's "The Religious Heritage of the British Northwest and the Rise of Mormonism," *Church History* 77 (March 2008): 73–104, and his "'Congenial to Almost Every Shade of Radicalism': The Delaware Valley and the Success of Early Mormonism," *Religion and American Culture* 17 (Summer 2007): 129–164, offer detailed case studies of certain groups of early Mormon converts. Steven Harper, "Infallible Proofs, Both Human and Divine: The Persuasiveness of Mormonism for Early Converts," *Religion and American Culture* 10 (Winter 2000): 991–118, draws some broader conclusions about the rational arguments of Mormon missionaries.

The Restorationist faith Joseph Smith discovered in Kirtland receives attention in Richard T. Hughes and Leonard Allen, *Illusions of Innocence: Protestant Primitivism in America, 1630–1875* (University of Chicago, 1988). John Wigger, *Taking Heaven by Storm: Methodism and the Rise of Popular Christianity in America* (Oxford University Press, 1998); Paul Conkin, *Cane Ridge: America's Pentecost* (Wisconsin University Press, 1990); and Ann Taves, *Fits, Trances, and Visions: Experiencing Religion and Explaining Experience from Wesley to James* (Princeton University Press, 1999) all explore the charismatic religion powerful in northeastern Ohio in the early nineteenth century.

On Joseph Smith's economic and ecclesiastical attempts to build Zion, Gregory A. Prince, *Power from on High: The Development of Mormon Priesthood* (Signature, 1995) and D. Michael Quinn, *The Mormon Hierarchy: Origins of Power* (Signature, 1994) discuss the construction of Joseph Smith's priesthood. The best study of the law of consecration and subsequent events to implement the United

Order in Utah is Leonard Arrington, Dean May, and Feramorz Fox, *Building the City of God: Community and Cooperation among the Mormons* (University of Illinois Press, 1992).

For the narrative of events in Kirtland and Ohio, Milton Backman, *The Heavens Resound: A History of the Latter-day Saints in Ohio, 1830–1838* (Deseret Book, 1983) has recently been eclipsed by Mark Staker's exhaustive *Hearken, O Ye People: The Historical Setting of Joseph Smith's Ohio Revelations* (Kofford Books, 2010). Alexander Baugh's *A Call to Arms: The 1838 Mormon Defense of Northern Missouri* (Brigham Young University Press, 2000) is a useful discussion of the events of the Missouri Mormon War slanted toward the Mormon perspective, as is Stephen Lesueur's *The 1838 Mormon War in Missouri* (University of Missouri Press, 1987), which is slanted toward the Missourian perspective.

THREE. CITY OF JOSEPH: 1839–1846

The basic studies of the Nauvoo period of Mormon history are Robert Flanders, *Nauvoo: Kingdom on the Mississippi* (University of Illinois Press, 1975) and Glen Leonard's more devotional but nonetheless exhaustive work *Nauvoo: A Place of Peace, a People of Promise* (Deseret Book, 2002), which succeeds as a social, economic, and cultural history. James B. Allen, Ronald K. Esplin, and David J. Whittaker's *Men with a Mission, 1837–1841: The Quorum of the Twelve Apostles in the British Isles* (Deseret Book, 1992) is a colorful account of the Quorum's mission to the British Isles.

The culture and everyday life of Nauvoo receive attention from Leonard, but I also relied on Terryl Givens, *People of Paradox: A History of Mormon Culture* (Oxford University Press, 2006) here and throughout the rest of my narrative. The origins and history of the Relief Society are examined in Jill Mulvay Derr, Janath Russell Cannon, and Maureen Ursenbach Beecher's essential *Women of Covenant: The Story of Relief Society* (Deseret Book, 2002), as well as in Linda King Newell and Valeen Tippetts Avery's *Mormon Enigma: Emma Hale Smith* (University of Illinois Press, 1984), in which the depiction of Emma's experiences with Nauvoo polygamy remains devastating.

On Nauvoo polygamy, Todd Compton, *In Sacred Loneliness: The Plural Wives of Joseph Smith* (Signature, 1997) exhaustively documents Joseph Smith's plural marriages. George D. Smith, *Nauvoo Polygamy: "But We Called It Celestial Marriage"* (Signature, 2009) seeks to do the same for other Mormon men who entered polygamy in Nauvoo. Richard van Wagoner's *Mormon Polygamy: A History* (Signature, 1989) offers a straightforward narrative history. My interpretation of polygamy in terms of community building relies on Bushman's *Rough Stone Rolling* and Lawrence Foster, *Women, Family, and Utopia: Communal Experiments of the Shakers, the Oneida Community, and the Mormons* (Syracuse University Press, 1991).

Joseph Smith's expanding Nauvoo theology, with its craving for community both spatial and temporal, its radical optimism about human nature, and its revised notions of God, should be understood in the context of American transcendentalism and Catholicism. Perry Miller's introduction to his edited collection *The Transcendentalists* (Harvard University Press, 1950) and the relevant sections of E. Brooks Holifield, *Theology in America: Christian Thought from the Age of the Puritans to the Civil War* (Yale University Press, 2005) are valuable. On American Catholicism, John McGreevey, *Catholicism and American Freedom* (Norton, 2004) is valuable, as are John Farina, *An American Experience of God: The Spirituality of Isaac Hecker* (Paulist, 1981) and Patrick Carey, *Orestes A. Brownson: American Religious Weathervane* (Eerdmans, 2004). On antebellum evangelical voluntarism and reform, see Ronald Walters, *American Reformers: 1815–1860* (Hill and Wang, 1997).

The unique doctrine and ordinances developed in Nauvoo have not received a great deal of analysis, though many commentators link them to older European traditions orbiting, ultimately, the divinization of humanity. The relevant sections of Catherine Albanese, *A Republic of Mind and Spirit: A Cultural History of American Metaphysical Religion* (Yale University Press, 2007) contain an interesting, if idiosyncratic, interpretation of the links connecting Freemasonry and Mormonism's spiritual quest; Brooke's *The Refiner's Fire* does likewise. Benjamin Park, "Salvation through a Tabernacle: Joseph Smith, Parley P. Pratt, and Early Mormon Theologies of Embodiment," *Dialogue: A Journal of Mormon Thought* 43 (Summer 2010): 1–44, roots these ideas in Anglo-American Protestant theology. David John Buerger, *Mysteries of Godliness: A History of Mormon Temple Worship* (Signature, 2002) documents the emergence of temple worship. Brown, *In Heaven as It Is on Earth* and Kathleen Flake, "Not to Be Riten: The Mormon Temple Rite as Oral Canon," *Journal of Ritual Studies* 9:2 (Summer 1995): 1–21, offer more sophisticated analyses of the rites.

D. Michael Quinn, *The Mormon Hierarchy* contains the most exhaustive discussion of the succession crisis following the death of Joseph Smith. Roger Launius, *Joseph Smith III: Pragmatic Prophet* (University of Illinois Press, 1995) is the best treatment of early RLDS history. Richard van Wagoner, *Sidney Rigdon: A Portrait of Religious Excess* (Signature, 1994) and Vickie Cleverley Speek, *God Has Made Us a Kingdom: James Strang and the Midwest Mormons* (Signature, 2006) examine some of the leadership alternatives to Brigham Young and the Quorum of the Twelve.

FOUR. COME, COME, YE SAINTS: 1846–1877

Any discussion of the Mormon trail should begin with Wallace Stegner's lyrical *The Gathering of Zion: The Story of the Mormon Trail* (McGraw-Hill, 1964), which captures both the extraordinary idealism and nobility of the trek as well as its blunders and tragedies. The definitive interpretation of the trek west as the Mormons' conscious attempt to claim the Biblical mantle of the children of Israel can be found in Jan Shipps's *Mormonism: The Story of a New Religious Tradition* (University of Illinois Press, 1984). Also useful are Carol Cornwall Madsen's documentary collection *Journey to Zion: Voices from the Mormon Trail* (Deseret Book, 1997); Stanley Kimball, *111 Days to Zion* (Deseret Book, 1978); and Leroy and Ann Hafen's enthusiastic *Handcarts to Zion: The Story of a Unique Western Migration, 1856–1860* (Arthur H. Clark, 1960). Leonard Arrington's *Brigham Young: American Moses* (Knopf, 1985) focuses on Young's institutional life; John Turner gives more attention to Young's personal, spiritual, and familial life in *Brigham Young: Pioneer Prophet* (Harvard University Press, 2012).

I ground my interpretation of the Mormon settlement of the West in the "new Western" history. Rather than an empty field for conquest and settlement, I see the West as a crowded place full of sharp elbows and competing agendas. Influential on my thinking are Patricia Nelson Limerick, *Legacy of Conquest: The Unbroken Past of the American West* (Norton, 1987) and Richard White, *It's Your Misfortune and None of My Own: A New History of the American West* (University of Oklahoma Press, 1991). Particularly relevant to Mormon history are W. Paul Reeve, *Making Space on the Western Frontier: Mormons, Miners, and Southern Paiutes* (University of Illinois Press, 2007), which illustrates the ways each group used strategies of settlement, economics, and politics as they struggled for control of southern Utah, and Jared Farmer, *On Zion's Mount: Mormons, Indians, and the American Landscape* (Harvard University Press, 2008), an environmental history of the settlement of the Great Basin and a study of the ways Mormons used cultural rituals to claim the land. Particularly useful to me on Mormon–Native American interactions are Armand Mauss, *All Abraham's Children: Changing Mormon Conceptions of Race and Lineage* (University of Illinois Press, 2005) and Scott Christensen, *Sagwich: Shoshone Chieftain, Mormon Elder, 1822–1887* (Utah State University Press, 1999).

The settlement of the Great Basin has received a great deal of attention from historians. Leonard Arrington's *Great Basin Kingdom: An Economic History of the Latter-day Saints, 1830–1900* (Harvard University Press, 1958) remains the basic work, and it is augmented by the essays discussing various aspects of the Mormon settlement in Thomas G. Alexander, ed., *Great Basin Kingdom Revisited* (Utah State University Press, 1991). Mormon settlement patterns are explored in Richard Francaviglia, *Believing in Place: A Spiritual Geography of the Great Basin* (University of Nevada, 2003) and Eugene Campbell, *Establishing Zion: The Mormon Church in the American West, 1847–1869* (Signature, 1988). The "Mormon village" is explored in Dean May, *Three Frontiers: Family, Land, and Society in the American West, 1850–1900* (Cambridge, 1994). The essays in Ronald Walker and Doris Dant, eds., *Nearly Everything Imaginable: The Everyday Life of Utah's Mormon*

Pioneers (Brigham Young University Press, 1999) offer invaluable glimpses of daily life in Mormon country.

The political conflicts that led to the Utah War have most recently been explored in David Bigler, *Forgotten Kingdom: The Mormon Theocracy in the American West, 1847–1896* (Arthur H. Clark, 1998); Will Bagley and David Bigler, *The Mormon Rebellion: America's First Civil War, 1857–1858* (University of Oklahoma, 2011); and most thoroughly in William MacKinnon, *At Sword's Point: A Documentary History of the Utah War to 1858* (Arthur H. Clark, 2008). Matthew Grow, *"Liberty to the Downtrodden": Thomas L. Kane, Romantic Reformer* (Yale University Press, 2008) explores these issues from Kane's non-Mormon perspective.

Ronald W. Walker, Richard E. Turley, and Glen M. Leonard, *Massacre at Mountain Meadows* (Oxford University Press, 2008) has become the definitive study of the Mountain Meadows Massacre, produced with the cooperation of the LDS church leadership (Turley currently serves as assistant church historian). It deepens and expands, though also largely confirms the conclusions of Juanita Brooks, *The Mountain Meadows Massacre* (Stanford University Press, 1950). Will Bagley, *Blood of the Prophets: Brigham Young and the Massacre at Mountain Meadows* (University of Oklahoma, 2002) assigns Brigham Young direct culpability for the tragedy.

FIVE. THE RISE AND FALL OF PLURAL MARRIAGE: 1852–1896

The definitive study of polygamy in the Utah period is Kathryn Daynes, *More Wives than One: Transformation of the Mormon Marriage System, 1840–1910* (University of Illinois Press, 2001). Most of the statistics in this chapter are drawn from Daynes's work. Jesse Embry, *Mormon Polygamous Families: Life in the Principle* (University of Utah Press, 1987) and B. Carmon Hardy, *Doing the Works of Abraham: Mormon Polygamy; Its Origin, Practice, and Demise* (Arthur H. Clark, 2007) are also valuable, as is Jeffrey Nichols's *Prostitution, Polygamy, and Power: Salt Lake City, 1847–1918* (University of Illinois Press, 2002).

A number of important works deal particularly with the experience of the women of polygamy. In 2010 Catherine Brekus delivered a plenary address to the Mormon History Association calling for increased attention to the agency of Mormon women exercised within, and even in support of, the seemingly painful boundaries of polygamy, later published as "Mormon Women and the Problem of Historical Agency," *Journal of Mormon History* 37:2 (Spring 2011). The essays in Claudia Bushman's edited volume *Mormon Sisters: Women in Early Utah* (Utah State University Press, 1997; originally published in 1976 by Emmeline Press) deftly explore this paradox. Mary Brown Firmage Woodward and Martha Sonntag Bradley's *4 Zinas: A Story of Mothers and Daughters on the Mormon Frontier* (Signature, 2000) delves into the experiences of a particular family—Zina Huntington and her mother, daughter, and granddaughter—to unfold the lives of four generations of Mormon women. Carol Cornwall Madsen's *An Advocate for Women: The Public Life of Emmeline B. Wells, 1870–1920* (Brigham Young University Press, 2005) is a monumental exploration of the life and activism of one of the central figures of late-nineteenth-century Utah. On the concept of social housekeeping and female activism in the Progressive era, see, for instance, Kathryn Kish Sklar, *Florence Kelley and the Nation's Work: The Rise of Women's Political Culture, 1830–1900* (Yale University Press, 1995).

The struggle over polygamy must be framed in the larger cultural, social, and political debates over marriage, federal power, and the law. Sarah Barringer Gordon's *The Mormon Question: Polygamy and Constitutional Conflict in Nineteenth-Century America* (University of North Carolina Press, 2001) informs my discussion greatly. Also valuable are Nancy Cott, *Public Vows: A History of Marriage and the Nation* (Harvard University Press, 2002) and Colleen McDannell, *The Christian Home in Victorian America, 1840–1900* (Indiana University Press, 1984). Patrick Q. Mason's *The Mormon Menace: Violence and Anti-Mormonism in the Postbellum South* (Oxford University Press, 2011) draws explicit parallels between anti-Mormonism and the nation's struggle over Reconstruction in the South, while Nathan B. Oman, "Natural Law and the Rhetoric of Empire: Reynolds v. United States, Polygamy, and Imperialism," *Washington University Law Review* 88 (2011): 661 connects American attempts to civilize Utah with the nation's imperial activities overseas. B. Carmon Hardy, *Solemn Covenant: The Mormon Polygamous Passage* (University of Illinois Press, 1992) is the standard examination of the slow demise of polygamy.

The Mormon Reformation receives its best discussions in Taysom, *Shakers, Mormons, and Religious Worlds* and Paul Peterson, *The Mormon Reformation* (Brigham Young University Press, 2002). Aaron Abell, *The Urban Impact on American Protestantism, 1865–1900* (Archon Press, 1962) and Paul Boyer, *Urban Masses and Moral Order in America, 1820–1920* (Harvard University Press, 1978) are standard works on the institutional church. Thomas G. Alexander has produced an excellent biography of Wilford Woodruff: *Things in Heaven and Earth: The Life and Times of Wilford Woodruff, a Mormon Prophet* (Signature, 1993).

SIX. ETERNAL PROGRESSION: 1890–1945

Excellent recent work on the American Progressive period includes T. J. Jackson Lears, *Rebirth of a Nation: The Making of Modern America, 1877–1920* (HarperCollins, 2009) and Maureen Flanagan, *America Reformed: Progressives and Progressivisms, 1890s–1920s* (Oxford University Press, 2007). The standard and essential study of

Mormonism in this period is Thomas G. Alexander, *Mormonism in Transition: A History of the Latter-day Saints, 1890–1930* (University of Illinois Press, 1986), which focuses on institutional, political, and economic reform, though it has key chapters on cultural and social issues. Alexander's interpretation of Joseph F. Smith and Heber J. Grant, which I somewhat follow, is reminiscent of Robert Weibe's *The Search for Order, 1877–1920* (Hill and Wang, 1966), which emphasized progressivism as an organizing force. Ethan Yorgason, *Transformation of the Mormon Culture Region* (University of Illinois Press, 2003) addresses the acculturation of the Mormons into American life in cultural and social ways.

In addition to these works, on Mormonism and American politics my discussion has been most informed by Kathleen Flake, *The Politics of American Religious Identity: The Seating of Reed Smoot, Mormon Apostle* (University of North Carolina Press, 2003); Jonathan Moyer, "Dancing with the Devil: The Making of the Utah-Republican Pact" (PhD dissertation, University of Utah, 2009); and Matthew Godfrey, *Religion, Politics, and Sugar: The Mormon Church, the Federal Government, and the Utah-Idaho Sugar Company, 1907–1921* (Utah State University Press, 2009), which emphasizes the challenges the Mormon church faced from Progressives suspicious of monopoly.

The abandonment of polygamy and the linguistic adaptations that accompanied it are addressed in Hardy, *Solemn Covenant*; Stephen C. Taysom, "A Uniform and Common Recollection: Joseph Smith's Legacy, Polygamy, and the Creation of Mormon Public Memory, 1852–2002," *Dialogue: A Journal of Mormon Thought* 35:3 (Fall 2002): 113–144; and D. Michael Quinn, "LDS Church Authority and New Plural Marriages, 1890–1904," *Dialogue: A Journal of Mormon Thought* 18:1 (Spring 1985): 9–105.

Though Heber J. Grant has yet to receive a thorough scholarly biography, Ronald Walker's *Qualities That Count: Heber J. Grant as Businessman, Missionary, and Apostle* (Brigham Young University Press, 2003) emphasizes Grant's Progressive credentials, confidence in organization, virtue, and rectitude. Garth Mangum and Bruce Blumell, *The Mormons' War on Poverty: A History of LDS Welfare, 1830–1990* (University of Utah Press, 1993) discusses the rise of the welfare program.

Alexander emphasizes that Mormon thinkers clarified the nature of God during this period. Truman Madsen's *Defender of the Faith: The B. H. Roberts Story* (Bookcraft, 1980) is devotional but nonetheless a reasonably sophisticated study of Roberts's thought. My own "The Crisis of Mormon Christology: History, Progress, and Protestantism, 1880–1930," *Fides et Historia: Journal of the Conference on Faith and History* 40 (Summer/Fall 2008) shows the ways Mormon theology engaged with Protestant theology to develop new ideas about eternal progression and human nature. Douglas Davies's *Joseph Smith, Jesus, and Satanic Opposition: Atonement, Evil and the Mormon Vision* (Ashgate, 2010) draws on the Progressive thought of Roberts and other thinkers to present a Mormon theology that emphasizes the free will's struggle against opposition, as does Blake Ostler's three-volume *Exploring Mormon Thought* (Kofford, 2001–08). On the Progressive Protestant theology to which these Mormons were responding, see William Hutchison, *The Modernist Impulse in American Protestantism* (Harvard University Press, 1976). Roberts and Talmage's controversy with Joseph Fielding Smith is discussed in Richard Sherlock and Jeffrey Keller, "We Can See No Advantage in a Continuation of the Discussion: The Roberts/Smith/Talmage Affair," *Dialogue: A Journal of Mormon Thought* 13:3 (Fall 1980): 63–78. Joseph Fielding Smith's background in Protestant fundamentalist literature is explored in Ronald Numbers, *The Creationists: The Evolution of Scientific Creationism* (University of California Press, 1993). The best study of fundamentalism itself is George Marsden, *Fundamentalism and American Culture* (Oxford University Press, 2005).

Eugene England discusses Orson Whitney and "home literature" in "Mormon Literature, Projects and Prospects," in *Mormon Americana: A Guide to Sources and Collections in the United States,* ed. David J. Whittaker (BYU Studies, 1995), 455–505.

The classic study of Mormon women's practices of anointing, blessing, and healing is Linda King Newell, "A Gift Given, a Gift Taken: Washing, Anointing, and Blessing the Sick among Mormon Women," in *The New Mormon History: Revisionist Essays on the Past,* ed. D. Michael Quinn (Signature, 1992), 101–18. It has recently been eclipsed by Jonathan Stapley and Kristine Wright's monumental "Female Ritual Healing in Mormonism," *Journal of Mormon History* 37:1 (Winter 2011): 1–85.

The origins of the Fundamentalist Church of Jesus Christ of Latter-day Saints are discussed in Martha Sonntag Bradley, *Kidnapped from That Land: The Government Raids on the Short Creek Polygamists* (University of Utah Press, 1993), and fundamentalist Mormon polygamy more generally in Brian Hales, *Modern Polygamy and Mormon Fundamentalism: The Generations after the Manifesto* (Kofford, 2006).

Lester E. Bush, "Mormonism's Negro Doctrine: An Historical Overview," *Dialogue: A Journal of Mormon Thought* 8 (Spring 1973): 11–68, may be the most influential historical article ever produced within the Mormon church: it was widely read by leaders of the church as they considered removing the restriction that kept members of African descent from attending the temple or receiving the priesthood. Other important works on race in the church include Mauss, *All Abraham's Children*; Newell Bringhurst, *Saints, Slaves, and Blacks: The Changing Place of Black People within Mormonism* (Greenwood Publishing, 1982); and Bringhurst and Darron T. Smith, eds., *Black and Mormon* (University of Illinois Press, 2006).

SEVEN. CORRELATION: 1945–1978

While nineteenth-century Mormon history has been graced with a number of solid historical narratives, there is no general narrative history of Mormonism after 1930. More generally, twentieth-century Mormon history has received staggeringly little attention compared to the nineteenth century. Those interested in narratives of twentieth-century Mormon history to date have had to rely on biographies and a few works by sociologists and other students of religion outside the historians' camp.

Three of the dominant figures of mid-twentieth-century Mormonism have recently received excellent biographies. D. Michael Quinn's *Elder Statesman: A Biography of J. Reuben Clark* (Signature, 2002) meticulously documents Clark's powerful influence in the First Presidency during the 1930s and 1940s. Gregory Prince and William Robert Wright's *David O. McKay and the Rise of Modern Mormonism* (University of Utah Press, 2002) is a history of the church during McKay's presidency as much as it is a biography of McKay himself, and it draws extensively on previously unavailable records collected by Claire Middlemiss, McKay's secretary. Edward Kimball's *Lengthen Your Stride: The Presidency of Spencer W. Kimball* (Deseret Book, 2005), by Kimball's son, provides extensive discussion of Kimball's reforms.

The emergence of Mormonism in the 1950s and 1960s as a "model minority," exemplified in David O. McKay's presidency, receives discussion in Patrick Allitt, *Religion in America since 1945* (Columbia University Press, 2003) and reflects the evolution Donald Meyer discusses in *The Positive Thinkers: Religion as Pop Psychology, from Mary Baker Eddy to Oral Roberts* (Pantheon Books, 1980). The sociologist Thomas O'Dea comments on Mormonism's balance of exclusivism with its desire to be a part of American society in *The Mormons* (Harvard University Press, 1957). Katie Clark Blakesley's "A Style of Our Own: Modesty and Mormon Women, 1951–2008," *Dialogue: A Journal of Mormon Thought* 42:2 (Spring 2009): 20–54, particularly discusses growing Mormon sartorial conservatism.

I build my arguments about the emergence of the Mormon value of "reverence," particularly exemplified in its music, on the work of Michael Hicks, *Mormonism and Music* (University of Illinois, 1989) and Kristine Haglund Harris, "Who Shall Sing If Not the Children? Primary Songbooks, 1880–1989," *Dialogue: A Journal of Mormon Thought* 37:4 (Winter 2004): 108–44. David Knowlton, "Belief, Metaphor, and Rhetoric: The Mormon Practice of Testimony Bearing," *Sunstone* 15:1 (April 1991): 20–27, discusses some aspects of contemporary Mormon piety, as does O'Dea, *The Mormons* and Mark Leone, *The Roots of Modern Mormonism* (Harvard University Press, 1979).

Mid-twentieth-century mission work in particular demands further attention from scholars. The demands of the growing international church are explored in James B. Allen, "Would Be Saints: West Africa before the 1978 Priesthood Revelation," *Journal of Mormon History* 17 (1991): 207–47. The sociologists Gordon and Gary Shepherd discuss their own 1960s missions in light of their academic training in *Mormon Passage: A Missionary Chronicle* (University of Illinois Press, 1998). The experiments of Alvin Dyer and his allies, particularly local mission president T. Bowring Woodbury, in the European mission are very critically examined in D. Michael Quinn's "I-Thou v. I-It Conversions: the Mormon Baseball Baptisms Era," *Sunstone* 16 (December 1993): 30–44.

The sociologist Armand Mauss's *The Angel and the Beehive: The Mormon Struggle with Assimilation* (University of Illinois Press, 1994) introduces the concept of "retrenchment," which I use to frame my discussion of the process of correlation. The administrative process is discussed in Arrington and Bitton, *Mormon Experience* and in Prince and Wright, *David O. McKay and the Rise of Modern Mormonism.* Jan Shipps's presidential address to the American Society of Church History, "From Peoplehood to Church Membership: Mormonism's Trajectory since World War II," *Church History* 76:2 (June 2007): 241–61, explores the ways correlation encouraged Mormons to conceive of themselves as part of an organization with particular duties and responsibilities.

The theology of Joseph Fielding Smith and Bruce R. McConkie has received the most sustained attention in O. Kendall White, *Mormon Neo-Orthodoxy: A Crisis Theology* (Signature, 1987). White argues that, in parallel to Protestant neo-orthodoxy that arose in Europe following the work of Karl Barth and Emil Brunner and in the United States in slightly different form following Reinhold Niebuhr and Paul Tillich, Mormon neo-orthodoxy in the 1950s and 1960s emphasized human incapacity, total dependence on God, and pessimism about civilization. While many Protestant neo-orthodox thinkers downplayed religious literalisms like the resurrection of Christ, those White labels Mormon neo-orthodox embraced such doctrines; they may thus be better compared to conservative evangelicals. Joel Carpenter, *Revive Us Again: The Reawakening of American Fundamentalism* (Oxford University Press, 1999) discusses contemporary evangelicals.

D. Michael Quinn, *The Mormon Hierarchy: Extensions of Power* (Signature, 1997) and Prince and Wright, *David O. McKay and the Rise of Modern Mormonism* contain the most sustained accounts of Ezra Taft Benson's political activities. Gary James Bergera and Ronald Priddis, *Brigham Young University: A House of Faith* (Signature, 1985) discusses the career of Ernest Wilkinson. The most extensive account of the church's campaign against the Equal Rights Amendment is Martha Sonntag Bradley, *Pedestals and Podiums: Utah Women, Religious Authority, and Equal Rights* (Signature, 2005).

The best account of the revocation of the priesthood restriction is Edward L.

Kimball, "Spencer W. Kimball and the Revelation on Priesthood," *BYU Studies* 47:2 (2008): 5–78. Also useful is Gregory Prince, "David O. McKay and Blacks: Building the Foundation for the 1978 Revelation," *Dialogue: A Journal of Mormon Thought* 35 (Spring 2002): 145–53.

EIGHT. TOWARD A GLOBAL CHURCH: 1978–2011

The most useful study of this period is Claudia Bushman, *Contemporary Mormonism: Latter-day Saints in Modern America* (Praeger, 2006). Ostling and Ostling, *Mormon America* is a deeply researched journalistic account of contemporary Mormonism. Susan Taber, *Mormon Lives: A Year in the Elkton Ward* (University of Illinois Press, 1993) is an intensely interesting compilation and analysis of oral histories gathered in a typical Mormon ward in Delaware over the course of a single year.

Rodney Stark's work on Mormonism—comprising not only his famous prediction but a number of studies of Mormon growth and organization—is collected in Reid Neilson, ed., *The Rise of Mormonism* (Columbia University Press, 2005). Gary Shepherd and Gordon Shepherd, "Sustaining a Lay Religion in a Modern Society: The Mormon Missionary Experience," in *Contemporary Mormonism,* ed. Marie Cornwall, Tim Heaton, and Lawrence Young (University of Illinois Press, 1994): 161–81; and Tania Rand Lyons, " 'Not Invited, But Welcome': The History and Impact of Church Policy on Sister Missionaries," *Dialogue: A Journal of Mormon Thought* 36:3 (Fall 2003):71–101, explore the experiences of missionaries. John-Charles Duffy, "The New Missionary Discussions and the Future of Correlation," *Sunstone* 138 (September 2005): 28–46, examines the introduction of the 2004 missionary handbook *Preach My Gospel.*

Philip Jenkins, "Letting Go: Understanding Mormon Growth in Africa," *Journal of Mormon History* 35:2 (Spring 2009): 1–26, is the single most focused evaluation of the drive and drag of Mormon growth overseas. Reid Neilson, *Early Mormon Missionary Activities in Japan, 1901–1924* (University of Utah Press, 2006) explores similar challenges in an earlier period; Neilson and Laurie Maffly-Kipp, eds., *Proclamation to the Pacific: Nineteenth-Century Mormonism and the Pacific Basin Frontier* (University of Utah Press, 2008) explores the story further. The anthropologist David Knowlton has done the most work on contemporary Mormon missions in Latin America; "Gringo, Jeringo: Anglo-Mormon Missionary Culture in Bolivia," in *Contemporary Mormonism,* ed. Cornwall, Heaton, and Young, 218–38, and "Missionaries and Terror: The Assassination of Two Elders in Bolivia," *Sunstone* 13 (August 1989): 10–14, are among the more important of his works. Nestor Curbelo's *The History of the Mormons in Argentina* (Kofford, 2009) is an important study originally published in Spanish.

G. Wesley Johnson and Marian Ashby Johnson, "On The Trail of the Twentieth Century Mormon Outmigration," *BYU Studies* 46:1 (2007): 41–83, uses statistical and survey research, combined with anecdotal data, to analyze the mid-twentieth-century Mormon diaspora from the Mormon cultural area in the American West. Jan Shipps, *The Scattering of the Gathered and the Gathering of the Scattered* (Dixie State College, 1991) explores this phenomenon in terms of theology and culture.

As the Mormons spread across the nation, they began also to get involved in politics and social movements. David Campbell and Robert Putnam, in *American Grace: How Religion Divides and Unites Us* (Simon and Schuster, 2010), use Mormonism as a particular example to explore the role of religion in American public life, charting the backlash that occurred after the passage of California's Proposition 8. Hugh Hewitt's access to Mitt Romney during the 2008 presidential campaign resulted in an admiring biography that discusses both generations of Romneys: *A Mormon in the White House?* (Trilennium, 2007). Newell Bringhurst and Craig Foster's *The Mormon Quest for the Presidency* (John Whitmer Books, 2008) places the Romney campaigns in the broader context of Mormonism's relationship with American politics. Jana Riess's *The Spiritual Traveler: Boston and New England* (HiddenSpring, 2002) discusses the Massachusetts temple controversy, as does Bushman, *Contemporary Mormonism*.

The various challenges that outmigration brought to the church are recent enough that primary as well as secondary sources are useful. Mormon engagement and disputation with evangelicals is ongoing. Stephen Robinson and Robert Millet have each published a number of works exploring the differences and similarities between Mormons and evangelicals. Of particular interest are Robinson and Craig Blomberg's *How Wide the Divide? A Mormon and an Evangelical in Conversation* (IVP Academic, 1997) and Millet's *A Different Jesus: The Christ of the Latter-day Saints* (Eerdmans, 2005). In 2002 Francis Beckwith, Carl Mosser, and Paul Owen, noted evangelical scholars, published *The New Mormon Challenge* (Zondervan, 2002), calling on evangelicals to educate themselves about Mormon theology and apologetics.

The Mormon feminist movement is still active, though neither so vocal nor so radical as it was in the 1970s and 1980s. After her excommunication, Sonia Johnson published an exposé, *From Housewife to Heretic* (Wildfire, 1989). Maxine Hanks's edited collection *Women and Authority: Emerging Mormon Feminism* (Signature, 1992) gathered much Mormon feminist writing in the 1980s and early 1990s. At roughly the same time Paul and Margaret Toscano published a speculative feminist Mormon theology, *Strangers in Paradox: Explorations in Mormon Theology* (Signature, 1990). Mary Farrell Bednarowski, *The Religious Imagination of American Women* (Indiana University Press, 1999) places Mormon feminism in context with that of other contemporary conservative Christian groups, in which well-educated, independent American women find ways to reconcile their public lives with a faith that often restricts their power relative to that of men.

More recently, controversy over gender and Mormonism has focused on issues of gay rights. D. Michael Quinn, *Same-Sex Dynamics among Nineteenth-Century Americans: A Mormon Example* (University of Illinois Press, 2001) seeks to locate the place of homosexual behavior in nineteenth-century Mormonism. Craig Harline, *Conversions: Two Family Stories from the Reformation and Modern America* (Yale University Press, 2011) explores, in part, the place of homosexuality in 1970s Mormonism. Douglas Winkler's *Lavender Sons of Zion: A History of Gay Men in Salt Lake City, 1950–1979* (University of Utah Press, 2008) explores homosexuality in mid-twentieth-century Mormonism.

The prominent Mormon intellectuals I've discussed in the text have all published widely. Eugene England published a number of essay collections; the best known is *Making Peace: Personal Essays* (Signature, 1995), while Leonard Arrington's *Adventures of a Church Historian* (University of Illinois Press, 1998) is a rather rollicking and frank memoir of his time as the official historian of the church. Richard Bushman's *On the Road with Joseph Smith: An Author's Diary* (Kofford, 2007) is a frank discussion of the genesis of Bushman's biography *Joseph Smith: Rough Stone Rolling* and the rather mixed response to it from the Mormon and the academic community.

In the spring of 1993, only months in advance of her excommunication, along with five other scholars, Lavina Fielding Anderson published an article entitled "The LDS Intellectual Community and Church Leadership: A Contemporary Chronology," *Dialogue: A Journal of Mormon Thought* 26:1 (Spring 1993): 7–64, charging various levels of church leadership with suppression and intimidation of Mormon intellectuals. More recently, however, signs of détente and cooperation have appeared. The "New Mormon History," the wave of Mormon scholarship that began in earnest in the 1970s, is discussed in Ronald Walker, David Whittaker, and James Allen, *Mormon History* (University of Illinois Press, 2001) and Jan Shipps, "Richard Lyman Bushman, the Story of Joseph Smith and Mormonism, and the New Mormon History," *Journal of American History* 94:2 (2007): 498–516. The church has sponsored the publication of a number of important historical projects, most prominently *The Joseph Smith Papers* (Church Historian's Press, 2008).

NOTES

INTRODUCTION

1 Parley P. Pratt, *The Autobiography of Parley Parker Pratt: One of the Twelve Apostles of the Church of Jesus Christ of Latter-day Saints* (New York: Russell Brothers, 1874), 38.

2 "Letters from a Mormonite," *The Unitarian* 1:5 (May 1834): 234.

3 Doctrine and Covenants 101:77–78, 80.

4 Jonathan Turner, *Mormonism in All Ages* (New York: Platt and Peters, 1842), 3.

5 Pratt, *Autobiography*, 108.

6 Parley P. Pratt, *The Angel of the Prairies: A Dream of the Future* (Salt Lake City: Abinadi Pratt, 1880), 15–16.

7 Brigham Young, "Epistle to the Brethren of the Church of Jesus Christ of Latter-day Saints," in *History of the Church of Jesus Christ of Latter-day Saints*, ed. B. H. Roberts (Salt Lake City: Deseret Book, 1964), 7:479.

8 Michael Luo, "Romney, Eye on Evangelicals, Defends His Faith," *New York Times* (December 7, 2007) A1.

9 Damon Linker, "The Big Test," *The New Republic* (January 1–15, 2007), 18–21; Jacob Weisberg, "Romney's Religion," Slate.com (December 20, 2006).

ONE. JOSEPH SMITH AND THE FIRST MORMONS

1 All of these titles appear in Matthews's conversations with Joseph Smith as recorded in Smith's journal for November 9–10, 1835. Dean C. Jessee, Mark

Ashurst-McGee, and Richard L. Jensen, eds., *The Joseph Smith Papers: Journals, Volume 1: 1832–1839* (Salt Lake City: Church Historian's Press, 2008), 92–95.

2   Lucy Mack Smith, *Lucy's Book: A Critical Edition of Lucy Mack Smith's Family Memoir*, ed. Lavina Fielding Anderson (Salt Lake City: Signature Books, 2001), 298–99, spelling as in original. This is the standard critical edition of Lucy Mack Smith, *Biographical Sketches of the Prophet Joseph Smith and His Progenitors for Many Generations*, which Lucy dictated to Martha Corey in 1845.

3   Anderson, ed., *Lucy's Book*, 307–8.

4   Anderson, ed., *Lucy's Book*, 310, 278.

5   Asael Smith to his children, April 10, 1799, reproduced in Richard Lloyd Anderson, *Joseph Smith's New England Heritage* (Salt Lake City: Deseret Book, 2003), 161–62.

6   Anderson, ed., *Lucy's Book*, 297, 319, 324–25.

7   Anderson, ed., *Lucy's Book*, 321.

8   Charles G. Finney, *Lectures on Revivals of Religion* (New York: Leavitt, Lord & Co., 1835), 9.

9   Anderson, ed., *Lucy's Book*, 344.

10   Alexander Neibaur Journal, May 24, 1844, in *The Papers of Joseph Smith*, ed. Dean C. Jessee (Salt Lake City: Deseret Book, 1989), 1:461.

11   "History" [1838], in *Papers*, ed. Jessee, 1:5.

12   "History" [1832], in *Papers*, ed. Jessee, 1:3.

13   "History" [1838], in *Papers*, ed. Jessee, 1:272.

14   "Joseph Smith—History," 1:32–36.

15   Anderson, ed., *Lucy's Book*, 345.

16   Isaac Hale Affidavit [1834] in Eber D. Howe, *Mormonism Unvailed* (Painesville, Ohio: published by the author, 1834), 264. Philastus Hurlbut, a journalist hostile to Mormonism, collected affidavits from many who knew Joseph Smith in the 1810s and 1820s.

17   "The Last Testimony of Sister Emma," *Saints' Herald* 26 (October 1, 1879), 289; this was an interview Emma gave to her son Joseph Smith III.

18   Isaac Hale Affidavit [1834] in Howe, *Mormonism Unvailed*, 264.

19   Anderson, ed., *Lucy's Book*, 379.

20   "Testimony of Martin Harris," transcribed by John Stevenson, September 4, 1870, cited in Joseph Grant Stevenson, "The Life of Edward Stevenson" (MA thesis, Brigham Young University, 1955), 163–64.

21   In 1844, this scrap was published as a broadside; the symbols on it do in fact appear reminiscent of Egyptian hieroglyphs but are not organized in any way that conveys coherent meaning. It is currently in possession of the

Community of Christ (formerly the Reorganized Church of Jesus Christ of Latter Day Saints).

22 "History" [1838], in *Papers,* ed. Jessee, 1:285.

23 "Last Testimony of Sister Emma," 290.

24 Anderson, ed., *Lucy's Book,* 417.

25 Doctrine and Covenants 3:2–3, 9.

26 Doctrine and Covenants 4:1.

27 David Whitmer, *An Address to All Believers in Christ* (Richmond, Mo.: n.p., 1887), 12.

28 "Last Testimony of Sister Emma," 290.

29 Moroni 10:32–33.

30 Alexander Campbell, *An Analysis of the Book of Mormon with an Examination of Its Internal and External Evidences, and a Refutation of Its Pretense to Divine Authority* (Boston: B. H. Green, 1832), 13.

31 "Testimony of the Three Witnesses," Book of Mormon.

32 *Messenger and Advocate* 1 (October 1834), 15.

33 Doctrine and Covenants 21:1, 1–4.

34 Dean C. Jessee, ed., "Joseph Knight's Recollection of Early Mormon History," *BYU Studies* 17:1 (Autumn 1976): 30.

35 Doctrine and Covenants 25:3–4.

TWO. LITTLE ZIONS

1 Doctrine and Covenants 76:20–21, 28, 70–71, 75, 103, 114.

2 Doctrine and Covenants 76 introduction.

3 Doctrine and Covenants 9:8.

4 Moses 7:18, 62–3; 4 Nephi 1:3.

5 Doctrine and Covenants 29:7–8.

6 Doctrine and Covenants 116:1.

7 Jan Shipps and John W. Welch, eds., *The Journals of William E. McLellin* (Urbana, Ill., and Provo, Utah: University of Illinois Press and Brigham Young University Press, 1994), 29–31. McLellin's records of his own half-dozen missions bear out these generalizations; see Welch's discussion in his introduction to the *Journals,* "The Acts of the Apostle William E. McLellin," 13–26.

8 All McLellin quotations are from Shipps and Welch, eds., *Journals of William E. McLellin,* 34–35. The German Reformed pastor Diedrich Willers observed that "they bear the name Mormonites" in a June 1830 letter. D. Michael Quinn, trans. and ed., "The First Months of Mormonism: A Contemporary View by Rev. Diedrich Willers," *New York History* 54 (July 1973): 317–33.

9   "Philo Dibble's Narrative," *Early Scenes in Church History* (Salt Lake City, Juvenile Instructor Office, 1882), 76–77.

10 Elizabeth Ann Whitney, "A Left from an Autobiography," *Woman's Exponent* (September 1, 1878), 51.

11 Quoted in Joseph Smith III and Heman Smith, *History of the Church of Jesus Christ of Latter Day Saints, 1805–1890* (Lamoni, Iowa: Herald House Publishing, 1897), 1:152–53.

12 Doctrine and Covenants 42:7, 30–35.

13 Doctrine and Covenants 42:30–36; 49:20.

14 Doctrine and Covenants 27:4–5.

15 Levi Hancock, "Autobiography [1803–1836]," Special Collections, Harold B. Lee Library, Brigham Young University, Provo, Utah.

16 "The History of Luke Johnson (by Himself)," *Latter-day Saints' Millennial Star* 26:53 (December 31, 1864), 834.

17 Pratt, *Autobiography,* 61; Doctrine and Covenants 43:2, 16–17.

18 Doctrine and Covenants 84:19–20.

19 Doctrine and Covenants 107:9, 33–36.

20 Doctrine and Covenants 91:12, 8, 11.

21 Doctrine and Covenants 109:8.

22 Edward W. Tullidge, *The Women of Mormondom* (New York: Tullidge and Crandall, 1877), 82.

23 "Autobiography of Jonathan Crosby," typescript, Utah State Historical Society, Salt Lake City, Utah.

24 W. W. Phelps to Sally Phelps, January 1836, *Journal History of the Church of Jesus Christ of Latter-day Saints,* Church History Library, Salt Lake City, Utah.

25 Manuscript History of the Church B–1 (September 1, 1834–November 2, 1838), 621–22, Church History Library, Salt Lake City, Utah.

26 Jessee, Ashurst-McGee, and Jensen, eds., *The Joseph Smith Papers: Journals, Volume 1: 1832–1839,* 221–22.

27 Ezra Booth, "Letter II," in Eber Howe, ed., *History of Mormonism* (Painesville, Ohio: published by the author, 1840), 181, 177.

28 Doctrine and Covenants 89:5, 8, 12.

29 Howe, ed., *History of Mormonism,* 229.

30 Josiah Gregg, *Commerce of the Praries: The Journal of a Santa Fe Trader* (1844; repr. Dallas: Southwest Press, 2006), 210.

31 *Latter-day Saints' Millennial Star* 33:14 (October 9, 1852), 514.

32 "Petition to Governor Daniel Dunklin," *Evening and the Morning Star* (December 1833), 114. This was the official Mormon newspaper that Phelps ran in Independence; it reprinted the Missourians' declaration.

33 Amos Hayden, *Early History of the Disciples in the Western Reserve, Ohio* (Cincinnati: Chase and Hall, 1876), 221.

34 Doctrine and Covenants 101:2, 4, 6, 9, 77, 80.

35 Doctrine and Covenants 103: 15.

36 Hancock, "Autobiography [1803–1836]."

37 Jessee, ed., "Joseph Knight's Recollection," 38–39.

38 Doctrine and Covenants 105:3.

39 "Autobiography of Jonathan Crosby," typescript, Utah State Historical Society, Salt Lake City, Utah.

40 Parley P. Pratt to Joseph Smith, May 23, 1837, reprinted in Arthur Deming, ed., *Naked Truths about Mormonism* 1:2 (April 1888), 4.

41 Donald Q. Cannon and Lyndon W. Cook, eds., *Far West Record: Minutes of the Church of Jesus Christ of Latter-day Saints, 1830–1844* (Salt Lake City: Deseret Book, 1983), 136.

42 Sidney Rigdon, *Oration Delivered by Mr. Rigdon on the 4th of July, 1838, at Far West, Caldwell Co., Missouri* (Far West, Mo.: Journal Office, 1838).

43 John Corrill, *A Brief History of the Church of Christ of Latter-Day Saints (commonly called Mormons)* (St. Louis: published by the author, 1839), 32.

44 Reproduced in John P. Greene, *Facts Relative to the Expulsion of the Mormons or Latter Day Saints, from the State of Missouri, under the "Exterminating Order"* (Cincinnati, Ohio: R. P. Brooks, 1839), 26.

THREE. CITY OF JOSEPH

1 "Mrs. Paul Selby," "Recollections of the Little Girl in the Forties," *Journal of the Illinois State Historical Society* 16 (1923–1924): 167–68.

2 Jesee W. Johnstun, "Reminiscences," Church History Library, Salt Lake City, Utah.

3 "Extracts of the Minutes of Conferences," *Times and Seasons* 1:1 (November 1839), 15.

4 Doctrine and Covenants 121:1–2; 122:7.

5 Turner, *Mormonism in All Ages,* 58.

6 Susan Staker, ed., *Waiting for World's End: The Diaries of Wilford Woodruff* (Salt Lake City: Signature Books, 1993), 23.

7 "To the Saints Scattered Abroad," *Times and Seasons* 1:10 (August 1840), 222.

8 *Latter-day Saints' Millennial Star* 2 (February 1832), 154.

9 Parley P. Pratt, *A Voice of Warning and Instruction to All People* (New York: W. Sandford, 1837); Parley P. Pratt, *History of the Late Persecution Inflicted by the State of Missouri upon the Mormons* (Detroit: Dawson and Bates, 1839).

10 "State Gubernatorial Convention," *Times and Seasons* 3:5 (January 1842), 651.

11 "Our City," *Times and Seasons* 5:5 (March 1844), 472.

12 Alexis de Tocqueville, *Alexis de Tocqueville: Democracy in America,* ed. Richard Heffner (New York: Mentor, 1956), 95.

13 Sarah Granger Kimball, "Auto-biography," *Woman's Exponent* 12:7 (September 1, 1883), 51.

14 Kimball, "Auto-biography," 51.

15 Minutes, March 17, 1842, Nauvoo Relief Society Minutes Book, Church History Library, Salt Lake City, Utah.

16 Ellen W. Douglas to parents, June 2, 1842, Ellen W. Parker Papers, Church History Library, Salt Lake City, Utah.

17 Maureen Ursenbach, ed., "Eliza R. Snow's Nauvoo Journal," *BYU Studies* 15:4 (Summer 1975): 413.

18 Doctrine and Covenants 124:40.

19 Vilate Kimball to Heber Kimball, October 11, 1840, Church History Library, Salt Lake City, Utah.

20 *Journal of Discourses* (Liverpool: Franklin D. Richards, 1854–1886), April 9, 1857, 5:85.

21 Abraham 3:22–24.

22 Andrew Ehat and Lyndon Cook, ed., *The Words of Joseph Smith* (Provo, Utah: Religious Studies Center, 1980), 541, 550, 544.

23 Doctrine and Covenants 130:22.

24 William Ellery Channing, "Likeness to God," *The Complete Works of W. E. Channing* (London: George Routledge, 1892), 230.

25 Charles Brownson, ed., *The Works of Orestes A. Brownson* (Detroit: Thorndike House, 1884), 12:359.

26 Doctrine and Covenants 132:7, 19, 45, 32.

27 Oliver Cowdery to Warren Cowdery, January 21, 1838, Oliver Cowdery Letterbook, Church History Library, Salt Lake City, Utah.

28 Zina D. H. Young, "Autobiographical Sketches" [n.d.], Zina Card Brown Family Collection, 1806–1972, Church History Library, Salt Lake City, Utah.

29 "Lucy Walker Kimball Affidavit, 7 December 1902," *Woman's Exponent* (January 1911), 43.

30 *Journal of Discourses,* November 9, 1881, 23:64.

31 *Journal of Discourses,* July 14, 1855, 3:266.

32 Pratt, *Autobiography,* 329.

33 Lyman Littlefield, ed., *Reminiscences of Latter-day Saints* (Logan, Utah: The Utah Journal Company, 1888), 46.

34 Helen Mar Kimball Whitney, *Why We Practice Plural Marriage* (Salt Lake City: Juvenile Instructor Office, 1884), 58–59, 22.

35 Helen Mar Kimball Whitney, "Autobiography, 1881 Mar. 30," typescript, Church History Library, Salt Lake City, Utah.

36   Littlefield, ed., *Reminiscences*, 46.

37   Emily D. P. Young, "Incidents in the Early Life of Emily Dow Partridge" [December 1876], Special Collections, Marriott Library, University of Utah, Salt Lake City, Utah.

38   "The Nauvoo Diaries of William Clayton," June 23, 1843, typescript, Church History Library, Salt Lake City, Utah.

39   Doctrine and Covenants 132:54.

40   "Nauvoo Diaries of William Clayton," July 12, 13, 1843.

41   "Last Testimony of Sister Emma," 289.

42   John C. Bennett, *A History of the Saints: or, an Expose of Joe Smith and Mormonism* (Boston: Leland and Whiting, 1842), 306–7.

43   "Theodemocracy," *Times and Seasons* 5:8 (April 15, 1844), 510.

44   Joseph Smith, *General Smith's Views of the Powers and Policy of the Government of the United States* (Nauvoo, Ill.: John Taylor, 1844), 5–8; *General Joseph Smith's Appeal to the Green Mountain Boys* (Nauvoo, Ill.: John Taylor, 1843), 3. Both of these were probably mostly written by W. W. Phelps, who often served as Joseph Smith's ghostwriter.

45   *Nauvoo Expositor* (June 7, 1844), 1.

46   "Extra," *Warsaw Signal* (June 11, 1844), 1.

47   Vilate Kimball to Heber Kimball, June 9, 1844, Kimball Family Correspondence, 1838–1871, Church History Library, Salt Lake City, Utah.

48   "The Answer of Governor Ford to the Warsaw Committee," *Nauvoo Neighbor* (July 3, 1844).

49   "The Death of the Modern Mahomet," *New York Herald* (July 8, 1844), 1.

50   "History of Joseph Smith," *Latter-day Saints' Millennial Star* 14:25 (April 1863), 215.

51   "The Mormon Conference," *Saints Herald* 5:1 (May 1860), 102.

52   "History of Joseph Smith," *Latter-day Saints' Millennial Star* 14:25 (April 1863), 216.

53   Doctrine and Covenants 136:22, 4.

54   George Alley to Joseph Alley, October 9, 1845, Church History Library, Salt Lake City, Utah.

55   "Elder Woodruff's Letter," *Times and Seasons* 6:23 (February 15, 1846), 1128.

56   *Warsaw Signal* (February 11, 1846), 1.

FOUR. COME, COME, YE SAINTS

1   Lawrence Clayton, ed., *William Clayton's Journal* (Salt Lake City: Clayton Family Association, 1921), 36.

2   Maureen U. Beecher, ed., *The Personal Writings of Eliza Roxcy Snow* (Salt Lake City: University of Utah Press, 1995), 114.

3   Quoted in Wallace Stegner, *The Gathering of Zion* (New York: McGraw-Hill, 1964), 59.

4   Quoted in Carol Cornwall Madsen, ed., *Journey to Zion: Voices from the Mormon Trail* (Salt Lake City: Deseret Book, 1997), 32.

5   Will Bagley, ed., *The Pioneer Camp of the Saints: The 1846 and 1847 Mormon Trail Journals of Thomas Bullock* (Logan: Utah State University Press, 2001), 124.

6   Bagley, ed., *Pioneer Camp of the Saints*.

7   Scott Kenney, ed., *Wilford Woodruff's Journal, 1833–1898* (Salt Lake City: Signature Books, 1984), 187, May 25, 1847.

8   Stegner, *Gathering of Zion*, 81.

9   Helen Mar Kimball Whitney, "Our Travels Beyond the Mississippi," *Woman's Exponent* 12 (December 1883), 83.

10 Quoted in Madsen, ed., *Journey to Zion,* 44.

11 "Epistle from the Quorum of the Twelve Apostles, 23 December 1847," *Latter-day Saints' Millennial Star* 10 (March 15, 1848), 82.

12 B. H. Roberts, *The Mormon Battalion: Its History and Achievements* (Salt Lake City: Juvenile Instructor, 1919) describes the statistics of the Battalion muster on 25–26.

13 Ronald Barney, ed., *The Mormon Vanguard Brigade of 1847: Norton Jacob's Record* (Logan: Utah State University Press, 2005), 229.

14 Everett Cooley, ed., "The Robert S. Bliss Journal," *Utah Historical Quarterly* 27 (October 1959): 389, 390.

15 Bagley, ed., *Pioneer Camp of the Saints*, 243–44.

16 Willard Richards to Orson Pratt, July 21, 1847, typescript, Church History Library, Salt Lake City, Utah.

17 *Latter-day Saints' Millennial Star* 17 (January 26, 1856), 52.

18 Twiss Bermingham diary, August 3, 1856, reproduced in Leroy and Ann Hafen, *Handcarts to Zion, 1856–1860* (Norman, Okla.: Arthur C. Clark, 1960), 72–73.

19 Sandra Ailey Petree, ed., *Recollections of Past Days: The Autobiography of Patience Loader* (Logan: Utah State University Press, 2006), 73.

20 "Captain Grant's Report from Devil's Gate," *Deseret News* (November 19, 1856).

21 *Journal of Discourses,* October 5, 1856, 4:113.

22 Clayton, ed., *William Clayton's Journal,* 326.

23 *Journal of Discourses,* September 10, 1854, 2:104.

24 *Journal of Discourses*, March 28, 1858, 7:47.

25 Brigham Young Diary, August 11, 1857, cited in Leonard Arrington, *Brigham Young: American Moses* (New York: Knopf, 1985), 254.

26 Brigham Young to Colonel Edmund Alexander, October 14, 1857, cited in Arrington, *Brigham Young,* 255.

27 Arthur Welchman, "Reminiscences [1854–1917]," June 1858, Church History Library, Salt Lake City, Utah.

28 James Henry Carleton, *Special Report on the Mountain Meadows Massacre, May 25, 1859* (Washington, D.C.: Government Printing Center, 1902), 15.

29 Brigham Young to Isaac C. Haight, September 10, 1857, Letterpress Copybook 3:827–28, Brigham Young Office Files, Church History Library, Salt Lake City, Utah.

30 James H. Haslam, interview by S. A. Kenner, reported by Josiah Rogerson, December 4, 1884, typescript, 11, in Josiah Rogerson, Transcripts and Notes of John D. Lee Trials, Church History Library, Salt Lake City, Utah.

FIVE. THE RISE AND FALL OF PLURAL MARRIAGE

1 George Q. Cannon, "Enduring to the End," October 5, 1890; reported in *Collected Discourses: Delivered by Wilford Woodruff, His Two Counselors, the Twelve Apostles, and Others,* vol. 2, edited and compiled by Brian H. Stuy (Woodland Hills, Utah: B.H.S. Publishing, 1988), 115–16.

2 *Journal of Discourses,* August 29, 1852, 1:58.

3 This poem, which Eliza titled "Invocation: Or the Eternal Father and Mother," has since been added to the official LDS hymnbook under the title "O My Father." *Hymns of the Church of Jesus Christ of Latter-day Saints* (Salt Lake City: Intellectual Reserve, 1985).

4 Orson Spencer, *Letters,* 6th ed. (Liverpool: Budge, 1879), 192; for a great deal more on this theme, see also his *Patriarchal Order* (Liverpool: Richards, 1853).

5 *Journal of Discourses,* August 29, 1852, 1:58.

6 Whitney, *Why We Practice Plural Marriage,* 26.

7 "Talmage on the Mormons," *New York Sun* (September 27, 1880).

8 Kenney, ed., *Wilford Woodruff's Journal, 1833–1898,* 8:126–127.

9 David John Journal, 1:418, cited in Kathryn Daynes, *More Wives Than One: The Transformation of the Mormon Marriage System, 1840–1910* (Urbana: University of Illinois Press, 2001), 72. The statistics that follow are drawn from Daynes's book.

10 *Semi-Annual Report of the General Conference of the Church of Jesus Christ of Latter-day Saints,* April 24, 1930 (Salt Lake City: Deseret News, 1897–1964), 185.

11 Whitney, *Why We Practice Plural Marriage,* 9.

12 Whitney, *Why We Practice Plural Marriage,* 22.

13   Donna Toland Smart, ed., *Mormon Midwife: The 1846–1888 Diaries of Patty Bartlett Sessions* (Logan: Utah State University Press, 1997), 63–64.

14   "Why? Ah, Why?" *Latter-day Saints' Millennial Star* 46:36 (November 17, 1874), 722.

15   Emmeline B. Wells, Journal, September 30, 1874, reprinted in *Women's Voices: An Untold History of the Latter-day Saints, 1830–1900,* ed. Jill Mulvay Derr, Audrey M. Godfrey, and Kenneth W. Godfrey (Salt Lake City: Deseret Book, 1982), 298.

16   James Daniel Richardson, *A Compilation of the Messages and Papers·of the Presidents* (New York: Bureau of National Literature, 1897), 10:4946.

17   Elizabeth Cady Stanton, *Eighty Years and More* (New York: European Publishing Company, 1898), 283–84.

18   "Miss E. R. Snow's Address to the Female Relief Societies of Weber County," *Latter-day Saints' Millennial Star* 33 (September 12, 1871), 578.

19   *Woman's Exponent* 5:6 (August 15, 1876), 44.

20   Whitney, *Why We Practice Plural Marriage,* 24.

21   "Zina D. H. Young Autobiography," 3.5, typescript, Zina D. H. Young collection, Church History Library, Salt Lake City, Utah.

22   Cited in Jesse C. Embry, *Mormon Polygamous Families: Life in the Principle* (Salt Lake City: University of Utah Press, 1987), 178.

23   Cited in Daynes, *More Wives Than One,* 156.

24   Levi Savage, *Journal of Levi Mathers Savage,* September 12, 1875 (Provo, Utah: Mimeographed by the Brigham Young University Extension Division, ca. 1955).

25   Edward Judson, *The Institutional Church* (New York: Lentilhon & Co., 1899), 30–31.

26   Susa Young Gates, *History of the Young Ladies Mutual Improvement Association* (Salt Lake City: Deseret News, 1911), 64–65.

27   Cited in William Hartley, "From Men to Boys: LDS Aaronic Priesthood Offices, 1829–1996," *Journal of Mormon History* 22 (Spring 1996): 103.

28   William Belmont Parker, *The Life and Public Services of Justin Smith Morrill* (Boston: Houghton Mifflin, 1924), 82–83.

29   Hubert Howe Bancroft, *History of Utah, 1540–1886* (San Francisco: The History Company, 1889), 381.

30   Samuel A. Cartwright and C. G. Forshey, based on the observations of Roberts Bartholemew, "Hereditary Descent, or Depravity of the Offspring of Polygamy among the Mormons," *DeBow's Review* 30 (1861), 203.

31   James Rusling, "Interview with President William McKinley," *Christian Advocate* (January 22, 1903), 17, reprinted in Daniel B. Schirmer, *The Philippines Reader* (Cambridge, Mass.: South End Press, 1987), 22.

32   Josiah Strong, *Our Country* (New York: Baker and Taylor, 1891), 116, 112.

33   Cited in Sarah Barringer Gordon, *The Mormon Question: Polygamy and Con-stitutional Conflict in Nineteenth-Century America* (Chapel Hill: University of North Carolina Press, 2001), 125.

34   Kenney, ed., *Wilford Woodruff's Journal,* 6:518–19.

35   B. H. Roberts, *The Life of John Taylor* (Salt Lake City: Cannon and Sons, 1892), 360–61.

36   Donald Godfrey and Brigham Card, eds., *The Diaries of Charles Ora Card,* February 12, 1887 (Salt Lake City: University of Utah Press, 1993).

37   "Remarks," *Deseret Weekly* (November 14, 1891), 11.

38   This statement has since been canonized; it appears in Mormon scripture as Official Declaration 1.

39   Ronald W. Walker, ed., "B. H. Roberts and the Woodruff Manifesto," *BYU Studies* 22 (Summer 1982): 365; Abraham Cannon diaries, July 10 and September 30, 1890, Special Collections, Harold B. Lee Library, Brigham Young University, Provo, Utah.

40   Joseph Dean Diary, October 6, 1890, Church History Library, Salt Lake City, Utah.

41   John Whittaker Diaries, October 6, 1890, John Whittaker Papers, 1867–1963, Marriott Library Special Collections, University of Utah, Salt Lake City, Utah.

42   "The New Revelation," *Salt Lake Tribune* (October 9, 1890), 1.

43   "Dedicatory Prayer," reprinted in James E. Talmage, *The House of the Lord* (Salt Lake City: Deseret News, 1912), 162.

SIX. ETERNAL PROGRESSION

1   Ronald J. Pestritto and William J. Atto, eds., *American Progressivism: A Reader* (Lanham, Md.: Rowman and Littlefield, 2008), 36.

2   Anthon H. Lund diary, March 30, 1899, cited in Thomas G. Alexander, *Mormonism in Transition: A History of the Latter-day Saints, 1890–1930* (Urbana: University of Illinois Press, 1985), 10.

3   *Proceedings before the Committee on Privileges and Elections in the Matter of the Protests against the Right of the Hon. Reed Smoot, a Senator from Utah, to Hold His Seat,* vol. 1 (Washington, D.C.: Government Printing Office, 1906), 31.

4   *Proceedings before the Committee on Privileges and Elections,* 313.

5   *Proceedings before the Committee on Privileges and Elections,* 99.

6   *Proceedings before the Committee on Privileges and Elections,* 98.

7   Merle Graffam, ed., *Salt Lake City School of the Prophets, Minute Book 1883,* reprint ed. (Salt Lake City: Pioneer Press, 1992), 27.

8   B. H. Roberts, "Comment on Dr. Reiser's Letter," *Improvement Era* 1 (May 1898), 7.

9   Franklin S. Richards, *The Admission of Utah: Replies of Hon. F. S. Richards to Statements in Opposition to the Admission of Utah as a State, Made Before the Committee on Territories of the United States Senate, Saturday, March 10, 1888* (Washington, D.C.: Gibson Brothers, 1888), 11.

10   James E. Talmage, *Articles of Faith* (Salt Lake City: Deseret News, 1899), 458. Like Talmage's later books *Jesus the Christ* (Salt Lake City: Deseret News, 1915) and *The House of the Lord* (Salt Lake City: Deseret News, 1909), *Articles of Faith* was published by the church, giving it semi-official status; all of his books remain in print, and several are included in the official library allowed to LDS missionaries.

11   James R. Clark, ed., *Messages of the First Presidency of the Church of Jesus Christ of Latter-day Saints* (Salt Lake City: Bookcraft, 1965–75), 5:329.

12   James E. Talmage, *The Vitality of Mormonism* (Boston: Gorham Press, 1919), 221, 223.

13   G. Homer Durham, ed., *Discourses of Wilford Woodruff* (Salt Lake City: Deseret Book, 1946), 157.

14   John Widtsoe, *Joseph Smith as Scientist* (Salt Lake City: General Young Men's Improvement Board, 1908), 1.

15   Doctrine and Covenants 88:36, 131:7–8.

16   Talmage, *Jesus the Christ,* 676.

17   "The Articles of Faith," Pearl of Great Price.

18   B. H. Roberts, *The Gospel* (Salt Lake City: Deseret News, 1888), 290. Gordon Shepherd and Gary Shepherd note that themes of "Experience" and "Eternal Progression" rose sharply in the General Conferences of the 1890–1919 era compared to earlier periods. Similarly, "Exaltation" as a theme spiked in those years compared to both preceding and following eras. See Shepherd and Shepherd, *A Kingdom Transformed: Themes in the Development of Mormonism* (Salt Lake City: University of Utah Press, 1984), 242.

19   B. H. Roberts, *The Mormon Doctrine of Deity* (Salt Lake City: Deseret News, 1903), 202; Talmage, *Jesus the Christ,* 8–9.

20   The First Presidency and the Twelve, "The Father and the Son: A Doctrinal Exposition," in *Messages of the First Presidency,* ed. Clark, 5:25; Roberts, *Doctrine of Deity,* 75–77; Roberts, *Gospel,* 261.

21   Nephi Anderson, *Added Upon* (Salt Lake City: Deseret News, 1898), 8.

22   Orson F. Whitney, "Home Literature," *Contributor* 9 (June 1888): 297–302.

23   Dedicatory Address, Cardston Temple, August 1923, reproduced in *Teachings of Presidents of the Church: Heber J. Grant* (Salt Lake City: Church of Jesus Christ of Latter-day Saints, 2002), 52.

24   Heber J. Grant, "Temperance—Inspirations to Progress," *Young Women's Journal* 20:9 (September 1908), 506.

25 First Presidency to Heber Q. Hale, March 28, 1923, cited in Alexander, *Mormonism in Transition,* 295.

26 Ellis Seymour Heninger Mission Diary, Southern States Mission, June 9, 1901, Special Collections, Harold B. Lee Library, Brigham Young University, Provo, Utah.

27 Claudia L. Bushman, ed., *Pansy's History: The Autobiography of Margaret E. P. Gordon, 1866–1966* (Logan: Utah State University Press, 2011), 205.

28 *Semi-Annual Report of the General Conference of the Church of Jesus Christ of Latter-day Saints,* April 6, 1921 (Salt Lake City: Deseret News, 1897–1964), 190–91.

29 Martha Hickman to Louise Robison, November 28, 1935; Robison to Hickman, December 5, 1935, both cited in Linda King Newell, "A Gift Given, a Gift Taken: Washing, Anointing, and Blessing the Sick among Mormon Women," in *The New Mormon History: Revisionist Essays on the Past,* ed. D. Michael Quinn (Salt Lake City: Signature, 1992), 115.

30 Roberts's dismissal of Beecher is in *The Gospel,* 3rd ed. (Salt Lake City: Deseret News, 1901), 271.

31 Joseph Fielding Smith, "Faith Leads to a Fullness of Truth and Righteousness," *Utah Genealogical and Historical Magazine* 21 (October 1930): 145–58.

32 James E. Talmage, *The Earth and Man* (Salt Lake City: The Church of Jesus Christ of Latter-day Saints, 1931), 4.

33 Heber J. Grant diary, January 25, 1931, Heber J. Grant Collection, Church Archives, Salt Lake City, Utah, cited in Alexander, *Mormonism in Transition,* 288.

34 First Presidency Minutes, April 7, 1931, cited in Trent D. Stephens and Jeffrey Meldrum, "Evolution and Mormonism: A Quest for Understanding," *BYU Studies* 45:1 (2006): 182–89.

SEVEN. CORRELATION

1 *Semi-Annual Report of the General Conference of the Church of Jesus Christ of Latter-day Saints,* October 6, 1940 (Salt Lake City: Deseret News, 1897–1964), 96.

2 "Prophet, Seer, and Innovator," *Time* (February 2, 1970), 50.

3 David O. McKay, "Reverence," *Instructor* 101 (October 1966): 371.

4 *Semi-Annual Report of the General Conference of the Church of Jesus Christ of Latter-day Saints,* October 6, 1955 (Salt Lake City: Deseret News, 1897–1964), 89. See also Marion Romney, "Reverence," *Ensign* (October 1976), 2, and Spencer W. Kimball, *We Should Be a Reverent People* (Salt Lake City: Church of Jesus Christ of Latter-day Saints, 1976).

5   *Semi-Annual Report of the General Conference of the Church of Jesus Christ of Latter-day Saints,* April 4, 1946 (Salt Lake City: Deseret News, 1897–1964), 317.

6   "Primary Leaders Challenged at Annual Conference," *Ensign* (June 1973), 68.

7   "Prophet, Seer, and Innovator," 50.

8   James B. Allen and Glen Leonard, *The Story of the Latter-day Saints* (Salt Lake City: Deseret Book, 1972), 364.

9   David O. McKay Diaries, June 23, 1952, cited in Gregory Prince and William Robert Wright, *David O. McKay and the Rise of Modern Mormonism* (Salt Lake City: University of Utah Press, 2005), 365–66. Though they are called "diaries," this material is in fact a vast collection of clippings, office records, memoranda, and other such data collected by McKay's secretary Clare Middlemiss; it was used for the first time in Prince and Wright's book.

10   David O. McKay Diaries, September 4, 1958, cited in Prince and Wright, *David O. McKay,* 370.

11   Adewole Ogunmokun to Missionary Department of the LDS Church, December 20, 1961, cited in James B. Allen, "Would Be Saints: West Africa before the 1978 Priesthood Revelation," *Journal of Mormon History* 17 (1991): 214.

12   David O. McKay Diaries, March 6, 1956, cited in Prince and Wright, *David O. McKay,* 145.

13   *Gospel Principles* (Salt Lake City: Church of Jesus Christ of Latter-day Saints, 2009), 139, 2.

14   Alvin R. Dyer, "The Challenging and Testifying Missionary," 1962, transcript, Church History Library, Salt Lake City, Utah, [4].

15   Billy Graham, *Peace with God* (1952; repr. Nashville: W Publishing Group, 2002), [9].

16   Alvin R. Dyer, "The Challenging and Testifying Missionary," in Dyer, *Messages to the Missionary* (Frankfurt, Germany: European Mission, 1961), 1.

17   Bruce R. McConkie to Eugene England, February 19, 1981. Photocopy in author's possession.

18   Bruce R. McConkie, *Mormon Doctrine* (Salt Lake City: Bookcraft, 1958), 5.

19   McConkie, *Mormon Doctrine,* 141.

20   McConkie, *Mormon Doctrine,* 238, emphasis in original.

21   McConkie, *Mormon Doctrine,* 658.

22   McConkie, *Mormon Doctrine,* 66, 347, 748.

23   McConkie, *Mormon Doctrine,* 603, 589, 374.

24   *For the Strength of Youth* (Salt Lake City: Deseret News, 1965).

25   These surveys are described in Armand Mauss, *The Angel and the Beehive: The Mormon Struggle with Assimilation* (Urbana: University of Illinois Press, 1994), 179.

26 "LDS Position on Abortion," *Deseret News* (January 12, 1991), B6.

27 Pew Forum on Religion and Public Life, "Religious Landscape Survey, Summary of Key Findings" (Washington, D.C.: Pew Research Center, 2008), 15.

28 Quoted in Lori Winder Stromberg, "LDS Position on the ERA: An Historical View," *Exponent II* 6 (Winter 1980): 2:6–7

29 Spencer W. Kimball, "The False Gods We Worship," *Ensign* (June 1976), 5.

30 Darius Gray and Margaret Blair Young, "Nobody Knows: The Untold Story of Black Mormons," *Dialogue: A Journal of Mormon Thought* 42:3 (Fall 2010): 113, 115.

31 "Official Declaration 2," Pearl of Great Price.

32 Bruce R. McConkie, "All Are Alike unto God," in *A Symposium on the Book of Mormon* (Salt Lake City: Church of Jesus Christ of Latter-day Saints, 1979), 2.

33 Nicole Warburton, "President Hinckley Calls Racism 'Ugly and Unacceptable,'" *Deseret News* (April 2, 2006), B1.

EIGHT. TOWARD A GLOBAL CHURCH

1 "A Portrait of Mormons in the United States" (Washington, D.C.: Pew Forum on Religion and Public Life, 2009).

2 Rodney Stark, *The Rise of Mormonism,* ed. Reid L. Neilson (New York: Columbia University Press, 2005), 22.

3 Roger Loomis, "Mormon Church Growth," a presentation at the Association for the Sociology of Religion, August 15, 2002; copy in author's possession. The 2004 figure comes from Peggy Fletcher Stack, "Unintended Consequence of Church's Raising the Bar," *Salt Lake Tribune* (July 26, 2005).

4 *Preach My Gospel: A Guide for Missionary Service* (Salt Lake City: Church of Jesus Christ of Latter-day Saints, 2005).

5 These numbers are in the *Deseret News Church Almanac* (Salt Lake City: Deseret News, 2010), passim.

6 These numbers were compiled by Claudia Bushman, *Contemporary Mormonism* (Westport, Conn.: Praeger, 2006), 72.

7 Gordon B. Hinckley, "Converts and Young Men," *Ensign* (May 1997), 47.

8 Philip Jenkins, "Letting Go: Understanding Mormon Growth in Africa," *Journal of Mormon History* 35:2 (Spring 2009): 1–26.

9 Quoted in E. Dale Lebaron, *All Are Alike unto God: Fascinating Conversion Stories of African Saints* (Salt Lake City: Bookcraft, 1990), 22.

10 Dallin H. Oaks, "Repentance and Change," *Ensign* (November 2003), 33.

11 "The Dinosaur Hunter," *Time* (April 6, 1959), 15.

12 Anthony Schinella, "Comments at Kennedy Memorial Service Open Temple Wounds," *Belmont Citizen Herald* (September 9, 2009).

13 A February 2007 Gallup poll placed the number of Americans who would not vote for a Mormon at 24 percent; in November 2006 a Rasmussen poll had the percentage at 43 percent. The Gallup number is in the lower range of most polls in the 2008 presidential campaign; the Rasmussen figure is quite high. The June 2011 number was reported in Michael Muskal, "Prejudice against Mormon Candidates Persists, Poll Shows," *Los Angeles Times* (June 20, 2011); the earlier numbers are recorded in George Gallup, *The Gallup Poll* (Lanham, Md.: Rowman and Littlefield, 2008), 78, and Thomas Burr, "Many Voters Say They Would Never Vote for a Mormon President," *Salt Lake Tribune* (November 20, 2006).

14 "Kingdom Come," *Time* (August 4, 1997), 56.

15 Gordon B. Hinckley, "Words of the Living Prophet," *Liahona* (September 1998), 16.

16 Ezra Taft Benson, "The Book of Mormon—Keystone of Our Religion," *Ensign* (January 1988), 6.

17 "The Living Christ," available at http://lds.org/library/display/0,4945,90-1-10-1,00.html, accessed October 1, 2011.

18 Shepherd and Shepherd, *Kingdom Transformed,* 101.

19 Stephen E. Robinson, *Believing Christ: The Parable of the Bicycle and Other Good News* (Salt Lake City: Deseret Book, 1992), 1, 4.

20 David Campbell and Robert Putnam, *American Grace: How Religion Divides and Unites Us* (New York: Simon and Schuster, 201), 244.

21 Spencer W. Kimball, "The True Way of Life and Salvation," *Ensign* (May 1978), 2.

22 Quentin L. Cook, "Our LDS Women Are Incredible!" *Ensign* (May 2011), 21.

23 "The Family: A Proclamation to the World," read in the General Relief Society Meeting, September 23, 1995; available on www.lds.org and in *Ensign* (November 1995), 102.

24 Spencer W. Kimball, *The Miracle of Forgiveness* (Salt Lake City: Bookcraft, 1969), 82.

25 Dallin H. Oaks, "Same Gender Attraction," *Ensign* (October 1995), 7.

26 Matis quoted in "Gay Mormon Suicides Mourned in Prop's Wake," *Sunstone* 118 (April 2001), 90–91.

27 Carrie Moore, "LDS Official Lauds Work for California's Prop 8," *Deseret News* (November 16, 2008), A1.

28 Nicholas Riccardi, "Mormons Feel the Backlash over Their Support of Prop 8," *Los Angeles Times* (November 17, 2008).

29 Eugene England, "The Possibility of Dialogue," *Dialogue: A Journal of Mormon Thought* 1:1 (Fall 1966): 2.

30 Boyd K. Packer, "The Mantle Is Far Far Greater Than the Intellect," *BYU Studies* 21:3 (Summer 1981): 5.

31 Dallin Oaks, "Alternative Voices," *Ensign* (May 1989), 27.

32 Gordon B. Hinckley, "This Is the Work of the Master," *Ensign* (May 1995), 69.

33 Gordon B. Hinckley, "The BYU Experience," BYU devotional address, November 4, 1997.

CONCLUSION

1 John Lahr, "God Squad," *The New Yorker* (April 4, 2011), 78.

BIBLIOGRAPHIC ESSAY

1 Doctrine and Covenants 47:3.

2 Davis Bitton, "B. H. Roberts as a Historian," *Dialogue: A Journal of Mormon Thought* 3 (Winter 1968): 25–44.

INDEX

ABOUT THE AUTHOR

MATTHEW BOWMAN received his PhD in American religious history from Georgetown University in May 2011, and a master's in American history from the University of Utah. His dissertation, "The Urban Pulpit: Evangelicals and the City in New York, 1880–1930," was funded by the prestigious Charlotte W. Newcombe Doctoral Dissertation Fellowship. His work on American evangelicalism and Mormonism has appeared in, among other places, *Religion and American Culture: A Journal of Interpretation,* the *Journal of the Early Republic,* and *The New Republic.* The associate editor of *Dialogue: A Journal of Mormon Thought,* he began teaching at Hampden-Sydney College in the fall of 2011.